𝕸𝖔𝖗𝖐𝖘 𝖇𝖊𝖆𝖗𝖎𝖓𝖌 𝖔𝖓 𝕭𝖎𝖇𝖑𝖎𝖈𝖆𝖑 𝕻𝖘𝖞𝖈𝖍𝖔𝖑𝖔𝖌𝖞,

PUBLISHED BY

T. & T. CLARK, 38 GEORGE STREET.

DELITZSCH (PROFESSOR) — A System of Biblical
PSYCHOLOGY. Second Edition. 8vo, 12s.

' This admirable volume ought to be read by every thinking clergyman. . . . .
There is much which will be of great value to studious clergymen, and we heartily wish
that the work may have a wide circulation.'—*Literary Churchman.*

HEARD (REV. J. B.)—The Tripartite Nature of Man—
SPIRIT, SOUL, AND BODY—Applied to Illustrate and Explain the
Doctrines of Original Sin, the New Birth, the Disembodied State, and
the Spiritual Body. With an Appendix on the Fatherhood of God.
Fourth Edition. Crown 8vo, 6s.

'A valuable and interesting treatise on the "Tripartite Nature of Man," the first
English theological work of any pretensions which has dealt with the subject in a
methodical and systematic manner.'—DEAN OF NORWICH.

BECK (J. T., D.D.)—Outlines of Biblical Psychology.
Crown 8vo, 4s.

'A useful, handy volume, which compresses into small space the results of scholarly
and elaborate investigations.'—*Baptist Magazine.*

MÜLLER (DR. JULIUS)—The Christian Doctrine of Sin.
An Entirely New Translation, from the Fifth German Edition, by
Rev. W. URWICK, M.A. Two Vols. 8vo, 21s.

'This work, majestic in its conception and thorough in its execution, has long been
very influential in German theology, and we welcome this new and admirable translation.'—*London Quarterly Review.*

MARTENSEN (BISHOP)—Christian Ethics. On the Concept
of Christian Ethics; The Postulates of Christian Ethics; The Fundamental Concepts of Ethics; and the Ethical Views of the World and
Life. 8vo, 10s. 6d.

'Of Bishop Martensen's *Christian Ethics* it is impossible to speak too highly. . . .
It is in every sense a masterly and philosophical production, and adapted in a singular
degree to the most prominent needs of our age.'—*Baptist Magazine.*

HARLESS (DR. C. A.)—System of Christian Ethics.
I. The Blessing of Salvation. II. The Possession of Salvation. III. The
Preservation of Salvation. 8vo, 10s. 6d.

'It would be difficult to find a more useful book to the Christian minister than the
volume before us. It is a thoroughly and profoundly Christian treatise. It is full of
ripe, deep, and fruitful thought, presented in a clear, compact, and attractive form.'—
British Quarterly Review.

WUTTKE (PROFESSOR)—Christian Ethics. Translated
from the German of Dr. ADOLPH WUTTKE, late Professor of Theology in
Halle. Vol. I. History of Ethics. Vol. II. Pure Ethics. Crown 8vo,
12s. 6d.

'Wuttke's *Ethics* should have a place in every pastor's library.'—Dr. HENGSTENBERG.

OEHLER (PROFESSOR)—The Theology of the Old
TESTAMENT. By Dr. G. F. OEHLER, Professor of Theology in Tübingen.
Two Vols. 8vo, 21s.

'Exhibiting in every page the most conscientious diligence.'—*British Quarterly
Review.*

AUGUSTINE (ST.)—Anti-Pelagian Writings. Three Vols.
8vo, 31s. 6d.

THE
CUNNINGHAM LECTURES,

PUBLISHED BY

T. & T. CLARK, 38 GEORGE STREET, EDINBURGH.

SECOND SERIES.

In demy 8vo, price 10*s.* 6*d.*,

THE DOCTRINE OF JUSTIFICATION:

AN OUTLINE OF ITS HISTORY IN THE CHURCH,
AND OF

ITS EXPOSITION FROM SCRIPTURE, WITH SPECIAL REFERENCE TO
RECENT ATTACKS ON THE THEOLOGY OF THE REFORMATION.

BY

JAMES BUCHANAN, D.D., LL.D.,
DIVINITY PROFESSOR, NEW COLLEGE, EDINBURGH.

THIRD SERIES.

In demy 8vo, price 10*s.* 6*d.*,

THE REVELATION OF LAW IN SCRIPTURE,

CONSIDERED WITH RESPECT BOTH TO ITS OWN NATURE AND
TO ITS RELATIVE PLACE IN SUCCESSIVE DISPENSATIONS.

BY

PATRICK FAIRBAIRN, D.D.,
PRINCIPAL AND PROFESSOR OF THEOLOGY, FREE CHURCH COLLEGE, GLASGOW.

FIFTH SERIES.

In demy 8vo, price 10*s.* 6*d.*,

DELIVERY AND DEVELOPMENT OF CHRISTIAN DOCTRINE.

BY

ROBERT RAINY, D.D.,
PRINCIPAL OF AND PROFESSOR OF DIVINITY AND CHURCH HISTORY
IN THE NEW COLLEGE, EDINBURGH.

SIXTH SERIES.

In One Volume, 8vo, price 12*s.*,

THE HUMILIATION OF CHRIST
IN ITS PHYSICAL, ETHICAL, AND OFFICIAL ASPECTS.

BY

ALEXANDER B. BRUCE, D.D.,
PROFESSOR OF DIVINITY, FREE CHURCH COLLEGE, GLASGOW.

THE BIBLE DOCTRINE OF MAN.

PRINTED BY MORRISON AND GIBB,

FOR

T. & T. CLARK, EDINBURGH.

LONDON, ...   HAMILTON, ADAMS, AND CO.

DUBLIN, ...   ROBERTSON AND CO.

NEW YORK,   . . .   SCRIBNER AND WELFORD.

THE

BIBLE DOCTRINE OF MAN.

𝕿𝖍𝖊 𝕾𝖊𝖛𝖊𝖓𝖙𝖍 𝕾𝖊𝖗𝖎𝖊𝖘 𝖔𝖋 𝖙𝖍𝖊 𝕮𝖚𝖓𝖓𝖎𝖓𝖌𝖍𝖆𝖒 𝕷𝖊𝖈𝖙𝖚𝖗𝖊𝖘.

BY

JOHN LAIDLAW, M.A.,

MINISTER OF FREE WEST CHURCH, ABERDEEN.

EDINBURGH:

T. & T. CLARK, 38 GEORGE STREET.

1879.

EXTRACT DECLARATION OF TRUST.

MARCH 1, 1862.

I, WILLIAM BINNY WEBSTER, late Surgeon in the H.E.I.C.S., presently residing in Edinburgh,—Considering that I feel deeply interested in the success of the Free Church College, Edinburgh, and am desirous of advancing the Theological Literature of Scotland, and for this end to establish a Lectureship similar to those of a like kind connected with the Church of England and the Congregational body in England, and that I have made over to the General Trustees of the Free Church of Scotland the sum of £2000 sterling, in trust, for the purpose of founding a Lectureship in memory of the late Reverend William Cunningham, D.D., Principal of the Free Church College, Edinburgh, and Professor of Divinity and Church History therein, and under the following conditions, namely,—*First*, The Lectureship shall bear the name, and be called, 'The Cunningham Lectureship.' *Second*, The Lecturer shall be a Minister or Professor of the Free Church of Scotland, and shall hold the appointment for not less than two years, nor more than three years, and be entitled for the period of his holding the appointment to the income of the endowment as declared by the General Trustees, it being understood that the Council after referred to may occasionally appoint a Minister or Professor from other denominations, provided this be approved of by not fewer than Eight Members of the Council, and it being further understood that the Council are to regulate the terms of payment of the Lecturer. *Third*, The Lecturer shall be at liberty to choose his own subject within the range of Apologetical, Doctrinal, Controversial, Exegetical, Pastoral, or Historical Theology, including what bears on Missions, Home and Foreign, subject to the consent of the Council. *Fourth*, The Lecturer shall be bound to deliver publicly at Edinburgh a Course of Lectures on the subjects thus chosen at some time immediately preceding the expiry of his appointment, and during the Session of the New College, Edinburgh ; the Lectures to be not fewer than six in number, and to be delivered in presence of the Professors and Students under such arrangements as the Council may appoint ; the Lecturer shall be bound also to print and publish, at his own risk, not fewer than 750 copies of the Lectures within a year after their delivery, and to deposit three copies of the same in the Library of the New College ; the form of the publication shall be regulated by the Council. *Fifth*, A Council shall be constituted, consisting of (first) Two Members of their own body, to be chosen annually in the month of March, by the Senatus of the New College, other than the Principal ; (second) Five Members to be chosen annually by the General Assembly, in addition to the Moderator of the said Free Church of Scotland ; together with (third) the Principal of the said New College for the time being, the Moderator of the said General Assembly for the time being, the Procurator or Law Adviser of the Church, and myself the said William Binny Webster, or such person as I may nominate to be my successor : the Principal of the said College to be Convener of the Council, and any Five Members duly convened to be entitled to act notwithstanding the non-election of others. *Sixth*, The duties of the Council shall be the following :—(first), To appoint the Lecturer and determine the period of his holding the appointment, the appointment to be made before the close of the Session of College immediately preceding the termination of the previous Lecturer's engagement ; (second), To arrange details as to the delivery of the Lectures, and to take charge of any additional income and expenditure of an incidental kind that may be connected therewith, it being understood that the obligation upon the Lecturer is simply to deliver the Course of Lectures free of expense to himself. *Seventh*, The Council shall be at liberty, on the expiry of five years, to make any alteration that experience may suggest as desirable in the details of this plan, provided such alterations shall be approved of by not fewer than Eight Members of the Council.

PREFACE.

TO the Council of the Cunningham Lectureship I owe an acknowledgment and an apology. I desire to express my sense of their great kindness in appointing the delivery of the Lectures for the spring of 1878 when it was discovered that to require it at the usual time in 1877 would have made the tenure of the appointment in my case a few weeks less than the minimum fixed by the deed. Further, I have to express my regret that the issue of the Lectures has been delayed several months beyond the statutory time for publication. I can only add by way of explanation, that the extension of the Notes entailed more labour than I had anticipated; and that for me all such work proceeds very slowly, since the doing of it has to be made compatible with the claims of the pulpit and of a considerable pastoral charge.

The book should explain its own method. But I may be allowed to indicate here in what way the mode and the order of treatment have been affected by the conception which I have been led to entertain of my subject. The aim of the Lectures is to give prominence to the psychological principles of Scripture, to those views of man and his nature which pervade the sacred writings. It does not, however, appear to me that the psychology of the Bible, or what may be

called its philosophy of man, can be successfully treated
as an abstract system. These natural views of man's
constitution are given to us in the record of a special
revelation which declares the divine dealings with man
in order to his redemption. They should be treated,
therefore, in close connection with the history and
development of those dealings. Accordingly, after
stating the Bible account of man's origin in Lecture
First, and some general principles of Bible psychology
in Lecture Second, I have devoted the remaining
Lectures to the exhibition of these psychological principles in the order of the great theological topics
concerning man. In Lecture Third they are illustrated
by the Scripture statement regarding man's original
image and primitive state; in Lecture Fourth by those
which describe his condition under sin; in Lecture
Fifth they are viewed in connection with regeneration;
and in Lecture Sixth in their bearing upon the future
life and resurrection.

The convenience of the reader has been consulted in
placing at the foot of the page those briefer notes and
references which are apposite to the immediate context,
and in relegating to the Appendix more extended
digests and citations upon topics introduced in the
Lectures.

I desire to acknowledge my great obligations to my
friend Professor S. D. F. Salmond, of the Free Church
College here, for his valuable assistance in revising the
sheets, and to Mr. W. Cruickshank, M.A., student of
theology, for his care in the preparation of the Index.

ABERDEEN, 30th October 1879.

CONTENTS.

———

LECTURE I.

INTRODUCTORY—THE BIBLE ACCOUNT OF MAN'S ORIGIN.

LECTURE II.

MAN'S NATURE—THE BIBLE PSYCHOLOGY.

LECTURE VI.

THE BIBLE VIEW OF MAN'S NATURE IN ITS BEARING ON A FUTURE LIFE.

APPENDIX.

NOTES ON LECTURE I.

NOTES ON LECTURE II.

NOTES ON LECTURE III.

LECTURE I.

INTRODUCTORY—THE BIBLE ACCOUNT OF MAN'S ORIGIN.

" Quæ vero hujus sunt generis, licet etiam in philosophia, et diligentiorem
et altiorem inquisitionem subire possint quam adhuc habetur, utcunque
tamen in fine religioni determinanda et diffinienda rectius transmitti
censemus. Aliter enim erroribus haud paucis et sensus illusionibus omnino
exponentur. Etenim cum Substantia Animæ in creatione sua non fuerit
extracta aut deducta ex massâ cœli et terræ, sed immediate inspirata a
Deo ; cumque leges cœli et terræ sint propria subjecta philosophiæ ; quo-
modo possit cognitio de Substantia Animæ Rationalis ex philosophia peti et
haberi? Quinimo ab eadem inspiratione divina hauriatur, a qua Substantia
Animæ primo emanavit."—BACON, *De. Augmentis Scientiarum*, lib. IV.
cap. iii. § 3.

Ps. VIII. 4–9.—" What is man, that Thou art mindful of him? and the son of man, that Thou visitest him? For Thou hast made him a little lower than the angels, and hast crowned him with glory and honour. Thou madest him to have dominion over the works of Thy hands; Thou hast put all *things* under his feet: all sheep and oxen, yea, and the beasts of the field; the fowl of the air, and the fish of the sea, *and whatsoever* passeth through the paths of the seas. O LORD our Lord, how excellent is Thy name in all the earth!"

LECTURE I.

THE scope of these lectures is to ascertain the doctrine of Scripture as to the nature and constitution of man. It will be at once understood that our subject is not Anthropology in the sense in which that forms a *topic* in the theological systems, but the Anthropology of the Bible in the stricter sense; that is to say, we seek some answer to the question, What views of man's nature and constitution are taught in Scripture, or are to be held as necessarily implied in its teaching?

Any study which may be classed under the head of Biblical Psychology has in most minds initial prejudices to overcome. The chief of these arises out of the extravagant claim which has sometimes been made on its behalf. To frame a complete and independent system or philosophy of man from the sacred writings is an impossible task. The attempt cannot commend itself to the judicious interpreter of Scripture. It is certain to foster one-sided views in theology, or to become a mere reflex of some prevailing philosophical school. It is an opposite extreme to say that Scripture affords us no knowledge of the soul's natural being,—that the texts on which a so-

B

called biblical psychology has been founded, do not
teach what the nature of man is, but only declare his
relation or bearing towards God.[1] No doubt the relation of man to God is that aspect in which the Bible
chiefly regards him. But for that reason its whole
structure rests on most important assumptions as to
what man was and is. Even should we adhere rigidly
to the view[2] that the Bible is to be construed as
giving us religious and spiritual, but no merely natural
knowledge, far less any scientific information, we
should still be compelled to admit that this religious
and spiritual teaching involves presuppositions regarding man and his nature which are of immense interest
for anthropology and psychology. These presuppositions cannot be separated from the substance of the
record. Let it be ever so strenuously maintained that
the religion of the Bible is the Bible, this religion
includes such relations of man to God, to the unseen,
to the everlasting, as manifestly to imply a very definite theory of his essential nature and constitution.
Let it be further remembered that the Bible is, upon its
own representation, the history of God's dealings with
man in a special course of religious and spiritual
communication; that therefore this record of revelation contains an account of man's origin, of his original
nature, of the changes which have befallen it, and of

---

[1] See v. Hofmann, *Der Schriftbeweis*, i. p. 284.

[2] Recently expressed thus : " That inspiration was not a general but a
functional endowment, and consequently limited to subjects in which religion is directly involved ; and that in those which stand outside it, the
writers of the different books in the Bible were left to the free use of their
ordinary faculties," etc.—Row's *Bampton Lecture*, 1877, p. 43. That a
writer should be more free to use his faculties when uninspired strikes us
as a very inadequate view of inspiration.

the changes which by divine grace have been and are
still to be wrought upon it. Such an account is
surely a contribution to the knowledge of man, and
to the history of the race. Is there not reason to
expect that, in the progress of such a revelation,
light should be shed on man's nature and constitution,
and that such information, apart from its saving and
spiritual purpose, should be of moment for the student
of psychology?

Far more, however, than any other department of
nature touched upon in the Bible, the nature of man
falls within the field of theology. Hence it becomes
us to inquire, in the interest of Scripture doctrine, in
what sense the Bible notion of man is authoritative,
uniform, and available for such treatment as we
propose.

How far Bible doctrine has in it a true knowledge
of man, formed for itself " in its own light out of
the revelations of the Spirit,"[1] how far the view
of man's constitution which pervades the Bible enters
into the subject-matter of the revelation, are questions
turning upon the relation between the natural and the
supernatural element in Scripture, or perhaps upon
the more general relation of natural to revealed truth.
It is quite what we should expect, that in a certain
school of theology the treatment of this biblical topic
appears as " the psychology of the Hebrews," and
that their science can have nothing to do with any
biblical psychology which professes to be more than
a view of the notions of the Hebrew people.   Such

---

[1] " In ihrem eigenen Licht aus den Aufschlüssen des Geistes."—Beck,
Umriss der biblischen Seelenlehre, Vorwort, p. vi. 3te Aufl. 1871.

questions, however, become most pregnant for those
who are interested in maintaining the really divine
character of the Bible revelation. For it is exactly
here that the authoritative character of the Bible
assumptions in regard to natural fact seems to form
an essential element in its claim to be from God. It
is in such regions as this that the maxim, "The religion of the Bible is the Bible," will not unlock all
difficulties. We cannot easily, or perhaps at all, draw
the line in what Scripture says of man between that
which is religious and that which is non-religious. If
we should say that the Bible notion of man as a
natural being must submit to the same criticism as
that which is contained in other ancient literature,
what are we to say of the information which the Bible
gives us about man's creation, the fall, the new birth,
the resurrection? Have these no bearing upon our
idea of man as a natural being? Have not these
entered into the very marrow of the philosophy of
man in all nations that know the Bible? That man
was made by God, and in His image; that the present
anomalies in man's nature are explained by a great
moral catastrophe which has affected his will; that
nevertheless his spirit stands in such relation to the
divine as to be capable of renovation and possession
by the Spirit of God; that soul and body alike are
essential to the totality of man, and are both brought
within the scope of redemption,—these are positions
which undoubtedly belong to the essence of the Bible
revelation, and which have also greatly influenced
the philosophical conception of human nature.

The view which would relegate all the elements of

natural knowledge contained in Scripture to the region
of the merely popular notions prevalent in the age
and mind of the writers, no doubt makes short work
with biblical psychology. But such a view involves
the widest issues with regard to the word of God.
In the highest of all interests it has to be resisted at
every point, and met with another and more adequate
theory, namely, one which will neither on the one hand
give up the statements of the Bible regarding natural
facts as subject to all the errors of their age, nor claim
for them on the other the anomalous character of
supernatural science.

Let us, for the sake of analogy, glance at a kindred
topic, namely, the Scripture account of the origin of
the world. The position to be maintained here by the
believer in revelation is one which refuses the dilemma
that the representations contained in the first chapter
of Genesis must be either scientifically correct or
altogether worthless. Their supremely religious
character, fundamental as they are to the whole
revelation, in teaching the being, unity, spirituality of
God and His relation to the creatures, places them in
a totally different region from that of science. They
must soar above and stand apart from the special
discoveries and provisional statements of any stage of
scientific attainment. To forget this has been the
great mistake of those who have sought to harmonize
science and Scripture, though the blame of the mistake
has often been misplaced. The complaint of science
is that theology has resisted her progress. Might not
the accusation be shifted, if not retorted? Is it not
theology that has been unfortunately encumbered with

physical science, or with the philosophemes which stood for science at some particular period? Interpreters of Scripture have allowed the prevailing theories of the day so to colour their statements of the Bible meaning, that natural discoverers of the next age have raised the cry, "The Bible with its theology stops the way!"—the fact being that it was not the Bible at all, nor even theology, which opposed itself to their discoveries, but only the ghost of defunct philosophical or scientific opinions, clothing themselves in the garments of religious thought.

The leading idea of the Bible cosmogony is not scientific, it is religious; yet as a cosmogony it gives principles of the becoming of things which, in their superiority to the corresponding ethnic conceptions, in their substantial agreement with science, contribute important proof of the divine character of the book in which they are found. Now, such a manner of accounting for the origin of those laws and principles which it is the province of human science to investigate, is inspiration. Coincidence, in such an account, with the findings of science in any one age, would have been as useless as correspondence to the ever varying results of it throughout the ages would have been impossible. But such a view of the world's becoming as satisfies religion, while it consists with the principles that science is discovering for itself, is a true and proper revelation on the subject.[1]

On this analogy would we define the character to be attached to the anthropology of the Bible. In answer to the question whether the Scripture view of man as

[1] See further on this point, Appendix, Note B.

a natural being is not the view of the times in which
the Scriptures were written, we reply that it is so, in
so far as man's notions of himself can furnish adequate
and correct foundation for revealed doctrine. For
everywhere in Scripture we find evidence of this marvellous quality, that its presuppositions on natural
subjects, and especially on the *Origines* of the world
and of man, though never given in the scientific form,
and not intended to teach science, justify themselves
in the face of scientific discoveries as these are suc-
cessively made. The writers of Holy Scripture, by
whatever method of poetic or prophetic elevation,
move in the domain of natural facts and principles
with a supernatural tact, which at once distinguishes
them from all other ancient writers on such subjects,
and places the Scriptures themselves above the reach
of scientific objections.

Some zealous upholders of biblical psychology seem
to assume that it was something directly descended
from heaven, bearing no relation to the natural
psychology of the times. But it is evident there must
have been such an adaptation, by the biblical writers,
of psychological terms in previous use as to be understood by those to whom their words first came. We
cannot afford here, or anywhere else, to forget that in
the Scripture the Holy Ghost speaks with a human
tongue, and therefore, in speaking of man, must have
employed such ideas and expressions regarding his
nature and constitution as convey a true and intelligible view of what these are. Such expressions and
ideas are undoubtedly those of the age in which the
writings arose, but they are at the same time so simple

and universal as to find easy access to the mind of
mankind everywhere and at all times.   And this simplicity speaks to another trait, namely, their uniformity.
The tendency of much recent scholarship is to disin-
tegrate the Scriptures, and accordingly objections have
been taken to the reception of a biblical notion of man,
on the ground that on all topics of natural knowledge
the standpoint of each Scripture writer must be considered independent.[1]   There is nothing more groundless.   The unity of Scripture is precisely one of those
facts not explained by Rationalism, but clear in a
moment when we regard Scripture as the record of a
continuous and consistent historical revelation.   And
the scope of that revelation being the redemption of
man, there is nothing which is more essentially bound
up with it, than that idea of man and his nature which
pervades the record.   It would, indeed, be very difficult to deny the uniformity of psychological view in the
Old Testament, were it only on the ground that at
the early period to which these writings belong, the
refinements of school philosophy, which introduce
diversity even where they bring ripeness, had not
begun to operate.   It cannot be denied that fresh
elements from without enter into the psychology of
the New Testament, and especially into that of St.
Paul; yet little doubt can remain on the mind of any
unprejudiced reader of Scripture, that a notion of

---

[1] *e.g.*, by H. Schultz : " Wenn man überhaupt von einer Lehre der Schrift
über solche dem Naturgebiete angehörige Sachen reden wollte, so würde
man bei jedem einzelnen biblischen Schriftsteller seine Ansicht über diese
Sachen, die nach der verschiedenen Bildung und Individualität voraus-
sichtlich verschieden sein würde, zu entwickeln haben."—*Die Voraussetzungen der christlichen Lehre von der Unsterblichkeit*, Göttingen 1861,
p. 72.

man pervades both the Old and the New Testament, popularly expressed, indeed, but uniform and consistent, though growing in its fulness with the growth of the biblical revelation itself.

Let us understand, then, what we may expect to attain in any study of biblical psychology. Dr. Delitzsch defines the scope of such study very fairly and modestly when he says its aim is "to bring out the views of Scripture regarding the nature, the life, and the life destinies of the soul, as these are determined in the history of its salvation."[1] We cannot agree with the same writer when he claims for it the rank of "an independent science," even within "the organism of theology."[2] It is really bound up with the theology which we call biblical. Far less can we allow that these Bible representations of man constitute an independent philosophy of human nature. To use them for such a purpose is to fall into an error like that of reading the Bible account of creation as a prophetic view of geological science. The friendly discussion between Delitzsch and the late Dr. v. Hofmann of Erlangen, as to the possibility of a Bible psychology, turns mainly on the form which such a study must assume. Notwithstanding the extreme position noticed above, Hofmann does not deny the existence in Scripture of disclosures deliberately anthropologic and psychologic. In his masterly treatise on *The Scripture Proof of Christian Doctrine*, he does not shrink from the discussion of texts involving the fundamental questions of our theme. He has no doubt that the presuppositions of Scripture on the

[1] *Biblische Psychologie*, p. 13.   [2] *Ibid.* p. 15.

subject can be grouped together, that is to say, that
they are consistent. He warns us only that we are
not to expect of them a scientific whole. Nor should
we forget that they come into view just as they are
used for the expression of facts which, though touching on the psychological region, do really belong to
another, namely, the theological. On the other hand,
Delitzsch, though premising that no system of psychology propounded in formal language is to be looked for
in the Bible, any more than of dogmatics or ethics,
zealously contends that a system can be found and
constructed. Under the name of Bible psychology he
understands a scientific representation of the doctrine
of Scripture on the psychical constitution of man as he
was created, and on the modes in which this constitution has been affected by sin and by redemption. It
seems as if Hofmann had overlooked the importance
and the purpose of that consistent idea of man's
constitution which underlies the Scripture teaching ;
while Delitzsch mistakes its purpose rather than exaggerates its importance.[1] That purpose is not to
teach the science of man, but it has a vital use in sub-
servience to theology, nevertheless. To trace that use,
in an induction of Scripture utterances, is the proper
scope and form of any study deserving the name of
biblical psychology.

A single word further of its necessity. The chief
argument for attempting a consistent and connected
view of man's nature, drawn from the Bible itself, is
easily stated. There never has been a theology which

---

[1] I subjoin the main paragraphs from each of these writers, that the
reader may judge for himself. See Appendix, Note A.

did not imply and implicitly base itself upon some philosophy of man. The influence of philosophy upon theology is proverbial. It is notorious how soon Christian doctrine, as discussed in the early Church, became coloured by Platonic speculations; how long the Aristotelic doctrine of the soul held sway in medieval and even in Reformation theology; how Leibnitz and Descartes became the lords of a system of Protestant orthodoxy. "No philosophy," says Dr. Charles Hodge, "has the right to control or modify the exposition of the doctrines of the Bible, except the philosophy of the Bible itself, that is, the principles which are therein asserted or assumed."[1] Yet with what *naïveté* do most of our theologians, not excluding the author now quoted, assume that the Bible stands exactly on the Cartesian postulates as to man, the world, and the soul! Beck very justly points out the vice of scientific theology in deriving those most essential conceptions of life, upon which Christianity has to build its unique doctrines of sin and redemption, not from the circle of thought which belongs to Christianity itself, but from some one totally different,—a mode which logically leads to results entirely opposed to Bible anthropology.[2] We can only rid ourselves of this vice by carefully observing those ideas of life and the soul which the Scriptures themselves assume in all their theological statements. To ascertain the "science of life," if it may be so called, which prevailed with the writers of Scripture, to put together such simple psychology as underlies their writings, cannot be an unnecessary task. Theology is not truly biblical so long as it is

---

[1] *Systematic Theology*, iii. 661.   [2] See *Umriss der biblischen Seelenlehre*, p. iv.

controlled by non-biblical philosophy; and such control
is inexcusable when it is seen that a view of human
nature available for the purpose of the theologian is
native to the source from which theology itself is
drawn.

The Bible notion of man ought to repay our study.
On the lowest ground it is of interest as a contribution
to the history of opinion regarding man and the soul.
Further, it is indispensable as a key to the theology of
the Bible, for into all those large portions of its teaching which concern man and his destiny, some natural
notion of man must enter. Finally, with believers in
revelation it is axiomatic, that revelation should throw
light on that nature which is the field of the divine
operations recorded in it. If Plato could sigh for
divine assistance as the only way by which the knowledge of the soul could be established, how carefully
should the Christian psychologist give heed to the
intimations of Scripture![1]

The further preliminary topic which we must discuss
in the present lecture is that of the origin of man.
What does the Bible say of man's coming into existence
at the first? The bearing of this upon all that follows
is very plain, for the lines of origin, nature, and destiny
run very close together. What a being is, and what
it is fitted to become, depend on how and with what
powers it has come into existence.

In describing the double account of the origination

---

[1] Τὰ μὲν οὖν περὶ ψυχῆς . . . τὸ μὲν ἀληθὲς ὡς εἴρηται, θεοῦ ξυμφήσαντος
τότ' ἂν οὕτω μόνως διισχυριζοίμεθα.—*Timæus*, 72 D.

"Concerning the soul . . . the truth can only be established, as we
have acknowledged, by the word of God."—*Jowett's Translation.*

of man given in the first and second chapters of
Genesis, we accept the fact that there are two distinct
creation-narratives or paragraphs contained in these
two chapters respectively.[1]   We take nothing to do
with theories that posit an Elohist writer for the one
and a Jahvist for the other.   Leaving the documentary
hypothesis to time and criticism, we begin with this
fairly accepted result, namely, that the human author of
Genesis found to his hand certain fragments of ancient
tradition, either recited from memory or preserved in
writing, which he embodied in this inspired book.   A
very similar piecing of documents or narratives' is
generally admitted in the New Testament at the beginning of the third Gospel.   But surely a history does not
cease to be the veritable product of its author because
it contains documentary or extracted material.   Nor
does inspiration, as we understand it, refuse to consist with the recital or insertion of older communica-
tions enshrined in the religious belief of those to
whom were committed the sacred oracles.   Accepting,
then, the two sections at the opening of the book of
Genesis as at least two distinct compositions, in each
of which a special phraseology has been maintained,
and naming them, for convenience sake, the first and
second narratives, we nevertheless do not admit that
they contain different accounts of the creation.   Such
an assumption is clearly beside the mark.   In the first
narrative we have the succession in creation of the
various elements, and then of the several orders of
animated beings.   In the second we have, not a different account of the creation, for the plain reason that

---

[1] The first contained in i. 1–ii. 3 ; the second in ii. 4–25.

in it we have no account of the creation at large. It makes no mention of the heavenly bodies, of land and water, of reptiles and fishes, all these having been described in the former narrative. Indeed, the introductory word of the second narrative, if we mark its use all through the book of Genesis, tells the tale quite distinctly, and should have prevented any misconception, for it means invariably not the birth or begetting of those named, but the history of their family.[1] So here, "the generations of the heavens and of the earth" means, not their creation at the first, but an account of certain transactions within the heavens and the earth; in short, the dealings of God with mankind. For this second narrative is plainly, as Ewald calls it, the history proper of the creation of mankind.[2]

Both narratives speak of the origin of man, and here, indeed, is their real point of unity and connection. We do not say that there are no difficulties in harmonizing the two. It is not clear whether the

[1] Gen. ii. 4, אֵלֶּה תֹלְדֹות : "These are the generations," i.e. what follows is the genealogical history, a formula which marks off this and the other nine sections which make up the rest of the book of Genesis—an orderly division and succession, affording strong presumption of its unity of plan and singleness of authorship. Hofmann lays great stress on the Sabbatic pause at the close of the first narrative, as bringing out the principle of a distinction between the act of creation and the history of that which is created. And now what follows is the history of that which is transacted between God and man. He says it is impossible, upon a comparison of all the passages where the phrase is used (note especially Gen. xxxvii. 2), to think that it can ever refer to what has preceded (Schriftbeweis, i. 206). The passages are Gen. v. 1, vi. 9, x. 1, xi. 10, xxv. 12, 19, xxxvi. 1, xxxvii. 2; see also Num. iii. 1.

[2] "Die eigentliche Menschen-schöpfungs-geschichte." In a series of papers in his Jahrbücher der biblischen Wissenschaft (1848, 1849), entitled, "Erklärung der biblischen Urgeschichte." In the first two papers of the series he discusses the double creation narrative of Genesis.

plants and animals, the formation of which is described along with that of Adam in the second chapter, are the same *flora* and *fauna* the rise of which is described as successive creation-acts in the sublime language of the first chapter.[1] But so far as man and his origin are concerned, the coincidence of the two narratives is plain. Lay them side by side at this point, and their relation becomes clear. The first gives us man's place in the succession of being and life upon the globe. On that grand opening page of the Bible stands a cosmogony which fitly prepares for all that follows in the book, and which shines with its steady light to-day in presence of the torch of science, as it shone on the Hebrew mind for centuries before Christianity came into the world. After the march of the elements—light and sky, and water and earth — after the preparation of the great platform of life, comes life itself, and that in the regular ascent which modern science has taught us to look upon as a law of nature. First vegetable life, then the creatures of the deep, then the fowls of the air, and, last of all, the animals of the land. At the summit man appears, the apex of the pyramid of earthly being. Who can doubt for a moment that we have in this arrangement a point in which theology and science meet? It matters little whether you read the arrangement as one of history or one of classification. If the account of the creation in that chapter be taken, in its more obvious sense, as chronological, then you have the convergence of two independent witnesses (science and Scripture) to the fact that man comes last and crowns the series; his

---

[1] See Appendix, Note B.

creation on the sixth day, at the close of the production of the land animals generally, corresponding with
his place, as ascertained by observation, in the latest of
the geological epochs.   On the other hand, were that
chapter taken merely as a pictorial classification, a
clothing of cosmic principles in dramatic garb, the
result would be still the same.   Man crowns the
edifice of nature and life—a principle attested by the
researches of biology and comparative anatomy, as
much as by those of geology and palæontology, namely,
that man is a compendium of nature, and of kin to
every creature that lives,—that man, in the words of
Oken, is the sum total of all animals, the equivalent
to the whole animal kingdom.[1]   In either case you
have a position as to which revelation and natural
knowledge are consciously at one—a fact at once of
religious and of scientific importance, for to give man
his true religious or theological place is to give him
also his true natural or scientific place.   The obvious
supremacy of man in the natural orders of the animal
kingdom corresponds with the central and final place
assigned him in the revealed system of religion.

This representation of man as "the paragon of
animals," this account of him appearing in line with
the other living beings of God's making,[2] though at

[1] Quoted by Hugh Miller, *Footprints of the Creator*, p. 279.
[2] The significance of this is brought out by Dawson, *Origin of the World
according to Revelation and Science*, Lond. 1877: " A fictitious writer
would probably have exalted man by assigning to him a separate day, and
by placing the whole animal kingdom together in respect of time. . . .
Geology and revelation coincide in referring the creation of man to the
close of the period in which mammals were introduced and became pre-
dominant, and in establishing a marked separation between that period and
the preceding one, in which the lower animals held undisputed sway,"
p. 241.

the summit of the line, is further heightened by a stroke of description which places man far above the other creatures. In the march of animated being previous to man there is a formula employed which indicates both mediate creation and generic distinction: "Let the waters bring forth the moving creatures . . . every living creature after his kind;" "Let the earth bring forth the living creature after his kind." But when we come to man, the formula is suddenly and brilliantly altered. Immediate rather than mediate origination is suggested. It is not, "Let the waters or the earth bring forth," but God said, "Let us make man." It is no longer "after his kind," on a typical form of his own; far less is it after the type of an inferior creature. God said, "Let us make man in our image, after our likeness." Reserving all that has to be said about the divine image as descriptive of man's nature and destiny, let us here note simply how much distinction the narrative attributes to his origination. For this distinction appears in the very form of the announcement. As to all the other products of creative power there is recorded in this first narrative simply a *fiat* with its *factum est*—"Let it be," and "It was." But in the case of man there is a purpose with its fulfilment; and that fulfilment is recorded with such majesty of language, with such threefold repetition, "a joyous tremor of representation,"[1] as to show how great stress the book laid upon this fact,—"So God created man in His own image, in the image of God created He him, male and female created He them."

---

[1] Ewald.

C

When we pass to the second narrative the point of view is changed—a fact noted long ago by Josephus, when he bids us mark how, at Gen. ii. 4, Moses began to "physiologize"—*naturam interpretari*, to explain the nature of things.[1] The remark is specially applicable to the account which follows of the production of man. For it is the formation of the individual first man which this second narrative proceeds to describe. Amid differences of detail, no doubt, the great features of the origin of mankind remain the same as in the former description. The close connection of man with earth and the mundane system of life is expressed in his name, Adam, from the *adamah*, the ground out of which he and the animals are alike formed or kneaded, as the potter kneads his clay.[2] His distinction above these, however, in his formation is no less clearly expressed. He is formed from "dust" of the ground, not from a clod of the earth; and into the nostrils of this form—"this quintessence of dust"— the Lord God Himself breathes the breath of lives, and man becomes a living soul. Let us note how this distinction of man from the animals is here brought out. It is neither in the principle of life, nor in its constitution. According to Scripture, the breath of the Almighty is the animating principle, not in man alone, but in the whole animal creation. And the result of that in-breathing, which was to constitute man "a living soul," is ascribed in the context to every creature possessing life. The only special mark by which man is

[1] *Antiqq.* I. i. 2: Καὶ δὴ καὶ Φυσιολογεῖν Μωϋσῆς μετὰ τὴν ἑβδόμην ἤρξατο, περὶ τῆς τοῦ ἀνθρώπου κατασκευῆς λέγων οὕτως κ.τ.λ.

[2] See further in Appendix, Note B.

distinguished, in this account of his creation, from the rest of the living creatures is the direct act of divine in-. breathing into his nostrils; that is to say, the communication of life in the case of man is described as a peculiar and distinct act of God. That this point, however, was deemed of the utmost moment is seen when we consider how the later Scripture writers dwell upon the immediate divine origination of man's breath, spirit, understanding, as constituting a peculiar connection between the Creator and this, the chiefest of His works.[1]

This second account of man's formation, then, while giving prominence to the details of his structure, while making still clearer than the first his affinity to earth and the kinship of the animal world to him, is as emphatic as the former in declaring his superior nature and his lordly position. Indeed, if we mark how it describes the preparation of the earth for man, —how it assigns the garden, and the trees, and the animals to his care and use; how it expresses not merely, like the former, a commission of man to rule, but an actual knowledge of and rule over the creatures on the part of the first man,—we shall not wonder that some consider it, with Ewald, as bringing out the preeminence of man even more distinctly than the former. At all events, the relation of the two accounts becomes very clear when we place them side by side. The first may be called cosmical, the second physiological. The former is the generic account of man's creation—of man the race, the ideal; the latter is the production of the actual man, of the historic Adam. The former spoke of the creative *fiat* which called man into existence;

---

[1] Job xxvii. 3, xxxii. 8, xxxiii. 4; Isa. xlii. 5; Zech. xii. 1.

this speaks of the plastic process through which the
Creator formed both man and woman—him from the
dust of the ground, her from the bone and flesh of
man.   The former spoke of them as to their type—in
the image of God; this, of the element in which
that type was realized—a material frame, informed by a
divinely-inbreathed spirit.   The former spoke of mankind at the head of the creatures, ruling over the
earth and them; this speaks of the home provided
for him, the work committed to him, the relationships
formed for him, and, finally, of the moral law under
which he was placed in his relation to God.   And no
unbiassed reader can see anything but unity in these
two accounts—a real and reasonable harmony, as distinguished from literal or verbal dovetailing; nor can
we doubt that the master hand which knit into that
marvellous whole—the book of Genesis—various paragraphs of precious tradition, enshrining the highest
spiritual truth, has placed these two accounts of the
creation of man side by side for the mutual light
which they shed on each other without absolute contact, and certainly without contradiction.[1]

The results of this twofold biblical account of man's
becoming are clear, definite, and intelligible.   His
origin is not emanation, but creation—formation out of
existing materials on the one side of his nature, out
of the blessed fulness of the divine life on the other.
His becoming is in the line of the natural order of
animated beings, but at its climax. His position among
them is central and supreme, but his nature stands
distinguished from them all in that it is formed after

[1] On the whole subject of the two narratives see Appendix, Note B.

the divine image. To examine the psychological value of the words describing man's formation in Gen. ii. 7, will fall in with the topics appropriate to our next Lecture. What elements in man's nature are denoted by his bearing the divine image will form the subject of inquiry in Lecture Third. Meantime, we offer a brief comparison of the Bible account of man's origin with that suggested by recent speculation.

It is not necessary to tell you that a prevailing theory on this subject fills the literary and scientific atmosphere of our time, and, indeed, so fills the air which we must all breathe, that we find it everywhere, even in the most popular literature. It is to the effect that man derives his present civilisation by long and slow progression from savage human ancestors; that these, again, were developed during an indefinite series of ages out of some form or family of the animal tribes; and in most instances these two branches of opinion as to man presuppose and naturally grow out of a theory of evolution applicable to all animated existence, namely, that in the course of ages too vast to be conceived, all living things were produced out of monads, or the simplest cellular forms of life. Such is the favourite hypothesis of our day regarding the origin of the animated world. Its reign in scientific circles has been despotic, jealous of any rival, intolerant of any dissent. We say "has been," for it has recently received severe checks, begins to show signs of age and some need already of readjustment to the advancing disclosures of fact.[1]

[1] See Appendix, Note C.

Upon the expounder of the biblical view of man's origin and nature, contradictory demands are apt to be made with regard to this theory.   There is, on the one part, an expectation that he should supply some *modus vivendi* between the commonly received findings of Scripture and the so-called views of science.   On the other part, it is rather desired that he should prove the first chapters of Genesis to have excluded this theory from any claim to be an admissible explanation of the beginnings of the human race.   The true hinge of all such questions we have already postulated, namely, that wherever the Bible touches the origin and nature of things, its standpoint is primarily spiritual and religious. So it is here.   The main scope of the creation-history of man is to teach his relation to the Creator, his place in the providential order of the world.   When we take up this position, other questions will fall into their proper place, and find in due course their appropriate solution.

The Scripture statement of a special divine act in the origination of man cannot certainly be divested of the appearance of opposition to the modern theory of evolution, with all its various consequences.   But if any *modus vivendi* is to be devised, it must come in the first place from the scientific side, for at every stage of its application to nature and fact, this theory has to satisfy a universal demand for proof.   Evolution, taking it in its highest and most abstract sense, may mean two very different things.   It may be offered as a solution of the entire complex of being.   It may be affirmed that on the hypothesis of "natural selection," only mechanical causes, working by the elimination of unsuccessful combinations and the "survival of the

fittest," are needed to derive all the diverse ranks of
animated nature from one primitive form of life, to
develop mind and civilisation from animal and savage
conditions.   But so long as it is impossible for men to
believe that an ordered world can be the result of
fortuitous arrangement; so long as the human mind
demands an adequate cause for the rise of life, for the
succession of species, for the entrance of an intelligent
being on the scene formerly occupied by the lower
animals only, so long will the theory in this form
be deemed incredible and almost unthinkable.   It
is discredited when brought to the touchstone of
every hypothesis, competency to explain the facts.
If, on the other hand, evolution be propounded not
as a "causal" but only as a "modal" theory of
creation, its reception may be very different.   If the
germ from which life, mind, spirit are all in succession
unfolded has really contained the "promise and
potency" of these from the first, then the origination
of the germ, viewed as the act of a First Cause or Will,
involves the glory and purpose of an entire series of
creations.   So far as the theory is conceivable, the
theistic view of creation has no quarrel with it.   It
reflects no less glory on the Creator and His work.   It
proposes no new cause of the origin of things, only a
fresh mode in the conception of their becoming.   And
the question of fact is whether this has been the
method of the Divine Worker.   The terms " development" and "evolution" are used in so many varying
senses, that we require to distinguish with some care
their various applications.   Sometimes they are loosely
employed to designate what has no necessary con-

nection with either, namely, the successive appearance
in the kosmos of living forms in orderly ascent.   This
is simply fact, not theory.   It is the Bible programme of
creation. It is attested by the earth's own geologic record.
Like many interesting facts in the structure of animals,
and in their physiology, it suggests a marvellous unity
of plan in the creation ; it means at least an orderly
unfolding of that plan by the supreme mind.   Whether
it is the key to the mode in which species originate is
the great scientific problem of our day.   There is certainly
a great preponderance of scientific opinion in favour of
the hypothesis that these successive forms of life were
derived each from each in ascending series.   But even
this idea of development was known in philosophy
before it appeared in science ; since the time of Leibnitz
it has never been considered necessarily alien to the
theistic or even to the Christian position.   The evolution hypothesis at present in vogue, namely, that of
derivation by natural selection, the actual rise of the
present animated world by slow emergence from lower
types of creation, plausible though it be in some of its
proofs, and undoubtedly grand in its conception, is
nevertheless surrounded with difficulties that can
hardly be exaggerated.   The practically infinite demand
which it makes upon the past duration of the globe is
the ground of the serious attack now made upon it by
mathematical physics.   Not less serious is the objection
taken a quarter of a century ago by Sedgwick, and now
renewed by Virchow, that however many analogies
may seem to favour it, not one direct and unmistakeable instance of transmutation of species has been
established.   The interval of time between these two

names marks more forcibly the absence of proof in a period specially devoted to this research. Then there are the physiological and geological difficulties, and the confessedly speculative elements in the theory itself. Yet it would be quite rash to say that in the abstract this theory of origins contradicts the Scriptures. The Bible should not be committed to any theory of the origin of species. The record of Genesis does not imply local, special, or successive creations for the various orders of animated being. On the contrary, a general sweep of creative process is suggested by it. The principle of mediate production is clearly recognised in it. The earth and the waters are called upon to bring forth the living creatures appropriate to each. The distinguishing feature of the biblical cosmogony is that it recognises two factors, the creative fiat and the creative process,—absolute divine origination on the one hand, and on the other the dependence of link upon link in the actual production of the world as it now appears. Thus it secures a pre-established harmony between faith and knowledge. Absolute origin it is the part of the former to receive. "Through faith we understand that the worlds were framed by the word of God." Mode and order in production, the structure of that which is produced, it is the province of science to investigate.

It cannot be concealed that the theory of evolution tends to grasp at universal dominion, that it virtually claims to be a theory of the universe. It is, as Virchow says, a new religion.[1] Yet in its spring and

---

[1] His words are: "A doctrine of such moment . . . the direct result of which is to form a sort of new religion."—*Freedom of Science*, p. 15.

essence it was only a biological theory. Its ablest defenders, at least in this country, are entitled to the advantages, such as they are, of that position. They do not apply it as if they assumed that life could have been evolved out of non-living matter. Some of its upholders—though these are not its consistent and main adherents—still further restrict it to the lower orders of life, believing it inapplicable to the genesis of the human race. Still more illogically, some think it might be used to account for man physical, though not for man mental and moral. It is evident that if it can account at all for the rise of man out of some kindred form of the animal tribes, it must account for him entirely. But it is when it enters the region of man's mental, moral, and religious history, that its want of success becomes conspicuous. And no wonder. It has, for example, to construct an entirely new psychology, in which all the complex processes of mind shall be evolved from elementary nervous movement in the animal frame. Its task in the domain of ethics is if possible still heavier. The rude outline of moral feeling in animals must be held to be the "germinal form" of all moral life. Out of struggle and self-preservation, which is its own chosen expression for the law of animal development, it must evolve the exactly opposite law of self-denial, which is the basis of human morality. It has to develop morality, that is to say, in a primarily non-moral animal by the gradual predominance of the social over the individual affections.[1] When we come to account for civilisation and religion, its method is at least equally paradoxical.

[1] See Professor Calderwood, in *Contemporary Review*, Dec. 1877.

It gives its primary and chief attention to those unfortunate branches of the human family which have hitherto failed to become civilised. It endeavours to fill out its conception of primitive man from observation of those presently existing races which are exceptions to that course of development proved by history to be normal to mankind.[1] Not to go farther with this enumeration of difficulties, let us rest our attention on what is most germane to our subject, the view which this theory gives of the starting-point of the human family; and let this be contrasted with the account we have already gathered from the sacred records.

Place for a moment before you the two delineations of primitive mankind presented to us by the Bible and by this modern theory respectively. Look on this picture and on that. The ideal man of the Scripture, "made a little lower than the angels," the typal man of the first creation-narrative, is portrayed to us in the second creation-narrative as the actual father of the race. The scene is a garden, the time is the morning of the world—that golden age upon which all poetry draws as upon an unfailing deposit in every human imagination. The figures are two, male and female, the prototypes of their kind; living a simple, primitive life, almost impossible for us to conceive to whom all comfort is an art and the product of civilisation; living in close fellowship with a pure and primitive nature in the vegetable and the animal kingdoms, but standing out above all other created beings in actual converse with their Maker; placed upon the way of ascent to

[1] See Appendix, Note C.

a still higher moral and spiritual position by a relation to Him of law, of obedience, of love. The Bible takes the bold and original course of starting mankind neither with civilisation on the one hand, nor with barbarism on the other, but with an Eden of innocence and simplicity far removed from either.

Take now that other delineation, the "joint product of modern philosophy and of antiquarian research." Instead of a type higher than the animal, and only lower than the angels, there is presented to us the type of the anthropoid ape; which itself is but a supposition, for this missing link between man and the quadrumana has never been found. Instead of regarding man as the goal of creation, and the earth as prepared and provided for him, you have to regard him as a variety in a certain animal family, coming to the front by accidental superiority to his fellows— the survivor of a struggle for existence. And instead of that picture of primitive humanity which satisfies reason, imagination, and faith, you have to accept as the ancestral specimen of the race "a coarse and filthy savage, repulsive in feature and gross in habits, warring with his fellow-savages, and warring yet more remorselessly with every living thing he could destroy, tearing half-cooked flesh, and cracking marrow bones with stone hammers, sheltering himself in damp and smoky caves, with no eye heavenward, and with only the first rude beginnings of the most important arts of life." [1]

Now we do not adduce this contrast as an appeal to feeling. Ask calmly which of the two beginnings

[1] Dawson, *Story of the Earth and Man*, p. 377.

accounts for man as he is, and can there be any hesitation? On the doctrine that he was made in the image
of God, we can understand all that is best in him,—
"how noble in reason! how infinite in faculty! in
form and moving how express and admirable! in
action how like an angel! in apprehension how like a
god!" On this doctrine, too, coupled with that other
Bible doctrine of a fall, we can explain his guilt, his
vileness, the degradation worse than animal to which
he can sink, on the familiar principle that the corruption of the best produces the worst. In short, the
Bible view of man's beginning and early history explains at once his greatness and his misery. But
the so-called scientific view accounts neither for what
is best in him nor for what is worst; it is impotent
to explain the rise of man as he is, from that which
it supposes to have preceded him. It is clear enough
that believers in the Bible are not called upon to make
any adjustment of their faith to this theory of the
origin of man. On the other hand, all who desire to
understand the human soul, to read human history
aright, to hope and to labour for the future of the
race, find in the Bible account of man's beginning an
intelligible position.

Let us never undervalue science, nor even scientific
hypothesis. The gold of fact will form at length the perfect ring of truth when the crust of suppositions which
have helped in its formation shall be dissipated into
dust and ashes. Whatever is true in the development
hypothesis will ultimately be seen to be in harmony
with all other ascertained truth. It has already led
scientific opinion to agree, with Theism and the Bible,

that the world must have had a definite beginning and an ordered process of becoming. It may yet win its way to a more solid position among laws of nature, and be proved to have had a place in the production and nurture of the human race. But this would be far from conflicting with the Bible. It would only more fully illustrate the idea of mediate creation which is so plainly indicated in the Bible cosmogony. It would only enlarge and enhance our idea of creative power that so much should be evolved out of so little, and thus be another and grander way of telling the glory of God. Meanwhile we have a revealed account of the origin of the world and of man which coincides with the instinctive beliefs of the human mind, with the plan of human history, with the faith and hope that are in God. With this account we can work and worship, and for the rest afford to wait. Knowledge and thought are advancing. "The world moves," and vainly do some seek with bars of iron or crooks of steel to hold it ever the same. "The world moves," but "The Word of the Lord endureth for ever."

LECTURE II.

MAN'S NATURE: THE BIBLE PSYCHOLOGY.

" Affections, Instincts, Principles and Powers,
  Impulse and Reason, Freedom and Control—
  So men, unravelling God's harmonious whole,
Rend in a thousand shreds this life of ours.

  Vain labour! Deep and broad, where none may see,
  Spring the foundations of that shadowy throne,
  Where man's one nature queen-like sits alone,
Centred in a majestic unity."

M. Arnold.

Gen. ii. 7.—"And the Lord God formed man *of* the dust of the ground, and breathed into his nostrils the breath of life, and man became a living soul."

1 Thess. v. 23.—"And the very God of peace sanctify you wholly ; and *I pray God* your whole spirit and soul and body be preserved blameless unto the coming of our Lord Jesus Christ."

Heb. iv. 12.—"For the word of God *is* quick, and powerful, and sharper than any two-edged sword, piercing even to the dividing asunder of soul and spirit, and of the joints and marrow, and *is* a discerner of the thoughts and intents of the heart."

1 Cor. ii. 14.—"But the natural (*lit.* soulish) man receiveth not the things of the Spirit of God : for they are foolishness unto him : neither can he know *them*, because they are spiritually discerned."

1 Cor. xv. 44.—"It is sown a natural (*lit.* soulish) body ; it is raised a spiritual body. There is a natural body, and there is a spiritual body."

LECTURE II.

LET us begin here with a summary of the principles on which all the psychological terms of Scripture are to be construed. " In this work," says the pioneer of modern biblical psychology,[1] " I take it for my guiding rule that everywhere in Scripture there reigns an accuracy and validity worthy of God." We are willing to accept this as our primary position. Holding the Bible to be substantially identical with that word of God which "pierces even to the dividing asunder" of the constituents of man's nature (Heb. iv. 12), we are prepared to give the utmost heed to its minutest shades of expression. Yet this we do in accordance with the views of inspiration already explained. As the chosen vehicle of the Divine speaker to men, the accuracy of Scripture language appears in spiritual sharpness and moral power. It is plain that in regard to psychology, for example, the Bible is marked by quite another kind of exactitude than that of the

---

[1] Magnus Friederich Roos, in his *Fundamenta Psychologiæ ex Sacrâ Scripturâ Collecta*, 1769. In the German version by Cremer, p. 4 (Stuttgart, 1857), the sentence runs: " Bei dieser Arbeit nahm ich mir zur Richtsnur: Kein Wörtlein sei von dem durch Gottes Geist getriebenen (Θεοπνεύστῳ) Verfasser auf's Gerathewohl hingesetzt, und es herrsche durchweg in der heiligen Schrift eine Gottes würdige Genauigkeit und Bündigkeit." The whole passage has been freely adapted by Beck in the preface to his own *Umriss der biblischen Seelenlehre.*

D

schools.   Indeed, its purpose requires that its teachings
be not cast in the scientific form.   According to the Tal-
mudic maxim, " The expressions used in the law are like
the ordinary language of mankind,"[1] it may be said of
the whole Bible that on all subjects it uses the language
of common life, a speech which men in all lands and
times can understand.   It is one of its divine charac-
teristics that by means of such expressions it conveys
discoveries of human nature which commend themselves to every man's conscience in the sight of God.
Yet on these very grounds the exact meaning and
consistent use of these expressions demand our closest
attention.

Again, the psychological ideas of Scripture must be
construed by us according to the manner of thought,
so far as we can apprehend it, of the writers themselves.
Now the writers of the Old Testament, from whom
those of the New derive in large part their phraseology,
are like the tongue in which they write, not philosophical.   Their psychology is not analytic.   The whole
character of their thinking should warn us against
expecting distinctions and divisions of human nature
in an abstract form.   Their tendency is to the concrete.
Their expressions, sensuous and symbolic, are " thrown
out" at mental and spiritual ideas.   They use a large
variety of terms for the same thing, according as it
is viewed from different points or conceived under
different emotional impressions.   Considering our
mental habits of analysis and abstraction, care must
be exercised in rendering their terms into modern
equivalents which are to have for us any intellectual

[1] De Sola's *New Translation of the Sacred Scrip.* i. 19.   1844.

validity. But to conclude on that account that the
expressions do neither justify nor repay accurate study,
is to fall into one of the shallowest blunders of the
Rationalistic school.   Once more, we shall certainly be
wrong if we persist in the old method of taking all
parts of Scripture as equally valid for our purpose,
and furnishing terms equally pliable and useful. We
should thus repeat the old error of the proof-text
system in theology, namely, that of finding all the
doctrines in every part of Scripture alike.[1] We must
be prepared to find growth in the use of psychological
terms in Scripture, and that from two several causes.
Acquaintance with culture outside of the Hebrew
nation has left its evident impress on the New Testament writers, and even on the later Old Testament
writers as compared with the earlier.   There is growth
from a more simple and popular to a more complex
and philosophical view of man's nature.   But the
other source of growth is more important.   There is a
progress in the revelation of which Scripture is the
record.   The proper influence of this fact upon theology has become an axiom of all enlightened study of
that science.   The fruits of that influence are already
seen in our rapidly multiplying essays in Old and New
Testament theology.   Its bearing on the study of the
sacred languages is also obvious.   Rothe has said that
"we may appropriately speak of a 'language of the

---

[1] H. Schultz complains of several otherwise meritorious works on
Biblical Psychology that they commit the error of regarding the entire
biblical writings, without more ado, as material of equal relevancy for the
study of man.—*Alt. T. Theologie*, i. 348. See also Böttcher's remark on
Beck: "Nuperrime, subtilius cæteris, nullo tamen ætatis discrimine facto."
—F. Böttcher, *De Inferis*, p. 14, Dresd. 1845.

Holy Ghost.' For in the Bible it is evident that the
Divine Spirit at work in revelation has always fashioned
for Himself, out of the language of those nationalities in
which the revelation had its chosen sphere, an entirely
peculiar religious dialect, moulding the linguistic elements which He found to hand, as well as the already
existing conceptions, into a form specially suited to His
purpose. Most clearly does the Greek of the New Testament exhibit this process."[1] Cremer, who cites this passage, adds: "The spirit of the language assumes a form
adequate to the new views which the Spirit of Christ
creates and works."[2] Without attention to this element
of progress, it is impossible to construct any adequate
biblical psychology. This alone explains the transition
from terms in the earlier Scriptures that are rather
physical than psychical, to those in the later Scriptures
that are more deeply charged with spiritual meaning. A
progressive religious revelation is intimately connected
with the growth of humanity, casts growing light upon
the nature and prospects of man, will therefore be in-
creasingly rich in statements and expressions bearing
upon the knowledge of man himself, and especially of
his inner being. It is in the latest records of such a
revelation that the terms expressive of the facts and
phenomena of man's nature should be correspond-

---

[1] "Man kann in der That mit gutem Fug von einer 'Sprache des heiligen
Geistes' reden. Denn es liegt in der Bibel offen vor unseren Augen, wie der
in der Offenbarung wirksame göttliche Geist jedesmal aus der Sprache des-
jenigen Volkskreises welcher den Schauplatz jener ausmachte, sich eine ganz
eigenthümliche religiöse Mundart gebildet hat, indem er die sprachlichen
Elemente die er vorfand, ebenso wie die schon vorhandenen Begriffe, zu
einer ihm eigenthümlich angemessenen Gestalt umformte. Am evidentesten
veranschaulicht das Griechische des Neuen Testamentes diesen Hergang."—
Zur Dogmatik, pp. 233, 234, 2te Aufl., Gotha 1869.

[2] Cremer's Lexicon, Vorrede.

ingly enriched, diversified, and distinguishable in their meaning.

Bearing in mind these simple maxims, we proceed to ask, What is the Bible view of man's constitution? It is only in the way of cursory discussion that it is possible here to indicate what we take to be the leading psychological ideas of the Scriptures. The announcement in Gen. ii. 7 is that which first claims our attention. Into this ground-text of biblical psychology the meaning of the various theories has been read, and round it numberless controversies have raged. The chief of these has been whether the passage, taken along with the allied expressions, entitles us to say that the Bible views man's nature as dual or tripartite in its constituents. But before discussing the "sufficiently famous"[1] *trichotomy*, as it is called, we must meet a question which recent speculation has brought up. Most advocates of a trichotomy of man allow it to be based upon a more radical dichotomy. But the newest question is, whether the Bible necessitates even this—whether, in short, we may not interpret its accounts of man's nature on the one substance hypothesis of modern positivism. If any part of Scripture seems in accord with this view, it is the earlier passages of the Old Testament, and prominently the one which stands at their head. The meaning, to a mind unprepossessed with theories, is sublimely simple. It declares that the Lord God formed the man, dust from the ground, and breathed into his nostrils the breath of life (or lives), and man became a living soul. Here are plainly two constitu-

---

[1] Olshausen, *Opusc. Theolog.* p. 145.

ents in the creation: the one from below, dust from
the ground; the other from above, the breath of life at
the inspiration of the Almighty. Yet from these two
facts results a unit. Man became an animated being.
Nothing can be more misleading than to identify "soul"
here with what it means in modern speech, or even
in later biblical language. "A living soul" is here
exactly equivalent to "a creature endowed with life,"
for the expression in these creation-narratives is used
of man and the lower animals in common. "Soul" in
the primitive Scripture usage means, not the "immaterial rational principle" of the philosophers, but
simply life embodied. So that in Gen. ii. 7 the unity
of the created product is emphatically expressed, and
the sufficient interpretation of the passage is, that the
divine inspiration awakes the already kneaded clay
into a living human being. Here is an account of
man's origin fitted to exclude certain dualistic views
of his nature with which the religion of revelation had
to contend. Whether the formation of his frame and
the in-breathing of his life be taken as successive or as
simultaneous moments in the process of his creation,
the description is exactly fitted to exclude that priority
of the soul which was necessary to the transmigration
taught by Oriental religions, and to the pre-existence
theory of the Greek schools. There is here no postpone-
ment or degradation of the earthly frame in favour of
the soul, as if the latter were the man, and the former
were only the prison-house into which he was sent,
or the husk in which he was for a time concealed.
According to the account in this text, the synthesis of
two factors, alike honourable, constitutes the man.

That neither the familiar antithesis, soul and body, nor any other pair of expressions by which we commonly render the dual elements in human nature, should expressly occur in this *locus classicus*, is a fact which may help to fix attention on the real character of the earlier Old Testament descriptions of man. The fact is not explained merely by the absence of analysis. Rather is it characteristic of these Scriptures to assert the *solidarité* of man's constitution, — that human individuality is of one piece, and is not composed of separate independent parts. This assertion is essential to the theology of the whole Bible—to its discovery of human sin and of a divine salvation. In a way quite unperceived by many believers in the doctrines, this idea of the unity of man binds into strictest consistency the Scripture account of his creation, the story of his fall, the character of his redemption, and all the leading features in the working out of his actual recovery from his regeneration to his resurrection.

All this, however, will not avail those who wish us to understand the Bible anthropology as giving a monistic view of man's nature, for an evident duality runs through the whole of its representations. But let us inquire how these dual elements are expressed in the Bible. The anthropology of the Greek and of some other ethnic schools rested on a dualistic scheme of the universe. Soul and body, mind and matter, were the representatives in man of contrary opposites in the constitution of things. So that for them, man, so far from being a unity, was a paradox, a mirror in little of that universe at large in which God and the world, the real and the phenomenal, were eternal opposites.

But the Bible philosophy of God, of the world, and of
man, rests on its grand and simple idea of creation
proper—an idea so familiar to us that we forget how
originally and essentially biblical it is. Its simplicity
must by no means lead us to confound it with the pantheistic doctrine of emanation ; for not out of God's own
essence or nature, but as the creation of His expressed
free will, do all things arise. As little is its duality to
be confounded with the dualism of the ethnic systems,
according to which the world is not created, but only
framed or fashioned, and exists therefore eternally in
contradistinction and counterpoise to the framer of it.
A duality, however, in the Bible philosophy there is. In
that sublime revelation of all things as the result of free
will and word in God,—" He spake, and it was done,"—
it is plain that the things made, good and perfect though
they are, stand in a line apart from and beneath their
Maker. This primal and fundamental antithesis runs
through all Bible thought,—antithesis of the Creator
and the creature, the infinite and the finite, the invisible
and the visible. This prepares us for the duality of terms
in which our passage describes the origination of man's
nature. It pointedly presents two aspects of it, the
earthly and the super-earthly,—that on the one side
which allies man to the animal creation, namely, that like
the lower animals he is formed from the ground ; that
on the other which represents man alone as receiving
his life by the immediate in-breathing of the Lord God.

We shall import into the passage a later meaning if
we insist on these contrasted aspects as a material and
an immaterial element in the modern sense of the terms,
if we identify the duality off-hand with that of body and

soul, much more if, led away by mere verbal parallelism (*aphar, nephesh, neshamah*), we read into Gen. ii. 7 the later trichotomy of body, soul, and spirit. The antithesis is clearly that of lower and higher, earthly and heavenly, animal and divine. It is not so much two elements, as two factors uniting in a single and harmonious result,—man became a living soul. Here, then, we have a duality or dichotomy no doubt substantially agreeing with that which has been current wherever man analyzes his own nature, but depending upon an antithesis native to the Scriptures. If we neglect this antithesis, if we identify it at once with the later philosophical contrast between body and soul, we shall miss the special light which it is fitted to throw upon the Scripture doctrine of man. We are told that the antithesis of material and immaterial was not developed till late in the progress of thought ; that the ancients, and even the fathers of the Christian Church, had no notion of an immaterial essence ; that the soul to them was a gas, a finer kind of matter than that of the body, but matter still; " that the sole theory of mind and body existing in the lower stages of culture is a *double materialism*," [1] and that, therefore, no antithesis of material and spiritual in the modern sense can be expected in the Bible definition of man. So far as these early passages are concerned, we agree. But the statement is much less important than it would seem ; for if we grasp this primal Bible antithesis of the earthly and super-earthly in man, if we note

---

[1] Bain, *Mind and Body*, p. 143 ; compare the hardy assertion, p. 158, that the conception of a proper immaterial or spiritual substance received no aid either from Judaism or Christianity.

how it rests on the unique account given by Revelation
of his origin, we shall be able at once to account for
the absence from the earlier Scriptures of our familiar
duality, matter and mind, and to see how for all religious
purposes this other supplied its place. We shall be able
to esteem it as a richer and fuller duality than the
mind and matter of the Greeks;—as, indeed, the only
conception which enables us to deal justly with our
subject.[1]

The pervading dual conception of man in the Old
Testament is that he is alternately viewed as fading
flesh on his earthly side, and on the other as upheld
by the Spirit of the Almighty; but this contrast of
flesh and spirit is primarily that of the animal and the
divine in man's first constitution. It is not to be
identified with the analysis of man's nature into a
material and an immaterial element. The antithesis
soul and body, in its modern or even its New Testament
sense, is absent from the Old Testament. It contains
no distinctive word for the human *body* as an organism,
but only an assemblage of terms, such as trunk, bones,
belly, flesh. The word for *soul* means radically life,
and metonymically the living person. But when used
for an element of human nature, it serves, with the help
of such terms as "heart," "spirit," "reins," to denote the
inner man. Only once, and that in a late writing,[2] is
there an expression used which favours the Greek idea
of body as the husk or clothing of the indwelling soul.

---

[1] See Appendix, Note E.

[2] Dan. vii. 15, "I Daniel was grieved in my spirit (רוּחִי) in the midst
of *my* body." But for "body" stands the Chaldee word נִדְנֶה, which
means literally the sheath of a sword. See Gesenius, *in voc.*

Indeed, we may say that neither together as making up human nature, nor in antithesis as contrasted constituents, are animal and spiritual in man even once expressed in the Old Testament as we should express them, by matter and mind, or by body and soul.

Instead of these terms we have a variety of dual expressions, such as "flesh and heart," "flesh and soul," and even of trinal terms, such as "flesh, heart, and soul," "heart, glory, and flesh," "eye, belly, and soul," to express in man the inner and the outer, the higher and the lower, the animating and the animated,—all resting upon the primal contrast of what is earth-derived and what is God-inbreathed.

So soon as we pass to the New Testament, we come upon those antithetic expressions which we ourselves familiarly use, soul and body, flesh and spirit,—Greek words moulded by Greek thought, but still derived in their use from the Septuagint, and therefore carrying with them their Old Testament force rather than the philosophical analysis of the Greek schools.

But we proceed now to consider whether this dual aspect of man, this biblical *dichotomy* (as we must call it for want of a better term), though vindicated against the false unity of monism, requires to be further modified in favour of a threefold division of man's nature. Here, as before, everything turns on the interpretation of terms. There is a pair of expressions which some find already in Gen. ii. 7, which certainly occur plentifully in the Old Testament as *nephesh* and *ruach*, in the Greek Scriptures as *psyche* and *pneuma*, in the modern languages as *Seele* and *Geist*, SOUL and SPIRIT. The distinction implied in this antithesis may be said to be the *crux* of biblical psychology, and the controversy concerning it has been very naturally, though rather unfairly, identified with that concerning the possibility of a Bible psychology at all. Is there a real distinction between these two terms in Scripture? If so, does the distinction indicate two separable natures, so that, with the corporeal presupposed, man may be said to be of tripartite nature? Or is it rather such a view of the immaterial nature of man as sunders that nature into two functions or faculties? Or, finally, is it a nomenclature to be explained and accounted for on principles entirely peculiar to the biblical writings?

The *Trichotomy* of body, soul, and spirit held an important place in the theology of some of the Greek Christian fathers; but in consequence of its seeming bias towards a Platonic doctrine of the soul and of evil, still more because of its use by Apollinaris to under-prop grave heresy as to the person of Christ, it fell into disfavour, and may be said to have been discarded from the time of Augustine till its revival within a quite modern period. It has recently received the support, or at least the favourable consideration, of a respectable school of evangelical thinkers on the Continent, represented by such names as those of Beck, Delitzsch, Göschel, Auberlen, and Oehler. That it has furnished a favourite scheme of thought for mystics and sectaries has not helped its fair investigation in our theological schools; and the pretension put forth for it by some of its votaries, that as a theological panacea it would heal the strife of centuries, has had the effect on the professional mind which is always produced by the advertisement of a quack remedy, not without that other effect on the common apprehension that after all there is probably something in it.[1]

Its crudest and most popularly known form is that which, taking *body* for the material part of our constitution, makes *soul* stand for the principle of animal life, and *spirit* for the rational and immortal nature. This is so plainly not the construction which any tolerable interpretation can put upon the Scripture passages, that such a tripartition could not be attributed to any theologian of repute. The views of Beck and Delitzsch are greatly more creditable attempts to frame a theory which will cover the Bible use of the terms. Let us briefly examine them.

Delitzsch holds both a dual and a tripartite division of human nature to be scriptural. He contends for three distinct or essential elements in man;[2] soul and spirit, though not distinct natures,[3] being nevertheless separable elements of the inner man,[4] and these such as to be substantially distinguished.[5] This position Delitzsch thinks of such cardinal importance to his system that he signalizes it thus: "The key of biblical psychology lies in the solution of the enigma, how is it to be conceived that spirit and soul can be of one nature and yet of distinct substance? When once I was enlightened upon this enigma, my confused materials for a biblical psychology formed themselves,

---

[1] See Appendix, Note F.

[2] "Drei verschiedene Bestandtheile," or "drei Wesensbestandtheile," *Biblische Psychologie*, pp. 90, 91.

[3] "Nicht verschiedene Wesen," p. 92.

[4] "Sondernde Bestandtheile der menschlichen Innerlichkeit," p. 92.

[5] "Substanziell zu unterscheiden," p. 95, where he explains that he does not take *substantia* to be the same as *essentia*.

as if spontaneously, into a systematic whole."[1]   This
light he endeavours to convey to his readers.   "Soul
and spirit are of one nature but of distinct substance,"[2]
"as the Son and the Spirit in the blessed Trinity are of
one nature with the Father, but still not the same
hypostases."   The soul is related to the spirit, as the
life to the principle of life, and as the effect to that
which produces it; as the brute soul is related to the
absolute spirit which brooded over the waters of chaos.
He quotes from Justin that as the body is the house of
the soul, so the soul is the house of the spirit; from
Irenæus, that the soul is the tabernacle of the spirit;
but his main and favourite analogy is that the human
soul is related to the human spirit, as the divine *Doxa*
is related to the triune divine nature.   The spirit is
the in-breathing of the Godhead, the soul is the out-
breathing of the spirit.   The spirit is *spiritus spiratus*,
and, as *spiritus spirans*, endows the body with soul.
The spirit is the internal of the soul, the soul is the
external of the spirit.   In the Old Testament the soul
is also called simply "the glory" (כָּבוֹד),[3] for the spirit
is the image of the triune Godhead, but the soul is
the copy of this image, and relates itself to the spirit
as the "seven spirits" (Rev. iv. 5) are related to the
Spirit of God.[4]

So much for his explanations and analogies.   The
main proofs he adduces for a scriptural trichotomy in
the sense now explained are the two well-known

---

[1] *Biblische Psychologie*, Vorrede, p. v.
[2] "Geist und Seele sind eines Wesens aber verschiedene Substanzen,"
p. 96.
[3] Gen. xlix. 6; Ps. vii. 6, xvi. 9, xxx. 13, lvii. 9, cviii. 2 (*orig.*).
[4] Pp. 97, 98 of *Bibl. Psych.*, or pp. 117, 119 of Clark's Transl.

passages, 1 Thess. v. 23 and Heb. iv. 12. On the first
of these he, in point of fact, yields the question by saying that "if any one prefers to say that by *pneuma*
and *psyche* the apostle is distinguishing the internal
condition of man's life, and especially of the Christian's
life, in respect of two several relations, this would not
be false, for the three constituents which he distinguishes are in no wise three essentially distinct
elements; [1] either spirit and soul, or soul and
body, belong to one another as of like nature, and
the apostle's view is in the last result certainly
dichotomic."

On Heb. iv. 12 he makes the exegetically happy
suggestion that there is a parallel in the passage
between the sensuous and the supersensuous in man,
and that both are here represented as bipartite, "soul
and spirit" in the one standing over against "joints
and marrow" in the other.[2] But clearly this exegesis
favours the conclusion that soul and spirit are two

[1] "Die drei Wesensbestandtheile, die er unterscheidet, sind keinesfalls
drei wesensverschiedene," p. 91; Clark's Transl. p. 110.

[2] "I maintain that the writer ascribes to the Word of God a dividing
activity of an ethical sort which extends to the whole spiritual-psychical
and corporeal nature of man; and that he regards as bipartite the unseen
supersensible element, as well as that which is sensuous and apparent to
the senses, inasmuch as he distinguishes ψυχή and πνεῦμα in the former,
in the latter the ἁρμοί which minister to the life of motion, and the μυελοί
which minister to that of sensation." — P. 92; comp. Clark's Transl.
p. 111.

In his Commentary, *in loc.*, he says: "The four terms (soul, spirit,
joints, marrow) appear to correspond to each other *chiastically, i.e.* ψυχή
answering to ἁρμοί, πνεῦμα to μυελοί, and the four together designating
man in his compound nature. The Divine Word is said to lay bare the
whole man thus described, before the eyes of God and before his own,
discovering by means of a strict analysis both his psychico-spiritual and his
inward corporeal condition."—Delitzsch *On the Epistle to the Hebrews,* vol. i.
p. 214; Clark's Transl.

several functions, relations, or aspects of the inner life
of man; as joints and marrow, the organs of motion
and sensation, are separable parts of his corporeal being,
but not distinct natures. The view of Delitzsch is, on
the whole, at least a strong and clear recognition that
Scripture maintains the duality of man. And for the
rest, it covers the fact that Scripture at times speaks
in tripartite language of that which is essentially only
twofold.

Beck's view is, that body and spirit are the two
radically distinct elements or principles. Soul is that
which unifies them; derived from the in-breathing of
the spirit, formed by the union of the breath of God's
Spirit with the body, it yet constitutes or is identical
with the human *ego*. Man is soul; he possesses body
and spirit; spirit is the principle and the power by
which life persists; soul is the seat, guide, and holder
of it, while body is its vessel and organ. The three
are specifically different, but they exist only in connection with one another. The proper foundation of
human nature, formed as it is out of spirit and earth,
is the Subject or Ego in the strict sense of the word,
that is the Soul, which connects the inward vital power
of the spirit with the outward vital organ of the body,
forming the two into one living individuality. So far
Beck. His treatise, *Umriss der biblischen Seelenlehre*,[1]
is extremely subtle, not always intelligible, and much
vitiated by entire disregard of the historical method;
Scripture being quoted as if the whole had been

[1] *Outlines of Biblical Psychology*, recently translated, Edinburgh, T. &
T. Clark, 1877. See especially p. 38 (or p. 35 of the original) for a
summary of his views.

written contemporaneously, and as if every text bore with equal directness on the nature of the soul.

It is plain that even these most strenuous defenders of a biblical trichotomy make no approach to the theory of a tripartite nature in man. They repudiate the attempt to revive the essential distinction of Occam, which represents man as possessed of two souls, one the seat of reason, the other of sensation and growth. In short, they are after all true Aristotelians as to the doctrine of the inner life, not Platonists. It is not two separate souls they find in the Scripture trichotomy.[1] And their position does not radically differ from that of the large number of writers, both in this country and on the Continent, who now willingly adopt the distinction between soul and spirit, as expressing two faculties or functions of the inner man. When, however, we examine the views of those who maintain that the distinction, though something less than that of two separate natures, is yet something more than merely of two relations, is really that of two departments in man's inward nature, we find much diversity in the mode of construing the distinction. Some tell us that *pneuma* represents the higher region of self-conscious spirit and self-determining will, *psyche* the lower region of appetite, perception, imagination, memory; the former that which belongs to man as man, the latter that which in the main is common to him with the brute.[2] Bishop

---

[1] Delitzsch says: "We thoroughly agree in this respect with Thomas Aquinas: 'Impossibile est, in uno homine esse plures animas per essentiam differentes, sed una tantum est anima intellectiva quæ vegetativæ et sensitivæ et intellectivæ officiis fungitur.'"—*Bibl. Psych.* p. 94; Clark, p. 114.

[2] Liddon, *Some Elements of Religion*, p. 92, Lond. 1873.

E

Ellicott puts it thus: "The spirit may be regarded
more as the realm of the intellectual forces, and the
shrine of the Holy Ghost; the soul may be regarded
more as the region of the feelings, affections, and im-
pulses, of all that peculiarly individualizes and per-
sonifies." [1] Others, again, reserving the term "body"
for those appetites which we have in common with
the brutes, take "soul" as denoting our moral and
intellectual faculties directed only towards objects of
the world, and "spirit" for the same faculties when
directed towards God and heavenly things. [2] Not
greatly different from this last, but more succinctly
expressed, is the view of Auberlen: "Body, soul, and
spirit are nothing else than the real basis of the three
ideal elements of man's being, world-consciousness,
self-consciousness, and God-consciousness." [3]

It would be easy enough to refute each of these proposed divisions by confronting it with one or more texts
which it will not cover. It is better to accept them
all as evidence that a trichotomic usage in Scripture
plainly there is, and that it requires recognition and
explanation. Only a patient investigation of its rise
will enable us to apprehend its force. That soul and
spirit denote distinct natures in man, or, as Delitzsch
has it, separable elements of one nature, or even, as
others, distinct faculties of the inner man, implies a
kind of analysis which is out of harmony with biblical
thought, and will not stand upon an impartial ex-

---

[1] *Destiny of the Creature, and other Sermons,* p. 123, Lond. 1863 ; also
in his *Commentary* on 1 Thess. v. 23.

[2] Dr. T. Arnold as quoted by Heard, *Tripartite Nature,* p. 161, note.

[3] Article "Geist," Herzog's *Real-Encyklop.* iv. 729. For an account of
some other forms of the Tripartition theory, see Appendix, Note F.

amination of the biblical phraseology. On the other
hand, that in the passages to be explained we have
nothing more than rhetorical accumulation of terms,
will not satisfy the facts. We must be guided by a
principle already suggested. The later inspired writers
adapted the growingly philosophical language of their
times to the enlarged ideas with which the spirit of
Revelation furnished them. Let us briefly trace that
growth in the case of the two terms in hand. *Pneuma*
and *psyche*, like *ruach* and *nephesh*, of which they are
the Greek equivalents, both originally refer to physical
life. *Ruach* and *nephesh* are easily distinguished, however, in this primal sense. *Nephesh* is the subject or
bearer of life, *ruach* is the principle of life; so that
in all the Old Testament references to the origin of
living beings, we find it possible to distinguish *nephesh*,
as life constituted in the creature, from *ruach*, as life
bestowed by the Creator. In most places the two
terms are used of man and animals alike. *Nephesh
hayyah* is a living creature in general; while both
ruach and the kindred term *neshamah* are used of the
principle as well of brute as of human life.[1] This
primary use of the two terms for physical life has
passed over from the Hebrew of the Old Testament to
the Greek equivalents in the New, and the primal distinction of the two terms *inter se* will suggest a reason
for their respective employment, even where the sense

---

[1] Compare נֶפֶשׁ חַיָּה, Gen. i. 30, ii. 7, with נִשְׁמַת חַיִּים, Gen. ii. 7; רוּחַ חַיִּים,
vi. 17, vii. 15, and נִשְׁמַת־רוּחַ חַיִּים, vii. 22. Compare also נֶפֶשׁ הַבָּשָׂר, Lev.
xvii. 11, with הָרוּחֹת לְכָל־בָּשָׂר, Numb. xvi. 22, xxvii. 16, for the distinctive
force of *nephesh* and *ruach* respectively. The application of *ruach* to the
divinely-given life-principle in general is not affected by such a passage as
Job xii. 10, "The soul of every living thing and the spirit of all mankind."

almost transcends the merely physical. *Psyche* will be the entire being as a constituted life: "He giveth His soul" (*psyche*, not *zoë*) "for the sheep."[1] *Pneuma* will be the life-principle as bestowed by and belonging to God: "He gave up the ghost."[2]

When, however, we pass from this primary to the secondary sense, in which both *ruach* (*pneuma*, spirit) on the one hand, and *nephesh* (*psyche*, soul) on the other, denote the whole inner life or hyperphysical nature in man, we find that they are freely interchanged and combined throughout the Old Testament and the first part of the New. This appears upon examination of three classes of passages. First, those where each term is used alone, as, "Why is thy spirit (*ruach*) so sad?"[3] "Why art thou cast down, my soul (*nephesh*)?"[4] "Jesus was troubled in spirit (*pneuma*);"[5] "My soul (*psyche*) is exceeding sorrowful."[6] Then, in those where either term is joined with body, as, "To destroy both soul and body;"[7] "The body without the spirit is dead."[8] Again, in those where the two terms occur together in the manner of other parallel terms of Hebrew poetry: "With my soul have I desired Thee in the night; yea, with my spirit within me will I seek Thee early;"[9] "My soul doth magnify the Lord, and my spirit hath rejoiced in God my Saviour;"[10] "Stand fast in one spirit, with one soul striving together for the faith of the gospel."[11] These last passages render it quite impossible to hold, for example, that spirit can mean exclusively the Godward side of

[1] John x. 11.   [2] John xix. 30.   [3] 1 Kings xxi. 5.   [4] Ps. xlii. 11.
[5] John xiii. 21.   [6] Matt. xxvi. 38.   [7] Matt. x. 28.   [8] Jas. ii. 26.
[9] Isa. xxvi. 9.   [10] Luke i. 46, 47.   [11] Philip. i. 27.

man's nature, and soul the rational or sensible. The
terms are parallel, though not equivalent. For the
underlying distinction found in their primary or
physical reference gives colour and propriety to their
usage all along; and firmly grasped, it will prepare
us to understand the expanded meaning which they
receive in the later New Testament thought. Spirit
is life as coming from God. Soul is life as constituted
in the man. Consequently, when the individual life
is to be made emphatic, "soul" is used. "Souls" in
Scripture freely denotes persons; "my soul" is the Ego,
the self, and when used like "heart" for the inner
man, and even for the feelings, has reference always to
the special individuality. "Spirit," on the other hand,
seldom or never used to denote the individual human
being, is primarily that imparted power by which the
individual lives. It fitly denotes, therefore, the innermost of the inner life, the higher aspect of the self or
personality.[1] Thus far, however, there is no apparent

[1] For confirmation of the correctness of this view, see Weiss, *Biblische
Theologie des N. Test.* 2te Aufl. p. 88 ; Oehler, *Theology of the Old Testament* (Edin., Clark, 1874), vol. i. pp. 216–220 ; Hofmann, *Schriftbeweis*,
i. 296, who, however, is careful to observe that we must not deny to
pneuma the force of personality on its higher side. That soul is oftener
used for person is to be explained, he thinks, thus : "Weil es näher liegt,
die Person nach ihrem so and so bedingten Einzelleben, als sie nach der
dasselbe so and so bedingenden Lebensmacht zu benennen." He is clear
that they can be distinguished as two sides of man's inner and moral life,
without making them two several constituents of human nature.

The distinction we are illustrating is well put by Ebrard in his *Comment.
ü. den Hebräer-Brief*, on the passage ch. iv. 12 ; and in Herzog, art. "Adam
u. seine Söhne." Olshausen in his well-known tract on the Trichotomy
has a glimpse of it, but really belongs to the older and less correct current
of interpreters. He says : "Πνεῦμα significat vim superiorem, agentem,
imperantem in homine, *ita ut simul origo ejus cœlestis indicetur ;* ψυχή
autem significat vim inferiorem, quæ agitur, movetur, in imperio tenetur,
nam media inter vim terrestrem et cœlestem collocata cogitatur ἡ ψυχή."—
Opuscula Theologica, p. 154.

design in the use of the terms to analyze the constituent parts of man's inner being. The purpose is
only to present the one indivisible thinking and feeling man in diverse aspects, as these terms originally
expressed man's life viewed from two different points.
Their use, therefore, up to this point cannot be held as
giving us a philosophical analysis of human nature
within the biblical writings. It is quite certain, however, that in the period between the production of the
Old Testament writings and those of the New, a use of
psyche and *pneuma* sprang up under the Alexandrian
influence, which led some of the apocryphal writers
and the Seventy to suggest for their national writings
a philosophical analysis of man's nature — a trichotomy, in short, corresponding to that of Plato, though
not identical with it. It is as undoubted that these
combined influences—the Greek philosophy and the
later Jewish schools—led the Christian writers of the
early centuries to adopt the analysis as a scriptural one;
hence also its revival in recent biblical psychology.

When we pass from the natural to the theological
use of these two terms in the New Testament, the
important question arises, whether the distinction to
be found between *pneuma* with its adjective on the
one hand, and *psyche* with its adjective on the other,
in the well-known group of texts, mainly Pauline, 1
Thess. v. 23, 1 Cor. ii. 14, xv. 44, Heb. iv. 12, Jude 19,
is identical with that of the Jewish schools, or owes
its force to another and higher influence. If the Old
Testament use of them, followed, as we learn from
the Gospels, by our Lord and the elder apostles, was
not analytic, was natural and real as opposed to

philosophical, then though Paul may be said to have
adopted the philosophical language of the Jewish
schools, he was rather redeeming the Old Testament terms out of their hands for a new purpose.
The parallel between his tripartite language and that
of the Platonists and Stoics is obvious enough. But
the difference is no less distinct. What he took from
them was sanctioned by the usage of the Septuagint;
what he added was an application of Old Testament
language to express the New Testament revelation of
grace.[1] The tripartition of Plato and the Platonizing
schools was part of a method for solving the problem
of evil. It was intended to account for divergent
moral forces in man, for the subjugation in him of
what is best by what is worst; and it did so by
assuming that there was in his formation a physical
element eternally opposed to the divine. In the
terms of the trichotomy, as derived from the Old
Testament, there was no such taint. They were fitted
to do a better thing than to account for man's evil—
namely, to express under the power of a new revelation
the way of his recovery. They were exactly suited to
express the new idea. One of them especially, "spirit"
($\pi\nu\epsilon\hat{v}\mu\alpha$), had never been debased by ethnic or erroneous
thought. It was never used in the Greek psychology.
Even Plato's highest principle is not $\pi\nu\epsilon\hat{v}\mu\alpha$, but $\nu o\hat{v}s$
and its derivatives. While, therefore, the idea of the
New Testament trichotomy was suggested by the usage
of the Greek and Græco-Jewish schools, the terms

[1] See Appendix, Note G. For some remarks on the apostle's relation to
the Stoics, see Lightfoot's dissertation on " St. Paul and Seneca," appended
to his *Commentary on Philippians;* also Sir Alex. Grant's *Ethics of
Aristotle,* vol. i., the preliminary essay on " The Ancient Stoics."

themselves were biblical. The meaning was at once
true to the simple psychology of the Old Testament, and
enlarged with fulness of New Testament revelation.
It is clear that the distinction between the psychical
man and the spiritual man, the psychical body and the
spiritual body, is one radical to the theology of Paul's
Epistles. But instead of being rooted in a philosophical analysis of the constituents of human nature,
it is mainly born of two disclosures of advancing
revealed thought. The one is the clear revelation of
the personality of a third hypostasis in the Godhead,
definitely and fully indicated in the New Testament
by the term Spirit, Holy Spirit of God, Spirit of Christ.
The other is the spiritual union of redeemed humanity
with God through Christ Jesus. The new life or
nature thus originated is variously called "the new
man," "a new creature," "the inner man," and
especially "the spirit" as contrasted with "the flesh."
Why this word *pneuma* should be adopted to express
the new nature in believers, or the indwelling of God
with man, is plain. The Third Person in the Trinity
is the agent in originating and maintaining this new
life, and with a rare felicity the same word (*ruach* of
the Old Testament, and *pneuma* of the New) denotes
the Holy Spirit of God and the heaven-derived life
in renewed man. It is an instance at once of the
elevating influence of revelation upon language, and
of that insight into the capacity and destinies of
human nature which the progress of revelation brings
with it. *Pneuma* and *psyche*, with their derivatives, thus
assume under the influence of New Testament theology
a new and enlarged significance. Besides denoting

physical life in common, yet with difference of aspect; besides denoting the inner life in general with corresponding difference of emphasis, they denote a moral and spiritual distinction. The psychical man is man as nature now constitutes him, and as sin has infected him. The spiritual man is man as grace has reconstituted him, and as God's Spirit dwells in him. The unrenewed man is "psychical not having the spirit."[1] The word of God divides and discriminates between that which is psychical and that which is spiritual.[2] The Christian is to be sanctified wholly in his threefold life,—the physical life of the body, the individual life of the soul, the inner life of the spirit; which latter two become again the basis of the natural and of the regenerate life respectively.[3] In the progress of redemption he shall exchange a body psychical or natural, which he has in common with all men as derived from Adam, for a body spiritual or glorified, adapted to his new nature and fashioned like unto the glorious body of his Lord; for the first head of the race was made a living *psyche*, but the second Adam is a life-giving *Pneuma*.[4]

According to this explanation, we do not base the Pauline psychology upon any school distinctions,

---

[1] ψυχικοί πνεῦμα μὴ ἔχοντες, Jude 19.

[2] Heb. iv. 12. See Delitzsch *in loc.;* also Ebrard, who says: "Von einer Trennung der Seele vom Geiste kann keine Rede sein. . . . Dagegen ergiebt sich ein trefflicher Sinn, wenn wir die Seele als ein tief innerlich im Menschen Liegendes, den Geist als ein noch tiefer Liegendes, und das Wort Gottes als ein in die Seele und von da noch tiefer, selbst in den Geist Eindringendes fassen." There is much to be said in favour of the penetrating rather than dissecting power as the thing attributed to the Word here. But that which penetrates, discriminates. See Hofmann's peculiarly ingenious remarks, *Schriftbeweis,* i. 296.

[3] 1 Thess. v. 23.   [4] 1 Cor. xv. 44, 45.

Platonist, Philonian, or Stoic.[1] We recognise it as
an essential part of St. Paul's inspired insight into
the relations of man's nature under the dispensation
of grace. Nevertheless we see how the simple and
natural use of the terms Soul and Spirit in the Old
Testament, and in the early usage of New Testament
times, prepared the way for this new meaning which
the spiritual system of the Pauline Epistles has poured
into them. The natural life as organically constituted,
the personal living being, was soul—*nephesh* or *psyche ;*
whereas life as emanating from the fountain, the
informing energy of the creature as derived from the
Creator, was spirit—*ruach* or *pneuma ;* and thus, when
a higher distinction became necessary, the man as he
was produced in nature was psychical or soulish, the
man as renewed from heaven was pneumatical or
spiritual. That is to say, the same word which
expressed the God-derived natural life came to express
the essence of the new life, the identity of the words
indicating an underlying biblical thought—namely,
that the immediate divine origination of man's being
in creation lays a ground for the immediate divine
renewal of his nature in redemption.

Not less important, for biblical psychology and theology, than the two terms already discussed, is the term
FLESH (בָּשָׂר, σάρξ).[2] It will be necessary to note its use
in two broadly distinct regions. There is (A) a natural

---

[1] In this opinion we are confirmed by such recent and keen inquirers
as Lüdemann, *Die Anthropologie des Apostels Paulus*, Kiel 1872, and
Pfleiderer, *Paulinismus*, Leipzig 1873. See more on this point in Lect. V.

[2] שְׁאֵר is sometimes used as equivalent to בָּשָׂר even in its psychological
sense ; see Ps. lxxiii. 26. More usually the relation of שְׁאֵר to בָּשָׂר is
like that of κρέας to σάρξ ; see, *e.g.*, Ps. lxxviii. 20, 27, comp. with ver. 39.

meaning, admitting of various shades of application, which runs through the whole Scripture. It bears also (B) a very definite ethical significance in certain well-known doctrinal passages of the New Testament, especially of the Pauline Epistles.

Under the first head (A), there are four shades of meaning which we may conveniently distinguish. There is (1) its literal meaning, *substance of a living body*, whether of men or beasts. From this radical meaning it comes to be a designation of the creature on one side, as "living soul" is on the other. If "soul" (*nephesh*) be an embodied life, "flesh" (*bāsar*) is ensouled matter; though we must never construe it as mere materiality, for in the life-principle which makes it flesh a higher element is presupposed. Under this use it denotes all terrestrial beings that possess sensational life.[1] From this there arises (2) its application to *human nature generally*, and the personal life attached to it. Man as clothed in corporeity is contrasted under the name "flesh" with purely spiritual being, and especially with God. Hence with reference to the weak, the finite, the perishable being which man is, does this expression pervade both the Old and the New Testament as a phrase for human kind.[2] The New Testament has the additional expression "flesh and blood" (σὰρξ καὶ αἷμα) to designate human nature on its earthly side, in contrast with the supersensible and the divine. The phrase, though without an exact equivalent in the Hebrew of

---

[1] *e.g.*, Gen. vii. 21.

[2] *e.g.*, Gen. vi. 3; Job xxxiv. 15; Ps. lvi. 5, lxxviii. 39; Isa. xl. 6–8; Jer. xvii. 5; 1 Cor. i. 29; 1 Pet. i. 24.

the Old Testament, is doubtless expressive of the
Old Testament idea, "The life of the flesh is in the
blood." Its special force, however, lies in contrasting
human nature with something greater than itself.[1]
When we come (3) to use "flesh" as a term of
contrast within the human being, it naturally stands
for *the corporeal or lower element* in man's constitution.
In the Old Testament it is used along with "heart"
or "soul" to express the entire constituents of man's
nature. So far, however, is it from being despised in
contrast with these higher elements, that it is joined
with them in the relation of the whole man to God and
to his future hopes.[2] In the New Testament its use
in this psychological sense for the lower element in
man without any ethical attribution, though not very
frequent, is quite clear. In a sufficient number of
passages it occurs coupled with spirit ($\pi\nu\epsilon\hat{\upsilon}\mu a$), to show
that flesh and spirit are used for the whole of man, the
simple natural elements of which he is made up, exactly
as "flesh and soul," "flesh and heart," are in the Old
Testament.[3] It is of considerable importance to point
out that even within the Pauline writings, where we
are afterwards to find the specifically ethical meaning
of flesh so current, a quite unethical use of "flesh"
($\sigma \acute{a} \rho \xi$) for the outward sensational part of human
existence, in contrast with the inner and spiritual, is
undeniable;[4] and even when the sinful state of man is

---

[1] *e.g.*, Matt. xvi. 17; 1 Cor. xv. 50; Gal. i. 16; Eph. vi. 12; Heb. ii.
14, to which may be added John i. 13.

[2] Ps. lxiii. 1, lxxxiv. 2, xvi. 9; Job xix. 26. A good example of the two,
bāsar and *nephesh*, used as the sole and even separable constituents of
human nature, like soul and body, is Job xiv. 22.

[3] Matt. xxvi. 41; Mark xiv. 38; comp. Luke xxiv. 39.

[4] Rom. ii. 28; 1 Cor. v. 5, vii. 28; 2 Cor. iv. 11, vii. 5, xii. 7; $\sigma \acute{a} \rho \xi$ is also

the subject under consideration, the whole of man is
designated by "flesh and mind" in one Pauline passage,
and by "flesh and spirit" in another.[1] The New
Testament has other pairs of expressions for the same
thing. It uses freely the Greek duality which has
become the modern one, "soul and body." And
though the Old Testament "soul and flesh" does not
recur, "body and spirit" can take its place.[2] These
phrases afford sufficient proof that the biblical view of
man's constitution is truly dichotomic. It may also
be observed that the use of "flesh and spirit" as really
equivalent to "soul and body" is an incidental confirmation of the view already advanced, that there is
no distinction of natures between soul and spirit,
though there is an obvious propriety in the ordinary
form of these dual combinations, where the inner and
the outer nature of man are respectively designated
according to fixed aspects of each. "Soul and body"
links the individuality with the organism; "flesh
and spirit" links the earthly substance in which life
inheres with the divine spark or principle of life.
The last use (4) of the term "flesh" in its merely
natural significance needs no more than to be named.
It is that so common in both Old and New Testament
for *relationship* or *connection*, by marriage, more usually
by birth; kinship—tribal, national, or universal.[3]

used by Paul of corporeal presence cognisable by the senses, as contrasted
with spiritual fellowship, *ἐν πνεύματι*, 2 Cor. v. 16, Col. ii. 1, 5, and, indeed,
of the earthly life of man without any moral qualification ; *e.g.*, Gal. ii. 20,
" The life which I now live in the flesh ; " so also Phil. i. 22.

[1] Eph. ii. 3 ; 2 Cor. vii. 1.

[2] 1 Cor. vi. 16, 17, vii. 34 ; 1 Cor. v. 3, like "flesh" and "spirit" in Col. ii. 5.

[3] *e.g.*, Gen. ii. 23, xxix. 14, xxxvii. 27 ; Judg. ix. 2 ; Rom. ix. 5, 8 ; 1 Cor.
x. 18 ; Eph. v. 29.

It is clear that in the four uses now considered there is nothing directly ethical, at least nothing which identifies the flesh with the principle of evil. "Not a single passage in the Old Testament can be adduced wherein בָּשָׂר is used to denote man's sensuous nature as the seat of an opposition against his spirit, and of a bias toward sin." [1] It is true that "flesh," used for human kind in contrast to higher beings and to God, brings out the frailty and finitude of man.   It is also true that "flesh" as a constituent of human nature means the perishable, animal, sensuous, and even sensual element of it; but which of these ideas is prominent in any passage must be learned from its connection and context.   It is further true that in its meaning of "natural kinship" there is often an implied contrast with something better, as, *e.g.*, "Israel after the flesh."   But the conclusive proof that nothing of moral depreciation is necessarily implied in this use of it, is its application to our Lord as designating His human in contrast to His divine nature: "Who was manifest in the flesh, justified in the spirit," "made of the seed of David according to the flesh." [2]

(B) It is evident, however, that throughout the Pauline Epistles, and especially in certain well-known passages, "flesh" is used for the principle, or for the seat of the principle, which in fallen human nature resists the divine law, which is contrasted with something ($\nu o \hat{v} s$) in man's own nature consenting unto the law, and which even in the regenerate makes war against the

---

[1] Müller, *The Christian Doctrine of Sin*, i. p. 323 (Clark's Translation, 2d edit.).

[2] 1 Tim. iii. 16; Rom. i. 3.

spirit. Here we have a very marked ethical significance given to the word. Nor is it the only term of
its kind used to denominate the evil principle in man's
nature as now under sin. "The old man," "the body
of sin," "the body of the flesh," "the law in the members," "our members which are upon earth," are
kindred expressions more or less closely denoting the
same thing, although "flesh" in its counterpoise to
"the mind" (νοῦς) in Rom. vii., and to "the spirit"
(πνεῦμα) in Rom. viii. and Gal. v., is the leading expression. Now, although it is not usual to construe
these phrases as asserting that the literal flesh or the
bodily organism is the seat or principle of sin,
although a metaphorical turn is generally given to
them, yet it must be admitted that it is exactly the
current and allowable character of the metaphor
which needs explanation.[1]   How is it that the terms
properly denoting the lower or corporeal element
in man's nature should come to denote the being
of sin in that nature?   The answer that it is
because the sensuous is either (a) the main seat
or (b) the original source of sin in man, although
it long contented negative divines, has become too
obviously shallow and incorrect even for some of them.
As to the elements in man's nature where sin has
(a) *its seat*, these are plainly not the sensuous or

---

[1] It seems to me that Hofmann, while strongly defending the thesis that
it is not from the body sin has its source, betrays his position to some extent by refusing to see that the Pauline phrases above quoted are metaphorical (see *Schriftbeweis*, i. p. 561, 2te Aufl.). Müller, on the other hand,
consistently maintains it,—*Christian Doctrine of Sin*, i. 330–332. How
"members which are upon earth," Col. iii. 5, followed by such an enumeration of sins, can be anything else than a metaphorical representation, it is
impossible to understand.

sensational alone. There are sinful desires of the
"mind" (διανοιῶν). There is filthiness of the "spirit"
(πνεύματος).[1] There are works called "of the flesh"
which have nothing to do with sensuality; *e.g.*,
"hatreds, variance, emulation, heresies."[2] The
apostle calls by the name of "fleshly wisdom" what
was evidently speculative tendency derived from the
Greek schools.[3] And there were heretics at Colossæ
whose ruling impulse he calls their "fleshly mind,"
though they were evidently extreme ascetics attached
to some form of Gnosticism.[4]

It might, indeed, be maintained that if we assume
the sensuous nature in man to be (*b*) *the principle* or
source of evil in him, it is easy to understand how the
whole man under its influence should receive the
denomination of "the flesh," or the "body of sin."
But this is an assumption which will not tally with
the treatment of man's corporeal nature in the sacred
writings. Any view implying the inherent evil of
matter is radically opposed to the whole biblical
philosophy. To derive moral evil in man from the
bodily side of his nature is as opposed to the Scripture
account of its beginning in the race as it is to our
experience of its first manifestations in the individual.
In Genesis the first sin is represented as the con-

---

[1] Eph. ii. 3 ; 2 Cor. vii. 1.

[2] Gal. v. 20 ; comp. also 1 Cor. iii. 1, 3, where the charge is "strife,
division," etc., not sensuality ; yet it is said, " Are ye not carnal?"

[3] Comp. 1 Cor. i. 21, 22, Ἑλληνες σοφίαν ζητοῦσιν, with ver. 26, σοφοὶ
κατὰ σάρκα. The phrase σοφία σαρκική occurs in another connection, 2 Cor.
i. 12.

[4] Col. ii. 18; comp. vers. 21, 22, 23. See Lightfoot's dissertation on
"The Colossian Heresy," prefixed to his *Commentary* on that epistle, 2d edit.
1876.

sequence of a primary rebellion against God.[1] The
first outbreaks of moral evil in children are selfishness,
anger, and self-will. Again, that the corporeal nature
is necessarily at strife with the spiritual is a view
which cannot be reconciled with the claims made upon
the body in the Christian system—with such precepts
as that believers are to "yield their members instruments of righteousness unto God,"[2] to present their
bodies a living sacrifice,[3] to regard their bodies as
the members of Christ and as the temple of the Holy
Ghost,[4] that the body is for the Lord and the Lord for
the body.[5] Still more impossible is it to reconcile with
such a view the Christian revelation concerning the
future of the redeemed, and the consummation of
redemption. If sin were the inevitable outcome of
man's possession of a body, redemption ought to cul-
minate in his deliverance from it, instead of in its change
and restoration to a higher form.[6] To say that the
matter of the body is or contains the principle of sin,
and then to say, as Paul does,[7] that the last result of
the Redeemer's Spirit indwelling in us shall be to
quicken these mortal bodies, would be flat self-contradiction. But the truth is, the view which connects sin
with the material body is neither Hebrew nor Christian.
It is essentially alien to the whole spirit of revelation.
Nevertheless, at a very early period in Christian history,
chiefly through the influence of the Greek and some of
the Latin fathers, it obtained such hold of Christian
thought that it continues to colour popular modes of
conception and speech to the present day. One of its

[1] See Lect. IV.   [2] Rom. vi. 13.   [3] Rom. xii. 1.   [4] 1 Cor. vi. 15, 19.
[5] 1 Cor. vi. 13.   [6] Phil. iii. 21.   [7] Rom. viii. 11.

F

most obvious examples is that men imagine they are
uttering a scriptural sentiment when they speak of
welcoming death as the liberation of the soul from the
body, the sentiment of Paul being exactly the reverse,
when he declares that even the redeemed who have
the first-fruits of the Spirit groan within themselves,
waiting for the adoption, *i.e.* for the redemption of
their body.[1] Two additional reasons why Paul cannot
be held as tracing man's evil to the corporeal element
may be summed up in the words of Julius Müller: "He
denies the presence of evil in Christ, who was partaker
of our fleshly nature,[2] and he recognises it in spirits
who are not partakers thereof.[3] Is it not, therefore, in
the highest degree probable that according to him evil
does not necessarily pertain to man's sensuous nature,
and that σάρξ denotes something different from this?"[4]

When, however, those who successfully refute this
mistaken derivation of the ethical force of σάρξ come to
give their own explanation of it, they fall for the most
part into mere tautology. If we say with Neander
that it represents "human nature in its estrangement
from the divine life,"[5] or with Müller that it is the
"tendency which turns towards the things of the
world and is thereby turned away from God,"[6] or with
Principal Tulloch that it means "all the evil activity
of human nature,"[7] we attain the profound conclusion
that the flesh is sinful human nature! If "flesh" be

---

[1] Rom. viii. 23.   [2] Gal. iv. 4 ; Heb. ii. 14.
[3] τὰ πνευματικὰ τῆς πονηρίας, Eph. vi. 12.
[4] *The Christian Doctrine of Sin*, i. p. 321.
[5] *Planting of Christianity*, i. p. 422 (Bohn's edit.).
[6] *Ut supra*, i. p. 326.
[7] Croall Lecture, 1876, p. 154. Dr. Tulloch also employs Neander's phrase.

a designation for sinfully-conditioned human nature, whence comes it that the term is appropriate? When σάρξ is defined as "the sinful propensity generally," or as "love of the world," it is quite fair to ask, as Pfleiderer does,[1] "how it would sound to say, 'In me, that is, in my tendency to sin in general, or in my love of the world, dwelleth no good thing.'" "If the 'flesh' be nothing else than just this condition of man's nature as we find it, this condition which is to be explained, then the whole of Paul's subtle and acute deduction would be nothing but the most wretched argument in a circle. People would give anything to explain away the idea of an impersonal principle of sin contained in the nature of man that precedes every sinful manifestation, and is the ultimate cause which infallibly produces it; and yet this is just the pith of the whole passage."[2] It is quite certain that Paul means to posit a principle of sin in man,— "the sin that dwelleth in me, the law in my members." It is further clear (notwithstanding the occasional use of the one for the other, e.g. "the flesh lusteth against the spirit"), that the law or principle of sin is one thing, and the flesh or native constitution of man in which it inheres is another. And it is certain that he as little develops the principle of sin out of the mere physical flesh as he identifies the one with the other. It is impossible to deny a very pointed reference to the lower element of human nature in

[1] *Der Paulinismus.* Ein Beitrag zur Geschichte der urchristlichen Theologie, p. 54, note.

[2] *Ibid.* p. 58. This book occupies vols. xiii. and xv. of the Theological Translation Fund Library. See Lecture V. for further reference to Pfleiderer's own position.

this important key-word of the Pauline theology; but the misleading idea in the minds of contending exegetes is, that the lower and higher elements were conceived of by Paul as by the Greeks or by ourselves, —that the antithesis, material and immaterial, is at the basis of the distinction. So long as this idea prevails, it will be impossible to get rid of the suspicion that in the "flesh" of the Pauline Epistles we have something which connects sin essentially with the material element in man's constitution. Dismiss that antithesis, substitute for it the proper Old Testament antithesis, —earthly and heavenly, natural and supernatural, that "flesh" is what nature evolves, "spirit" what God bestows,—then we can see how the idea of "flesh," even when ethically intensified to the utmost, is appreciably distinct from the Oriental or Greek idea of evil as necessarily residing in matter. The great word of John iii. 6 is the source of the apostolic doctrine on this subject: "That which is born of the flesh is flesh." "Flesh" has become the proper designation of the race, as self-evolved and self-continued. Human nature as now constituted can produce nothing but its like, and that like is now sinful. "Flesh," therefore, may be appropriately used for the principle of corrupt nature in the individual man, for the obvious reason that it is in the course of the flesh, or of the ordinary production of human nature, that the evil principle invariably originates and comes to light. Thus the phrase is some explanation of the condition of man's nature, which it describes. It is no objection to this view, but rather a confirmation of its correctness, that it grounds the Pauline use of σάρξ for sinful human

nature on the underlying doctrine of hereditary corruption,—the primary assumptions of apostolic doctrine
regarding man being always that "God made man
upright," and that "by one man sin entered into the
world."[1]

We thus see how the secondary, *i.e.* the ethical or

---

[1] Hofmann, whose whole discussion of Rom. vii. 14 *et seqq.* (*Schriftbeweis,*
i. 548, etc.) is most interesting, has clearly perceived how this question
about the ethical force of σάρξ in Paul runs back into that still subtler one
of the appropriation by each responsible human being of the sinful tendency
which he inherits. See this touched upon *infra*, Lect. IV. "Let us
abide by this," says Hofmann, "that 'flesh' signifies human nature in
that condition in which it is now found in consequence of the sin of the
first man. Let us duly emphasize it, that the nature of man is that of a
corporeal being, but of a corporeal being intended to be personal, so that
the ungodly impulse of the inborn nature converts itself into an ungodly
relation of the Ego (or person) possessing that nature; then we shall have
no difficulty with passages, such as Gal. v. 19, etc., where sins not of the
sensual order are called 'works of the flesh,'" p. 559; and similarly at
p. 561, in a paragraph beginning, "Allerdings ist die Quelle der Sünde
nicht, wie man mich hat lehren lassen, im Leibe, sondern im Willen." All
this may look like leaving "flesh" to the old tautological interpretation,
"sinfully-conditioned human nature," were it not for the suggestion, "conditioned by inheritance;" and as birth-condition is, as we have seen at p.
77, a proper meaning of the biblical term "flesh," no unnatural force is
put upon the term in this its spiritual or ethical significance.

I find this view well supported in a brief article on Σάρξ in the *Biblio-
theca Sacra*, Jan. 1875, by E. P. Gould:

"What, then, is the reason of this use of σάρξ to denote man's sinful
nature? . . . Humanity, which on the natural side owes its continuance
to the σάρξ, is itself called σάρξ. Natural and sarkikal are therefore convertible terms in reference to man. On the other side, the Spirit, πνεῦμα,
is that through which man is connected with the divine and supernatural,
and specially in the new birth. It is there that the Divine Spirit works,
implanting the germs of a new life; and so spiritual and divine or supernatural are also convertible terms in regard to man. To this let it be
added that the natural man, connected with the race through the σάρξ, is
sinful, while the new man, connected with God through the πνεῦμα, is
holy; and does it seem strange that σάρξ should itself be used to denote the
sinful natural man, and πνεῦμα the holy renewed man? It is simply resolved
into this: the former is that through which man, in his natural state, is
descended from a sinful race, and inherits a sinful nature, and it is used to
denote that nature; while the latter is that through which and in which God
implants a new divine life of holiness, and it is used to denote that life."

theological meaning of σάρξ has a certain reasoned connection with its primary or natural meaning. But we make no apology for any want of complete continuity in the transition. It is not our view of the thoughts and language of the Bible that the religious or spiritual is developed by the human writers of it out of the natural or philosophical language of their time, and that critics can trace the development. We hold it a worthier view that the Spirit of revelation poured new and intenser meanings, as revelation advanced, into the earlier and simpler language. The rise of the Pauline phrase, "the flesh," for human nature under sin, is in our view another striking instance of this method of the inspired writers, or rather of the Spirit of inspiration in them.

The last of the leading terms in biblical psychology which I shall notice here is HEART (לֵב, καρδία). This term is the one least disputed in its meaning, and which undergoes the least amount of change within the cycle of its use in Scripture. Indeed, it may be held to be common to all parts of the Bible in the same sense. It only concerns the modern reader to note what that sense is, and to distinguish it, in one or two particulars, from the modern use of the word. Its prominence as a psychological term in the Bible and in other ancient books is due, doubtless, to the centrality of the physical organ which it primarily denotes, and which, to the mind of antiquity, bulked so much more in the human frame than the brain. Since, in Bible phrase, "the life is in the blood," that organ which formed the centre of the distribution of the blood must have the most important place in the

whole system. By a very easy transition, therefore,
"heart" came to signify the seat of man's collective
energies, the focus of the personal life. As from the
fleshly heart goes forth the blood in which is the
animal life, so from the heart of the human soul goes
forth the entire mental and moral activity. By a sort
of metaphorical anticipation of Harvey's famous discovery, the heart is also that to which all the actions
of the human soul return (in the condensed language
of Roos, "*In corde actiones animæ humanæ ad ipsam
redeunt*"). In the heart the soul is at home with itself,
becomes conscious of its doing and suffering as its own.
"The heart knoweth the bitterness of its soul," or, "of
its self." [1] It is therefore the organ of conscience, of
self-knowledge, and indeed of all knowledge. For we
must note well that, in contradistinction to modern
usage, heart includes the rational and intellectual as
well as all other movements of the soul. It is only in
the later scriptures that the Greek habit of distinguishing the rational from the emotional finds a place in the
sacred language. Now, because it is the focus of the
personal life, the work-place for the personal appropriation and assimilation of every influence, in the heart
lies the moral and religious condition of the man. Only
what enters the heart forms a possession of moral
worth, and only what comes from the heart is a moral
production. On the one hand, therefore, the Bible
places human depravity in the heart, because sin is a
principle which has penetrated to the centre, and
thence corrupts the whole circuit of life. On the other
hand, it regards the heart as the sphere of divine

---

[1] Prov. xiv. 10.

ınfluences, the starting-point of all moral renovation:
"The work of the law written in their hearts;"[1] "A
new heart will I give you;"[2] "Purifying their hearts
by faith."[3]   Once more, the heart, as lying deep
within, contains "the hidden man,"[4] the real man.   It
represents the proper character of the personality, but
conceals it; hence it is contrasted with the outward
appearance, and is declared to be the index of character only to Him who "searches the heart and tries
the reins of the children of men."[5]

It is impossible, in so rapid a sketch as this,
to trace the introduction and history of such additional terms as Mind, Understanding, Conscience
(νοῦς, διάνοια, σύνεσις, συνείδησις), which the greater
analytic perfection of Greek thought, with its attention to the intellective element in man, has brought
into the language of the New Testament through
the medium of the Septuagint.   The Old Testament did not distinguish that element by a radical
term, as it did Spirit, Soul, Heart, but only by derivatives, such as (binah, בִּינָה) Understanding; and even
this with the effect of giving to "knowledge" the
turn "prudence" or "good sense."   Such, moreover,
was the influence of the Old Testament spirit on the
Seventy, and much more on the writers of the New
Testament, that although the above-named words of
greater precision are introduced, yet *heart* (καρδία)

---

[1] Rom. ii. 15.   [2] Ezek. xxxvi. 26.   [3] Acts xv. 9.   [4] 1 Pet. iii. 4.
[5] 1 Sam. xvi. 7 ; Jer. xvii. 10, xx. 12.   On "the heart" as the seat of sin,
see *infra*, Lect. IV.   The whole subject is well discussed by Oehler in
Herzog, art. "Herz;" also in his *O. T. Theology*, i. pp. 221–227; by Roos,
Grundzüge der Seelenlehre, pp. 89–175 ; and by Beck, *Biblische Seelenlehre*,
pp. 70–126.

retains in the Greek of both Testaments the old
Homeric breadth of meaning, and largely represents
the corresponding term (*leb*, לֵב) of the older scriptures.[1]

Mind, Reason, Understanding (νοῦς with its congeners,
διάνοια, ἔννοια, νόημα ; also σύνεσις, διαλογισμός, etc.), are
not used with any psychological refinement in the sacred
writings. It is quite impossible, for example, to follow
Olshausen[2] when he attempts to show that νοῦς and
σύνεσις, with their corresponding verbs, as used in the
New Testament, represent the Kantian distinction
between *Vernunft* and *Verstand*, familiarized to us in
English by Coleridge as that between Reason and Understanding,—the former being the higher intuitive or
spiritual perception, the latter the lower, or dialectic
judgment. It is quite plain, from a glance at the passages, that the terms are really interchangeable.[3] Some

---

[1] One of the most obvious examples of both these facts, viz. that καρδία
is retained in the New Testament with much of its archaic force, and yet
that need was felt of terms more distinctly marking out the *rational* in
man, is to be seen in the various renderings of the great commandment,
"Thou shalt love the Lord thy God with all thy heart, and with all thy
soul, and with all thy might." In the original of Deut. vi. 5 the three
terms are :

מְאֹד,   נֶפֶשׁ,   לֵבָב

In the Septuagint they run thus :	διάνοια,	ψυχή,	δύναμις.

In Matt. xxii. 37, with noticeable

change, ...	καρδία,	ψυχή,	διάνοια.
Mark has two renderings, . {xii. 30,	καρδία,	ψυχή,	διάνοια,	ἰσχύς.
{xii. 33,	καρδία,	σύνεσις,	ψυχή,	ἰσχύς.
Luke x. 27, ...	καρδία,	ψυχή,	ἰσχύς,	διάνοια.

Godet (Comm. *in loc.*) calls attention to the Alexandrine variation in Luke,
which, retaining ἐκ before καρδία, inserts ἐν before the other three terms.
This he thinks emphasizes καρδία as the *focus* of the moral life, and indicates the other three as its principal directions.

[2] *Opuscula Theologica*, p. 156.

[3] Mark viii. 17 ; Matt. xiii. 14, 15. That σύνεσις cannot be confined to
the things earthly is plain from Col. i. 9 ; Eph. iii. 3, 4 ; 2 Tim. ii. 7. In
this last passage, νοῦς and σύνεσις take almost the reverse force from that
suggested by Olshausen.

of the other terms, as νόημα, φρόνημα, διαλογισμός,
" thoughts," " thinkings," are used very much at convenience to represent the contents or products of the
inner life, what the Old Testament calls the imaginations
of the thoughts of the heart (יֵצֶר לֵב).   But there is one
special use of *mind* (νοῦς) in the Pauline writings which
deserves notice.   Paul's highest element in the trichotomic expression of man's nature is undoubtedly
" spirit " (πνεῦμα).   But this entirely original biblical
phrase for the highest aspects of man's life is almost
inseparable from the idea of man's relation to God,
whether in creation or in redemption.   Accordingly,
when he wishes to contrast man's own highest sense
of right or faculty of knowledge with other powers,
sinful or spiritual, he adopts the word (νοῦς) which represents the highest element in man according to the
philosophers.   This is brought out in two leading
passages, in the one of which νοῦς, the " mind," is
contrasted with the " flesh " in the struggle against
sin (Rom. vii. 23, 25) ; in the other it is contrasted
with the spirit, when *pneuma* represents the inner
man under control of a spiritual or prophetic afflatus
(1 Cor. xiv. 14, 15, 19).   Thus, *mind* (*nous*) becomes
a convenient and appropriate term for highest natural
faculty in man, moral and intellectual, but so purely
natural that it can be either "mind of the flesh"
(Col. ii. 18), or awakened by the law, which will then
be the "law of the mind" (Rom. vii. 23), or renewed
in the spirit (Rom. xii. 2 ; Eph. iv. 23).

Through a somewhat similar current of influences,
which may be expressed generally as the necessity for
greater analytic precision, what was in the Old Tes-

tament denoted by "heart" (*leb*), and by the several
verbs for the active side of man's inner life, has to
appear in the Greek of the New Testament as *will*
(ἐθέλειν, θέλημα) and *conscience* (συνείδησις). The word
conscience takes its place in the New Testament beside
heart (καρδία) as the critical or self-judging function of
the inner man ("hearts sprinkled from an evil conscience "[1]). Therefore, as *mind* (νοῦς) is the highest
faculty of the soul, and *conscience* (συνείδησις) of the
heart, the intensest corruption of the whole nature
can be described as the defilement even of the mind
and of the conscience.[2]

To sum up : no one need be at any loss to grasp the
simple psychology of the Bible who keeps well in view
the original signification and subsequent growth of the
four leading terms SPIRIT (רוּחַ, πνεῦμα), SOUL (נֶפֶשׁ, ψυχή),
FLESH (בָּשָׂר, σάρξ), HEART (לֵב, καρδία). These are the
voces signatæ of the entire Scripture view of man's
nature and constitution. They are all grouped round
the idea of life or of a living being. The first two,
soul and *spirit*, represent in different ways the life
itself of a living being (not life in the abstract). The
last two, *flesh* and *heart*, denote respectively the life-
environment and the life-organ; the former that in
which life inheres, the latter that through which it
acts. So much for their simple and primitive meaning.
In their secondary meaning (which again in the case
of the first three—*spirit, soul, flesh*—becomes the basis
of a tertiary, viz. an ethical or theological meaning in

---

[1] Heb. x. 22.
[2] Tit. i. 15. For further notes on some of these psychological terms of
Scripture, see Appendix, Note H.

the latest development of inspired thought) they are
to be grouped as follows. *Spirit, soul,* and *flesh* are
expressions for man's nature viewed from different
points. They are not three natures. Man's one nature
is really expressed by each of them, so that each alone
may designate the human being. Thus man is *flesh,*
as an embodied perishable creature: " All flesh is
grass." He is *soul,* as a living being, an individual responsible creature: " All souls are mine;"[1] " There
were added about three thousand souls."[2] Once more,
he is *spirit.* More commonly, however, he is said to
have it, as his life-principle derived from God. He is
of the spiritual order—that, namely, of God and
angels. But "spirits" designates men only as disembodied: " The spirits of just men made perfect,"[3]
"spirits in prison,"[4] exactly as we read "souls under
the altar."[5] *Heart* stands outside of this triad, because
man is never called " a heart," nor men spoken of as
"hearts." *Heart* never denotes the personal subject,
but always the personal organ.

Again, they may be grouped thus: *Spirit, soul, heart,*
may be used each of them to indicate one side of man's
double-sided nature, viz. his higher or inner life. Over
against them stands *flesh,* as representing that nature
on the lower or outer side, so that any one of the first
three combined with *flesh* will express, dichotomically,
the whole of man—flesh and spirit, flesh and soul, or
flesh and heart.

Then, looking at the first three once more, not in
relation to *flesh* but in their mutual relations to "life,"

---

[1] Ezek. xviii. 4.   [2] Acts ii. 41.   [3] Heb. xii. 23.
[4] 1 Pet. iii. 19.   [5] Rev. vi. 9.

we get that correct and convenient division suggested by
Beck and followed by most competent inquirers since,
—a clear and intelligible result, which justifies itself
throughout the whole Scripture, viz. that *spirit* represents the principle of life, *soul* the subject of life, and
heart the organ of life; definitions which will be found
to apply accurately to all the three constituent lives
which the human being can lead—(*a*) the physical, (*b*)
the mental and moral, (*c*) the spiritual and religious.

The general result is a view of man essentially
bipartite, corresponding to the generally accepted
position, which is native and almost instinctive to the
human mind, that man consists of flesh and spirit, or
of body and soul; although the Scripture lays stress
upon the oneness of man's constitution, a fact obscured
and sometimes betrayed by the kind of dualism which
has prevailed even in Christian theology. Besides this,
however, it is undoubted, as we have shown, that a
trichotomic usage arose, which prevails in the Pauline
Epistles, where *soul* and *spirit* are represented as diverse
aspects of man's inner being—a division brought to
light mainly in consequence of the spiritual distinction
which is based upon it. The trichotomy of the sacred
writings, *spirit, soul,* and *body,* is to be distinguished
from that of Plato, from which it differs entirely both
as to content and form, Plato's being the ascription to
man of three souls, the *rational,* the *irascible,* and the
appetitive; also from that of the Stoics, which in its
ripest form associated with the fleshly a psychic or
pneumatic, and a noetic or governing principle, and
which in its simplest terms was a tripartition into *mind,
soul,* and *body.* Finally, it differs from the famous

Plotinian triad, the neo-Platonic offset to the Christian
Trinity, which consisted of the *One* or absolute principle,
the *mind* and the *soul*, "body" being the product of the
last.[1]   Hence the important distinction in form as well
as in content which belongs to the Pauline or scriptural
trichotomy.   That distinction lies in the use of *spirit*
for the highest element or aspect of man's nature.   In
this the biblical psychology stands entirely alone, and
is thoroughly consistent with itself from first to last.
Pneuma is not so used by Plato, by Philo, by the earlier
Stoics, by Plotinus and the neo-Platonists, nor indeed
anywhere out of the circle of Bible thought.   The
great and peculiar affirmation of Scripture in regard to
man's nature is this attribution to him, as the highest
in him, of that which is common to man with God.
What this *spirit* (*pneuma*) of the biblical psychology is,
however, we must be careful properly to state.   Regard
to accurate Scripture interpretation forbids us to distinguish *pneuma* otherwise than as the God-given
principle of man's life, physical, mental, and spiritual.
To make *pneuma* a nature or life-element,—the spiritual,
for instance, in contrast to the other two, the physical
and the rational,—is to fall at once into a false and unbiblical analysis.   The theory that *pneuma* is a separable
constituent of man's being, which can be wanting, dead,
or dormant on the one hand, restored or confirmed on
the other, so as to explain the fallen, regenerate, and
immortal states of man respectively, is temptingly
simple, as such arbitrary suppositions often are, but it
wants the foundation of fact, and leads to grossly
unscriptural conclusions.[2]   It is also a mistake, though

[1] See Appendix, Note G.   [2] See Appendix, Note F.

one by no means so serious, to make *pneuma* the faculty
of God-consciousness or the organ of religion in man,
deadened by the fall, awakened in regeneration, and
perfected in the life to come. It is evident, on a general
view of the facts, that we cannot assign religion to any
single faculty or power in man as its exclusive function.
The intellect, the affections, and the will are seen to
be all concerned in it.[1] It is equally evident that no
such use or application of *pneuma* marks the language
of Scripture. It is not the *pneuma* only which in the
words of the Psalms and Prophets is the organ of the
spiritual or religious mind; heart, soul, and even flesh
cry out for the living God. On the other hand,
the functions of the *pneuma* are not confined to the
religious consciousness or conscience toward God; it
has the faculty of self-cognisance as well. Indeed, the
whole character of the Bible psychology is mistaken
in such attempts to distinguish spirit, soul, heart as
separate faculties. They are diverse aspects of one
indivisible inner life.

In spite of these errors and exaggerations, it is important that we recognise what some of those who have
fallen into them do with truth maintain, namely, that
the distinctive feature of the biblical psychology lies
in its doctrine of the *pneuma* in man. By this term the
Bible designates, as we have shown, (*a*) from the first,
the divine origination even of his physical life; then (*b*),
the innermost aspect of his inward natural life; finally,
in the latest system of Scripture thought, (*c*) the
regenerate or spiritual life in which man is linked anew

---

[1] For some good remarks on this subject, see pp. 54–59 of Dr. Alliott's
Psychology and Theology, the Congregational Lecture for 1854.

to God through Christ Jesus.   Parallel to this doctrine
of the *pneuma* in man runs a higher line of Bible
teaching concerning God.   He is the God of the spirits
of all flesh, the Father of spirits.   God is *Pneuma*.
Pneuma, with appropriate epithets, becomes the designation of the Third Person of the Trinity.   And it is one
of the central doctrines of Christianity concerning the
theanthropic person of the Son, that He becomes, as
head of the new humanity, a life-giving *Pneuma*, "a
quickening Spirit."   At every point in the unfolding
of the Bible anthropology, this doctrine of the *pneuma*
in man will be seen to be peculiar to and distinctive
of the whole revelation.   It forms a central element
of the Divine Image.   It explains the nature of that
moral movement which we designate the Fall.   It
enters into the psychology of Regeneration, and into
the Scripture doctrine of man's future Life.   It is
with these topics that our four remaining lectures
must be occupied.

LECTURE III.

THE DIVINE IMAGE, AND MAN'S PRIMITIVE STATE.

Ἀλλὰ καὶ ἐὰν φῆς, Δεῖξόν μοι τὸν Θεόν σου· κἀγώ σοι εἴποιμι ἂν Δεῖξόν μοι τὸν ἄνθρωπόν σου, κἀγώ σοι δείξω τὸν Θεόν μου.—THEOPHILUS OF ANTIOCH, *Ad Autolyc.* lib. i. c. 2.

" In solâ creaturâ rationali invenitur similitudo Dei per modum Imaginis . . . . in aliis autem creaturis per modum Vestigii."—AQUINAS, *Summa* I. *q.* 93, *ar.* 6.

" Whereas in other creatures we have but the trace of His footsteps, in man we have the draught of His hand."—BP. SOUTH.

GEN. i. 26.—"And God said, Let us make man in our image, after our likeness: and let them have dominion over the fish of the sea, and over the fowl of the air, and over the cattle, and over all the earth, and over every creeping thing that creepeth upon the earth."

GEN. i. 27.—"So God created man in His *own* image, in the image of God created He him; male and female created He them."

GEN. v. 1.—"This *is* the book of the generations of Adam. In the day that God created man, in the likeness of God made He him."

GEN. v. 3.—"And Adam lived an hundred and thirty years, and begat *a son* in his own likeness, after his image; and called his name Seth."

GEN. ix. 6.—"Whoso sheddeth man's blood, by man shall his blood be shed: for in the image of God made He man."

JAMES iii. 9.—"Therewith bless we God, even the Father; and therewith curse we men, which are made after the similitude of God."

EPH. iv. 24.—"And that ye put on the new man, which after God is created in righteousness and true holiness."

COL. iii. 10.—"And have put on the new *man*, which is renewed in knowledge after the image of Him that created him."

LECTURE III.

THE doctrine of the divine image connects itself most intimately with the two questions already discussed—namely, with the Bible account of man's origin, and with the scriptural idea of man's constitution. In itself, indeed, it is the foundation of our entire theology and of revealed religion. For a religion in which God reveals Himself to man in order to reconcile and restore man to Himself, proceeds upon the fact that man was so constituted originally as to be capable of becoming the subject of such revelation and redemption.

The doctrine is found exactly where we should expect to find it,—on the forefront of the sacred records; and in its simplicity and grandeur it is worthy of the place which it occupies. We have to look at it, first, as a biblical definition of human nature, as expressing the type or ideal after which man was formed. Then we have to consider the Bible record of man's primitive state, that we may learn in what sense and to what extent the divine image was actually manifest in man unfallen.

Let us glance briefly at the leading Scripture passages in which the doctrine is expressed, before detailing in historical order the doctrinal views which have been drawn from these.

I.

The prime text, Gen. i. 26, 27, we have already discussed as an account of man's origin. Looking at it now as a description of his ideal, we note especially two things brought out by its textual connection. Instead of the expression, "after his kind," used of all the other creatures, it substitutes, as the archetype of man's formation, the image and similitude of God. Again, instead of the origination of an order of beings, each of which is a nameless specimen or example of its kind, what we find here is the origination of a person who holds a momentous place in the history of the world. As to the two terms, "image" and "likeness," it has only to be remarked that while both occur in ver. 26, "image" (*Tselem*) alone is thrice repeated in ver. 27, and "likeness" (*Demuth*) alone is found in Gen. v. 1. This discourages the attempt of some ancient and modern writers to base important theoretical distinctions on the use of these words here. Especially futile is it to identify *Tselem* with the permanent, and *Demuth* with the perishable element in the divine image. The double expression belongs to the strength and emphasis with which the fact of man's creation in Godlikeness is set forth in this remarkable text. Likeness added to image tells that the divine image which man bears is one corresponding to the original pattern.[1] For the rest, the light which the passage in its connection throws on the

[1] Oehler's *Theology of the Old Testament,* i. 211 (Clark, Edin. 1874).

contents of the divine image is chiefly relational. The central and supreme place assigned to man among the other creatures is explanatory of his image on the one side, as the solemn and majestic record of his creation is on the other. By the latter is suggested man's nearness and kinship to his Maker; by the former, his superiority and supremacy over the things made.

The divine image, so far from being peculiar to the first man, or wholly lost to the race by his sin, is spoken of in Gen. v. 1–3 as natural and capable of transmission. The statement of this passage is, that Adam, whom God had created in His likeness (*Demuth*), begat progeny in his own likeness and image. The significance of the connection appears when we observe the method of the narrative. It is done with the generation of Cain. That race is ruled out, and appears no more in the history. This chapter begins with a fresh "Book of Generations" (*Sepher Toledoth*) to carry on the account of Adam's family by Seth—the genealogy of the pious, of those who "began to call upon the name of the Lord." Accordingly, it here recalls Adam's own creation in the likeness of God; exactly as Luke traces up our Lord's genealogy to Adam through Seth: "Which was of Adam, which was of God." The subject, then, as Hofmann says, is not the moral similarity of Adam's son to his father, but the homogeneity of father and son, by virtue of which the race, so long as it propagated itself naturally, and not in the manner recorded in Gen. vi. 1, remains like itself, and as it was created by God at the first.[1]

From passages such as Gen. ix. 6 and James iii. 9,

---

[1] *Schriftbeweis*, i. 287, 288.

which unmistakeably speak of man as he now is, it is clear that the Image is the inalienable property of the race. To all generations is it asserted in these two texts that offence against our fellow-man, either by the murderous hand or by the slandering tongue, is an offence against the Divine Majesty; for man is made in the image, after the similitude of God. Gen. ix. 6 is valuable for its assertion that this image confers a sacredness on human life; that for this reason man is to protect and avenge the life of his fellow-man, and strive to secure the supremacy of his race over the earth. Thus it lays a foundation for those principles of jurisprudence on this subject which now rule the civilised world. It is not simply that human life is more precious than that of animals. It is not merely that man is brother to man. The principle here asserted rises far above that of blood-revenge in its most refined form. It asserts that man's life belongs to God: "At the hand of every man's brother will I require the life of man." It confers upon the execution of human justice, in the case of murder, the sacredness of a divine judgment. This very practical result from the idea of the divine image in man helps us to understand the idea itself; for murder assails man's personality, his sovereignty, and this the text declares to be that divinity which ought to hedge him about from the hand of his fellow. James iii. 9 bears a close resemblance in its effect to Gen. ix. 6. It refers to men as they are,—our brother-men, the children of the Lord and Father. It declares that the cursing tongue sins against that similitude of God which is inherent in mankind by creation.

In Ps. viii. the point of view is neither distinctively before sin nor after sin. It is one abstracted from moral history. This psalm, in praising the excellence of the divine name on earth, occupies itself chiefly with man. It boldly grapples with that constant problem of human thought, the apparent insignificance and the real centrality of man. It reconciles the two by throwing us back on his original constitution. First, his near approach to a divine standing. This mortal man has been constituted a little less than divine : "Thou hast made him (or, set him) a little lower than Elohim." If we take "Elohim" here as abstract, equivalent to "divinity" (numen, göttliches Wesen), we can see how the translation of the LXX. finds a legitimate foundation. If the meaning be that man, as spiritual, is of the same kind or order of being as God and angels, though subordinated to other members of that order in his degree, then it is conceivable how the expression could be rendered, "Thou hast made him a little lower than the angels," and also how the writer to the Hebrews found this expression exactly suited to his argument when he desired to set forth the dispensational subordination of man to angels at a certain point in his religious development ; which point was occupied by Jesus when, as man's representative, He was under the law.[1] The second assertion of man's original dignity in the psalm is that he is the representative of divine rule here below. Man is crowned a king, and the earth, with the works of divine wisdom which

[1] I have been favoured with the sight of an unpublished lecture by Prof. W. Robertson Smith on Ps. viii., in which this view of the reference to angels is maintained in a way which seems to me original.

fill it, is his kingdom. Man's rule in it is described with much concentrated poetry—a rule extending from the domestic animals immediately around him to the remotest bounds of animate and inanimate creation. The Godlike in man, then, is his constitution "a little lower than divine," on the one hand, and his rule over the divine works on the other. The glory of God in man is brought out by man's greatness in littleness. The excellence which the psalm ascribes to Jehovah's name in all the earth, is that He should mirror Himself in such a one as man, and bring praises even out of the mouths of babes and sucklings. Now, though in all this there is no express mention of the image, yet these two things so exactly correspond to the likeness and the dominion in Gen. i. 27, 28, that we may well call the psalm, with Delitzsch, "a lyric echo of that account of man's creation."

A single expression of St. Paul condenses this interpretation, and illustrates the connection of Ps. viii. with Gen. i. 27. He speaks of man as "the image and glory of God."[1] True, it is ἀνήρ, not ἄνθρωπος, of whom this is affirmed; but the writer plainly has his eye also upon that second record[2] where the man is created first and directly, the woman through the man, so that whatever he is, she is more refinedly, for she is "the glory of the man." The combined expression, "image and glory," amounts then to this: the divine likeness is man's title to royalty on earth.[3] The dominion is that which manifests or reveals the fact that man bears the image of his Maker,—he is the glory of God.

---

[1] 1 Cor. xi. 7.   [2] Gen. ii. 7–25.
[3] " Des Menschenkönigs diploma," quoted by Oosterzee.

Of the passages already considered, Gen. i. 26, 27
alone belongs to the section of Scripture history before
the fall. Ps. viii. is ideal, not historical. The other
passages cited (Gen. v. 3, ix. 6; Jas. iii. 9) speak of
man as he now is, and clearly warrant the inference
that there is a sense in which the divine image is
inalienable from man. It is further worthy of notice,
that of the many Scripture expressions denoting the
depth of man's fall, there is no one which describes
the effect of sin upon God's image in man. St. Paul's
axiom, that " all have sinned and come short (ὑστεροῦν-
ται) of the glory of God," is the nearest allusion to it.
Indeed, the formula never occurs in any description of
man's now depraved nature and fallen state. It is
when redemption is the theme that Scripture resumes
the language which implies a correspondence and conformity between the human and the divine.

Thus we come to the two classical texts on the
renewal of the image in man through Christ—namely,
Eph. iv. 24, Col. iii. 10. These have the closest
bearing on the ethical contents of the image. We
must, however, repel the assumption that they were
meant to define primarily what the divine image was
in Adam. They treat expressly of the new man. The
distinct and intended parallelism between the old man
and the new in both passages leaves us no room to
doubt that the creation signified is not the formation
of man at the beginning, but the new creation in
Christ Jesus, and that the result described is the
" new creature "[1] of 2 Cor. v. 17. That result consists
in "righteousness," _i.e._ such rectitude as justice

[1] καινὴ κτίσις.

demands, and "holiness," *i.e.* purity, the fulness of
God in the soul; and both these are "true" or "of.
the truth," as contrasted with the "lusts of deceitful-
ness" in the old man, and are effects of "the truth in
Jesus" and of renewal in the "spirit of the mind."
The expression, "after God," in Eph. iv. 24,[1] denotes
the divine ideal of the new creation, its formation
in righteousness and holiness as contrasted with
the character of ordinary nature.[2]   The Author or
Creator referred to in Col. iii. 10[3] can be no other
than the God of grace, for the result is that new
creation where Christ is all in all.   The image according to which is formed this new creation, where "all
things are of God in Christ Jesus,"[4] can be no other
than that "image of His Son,"[5] who, again, is the
"image of the invisible God."[6]   But while the creation
of grace is thus the only direct subject of affirmation
in both these passages, the language fairly implies that
man was originally constituted in a divine image, of
which righteousness and holiness in truth or knowledge were essential features.   We are to guard against
the extreme view, which takes these texts as definitions
of the divine image in Adam, as implying that all the
features of the image borne by the new creature were
already in our first parents so as to be lost by them.
When we content ourselves with the assertion that
this description of the "new man" presupposes corresponding outlines in the first man which were broken
off and blurred by sin, and which are now for the first

---

[1] κατὰ Θεόν.

[2] κατὰ τὴν προτέραν ἀναστροφήν, ver. 22.

[3] τοῦ κτίσαντος.

[4] Conf. 2 Cor. v. 17, 18 ; Col. iii. 10, 11.

[5] Rom. viii. 29.

[6] Col. i. 15.

time fully realized in man redeemed and renewed, a
sound exegesis will bear us out.

There are other passages referring to man's regenerated nature, where, though the image is not expressly
mentioned, the doctrine of it is assumed. The expressions in Matt. v. 48, Luke vi. 36, and 1 Pet. i. 15, 16,
in which believers are exhorted to be "perfect," "merci-
ful," "holy," as their Father in heaven, point to a
similarity or congruity between the natures that are
compared; though interpreters, almost without exception, remark that ὥς, καθὼς κ.τ.λ. denote not equality
but similitude, likeness not in degree but in kind. In
2 Pet. i. 4 it is said to be the aim of the supernatural
arrangement of grace that we might become "partakers
of the divine nature."[1] But this appears from the context to refer not so much to the presence of a divine
element in the new creature, or to the indwelling of the
Divine Spirit in a regenerate heart, as to the moral
conformity which that "divine power" produces. The
expression, however, is valuable as showing that man's
participation in the divine nature is implied in his
original constitution, and promoted by all restoration
and development of that constitution.[2]

What light these texts cast on the thing meant by
this grand formula of the divine image is the main
question—one of " preponderating import not merely
for Anthropology, but also for Christology and Soteri-
ology, and one which in the course of centuries has
been answered in the most diverse ways."[3] We attempt

---

[1] θείας κοινωνοὶ φύσεως.

[2] For further remarks on some of the passages cited in this section, see
Appendix, Note I.

[3] Van Oosterzee, *Christian Dogmatics*, p. 374. Hodder & Stoughton, 1874.

an answer, therefore, in connection with a rapid historical sketch of those views.

II.

Recalling our exact aim, which is to ascertain what ideas of man and his nature are involved in the biblical theology concerning his creation, fall, and redemption, we find that this first topic of his original image and primitive state has become much involved with dogmatic presuppositions. Partly has this arisen from the brevity of the Scripture statements. The primitive state of man became a favourite battle-ground of theologians, because it was like unexplored territory, which in maps the geographer can fill up at his pleasure. Theologians in their systems could draw up and deploy, in this comparatively empty space, the principles which they were afterwards to bring into action in more crowded departments. The doctrine of the image became a great topic, so soon as sin and grace were the key-positions in theological controversy, because the idea formed of man's original nature and endowments had a direct bearing on the measure of the loss caused by the fall, and upon the consequent necessity and nature of redemption.

From the earliest to the latest times, need has been felt of attaching a twofold meaning to the image; and the double terms of the great proto-text seemed to give it express Scripture authority. Justin Martyr and Irenæus refer image (*Tselem*) to the bodily form, likeness (*Demuth*) to the spirit. The Alexandrian fathers prefer to understand κατ' εἰκόνα of the rational

basis of man's nature, καθ᾽ ὁμοίωσιν of its free development. Augustine distinguished them as *cognitio veritatis*
and *amor virtutis;* the Schoolmen, as "natural attributes" and "moral conformity." We have already
said that the exegesis is incompetent.[1] It is only
another instance of the habit of interpreters to import
dogmatic results into the simple and uncritical language
of the earlier scriptures.

The distinction itself, however, between a natural
and a moral element in the image, between a constitutional potentiality and an ethical realization, has
proved itself valid at every stage of thought on the
subject, though the form of the distinction has varied
with the movements of theology. The great controversy
concerning sin and grace, which, as we have said, first
brought the doctrine of the image into prominence, for
long determined that the distinction should turn on
what remained after the fall and what was lost by the
fall. The Greek fathers had emphasized that which
is permanent, and are accordingly said to place the
image in the free-will and immaterial nature of man.
The Latin fathers emphasize that in the image which
perished by sin. When necessity arose of formulating
into a dogma the relation between the two, that which
the Schoolmen evolved for the Latin Church took the
shape that man was created *in puris naturalibus* with
a bent to religion; upon which was added, as a supernatural gift, original righteousness, to keep the lower
nature in check, and to effect the production of actual
holiness. The effect of the fall upon each of these
respectively was thus defined. Through sin the natural

---

[1] See p. 100 *supra.*

Godward bent was only weakened, the supernatural gift was quite lost.

When the strife concerning the doctrines of grace took a new departure at the Reformation, the Evangelical Church had to replace the medieval view by a fresh assertion that the image of God was wholly created and natural; yet that a quite lost condition of innocence and holiness, the very power to recover which has departed from fallen man, formed an original element in it. This position Protestants had to maintain against Romish controversialists on the one hand, and Socinians on the other. These were not so much two extremes, as two diverse modes of Pelagianizing. The more subtle is that of the Romanists, who seem to exalt the divine image in man by adding to it that peculiar feature which they call supernatural. But an endowment not essentially belonging to human nature, magically given and taken, passing soon away, could not be thought of as proper to the divine image. Hence Bellarmin, availing himself of the old verbal distinction, framed the well-known formula, "Adamum peccando non imaginem Dei sed similitudinem perdidisse." On this theory man is left by the fall much as he was upon his natural creation, and before the bestowal of the *donum superadditum*,—that is, with a certain ability, though now damaged, to love and serve God. The other Pelagian tendency which the Reformers had to oppose was that which explained away the image into an expression of man's original or general superiority, together with his moral innocence. The Socinians, who, according to Principal Cunningham, "usually contrive to find in the lowest deep a lower deep,"

viewed it as consisting only in dominion over the
other creatures. In contrast with this, it was necessary for evangelical divines to bring out the Scripture
doctrine of the image, as embracing those features of
perfect conformity to the divine character and law
which were lost by sin, and which it is the object of
redemption to restore. It concerned them to show
that not merely a certain attained state of holiness,
now lost, belonged to primitive man, but that an
"original righteousness," which is now wanting, must
have entered into his constitution as created.

With all this, Protestant theologians of both the
great sections were careful to maintain both the wider
and the stricter sense of the image. In the former
sense, it stands for the essence of the soul endowed
with the faculty of knowing and willing, the general
congruity and analogy between the nature of God and
of man, and man's dominion over the creatures. In
the latter sense, it stands for that moral conformity
to God which man lost by the fall. The Reformed
divines are somewhat more distinct than the Lutherans
in maintaining that the image embraced those natural
and indestructible features of likeness to God which
survive the fall. Calvin is clear that it includes all
that excellence by which man surpasses all other
species of living beings; though he argues that what
holds the principal place in the renovation of the
divine image must have held the like place in the
formation of it at the first.[1]   Turretin also is very

[1] " Principium quod nuper posui retineo, patere Dei effigiem ad totam
præstantiam, quâ eminet hominis natura inter omnes animantium species."
Again, " Dei imago est integra naturæ humanæ præstantia, quæ refulsit in
Adam ante defectionem."—*Instit.* I. xv. 3, 4.

clear that a certain part of the divine image must be
held to belong to the substance of the soul, and hence
is not lost by the fall.[1] Divines of the evangelical
school in the centuries following the Reformation continued to uphold this distinction between what was
loseable in the divine image and what was not.
When the great Puritan, John Howe, describes it in
The Living Temple as now defaced and torn down, he
says: "We speak not now of the *natural image* of God
in man, or the representation the soul hath of its
Maker in the spiritual, intelligent, vital, and immortal
nature thereof, which image, we know, cannot be lost,
but its resemblance of Him in the excellencies which
appear to be lost, and which were his duty,—a *debitum
inesse*,—and could not be lost but by his own great
default."[2] More accurately and philosophically it is
expressed by Jonathan Edwards thus: The *natural
image* of God consists very much in that by which
God in His creation distinguished man from the beasts,
viz. in those faculties and principles of nature whereby
he is capable of moral agency; whereas the *spiritual
and moral image*, wherein man was made at the first,
consisted in that moral excellency with which he was
endowed.[3]

The elements now commonly recognised by evangelical divines as forming the divine image, when they
speak with special regard to the ethical content of the
expression, are moral capacity and actual conformity

[1] F. Turret. *Instit. Theologiæ Elencticæ*, Loc. V. Q. x. § 7.

[2] *Living Temple*, pt. II. c. iv. sec. 2. *Debitum inesse* was a technical
phrase for what was inherent quality of man's proper nature, *due to it*,
because necessary to its completeness or perfection.

[3] *On the Freedom of the Will*, pt. i. sec. 5.

or man's intellectual and moral nature on the one
hand, and his original moral perfection on the other.
It would, no doubt, have been very convenient and
clear if Protestant divines could have agreed to say
that the inalienable divine features in man constituted
the *image*, and those actually lost by sin the *similitude*;
but it was no mere superstitious dread of seeming to
agree in phraseology with Romanists which prevented
them. The fallacy of the Scholastic distinction between
the *image*, as consisting in the natural attributes of the
soul, which are retained, and the *similitude*, in the moral
conformity, which was lost, had emerged in the course
of discussion.   For if we understand man's *moral
capacity* as " perfect adaptation to the end for which
he was made, and to the sphere in which he was
designed to move," the fall cannot be said to have
left that *moral capacity* unimpaired, nor to have destroyed only the *actual conformity*. Neither will Protestant divines allow that the actual moral likeness
was other than an essential part of the divine image
in man. They will neither sublimate it with the
Romanists to a supernatural and additional endowment, nor precipitate it with the Socinians to a mere
natural innocency. They maintain that there was,
from the first, an " uprightness " in man, a positive
spiritual goodness, constituting the most important
part of the divine image in which he was made.   In
this they are most true to the Scripture ideal of the
dignity of man's nature, and, quite contrary to what
is often supposed of them, are most interested in
bringing out clearly the surviving vestiges of the
divine image in man as now fallen. In other words,

H

it appears that, however convenient the distinction in thought between the natural and the moral aspect of the image, it does not coincide with the actual division between that in the image which is permanent and that which has been lost by sin. For it is evident that man's entire moral and intellectual endowments, together with his place in creation, which constitute the divine image in the wider sense, are not unaffected by the fall; while, on the other hand, his original possession of the divine similitude in righteousness and true holiness, or, the image in its stricter sense, is not so lost by sin but that man is capable of renewal in it through grace.

It would be easy enough to pass from all this with the remark that these are idle and obsolete battles about words. But it is not so. These controversies turn on deep and essential differences in the conception of man and creation. Hence their importance to our theme. The controversy between Romanists and Protestants, though seeming to hinge upon such questions as, whether man's original righteousness was concreated or subsequently bestowed, whether it was, in the strict sense, a natural endowment or a supernatural gift, is really a controversy between the Augustinian and the Pelagian view of human nature in its ruin and redemption. This controversy is oft misunderstood in its bearing upon the idea of man. Augustinians, whether Lutheran or Calvinistic, take the high view of man's original, and, in consequence, the dark view of man's fallen state. Pelagians of all shades — Romanist, Socinian, or Remonstrant—take the more liberal or flattering view of man's fallen state, but the low view of man's original nature. It is common, however, to represent the evangelical school of theology as that which vilifies human nature, the liberal as that which exalts it, whereas precisely the reverse of this is the fact.

The Pelagian theory, as represented, for example, by Romish divines, is that the elements of human nature, lower and higher, flesh and spirit, were from the first so balanced against each other that an abnormal restraint, in the form of a supernatural gift of original righteousness, was added in our first parents to keep the lower in check. This once set aside by the fall, the constitution of man fallen does not differ very greatly from that in which he was created. In other words, the nature of man has not fallen far, because it had not far to fall. The Augustinian maintains that man's original state is one not of supernatural rectitude, but of uprightness by nature; and, consequently, that when man in the exercise of his free will departed from God, a great shock was given to the moral universe, a very great ruin befel man's own moral constitution. That is to say, the underlying hypothesis of these two radically diverse lines in theology is a low view of man's original nature in the one case, a high view of it in the other; and the low view belongs to those who make it their boast to take a more favourable estimate of human nature than their opponents. But this is not all. The origin of these tendencies lies farther back. They depend upon views of the universe that are respectively dualistic and ethnic on the one hand, monotheistic and scriptural on the other. To the Pelagian, evil seems as natural as good. His scheme of thought involves him in the Manichæism from which Augustine had escaped, and which he hated, or at least in the Neo - Platonism, which sees in the universe a cosmos or order, evolved out of primary ataxia or disorder, and finds evil something inherent and inexpugnable.[1] The Augustinian view of the world is that which coincides with Scripture; namely, that a Being entirely good is the sole author of nature and the immediate originator of man. The Bible view of man's constitution fits into its exquisite picture of the primeval world. Nature is not evil, either in whole or in part. Pleasantness, innocence, perfection, are the features of the scene. "God saw everything that He had made, and behold it was very good." In the centre of that picture is man, made in the image of the Supreme Good Himself.

Modern philosophical divines take a less strictly theological view of this great formula than did the Reformers, but make strenuous endeavours to interpret the divine image on its metaphysical and ethical sides. When we sift and summarize the views of Schleiermacher, Hofmann, Julius Müller, Oehler, Delitzsch, we find ourselves in a region of thought differing very considerably from that of the previous ages.[2] These more recent thinkers take their stand upon the permanent aspect of the divine image. Indeed, it has been successfully made out that this biblical definition

---

[1] Μεμιγμένη γὰρ οὖν δὴ ἡ τοῦδε τοῦ κόσμου φύσις, ἔκ τε νοῦ καὶ ἀνάγκης. Καὶ ὅσα παρὰ Θεοῦ εἰς αὐτὸν ἥκει, ἀγαθά· τὰ δὲ κακά, ἐκ τῆς ἀρχαίας φύσεως, τὴν ὕλην λέγων τὴν ὑποκειμένην, οὔπω κοσμηθεῖσαν εἰ θεῷτο.—Plotini, Ennead, I. viii. 77.

[2] See Appendix, Note J.

of man's nature is given as his distinction among
created beings, rather than as the distinction of man
unfallen from man fallen. This can be maintained in
perfect consistency with the Scripture view of the fall;
and, in truth, when properly handled, helps to explain
the complex effects which follow upon the entrance of
sin. But whereas at one period in the history of
Reformed theology it was important, in discussing the
image, to direct attention to the greatness of the loss
which human nature sustained by the fall, it is now of
more immediate moment to insist strongly on the
divine image as man's original type and inalienable
distinction from all other creatures on earth.

Delivered from the old strife as to how much of
the image was lost by the fall, and how much retained
after it, theologians have less occasion to specify in
what elements or constituents of man's nature the
image resides. They are more free to look at the
general analogy or congruity between God and man
which Scripture presents, and therefore to proceed in
the simple and non-analytic method of the Bible itself.
Yet the subject has lost none of its importance. The
greatest of modern controversies turns upon it; for
the battle of the supernatural has the key of its position in the nature of man. Whether there be anything in the universe above mere physical causation
and succession is the vital question for the philosophy
and theology of our day. But the denial of a divine
supernatural is logically impossible, so long as man's
own being cannot be explained without allowing to
it something which transcends mere physical nature.
The Bible, by putting man in the rank of the *Elohim*,

by co-ordinating the human and the divine so far as to
make the one the image of the other, holds the citadel
of this controversy, and shows us how great is its
strength.   Let us ask, then, how the Bible idea of God
and the Bible idea of man cast light on each other.

The Scripture never speaks of the divine image in
man, but always of man as formed after the divine
image.   And this indicates a profound principle of
biblical thought.   It presupposes God, to account for
man.   It never sets us the "Sisyphus task" of proving
God and the supernatural from man and nature.[1]
Thus, by "the divine image," the Bible does not mean
those elements in man from which an idea of God
may be framed, but conversely those features in the
Divine Being of which man is a copy.   If we read
what the Bible says of God in relation to the world,
and what of God in Himself, we shall get leading lines
for its delineation of man; always premising that of
the Divine Idea man is a created copy, not, like the
Logos, an essential image.

And, first, of the analogy between the relation of
God to the universe, and the relation of man to the
other creatures.   Students of revelation are but slowly
learning to appreciate the magnificence and breadth
of its discovery of God.   Nowhere is this breadth
more remarkable than in its description of the relation
of God to the world.   A true biblical theism, avoid-
ing the extremes in speculation of which pantheism

[1] "It seems to me that both the sceptic and dogmatic schools of thought
alike assume erroneously that the true method of procedure is this : ' Grant-
ing man and nature, to prove God and the supernatural,'—a Sisyphus
task which I am sure must for ever fail."—R. Holt Hutton, *Essays, Theological and Literary*, vol. i. p. 219, 2d edit., London, 1877.

on the one hand and deism on the other are examples,
yet gathering up all in these speculative views that is
true, can represent God as at once the Maker and the
Upholder of the world. In other words, the Bible
represents God's relation to the world as at once
immanent and transcendent. He is spoken of as
creating it and ceasing, yet not ceasing to inform it;
as in the world, but not of it; as making all things
for Himself, yet giving Himself to all things. Man,
on the other hand, in relation to nature around him,
is a created copy of God in His relation to the universe. This is brought out by the position assigned
him in the order of creation. He appears last, as the
scope and end of all things earthly,—the *terminus ad
quem*,—and therefore as the similitude of God, who is
the " archetypal purpose of the universe." [1]   Still more
clearly is it set 'forth by the place claimed for him
among the beings created, what theologians call "his
dominion over the creatures." As described in the
purpose and fiat of his creation at the first,[2] in the
renewal of that commission after the flood,[3] in the
ideal picture of Ps. viii., in the redemption-victory
foreshadowed in 1 Cor. xv. 22–28, man is set on earth
as the instrument and imitator of God, to appropriate
nature consciously and formatively to himself. To
this world of earth man is, in a sense, what God is
to the world at large. Its various grades of being
lead to him and look up to him. Its provisions and
arrangements have respect to his use. Its forces and

---

[1] " Der Mensch sei zum geschöpflichen Abbilde Gottes des urbildlichen
Weltziels geschaffen."—Hofmann, *Schriftbeweis*, i. 290, etc.
[2] Gen. i. and ii.   [3] Gen. ix. 1–7.

treasures serve his purposes. He modifies its races of plants and animals. He discovers and utilizes its laws. He subdues nature and her tribes. He makes earthly existence and human toil things sacred to God, since he is God's vicegerent and representative here below. He stands, in short, in the midst of the material processes of nature and the humbler denizens of the world as the divine shadow or second self,—"the image and glory of God." At the same time, these scriptures bring out the relation of man to Him who made the world. The being who is set in the midst of the garden to till the ground, in the midst of the creatures to understand and name the animals, to dress the fairest of God's earth and keep it, is to carry back to God the praises of that world over which He has made him lord. In reading the laws of nature, he is "thinking after Him the thoughts of God." In imitating the works of nature he is expressing the law of God written on his intellect; in subduing, improving, civilising, he is exercising towards God nature's best homage. And he ought to go much farther. As a living temple in the midst of nature, he ought to make its dumbness vocal and its voices articulate, to translate its animal gladness into intelligent thanksgiving, its irrational yet instinctive homage into a full-souled, high-hearted worship: "O Lord our Lord, how excellent is Thy name in all the earth!"

Advancing from the Scripture view of God's relation to the world to its view of what He is in Himself, we find those grandly simple definitions of the Divine Being: God is "Spirit," "Light," "Love." Let us see how these may find a parallel in man, the created copy.

It corresponds with all we have traced of the biblical psychology, that it is on the side of *Spirit* man should primarily exhibit an analogy with the divine nature. It is the only element in man's constitution which is properly ascribed to God. He is Spirit. Absolutely and supremely, spiritual existence is affirmed of God. He is said, moreover, to be the Father of spirits, and the God of the spirits of all flesh; indicating that the spiritual world, including man in so far as he is spiritual, stands in a closer relation to God than the corporeal. We have already sufficiently guarded against the Platonizing form of this idea—a form given to it by some of the Greek fathers, who made *pneuma* something physical connecting man with God. This form of statement easily leads to the conclusion, that through the fall human nature has been constitutionally altered by the loss of a part or element; whereas the Bible doctrine is that man's nature is morally lowered by the loss of its purity. The standpoint of the Bible psychology is always that of the divine origination of man. His life—animal, intellectual, moral—is spiritual, because specially in - breathed of God. The " spirit in man " is the " inspiration of the Almighty," and man is spiritual in so far as he lives and acts according to his divine origin and basis of life. Thus does Scripture teach that the spiritual nature which man has, the spirit of man which is in him, affords a parallel or analogy to the absolute and supreme Spirit which God is.

We find, accordingly, that the Bible makes *Intellect* or *Rationality* in man—not only a function of " spirit " in him, but a function flowing from and corresponding to something in God. It is the breath of the Almighty that giveth man instruction and understanding. The scene in the garden, when the Lord God brought the animals to Adam to be named, presents this idea in a pictorial form. That "admirable philosophy lecture," as Bishop Bull has it, which Adam, appointed by God Himself, read on all the other animals, denotes the correspondence of divine and human intelligence : "Whatsoever Adam called any living creature, that was the name thereof." [1] "I think, O Socrates, that the truest account of these matters is, that some power more than human gave the first names to things, so as to make them necessarily correct." [2] Similar is the ascription to the artificers of the tabernacle, of wisdom, understanding, cunning workmanship, together with the Spirit of God. [3] Thus all scientific knowledge and artistic skill, all the results of reason, Scripture ascribes to divine assistance ; not from a vague sentiment of piety, but in right of its consistent theory that the spirit in man corresponds to the Spirit of his Maker, and is sustained by it. Teaching like this is a foundation for the loftiest philosophy of man. It is at once an assertion of the preciousness of the individual and a prediction of the progress of the race. The true idea of human greatness we owe not to modern thought, but to the primary axioms of revelation. [4]

---

[1] Gen. ii. 19.

[2] Οἶμαι μὲν ἐγὼ τὸν ἀληθέστατον λόγον περὶ τούτων εἶναι, ὦ Σώκρατες, μείζω τινὰ δύναμιν εἶναι ἢ ἀνθρωπείαν τὴν θεμένην τὰ πρῶτα ὀνόματα τοῖς πράγμασιν, ὥστε ἀναγκαῖον εἶναι αὐτὰ ὀρθῶς ἔχειν.—Plato, Cratylus, 438, C.

[3] רוּחַ אֱלֹהִים, Ex. xxxi. 3.

[4] "It is indeed an extraordinary anomaly that a truth for which we are indebted to Scripture alone has become the very watchword of infidelity, and that the enthusiasts of unbelief, its poets, dreamers, and political agi-

Another point of analogy between the divine and the human spirit the Bible finds in *Self-consciousness.* "A candle of the Lord is the spirit of man searching through all the chambers of the heart."[1] The phrase "candle of the Lord" may assert divine origination— the light in man which the Lord has kindled—or divine possession — the light which is His, the true light which lighteth every man—or both; but the characteristic of the human spirit to which it affixes the description is its self-penetrating power, that it searches the innermost regions of the human being.[2] With a very similar figure, moral consciousness or conscience is denoted in the New Testament as "the eye," "the light of the body," "the light within." Still more explicitly is it asserted that the spirit of the man which is in him alone knows the things of the man, and is therefore analogous to the Divine Spirit, which alone knoweth the things of God.[3] This analogy is, in yet another text, strengthened by the idea of correspondence or communication. "The Spirit itself beareth witness with our spirit that we are the children of God."[4] It may be fairly inferred from these passages that the Bible regards self-conscious-

tators, should have gone mad upon an idea which is historically the gift of revelation to mankind—the greatness of man as such."—J. B. Mozley, *Ruling Ideas in Early Ages*, p. 232, Lond. 1877.

"The sacred representation of man's original relationship to God excels in sublimity, truth, and force. . . . Ancient philosophers have already felt, and in some degree expressed this truth; but revelation has been the first to give to that feeling its just expression and its highest meaning. It teaches us to think humbly of ourselves, but loftily of mankind."—Van Oosterzee, *Christian Dogmatics*, p. 377. See Appendix, Note K, for some additional illustrations of the Image in man's rationality.

[1] Prov. xx. 27.   [2] חַדְרֵי־בָטֶן, ταμιεῖα κοιλίας.

[3] 1 Cor. ii. 11.   [4] Rom. viii. 16.

ness in man as an essential feature of the divine similitude.[1]

From self-consciousness it is a short step to *Personality*.[2] It is a truism that self-conscious free personality is the Bible representation of God. Pervading every line of Scripture, from the first to the last, runs the assumption that God is personal. It is easy enough to call this anthropomorphism. But the Bible, as a revelation from God to man, begins with God. And its own account of its doctrine is not that it gives a God fashioned like unto man, but that God can reveal Himself to man, because man is made in the likeness of God. No wonder on this showing that man should be taught to think of God as Person, Will, Holiness, Love,—ideas of which he finds some copies in his own constitution, since that constitution is framed upon the divine model. It is not in any metaphysical formula that the Bible claims personality in man as the image of something in God, but in its profound principle of the relation between God and man, *i.e.* between God and the individual human being, as well as between God and the human race. This principle is asserted, for example, in Num. xvi. 22, where the relation of God to the spirits of all flesh is pleaded as a reason for His dealing with one man who

---

[1] " Dies Vermögen des Selbstbewusstseins ist nun aber der wesentlichste Theil des göttlichen Ebenbildes; und darum wird es eine Leuchte Gottes genannt weil sich hierin besonders deutlich der menschliche Geist als ein Abglanz des göttlichen bekundet."—Delitzsch, *Biblische Psychologie* (quoted from Elster), p. 154, 2te Aufl.

[2] " Das Personbildende des Menschen d. h. dasjenige, vermöge dessen er sich selbst wissendes und sich aus sich selbst bestimmendes Wesen ist, ist sein Geist, denn die gottgehauchte נְשָׁמָה ist die Gottesleuchte welche alle Kammern seines Inwendigen durchspäht."—Delitzsch, *ibid.*

has sinned, rather than that He should punish a whole people. It is repeated in Num. xxvii. 16 as a reason why God should choose a particular leader for the congregation. The same argument of divine property in man is made the foundation of a splendid declaration by the prophet Ezekiel[1] of God's moral dealing with individuals, as contrasted with the unbroken federalism on which Israel presumed to reckon. The right of God in each soul (where *nephesh* denotes the human being, "all souls are mine") is made the ground of the divine prerogative to exercise in each individual case both punishment and pardon. The other side of this relation is presented in those passages which speak of man as existing for God, even the Father,[2] as sought for his worship,[3] as redeemed to an eternal life which consists in the knowledge of the Father and the Son.[4] Even in his present fallen condition, and under the most unfavourable forms of that condition, St. Paul represents man as being the offspring of God, to this effect, "If haply we may feel after Him, and find Him."[5] In this passage the entire inwardness of the resemblance between the offspring and the great Parent is made a reason against the artistic efforts of the Greek paganism to humanize the divine. Since man is the offspring of God, he ought not to think that he can frame an outward image of God,—a far better one lies deep within. The relationship of man with God ought to be thought of not as physical, but as moral. The sentiment that we are the divine offspring is quoted to

---

[1] Ezek. xviii.　　[2] εἰς αὐτόν, 1 Cor. viii. 6.　　[3] John iv. 23.
[4] John xvii. 3.　　[5] Acts xvii. 27–29.

illustrate the fact that mankind has been destined to seek God, who was not far from them, *i.e.* who has made Himself cognisable and conceivable by them. Only personal beings can feel after and find a personal God, and in so doing their likeness to Him is affirmed and confirmed.

We cannot properly ground these analogies between the divine and the human without a glance at the Trinity in unity. This doctrine is one of the most prolific and far-reaching among the discoveries of revelation. Fully to receive it, influences most profoundly every part of our theological system and of our practical religion. It is that which sets the theism of the Bible on a ground of vantage far above all the partial systems of the philosophers. It is the consummation and the only perfect protection of Theism. It alone clears the relation of God to the world from all the defects of Deism, Polytheism, and Pantheism respectively. It alone furnishes the connecting link between God and man in the person of the Incarnate Logos. It alone provides for the absolute truth of that entirely biblical definition, "God is Love." The God of the Bible is a totally different being from the solitary God of the deist. How the God of deism can be a loving God it is hard to conceive; that he should ever be declared to be Love in his very essence is inconceivable. For in this philosophic figment which has too oft usurped the place of God even in Christian theology, knowledge and power are in a sense superior to love. In the God of the Bible, on the other hand, absolute being, unbeginning and self-sufficing existence, are united in the most marvellous way to essential relativity and unbeginning love. And it is the Trinity in unity which gives us this grand conception. The inter-trinitarian relations are coeval with Godhead. God is not first solitary existence, then power in creation, then love to the created, then pity for the fallen,—these latter being secondary effluences from a God who is in the first place self-centred. On the contrary, God is essential and eternal Love. Love in exercise from eternity has laid the foundations of all that God is to His creatures, and especially to man. Hence the bearing of the doctrine of the Trinity upon that of the divine image. "We are apt to take the word 'Father' as metaphorical in its application to God, a metaphor derived from human parentage."[1] The doctrine of the Trinity implies the converse. If there be an Eternal Son, there must have been an Eternal Father,—an absolute and essential Fatherhood must belong to Godhead. The most sacred human relationships, therefore, are copies of realities eternally existing in God. The relations of man to God and to his fellow-man have their archetype in relations which lie within the essence of the Godhead. For the divine original, after which man is made, is thus presented not as mere sovereign will, but as eternal love; not as exclusive life in the absolute and infinite, but as that fulness of life which cannot be without a perfect union of distinct personalities.

Let us note that exactly here some light arises

---

[1] R. H. Hutton, *Essays*, vol. i. p. 235, in an extremely interesting passage contrasting the Unitarian with the Catholic and Evangelical conception of God.

on that subtle element of personality in man. Instead of saying that personality is not strictly, but only by way of accommodation, ascribed to the Persons of the Godhead,—as if person were more properly used when applied to man,—ought we not on the analogy just suggested to say the reverse? Ought we not to say that personality in its proper and archetypal sense as inherent in God is discovered to us through the Trinity in unity, and that herein is revealed at once the personality of God and the image of that personality in man? The absolutely solitary God of natural religion is not one whose personality receives any illumination to our minds from our own, for no such absolute, self-centred, self-sufficing personality is conceivable among men. If this be personality at all (for can person be realized without another in whom it shall be reflected?), it is such as has no shadow of a copy among us. There has never been any Adam made in the image of the God of deism. Every human being has a consciousness of freedom and personality, given only along with a sense of relation and inter-dependence, which finds its prototype not in the God of the philosophers, but in the God of the Bible. The God who is essentially Three-in-one, an inter-linked personality—this God alone furnishes the mould on which our personality could be formed.

Thus we seem to get a full meaning for those words: " Let us make man in our image after our likeness." The emphasis on plurality in the Maker is very poorly accounted for by those who would exclude a Trinitarian interpretation, either by reading it as the sovereign " we " on the one hand, or " we, the divine order,"

meaning God and angels, on the other. In the light
of the entire biblical delineation of God, the words
have no strain put upon them, but are only seen to be
divinely pregnant, if we hold them as now indicating
to us that man was created an image of *something
inter-trinitarian*. And if we reject, as we must do, the
patristic scholasticism of finding that something in the
individual constitution,—in the "three souls" of the
Platonists, or in the three elements of the trichotomy,
—we are fully borne out in Scripture when we put it
that the inter-trinitarian relations of Godhead find a
copy in man's personality, as related to God on the
one hand and to his fellow-men on the other.[1]

Having traced the divine similitude in which man
was formed on its natural side, we should now pass on
to its moral aspect. It is plain that the former belongs
to what is permanent in the image, in the modified sense
in which that distinction can be accepted.[2] Man's self-
conscious, free personality, illustrated as it is by his
place in creation, is that God-likeness which belongs
to him as such, and is inalienable. When we come to
speak of what is supremely divine, viz. that God is Holy
Love, we can no more say that man as he is will be
found to bear the likeness of God. But we have still to
take note of the Bible doctrine that man was created
in uprightness.[3] This doctrine sufficiently asserts the
capacity of man's nature, even though now fallen, for
receiving the moral image of God; the possibility
of the restoration of that image, nay, of its renewal

---

[1] The question will suggest itself here, What relation, then, does the
image of God in man bear to Him who is the image of the invisible God?
See Appendix, Note L.

[2] See p. 113.   [3] Eccles. vii. 29.

I

by grace in a degree higher than that of its original
creation. Here, however, we are restricted to a discussion of the image as the Bible declares it to have been
bestowed on Adam, and accordingly are brought to our
concluding question on this theme, viz. To what extent
the primitive state, as described in Scripture, reveals
in the first human beings the moral likeness of God.

III.

The idea of man conveyed to us in the narrative of
his creation is, as we have seen, one that connects him
with earth and the creatures on the one side, and with
God on the other.   It sets him before us as God's representative here below.   In keeping with this original idea
of man is the primitive state which the Bible goes on
to depict.   That state is one of happiness.   It is one
of undisturbed alliance with nature.   It is one where
work was without toil, where life was bright and joyous
in the consciousness of security and strength, where
mastery over the world was a natural inheritance conveyed by the divine blessing.   In this delicious picture
there is presented to us a human family, consisting of the
first pair, living in a relation to the vegetable world of
sustenance from it without pain and labour, in a relation to the animal world of artless familiarity, in a relation to God of filial dependence, implicit obedience,
and fearless intercourse; to which is added, as the
narrative proceeds, a special engagement, founded upon
a testing inhibition, and guarded by a divine sanction.[1]

[1] That this state of human blessedness is real, and not merely ideal, is
confirmed by the consideration that in all literature, profane and sacred
alike, the conception of it takes the form of a reminiscence—it is spoken of
as a state which once was. This argument is happily put in the late Isaac

It is not necessary to discuss the physical and intellectual conditions of this delineation. It is self-luminous in its brief, felicitous, and original view of a state which is neither cultured nor animal, neither civilisation nor barbarism, but exactly that paradisaic state which man's natural endowment would lead us to expect, upon the important supposition that he was created in the divine likeness as to the moral and spiritual elements of his nature. On that idea, man could not really begin otherwise than as holy and happy. To state this view, so radical to the entire biblical theology, without exaggeration, yet without dilution, is what the subject demands of us.

For it is here that theologians, under the pressure of dogmatic necessities, have departed from the simplicity and modesty of the Scripture narrative.[1] Their whole

Taylor's *Spirit of the Hebrew Poetry*, in a chapter headed, "The Tradition of a Paradise is the Germ of Poetry." It is hardly needful to say that in our view a historic paradise is demanded by the whole system of revealed doctrine concerning man. Ewald, in the second of the papers referred to at p. 30, note, says, "Peace, as God meant it, is the primitive state of humanity —a state towards which, though it has long since fled, humanity still ever yearns again; the hope of which forms the rosy fringe of the future, and to restore which is the effort and the aim of all true religion."

[1] I refer not merely to the romancing descriptions of the first man to be found in the fathers and in some mediæval writers. South's famous sermon on Gen. i. 27 (see *Works*, i. p. 26, Oxford edition, 1842) is a comparatively modern example of these: "Discourse was then almost as quick as intuition, . . . it could sooner determine than now it can dispute. There is as much difference between the clear representations of the understanding then, and the obscure discoveries that it makes now, as there is between the prospect of a casement and of a keyhole. . . . We may guess at the stateliness of the building by the magnificence of the ruins. . . . An Aristotle was but the rubbish of an Adam, and Athens but the rudiments of Paradise." All such rhetoric with reference to the splendour of the first man's natural and intellectual powers is based upon an unwarranted view of his spiritual position. But this last is to be found even in writers who avoid these other absurdities. The temptation under which theologians have overpressed their text here is suggested by Dr. Rainy (*Delivery and Development of Doctrine*,

conception of the primitive man of the Bible is overcharged. In particular, they are wont to ascribe to
man in Eden a degree, if not a kind, of moral and
spiritual perfection which not only has no basis in
Scripture, but which encumbers theology with an
unworkable hypothesis,—a doketic Adam, an ideal first
man, of whom his creators find it afterwards difficult
to dispose. If we take the Romanist view that this
high state was maintained by a supernatural endowment (*donum superadditum*), or even the Lutheran one
of a direct spiritual guidance, we are at a loss to
understand how the fall was possible, except through
a capricious or causeless withdrawal of the divine help,
which cannot be admitted. If we take the more
moderate position that goodness was concreated, that
Adam was so made as naturally to love and serve God,
we have still no means of understanding how he had
arrived at a spiritual condition so high as theologians are
wont to ascribe to him, except upon the supposition of
a time and progress nowhere granted in the narrative.

If we assume that man's personality and free will
are essential to him, an initial state of perfected holiness is inconceivable, or, if insisted on, would simply
render it inconceivable how he should have fallen. In
that case, moreover, " original righteousness," which
is not a Scripture expression, would have to be read
with a sense given to the word " righteousness " no-

p. 329): " Orthodox systematic writers are led to depict the unfallen state
in an exaggerated manner by way of bringing out more forcibly the ruin of
the fall." No doubt, also, there is a disposition, for other theological reasons,
to presuppose at the head of the human race a moral and spiritual giant,
who is as much a myth as the physically gigantic Adam of the Rabbinical
and Mussulman tales. We must adhere to the Scripture.

where else, viz. not of a character formed and acquired, not of a habit of confirmed and faultless rectitude, but of some sudden preternatural endowment. The modest statement of Scripture, that " God made man upright," supplies us with a theory of original uprightness, which is what more cautious divines really mean by *justitia originalis*. This much, however, be it remembered, is essential to the whole Bible view of man. It cannot be given up without " transforming the scheme of man's relations and obligations from end to end."[1] Not only so, it has an "inward sentence" on its side. The conscience requires and approves of the position that man's primitive condition was sinless, for we instinctively feel that to be sinful is not a natural but a fallen state. But the Bible account carries us farther. It represents the state of the first man as more than innocence, certainly more than that of balance between good and evil. The theories of equilibrium are plainly unscriptural, whether the unstable equilibrium of Socinus and Schleiermacher, or the equilibrium, stable by miracle, of the Roman Church. They are based upon the anti-scriptural assumption of a concreated strife in man between his higher and his lower powers. The Bible starts man with no schism at the root of his being of which the fall would be an almost necessary consequence, but with a positive rightness, a living commencement of being right and doing good. This leaves room for trial, and all theologians admit that man in Eden was on his probation; was *viator*, and not

---

[1] Dr. Rainy, *loc. cit.*, who also says, " It must be admitted that, beyond the fact of a yet unfallen state, Scripture does not give us much material bearing directly on the primitive condition of man." See further as to this, Appendix, Note M.

comprehensor; was on the way to a confirmed moral and spiritual condition, but had not attained the goal. If, in addition to the fact that man was made upright, the phrase " original righteousness " be meant to include the divine approval of man in the state of his creation, we have Scripture ground for it. The Creator, pronouncing all that He had made to be " very good," approves man as good, *i.e.* as fulfilling the end of his creation so far as a beginning and growing moral creature could be said to fulfil it. We thus obtain an account of man's creation in the divine image on its ethical side. Knowledge, righteousness, and true holiness were in germ essential to man's nature, but they had to be freely developed. " He was in principle perfect, . . . potentially, Adam was everything which he must primarily have been, but actually he had still to become all of which the germs had been implanted in him."[1] Moral capacity and actual conformity being both implied in this likeness to his Creator, the latter is that in which he received power to fashion himself. The only full realization of the likeness would have been his continuous appropriation of the divine will as his own. He has lost it through the fall, in the sense that he has sinned and come short of its attainment. And this has entailed further consequences. For though he has not lost capacity for the likeness, he has lost the ability of himself to recover it, and for this is now wholly dependent upon a Redeemer in his own nature.

One last word regarding dogmatic exaggeration.

---

[1] Van Oosterzee, *Christian Dogmatics*, p. 381, Hodder & Stoughton, Lond. 1874.

Tempted to draw their view of the first Adam from
the description of man as renewed in the Second Adam,
theologians seem to make the outcome of redemption
merely the recovery of what was lost by the fall.
This is a strained interpretation.   It puts a strain
upon Scripture to imply that Adam actually had
attained that to which Christ brings us by His grace.
It detracts from the greatness of redemption, as if it
required all the energy of divine wisdom, love, and
power to bring back what sin and Satan took away.[1] It
is inconsistent with that gradual rise and march in the
divine dealings toward man of which the Bible is full.
To make the entire history of redemption a mere eddy
in the stream of divine developments, to place redeemed
humanity in Christ only after all where Adam began,
is a view that falls short of the breadth and grandeur
of the Scripture representation.   Scripture conveys not
obscurely the idea that the type of redeemed man is
higher than that of man unfallen; that the second
creation, when completed, shall excel what the first had
been even had it remained unsullied by sin; that as
we have borne the image of the earthly, we shall also
bear the image of the heavenly; and that when earth
and heavens are dissolved, " we look for new heavens
and a new earth wherein dwelleth righteousness."[2]

---

[1] " It cannot be proved that the new creation in Christ is nothing more
than the restoration of the state wherein Adam was at first created. There
is, indeed, a relationship between the two; the divine image wrought by
Christ's redemption is the only true realization of the image wherein man
was at first created. Man was originally given the one, in order that he
might attain the other, if not directly, by continuing faithful in obedience
and fellowship with God, yet indirectly after his fall by means of redemption.
But it is evident that from the very nature of this relationship the two are
not identical."—Müller, *Christian Doctrine of Sin* (Clark, 2d ed.), ii. 352,353.

[2] 2 Pet. iii. 13.

The value of this great Bible definition of man's nature, that he was made in the image of God, has now been illustrated in detail.

1. It is of vital moment, in face of modern anthropological theories, as answering to the fact, that while man is one side of him earthly, animal, and mortal, he takes rank on the other by his essence as spiritual being and free personality above physical causation and succession. In relation to mere physical nature, man is supernatural, and so bears the likeness of the Supreme Supernatural or of God.

2. That this image of God, in which man was made, had for one of its essential elements uprightness, or moral conformity to his Maker, is a position of inestimable worth in its bearing on the origin and nature of moral evil. That the constitution of man, like everything else in creation, was from the first very good, is essential to the monotheism of the Bible, as contrasted with the dualism of the ethnic religions and of much modern speculation.

These two biblical positions present the image in twofold aspect as natural and ethical, potential and actual, or however else we may choose to express what is after all a " doublefaced unity "—a thing inalienable from man even as fallen, yet so affected by sin that only a supernatural redemption can restore it. How worthy of being the religious book of the human race is that which on its opening page foretells man's mental and practical progress by declaring that he was made to replenish the earth and subdue it; which vouches for the possibility of his moral renovation in the still more profound doctrine that he was constituted after the similitude of God!

LECTURE IV.

MAN FALLEN : HIS NATURE UNDER SIN AND DEATH.

" Il y a deux vérités de foi également constantes : l'une, que l'homme dans l'état de la création ou dans celui de la grâce, est élevé au-dessus de toute la nature, rendu semblable à Dieu, et participant de la divinité ; l'autre, qu'en l'état de corruption et du péché, il est déchu de cet état et rendu semblable aux bêtes."

" Ainsi tout l'univers apprend à l'homme ou qu'il est corrompu ou qu'il est racheté ; tout lui apprend sa grandeur ou sa misère. . . . Les hommes sont tout ensemble indignes de Dieu et capables de Dieu—indignes par leur corruption, capables par leur première nature."—PASCAL, *Pensées*, pp. 292, 294, 295 (Molinier), Paris, 1877.

> " The candid incline to surmise of late
>   That the Christian faith may be false, I find ;
>
> .   .   .   .
>
>   I still to suppose it true, for my part,
>   See reasons on reasons ; this, to begin :
>   'Tis the faith that launched point-blank her dart
>   At the head of a lie—taught Original Sin,
>   The Corruption of Man's Heart."
>
> ROBERT BROWNING,
> *Dramatis Personæ.*

ECCLES. vii. 29.—" Lo, this only have I found, that God hath made man upright ; but they have sought out many inventions."

GEN. vi. 5.—" And God saw that the wickedness of man *was* great in the earth, and *that* every imagination of the thoughts of his heart *was* only evil continually."

GEN. viii. 21.—" The imagination of man's heart *is* evil from his youth."

JER. xvii. 9.—" The heart is deceitful above all *things*, and desperately wicked : who can know it ? "

MATT. xv. 19.—" For out of the heart proceed evil thoughts," etc.

JOHN iii. 6.—" That which is born of the flesh is flesh ; and that which is born of the Spirit is spirit."

ROM. v. 12.—" Wherefore, as by one man sin entered into the world, and death by sin ; and so death passed upon all men, for that all have sinned."

LECTURE IV.

MAN FALLEN : HIS NATURE UNDER SIN AND DEATH.

WE go on now to consider what light the Scripture
account of the fall throws upon its view of
man's constitution, and, conversely, how far the simple
psychology of the Bible may help us to ascertain the
significance of the Scripture doctrine concerning sin
and death. It is but a few hints we can supply on
each topic. The doctrines of the fall and sin are
exclusively biblical ideas ; or at least they are only
fully conceived and applied in the biblical scheme of
religious thought. These doctrines are solvents, not
sources of difficulty. Into the problem of evil Scripture introduces elements of explanation. It accounts
for man's present moral and physical condition, for
the broad phenomena of life and death, in a way that
is thinkable and intelligible. Pascal has said that the
Christian faith has mainly two things to establish,—
the corruption of human nature, and its redemption
by Jesus Christ.[1] The first of these has been most
thoroughly brought out in connection with the second.
The evil which is in man has been most entirely probed

---

[1] "La foi chrétienne ne va principalement qu'à établir ces deux choses,
la corruption de la nature et la Redemption de Jésus-Christ."—Pascal,
Pensées, Préface générale, p. 10 (Faugère).

and sounded in connection with that power above
man which the gospel brings to his help. This is a
principle at once profound and beneficent. Knowledge
is not given to man for its own mere sake; it is when
an end of use and benefit is to be served that knowledge comes. Naturalists could never dredge the
deepest beds of ocean for the mere love of science, till
the practical needs of the telegraph led to the sinking
of the deep-sea line. Men first learned the structure
of their own bodies not from the pure love of knowing,
but because the necessities of human disease made such
knowledge the indispensable handmaid of the healing
art. We may be asked, Why go to a book so simple
and practical as the Bible for the solution of the
mysterious problems of moral evil, or for any theory of
the being of man? We answer that we do so relying
upon the surest analogy. It is because revelation has
proved such an instrument for man's renovation and
recovery to God, because it has achieved the only success in the remedy of man's evil, that we are entitled
to expect in it profounder views than anywhere else as
to what man and his evils are.

I. Nothing is more characteristic of the Bible than
the manner in which it accounts for the ORIGIN of
man's evil. It differs from those ethnic religions,
which sought the root of evil in the elements of the
world, as if good and ill were alike of its essence; from
those ancient and modern sages who find it in the
make of the creature man; from those modern philosophers who place it in the tendency of a being typi-
cally lower than now appears to revert to his original
savage or bestial condition. The origin of evil within

the human sphere is, according to Scripture, a fall—
an unnatural movement. And this is a practically
hopeful, as well as a speculatively high view of man's
nature, even as fallen. On the other views just named,
it is hard to see how evil could be aught but inevitable, how it ever could be removed or even remedied.
The Bible represents the ills in which man is involved
not as the necessary faults of a being low, earthly, and
animal by his constitution, but as effects from the fall
of a being made in the image of God. Our religion
can deal hopefully with ignorance, barbarism, vice,
and crime, because it views these not as the nature of
man into which he tends to relapse, but as contrary
to the nature and ideal of his creation, as a defilement
and degradation of that which radically bears the
stamp of God.

Let us keep our eye, then, on the speculative significance of this Bible doctrine of a fall, when we are
considering the nature of man as now under sin.
The Bible descriptions of fallen human nature are
drawn in very dark lines. But let us not forget that
what is so described is "not pravity but depravity;"[1]
that it is not nature, but un-nature; that when Scripture speaks of the nature of fallen man, it does not
mean the nature in which, nor the nature in the midst
of which God created him. All flesh has now corrupted his way upon the earth; that which is born of
the flesh is flesh. It is in this sense that, according
to Scripture, man is now a child of wrath by nature.[2]

[1] Dr. John Duncan, *Colloquia Peripatetica*, p. 120.
[2] "Very many pious people do not rise high enough in their anthropology. They ascend to the fall, and forget the higher fact that we fell from
a height where we were fitted to dwell, and where we were intended to

It is also of importance to observe that the fall is wholly a moral crisis, taking place within the sphere of man's free will. Physical evil is always viewed in Scripture as a consequence of moral evil. The whole creation was very good. There is no physical necessity of sinning suggested by anything in the Bible from beginning to end. Sin is consistently represented as a free movement in the creature. " God made man upright, but they have sought out many inventions."[1] "They are all gone aside."[2] Though sin makes its first appearance in connection with the physical world, and as a bodily act, yet is it no mere natural result of the presentation of the forbidden fruit to the senses. A clear and full view of the temptation narrative leads one to look upon the first sin not as a sensual slip, but as a moral revolt. "Its point of departure," as Delitzsch says, "was in the spirit."[3] It arose with an external suggestion, and upon an external occasion; but it was an inward crisis. The motives most efficient in bringing it about were ambitious desire of a short road to divine knowledge, doubt of the divine love. When these had

remain. And Jesus Christ has come that He might raise us even higher than to that height, and make us sit in the 'super-celestial ' with Himself."
—*Colloquia Peripatetica*, p. 121.

[1] Eccles. vii. 29. " ' They seek many arts' (*Künste*, Luther), properly calculations, inventions, devices, viz. of means and ways by which they go astray from the normal natural development into abnormities. In other words, inventive refined degeneracy has come into the place of moral simplicity."—Delitzsch, *in loc.*, Clark's transl. p. 335.

[2] Ps. xiv. 3. "Gone aside," "gone out of the way," ἐξέκλιναν, Sept. Note the absolute sense in which the verb סוּר is used in other places, as *e.g.* Deut. xi. 16 ; Jer. v. 23 ; Dan. ix. 11. A kind of *vox signata* for the initial movement of sin. It is the revolt, the departing, the turning aside.

[3] " Der Ausgangspunkt der Ursünde war also im Geiste."—*Psychologie*, p. 124.

conceived, the sin which they brought forth was disregard of the limit which divine love had imposed, or transgression of the law. Sin, therefore, is carefully represented in Scripture as arising, not out of nature, not out of anything in man's own constitution, far less out of the constitution of things around him, but from an act beyond nature—an act of the human spirit freely departing from God by traversing His law. In so far as Scripture accounts for the entrance of evil into the human world, it refers it to the suggestion of an alien will, to the influence of a higher spirit previously fallen, thereby indicating that the possibility of sinning belongs to spiritual creatures. But the chief result of the Scripture teaching here as to origins is, that it traces all human evils to a source beneath the scientific level, deeper than all observed sequence, to a preternatural root in the revolt of the human will against God;[1] as it also reveals for this root-evil a supernatural remedy in a divine-human Redeemer.

We are to note, then, that the fall—an unnatural movement—was an act of man's spirit, of his free will, and was above all things sin because it was transgression of the divine law and departure from God. It was possible to man because of his possession of free spiritual personality. To any nature lower in the scale of being than man, sin was impossible. It is mere perversion of thought and language, however, to represent man's experience of moral evil as not a fall but a rise. That sin was possible to man belongs,

[1] It is usual to say that the Bible does not solve the problem of the origin of evil, but profound thinkers find that this element of insolubility enters into the nature of evil. See Appendix, Note N.

indeed, to the height on which his nature was originated, but that it became actual was loss and ruin.
The greatness of the ruin, the gravity of the shock,
Scripture consistently represents as the correlate of his
original dignity.   The Bible account of the fall and
sin, instead of vilifying human nature, implies the
highest view of man and his constitution.   The present degradation of the edifice consists largely in the
fact that it no longer serves the purpose of its erec-
tion—a temple of the living God.   The music of man's
life is no longer in harmony with the divine order and
glory to which it was set, therefore are the sweet bells
so jangled and out of tune.

The first sin, although suggested by an alien evil
spirit, marked itself as a voluntary act of departure
from God.   The deliberateness of the act on Adam's
part is specially asserted: "And Adam was not de-
ceived." [1]   Accordingly, this representation is the one
which is central for the whole Bible view of sin and
its effects.   It is the main element in its description
of universal sinfulness: "There is none that seeketh
after God." [2]   If we maintain clearly these two positions, that the fall of man was an act of his free will,
and that the act was sin because it was transgression
of divine law and revolt from personal divine authority,
all the other elements of Bible truth on the subject will
take their proper places.   From this view of the fall as
primarily a spiritual and religious catastrophe, all the
rest of the scriptural teaching about man's evil depends.

The sublimely simple narrative [3] of the immediate

[1] 1 Tim. ii. 14.   [2] Rom. iii. 11.
[3] See on the temptation narrative, Appendix, Note O.

consequences of the first sin represents it as rending in a moment the veil of ideal glory in which man, as a self-conscious, free, yet holy being, had moved in his primal state. The spiritual animal, having spiritually fallen, becomes at once rudely conscious of the mere flesh: "The eyes of them both were opened, and they knew that they were naked."[1] The friend and fellow of the Most High flees from His voice and hides himself from His presence: "Adam and his wife hid themselves from the presence of the Lord God amongst the trees of the garden."[2] Sensual shame and superstitious fear are the prompt first tokens of the fall of a being who is created eminently spiritual and religious. The whole position of man towards God is changed. He has parted from His fellowship, and must therefore be driven out of Paradise. And his relation to nature and to the world is altered, as well as his relation to God. In the divine sentence immediately following on the first sin,—a sentence of degradation and final destruction for the serpent, of sorrow in conception for woman, of painful toil and ultimate return to dust for mankind,—we recognise, as we should expect, the effects of the fall upon nature and man together. The revolt of the being made in God's image, with dominion over the creatures, was a cosmic event, and has a disturbing effect upon the cosmos, "as when a kingdom falls with its king."[3] Upon this hint in the sacred narrative is founded St. Paul's doctrine of nature's sympathetic suffering with fallen man.

The description of the spread of sin, and its effects

---

[1] Gen. iii. 7.　　　　　　[2] Gen. iii. 8.
[3] Baader, quoted by Van Oosterzee.

among Adam's posterity, brings out the same general principles, viz. that sin is no mere weakening, but an active and energetic perversion of our moral nature; that it originates in the revolt of a spiritual personality against God and His law, and that this revolt carries in it the seeds of its own punishment. It is not followed in Adam's case by an instantaneous and literal death on the day of his transgression. It is not followed by the eclipse of his intellectual powers. There is a sense in which his spiritual fall is an advance in knowledge; but it is followed by the immediate cessation of that divine fellowship and paradisaic felicity in which he was created. So with his posterity. There is not at first any marked degradation of their constitution as creatures. Instead of physical degradation, there is in the immediate descendants of the first man great physical splendour. Instead of intellectual extinction, there springs up a brilliant civilisation. In the line of the first murderer we have the early rise and growth of agriculture, cattle-breeding, city-building, music, and other arts. Instead of decay, feebleness, and early death, the narrative suggests gigantic strength and marvellous longevity. Upon that further step in the development of the race which is enigmatically described as the inter-marriage of the sons of God with the daughters of men, evil became more rampant.[1] The power and prevalence of sin was manifested in monstrous crimes, high-handed and clamant vices—the iniquities, therefore, of a race physically strong and mentally active. "The earth also was corrupt before God, and the

---

[1] Gen. vi. 2.

earth was filled with violence. And God looked upon
the earth, and, behold, it was corrupt; for all flesh
(*i.e.* the whole human race) had corrupted his way
upon the earth."[1] This description is eminently consistent with that view of sin's origin which represents
it as a religious fall. The physical force, the longevity, the rapid progress of the first men in the sacred
narrative, is quite inconsistent with any theory of
man's evil as arising out of weakness or want of
balance in his original constitution; as coming into
human nature entirely by the animal side; as the prevalence of the flesh over the spirit. But it is perfectly
consistent with the view that sin began as a spiritual
revolt in a creature made in God's image, the consequences of which should slowly broaden down among
his descendants, to shorten life, to break up and dis-
perse the race, to produce physical degradation, savage
ignorance, and at last brutality. These final results,
however, were only partial. The loss of the preserv-
ing salt of spirituality would no doubt have made
these effects universal had it not been counter-checked
by a redemptive process centred in one chosen people,
sustained in a providential *economy of preparation*
among all nations, and now spreading itself among the
foremost and governing races of mankind.

In connection with these words: " Behold, the man
is become as one of us, to know good and evil," it
may be proper to take note of the question whether
the fall was an advance of any sort. The only thing
about that view which has reason is that self-determi-
nation must be a moral movement. We have already

[1] Gen. vi. 11, 12.

decided that moral indifference or equilibrium is not, according to Scripture, a thinkable view of man's original state, that a human being without moral quality is no such being as God could create. Yet though we cannot start with moral indifference, though we posit original uprightness (יָשָׁר, straight, *rectus*), the Scripture makes it sufficiently plain that there lay before man in his primitive state such a self-determining act or series of acts as would have led him out of moral childhood or pupilage into moral perfection and holy manhood. From this state of pupilage he would have emerged by self-denial and obedience. But it is true that he did emerge from it the wrong way, by his act of self-assertion and transgression of law in the fall. There was a portion of truth in the tempter's plea that there should be a gain of knowledge by disobedience. The idea of moral progress in Adam's case implied a self-determining act in the matter of the commandment. And the fall was such an act: it brought him at once out of the childlike *naïveté* of the paradisaic state. But so far is this from supporting the theory that evil enters as a necessary factor into human development, that it only rightly states the truth of which that theory is a perversion.

II. From this account of the first sin and its effects we pass to the scriptural accounts of the UNIVERSAL PREVALENCE of sin in the race. As to the fact, Scripture and experience agree. The absolute universality of sin is so frequently and emphatically affirmed in Scripture, that detailed proof is unnecessary. The testimony of human experience is vividly represented by ancient non - Christian writers. On two points

their evidence is overcharged, and has to be corrected
by revelation. The one is that which leads them to
throw the burden of evil on nature, or on the Author
of nature. "Some of the ethnic philosophers," to use
the language of Howe, "have been so far from denying
a corruption and depravation of nature in man, that
they have overstrained the matter, and thought vicious
inclination more deeply natural than indeed it is." [1]
The other is, that their account of the universality and
increase of evil leads to a fatalistic despair of humanity,
and is at variance with fact. If Horace's maxim were
true, that each generation of men is worse than the
preceding, the race ought long ago to have been
extinct. The fact not present to the mind of the
pagan world is, that humanity is under a remedial
economy which has its centre in revealed religion.
But the truth with which we have to do now is that
which Scripture posits to account for the universal
prevalence of sin. It exactly coincides with observation, and falls in with the known laws of nature, viz.
that moral evil is hereditary, *vitium originis*. It is a
proof of the inner unity of Scripture thought, that its
teaching as to the presence of sin throughout the
world is so thoroughly in accordance with its teaching
as to man's origin and nature. Evil, according to the
Bible, is no inherent part of man's nature as created;
yet its actual prevalence among mankind is explained
in perfect consistency with this initial truth. The
universality of sin is a corollary and consequent from
the unity of the race.[2] The fact of that unity has a
most direct theological interest. The ethnic doctrine

[1] *The Living Temple*, Pt. II. c. iv.   [2] See Note D, in Appendix.

of Autochthones, " men sprung of the soil," the theory,
recently favoured but now abandoned, of several
starting-points for the human race, taken in connection
with the fact of universal sinfulness, would go to make
moral evil something original in man's constitution—
a characteristic of the whole *genus homo*. " Only on
the supposition of first parents can evil be regarded as
something which was introduced afterwards, and which
has penetrated through to all." [1] Evil is not necessary,
eternal, and irremediable. Hence the emphasis of the
Scripture position, that " by one man sin entered into
the world." [2] Men are sinners by birth, by generation,
not by constitution.

How this hereditary depravity connects itself with
the consciousness of personal guilt is a problem
of much psychological interest.   That conscience
charges sin upon each individual, although each has
become a sinner through his connection with the race ;
that a truly awakened soul charges itself not only
with its own conscious sin, but with a sinful disposition ; and that the inherited sin is not a palliation but
an aggravation of the evil,—these are facts which
have occupied the most profound and serious thinkers
from the dawn of Christian theology. We note the
views of those only who admit the facts. There is no
means of testing the proposed explanations directly by
Scripture proof, but we may judge them by their bearing upon doctrines otherwise established by Scripture.
They may be divided, as Julius Müller suggests, into
the organic or substantial theory on the one side, and
that which is atomic or subjective on the other. The

[1] Martensen, *Dogmatics*, p. 150 (Clark's Transl.).   [2] Rom. v. 12.

former, which from the time of Augustine to the
present day has been held in various forms, amounts
in brief to this, that all human beings are contained in
the first man.   We are not at present concerned with
the theological dogma that Adam represented his
posterity in covenant.   We leave this federal unity or
identity out of account for the moment.   It has no
direct bearing on the subjective question, which alone
we are considering, how hereditary depravity involves
personal guilt.   The theory we are describing asserts
that the unity of the human race involves community
of essence, or at least such identity as belongs to a
tree or other complex organism.   Consequently, each
individual is not only a member of the race, but the
beginning of the race is his beginning.   And since the
beginner of the race has sinned, his sin is the sin of
all who descend from him.   This view of each having
sinned in Adam because of an essential or numerical
oneness in the race, is a mere philosophical theory,
— sometimes the product of Realism, sometimes of
this combined with Traducianism, sometimes held upon
a peculiar and independent position.[1]   But it is quite

[1] Neander thinks that Augustine's view of Adam, as bearing in himself
germinally the entire human race, was determined by his Platonico-Aris-
totelian Realism [see *Church History*, Bohn's edit. iv. 350].   Jonathan
Edwards holds that the oneness or identity of the posterity of Adam with
their progenitor is simply a oneness established by the divine constitution.
It is from Hofmann that we have cited the modern realistic theory as above
described.   He says : " Wir brauchen keine künstliche Annahme, wie dass
alle von Adam Stammenden in ihm gewesen, oder dass er als Bundeshaupt
des menschlichen Geschlechts gesündigt habe, sondern bleiben bei der ein-
fachen Thatsache jener Einheit des Menschengeschlechts, vermöge welcher
jeder Einzelne nicht nur Glied des Geschlechts, sondern auch der Anfang
desselben sein Anfang ist.   Nicht hat der Einzelne die Sünde Adam's
mitgethan, sondern weil der Anfänger des Geschlechts sie gethan hat, so
ist sie die Sünde aller, welche von ihm stammen."—*Schriftbeweis*, i. 540.

unnecessary for the support of the great Protestant
doctrine of imputation, which rests securely enough
upon the fact of a representative unity. The theory
of numerical unity exposes its upholders to the absurd
conclusion that men personally acted thousands of
years before they were born, or entangles them in
materialistic views of the soul. And in most of its
forms it renders inconceivable the entrance into the
race of a truly human and yet sinless Redeemer.

As an example of the opposite, namely, the atomic
view, may be cited the theory of Julius Müller himself.
It is that we must hold each sinful human being to
have exercised a personal self-decision in that extra-
temporal existence which he assumes to belong to
created personality, and thus to have served himself
heir to the sin of the first man. In other words, that
" each one who in this life is tainted by sin has in a life
beyond the bounds of time wilfully turned away from
the divine light to the darkness of self-absorbed selfishness."[1]   Not to speak of its fantastic and startling
appearance, it is plain that this view derives no support either from consciousness or from Scripture. But
what is still more conclusive against this and all other
attempts to account for the first consciousness of sin
on the lines of individualism, is the inadequate theory
of guilt which they involve, namely, that in order to
render man justly responsible for acts determined by
an internal state or character, that state must be self-
produced. This theory is contrary to common judgment, to conscience, and to the analogy of the leading
doctrines of Scripture. According to all known human

[1] *The Christian Doctrine of Sin,* ii. 359 (Clark, 2d edit.).

and divine modes of reckoning, a being is reckoned good or bad because he is so, however he may have come into the state or constitution which produces such moral character.

The Augustinian or Protestant doctrine of imputation must not be identified with either or any of these theories. Its basis is the federal unity of the race—a fact supported by independent Scripture proof, and which tends to explain the existence of corruption in all as a just consequence of the sin of their covenant head. How depravity becomes guilt in each, the doctrine of imputation does not profess to explain. Most of its adherents have leaned to the organic or substantial view of the human race. It was long put in a form sanctioned by Anselm, Odo, and Aquinas: " In Adam a person made nature sinful; in his posterity nature made persons sinful." [1] This suggests the idea of humanity as an essence or species standing by itself, so that in the first man's sin the individual ruled the nature, but ever since the nature rules the individual. In this way there can be penalty where there is no guilt in the sense of moral culpability, and there can be guilt in the sense of legal exposure to penalty where there is no personal sin. This view is not philosophically complete. But Augustine long ago perceived that we must distinguish the fact from all explanations offered. He knew how to distinguish the conviction that sin and guilt had spread from the first man to all, from his own realistic speculations regarding the propagation of guilt and penalty. In like manner,

[1] Hence the formula, " Natura a primis personis corrupta, corrumpit cæteras personas."—Müller, ii. 312.

he saw how easily the question concerning the propagation of a sinful nature would connect itself with another philosophical question respecting the origin of individual souls. But he declined to allow a vital point of Scripture doctrine to be confused with mere speculations which were indifferent to faith. He refused to decide for Creationism or Traducianism on scriptural grounds, for he could find none such. He perceived the strength of the former on philosophical grounds, however much the latter might seem to favour his own theological system. In the same way, Protestant divines of both the great communions agree in maintaining the doctrines of depravity and of imputation; yet, for the most part, Lutherans favour Traducianism, and Reformed theologians Creationism. These facts remove the question out of the region of opinions having any theological value. Nor will biblical psychology enable us to decide for the one or the other of these theories as to the origin of the soul. The whole mode of conception out of which the strife arose, involving a sharp distinction between material and immaterial substance, is other and later than the biblical. The Bible account of man includes both. Its dualism is precisely that of the earthly and the heavenly —that which man derives from his race, and that which he is at the hands of God. At first formed of the dust, yet God-inbreathed, so now he is begotten of human parents, but formed in the womb by the Almighty, and the spirit within him is a divine product.[1] Yet, though Scripture thus favours the ascription of the higher elements in men to an immediate divine act at their

[1] Comp. Ps. li. 5, cxxxix. 13–16; Isa. xlii. 5; Zech. xii. 1.

origination, it will not enable us to gather from the account of their formation how evil arises within each.[1]

Scripture, however, is an unmistakeable witness to the fact that each of us, as he is quickened to discern himself and his nature, appropriates a sense of guilt derived from the sinfulness of the race. Thus the writer of the 51st Psalm, having stated as the head and front of his offending that it was sin against God, goes on in the next clause to adduce his birth-sin as an aggravation of the case. "Not only have I done such things, but I am the inheritor of a nature which produces them." A self-ignorant man might have said: "It is true that I have done these wrongs and come by these slips, but I have a good heart. These doings are not the exponents of my real self." A man untaught in the mystery of human evil would have said: "I have sinned, but my inherited sinfulness is some excuse for me." This penitent taught of God says: "I have sinned, but what is worse, I am by nature a sinner, and in sin did my mother conceive me. If such deeds be the streams, how foul must be the source of them!" Thus he clears God, accuses himself, and does truth in the inward part. Now this is substantially a doctrinal testimony. If the depravity which we bring with us into the world were not sinful, it would to some extent excuse our actual sins. But it is never adduced in the Scripture as a palliation, rather as an enhancement of our evil. The same thing is implied in saying that we are " the children of wrath

---

[1] "Nous ne concevons ni l'état glorieux d'Adam, ni la nature de son péché, ni la transmission qui s'en est faite en nous. Ce sont choses qui se sont passées dans l'état d'une nature toute differente de la nôtre, et qui passent l'état de notre capacité présente."—Pascal, *Pensées*, p. 295 (Molinier).

by nature." Guiltiness in the "nature" is the necessary correlative of "wrath," which is God's righteous
displeasure. The doctrinal expression of such Bible
statements is nothing else than that profound, apparently paradoxical, and much maligned position of the
Protestant Evangelical Church,—that original sin is no
mere disease nor flaw in our origin, but is really sinful;
that inborn depravity is not only an evil and a sickness,
but entails guilt.

III. From the origin of sin and the propagation of
it in the race, we pass to the SEAT AND DOMINION of it
in man. In regard to the latter, the Old Testament
keeps very much to facts and instances instead of
laying down dogmatic positions. The early narrative
details special instances of its prevalence in particular
men and races; and throughout the whole history its
hold on man appears "not more from the dominion it
exerts over evil men, than from the energy with which
it rises up in men who are, on the whole, servants of
God."[1] The characteristic candour of Scripture in
relating the faults and sins of the patriarchs and saints
must not, however, be denuded of doctrinal intention
to teach historically the great lines of sin and grace.
Although it is only when we come to the New Testament that the opposition of flesh and spirit in human
experience is crystallized into a doctrine, yet passages
in the Old Testament lay a foundation for it, beginning
with that immediately following the fall, when the
Lord says, "My Spirit shall not always strive with
man, for that he also is flesh."[2] To trace the progressive import of the expressions "flesh" and "spirit"

[1] Rainy, *Delivery and Development of Doctrine*, p. 334.   [2] Gen. vi. 3.

would confirm the view already advanced, that " flesh "
in its ethical meaning denotes not the animal character
of sin, nor its carnal seat, but the·inherited or birth-
condition of our nature.[1] The " flesh," in this its higher
or secondary import, is human nature as generated in
the race—a view confirmed by the Bible account of
the progress of corruption in man's early history, and
by the experience of the rise of sin in every individual
life. The further consideration of the sense in which
" flesh " seems to be identified with indwelling sin,
especially in Pauline phraseology, we postpone till it
can be looked at in its relation to grace.[2]

When we ask what is the doctrine of Scripture
regarding the seat of sin in man's constitution, and the
degree in which it has affected that constitution, we
have to consider the ascription all through the Bible
of sin and its corruption to the human heart. A well-
known and much quoted chain of such passages runs
across the whole breadth of Scripture. Some of its
main links are to be found in the assertion of universal
and hereditary corruption, Gen. vi. 5, viii. 21: "The
imagination " (יֵצֶר, including all inward product, desires,
and purposes) "of man's heart is evil from his youth;"
in the words of the Preacher: "The heart of the sons
of men is full of evil;"[3] in those of the prophet: "The
heart is treacherous above all things, and malignant; who can know it?"[4] and in the saying of our
Lord: "Out of the heart proceed evil thoughts," etc.[5]

---

[1] *Supra*, pp. 84, 85.   [2] See Lect. V.   [3] Eccles. ix. 3.
[4] Jer. xvii. 9. אָנֻשׁ, " malignant," in the sense used when speaking of a
disease or a wound, and rendered " incurable " in Jer. xv. 18, Job xxxiv.
6, Micah i. 9.
[5] Matt. xv. 19.

These scriptures present a view of man's sin full of inward penetration. They speak of the evil as "being from within, not from without—a part of the self-life, and not of the accidental or external life."[1] It is a view at once broad and deep. It asserts the universality of the evil and its radical character in one single formula. Individual differences and degrees in wrong are fully admitted in the Bible utterances, but the leading assertion is common and universal wrongness at the heart. Now what is "the heart" in Scripture language? The proper appreciation of the phrase will help us to state correctly the Bible doctrine of human corruption. Deriving its import from its physical analogue, "heart" in the language of biblical psychology means the focus of the personal and moral life. It never denotes the personal subject, always the personal organ. All the soul's motions of life proceed from it, and re-act upon it. The Bible term "heart" might be read as it is used in the popular speech of men, were only this peculiarity kept well in view, that in biblical usage it includes the intellectual as well as all other movements of the soul. No doubt, however, while regarded as the home of every inward phenomenon, mental, emotional, moral, it more particularly denotes that which constitutes character. It is that which determines the whole moral being: "Out of it are the issues of life."[2]

Plainly, therefore, when the heart is spoken of as the seat of sin, this indicates the radical nature of human corruption. It consists not in words, acts, appearances. These merely show it, for it reigns

[1] Tulloch, *Croall Lecture*, p. 123.
[2] Prov. iv. 23. On the term "heart," see Lect. II. pp. 86–88.

within.   It has tainted the roots of life, the formative
sources of character.[1]   This explains its influence on all
the powers and faculties, its blinding effect upon self-
consciousness,—for " who can understand his errors ? "
the radical nature of the change needed to remove it,
the energy of that whole divine process which constitutes redemption; for the sin, from which God is
risen up to redeem us, sits where God alone ought to
dwell, at the source of our moral and spiritual being.

This language, however, while confirming the evangelical doctrine of human corruption, corrects some
mistakes and exaggerations.   It is of interest to find
that the very words of Scripture, when thus carefully
observed, exclude, for example, the exaggerated dogma
of Flacius, that sin is a corruption of the nature of the
soul.[2]   For heart never means the being or constitution
of the soul, always only its sources and principles of
action.   This language is also clear in affirming that
sin is not seated in any special faculty or part of our
nature, but at the centre of the whole.   Heart, no
doubt, is emphatically τὸ πρακτικόν, the practical principle of the soul's operations.   But we shall at once
introduce confusion into the Bible doctrine of sin, and,
indeed, into its whole doctrine of man, if we use
"heart" as excluding the rational or intellectual
element.   It is usual to say that " the Scriptures do
not make the broad distinction between the under-

---

[1] " This goes far beyond the superficial doctrine which makes man a
morally indifferent being, in whose choice it lies at each moment to be
either good or bad.   This book understands sin as a principle which has
penetrated to the centre, and from thence corrupts the whole circuit of
life."—Oehler, *Theology of the Old Testament*, i. 223 (Clark).

[2] Of which see more in Lect. V.

standing and the heart which is common in our philosophy." [1]   It would be better to say that "mind" and
"heart," as these terms are used through the Bible
generally, never do imply that distinction between the
intellectual and the emotional nature which we denote
by them even in popular language, much less the
stricter division of man's faculties into the understanding and the will, or into the intellectual and the
active powers.   The Scripture doctrine of corruption,
therefore, in accordance with its own simple psychology, is this, that the heart, i.e. the fountain of man's
being, is corrupt, and therefore all its actings, or, as
we should say, the whole soul in all its powers and
faculties, perverted.   A proper application of this principle will deliver us from the question whether the
power of depravity lies mainly in the evil affections
or in the darkened understanding; as also from the
correlative question, whether saving faith is an emotion
of the heart or an assent of the understanding.   Much
more will it keep us from the error of supposing that
man's corruption is only a practical bias, leaving the
judgment pure and uncontaminated by evil.   Scripture
gives no countenance to such distinctions, both because
it recognises the whole soul under the name "heart"
as the seat of depravity, and because it proceeds upon
a different psychology from those which afford play for
such controversies. [2]

[1] Hodge, *Systematic Theology*, ii. 255.

[2] "The heart in the Scripture is variously used; sometimes for the mind
and understanding, sometimes for the will, sometimes for the affections,
sometimes for the conscience, sometimes for the whole soul. Generally it
denotes the whole soul of man and all the faculties of it, not absolutely, but
as they are all one principle of moral operations, as they all concur in our
doing good or evil. . . . And in this sense it is that we say the seat and

Once more, let us observe that while the Scripture
statement is so strong in asserting a corruption of
man's whole nature, and in assigning that corruption
to the centre and fountain of his moral life, and while
the force of that statement is vainly sought to be
evaded or softened down, yet the Scripture asserts no
corruption, depravation, or destruction of his natures,
faculties, or powers as such.   It recognises a constitution which, in relation to the end for which man was
made, is wholly gone wrong, and has no power to right
itself.   But this just strength of statement is entirely
misapplied when the Scripture language is transferred
literally to the wholly different region of human
psychology, and the powers of the soul are held to be
corrupted as powers and faculties.   The great Protestant theologians have always perceived this, and have
accordingly repressed as unscriptural all such extremes.
They have usually repelled the error by saying that,
while man since the fall can do no good in any divine
relation, his natural and civil actions may be correct
and virtuous.[1]   Not only so, but maintaining the

subject of this law of sin is the heart of man."—Owen, *On Indwelling Sin;
Works* (Goold's edit.), vi. 170.

Edwards, speaking not of sin, but of grace, uses " heart " in its scriptural
inclusiveness, thus : " Spiritual understanding consists primarily in a cordial
sense, or *a sense of heart, of that spiritual beauty.* I say *a sense of heart,*
for it is not speculation merely that is concerned in this kind of understanding; nor can there be a clear distinction made between the two
faculties of understanding and will, as acting distinctly and separately, in
this matter."—Jon. Edwards, *On Religious Affections; Works,* i. 283 (Lond.
1840).

[1] Commenting on Mark x. 21, " *Intuitus eum Jesus dilexit,*" Calvin says :
" Interdum vero Deus, quos non probat, nec justificat, amare dicitur : nam
quia illi grata est humani generis conservatio (quæ justitia, æquitate,
moderatione, prudentia, fide, temperantia constat) politicas virtutes amare
dicitur, non quod salutis vel gratiæ meritoriæ sint, sed quia ad finem spec-
tant illi probatum."

L

validity of man's natural faculties and of their operation on natural things,—the denial of which would be
a universal pyrrhonism,—it has been an essential of
the evangelical theology to maintain, further, that
there is possible to fallen man a natural knowledge
of God, and even a natural acquaintance with truth
supernaturally revealed, as contrasted with a spiritual
and saving knowledge of God and things divine.   This
position was strongly contended for by the orthodox
theologians of the seventeenth century in opposition to
the Socinians, who denied it.   Its value consists in its
forming the proper foundation of natural theology, as
well as in its being an essential part of the Scripture
doctrine of the divine image.[1]

The Scripture view of the fall, as we have seen, is
that it was radical and fatal as regards man's relation
to God.   The consistency of this with the maintenance
of validity in fallen man's natural faculties, and of the
goodness of his actions in a natural sense, is sometimes
stated in this form, namely, that it is the constitutional working of man in his moral and religious life
that is vitiated by sin, but not his parts and faculties.
As if we should note that a timepiece may cease to
give accurate time and yet be unimpaired in its wheels,
plates, jewels, and other constituent portions.   The
analogy has only to be carried out, however, to suggest
the complete statement.   If a watch or other timepiece
fail of its chief end, and be laid aside from its proper
use of keeping time, it is certain that its wheels, plates,

---

[1] See the pamphlet of Prof. James Macgregor, entitled *A Vindication of
Natural Theology*, Elliot, Edin. 1859, the surviving monument of a now
forgotten controversy in the Glasgow F. C. College case.

and jewels will not long remain untarnished. So the fall affects indirectly the natural powers of man, as it directly affects his spiritual condition. It is most evident that the working of sin, and especially of vice, bedarkens the understanding and blunts the judgment even in common things; that it not only sears the conscience, but deadens the natural affections; in short, that the failure of human nature to attain the chief end of its constitution carries with it consequences which affect even its constituent parts.

Very carefully have evangelical divines brought out the breadth and harmony of Scripture statement as to the two positions covered in this and the preceding lecture, namely, that man though fallen is still in a natural sense constituted in the image of God, but that in a spiritual sense that constitution is through sin totally ruined; and hence, that though the natural powers and faculties have still the stamp of God, are not in themselves sinful, they are all indirectly under sin's power and suffer from its effects. The eloquent passage in Howe's *Living Temple* is well remembered, but it is not always observed with what exquisite balance it keeps both these lines of truth in view. "That God hath withdrawn Himself and left this His temple desolate, we have many sad and plain proofs before us. The stately ruins are visible to every eye that bear in their front (yet extant) this doleful inscription, '*Here God once dwelt.*' Enough appears of the admirable frame and structure of the soul of man to show the Divine Presence did sometime reside in it; more than enough of vicious deformity to proclaim He is now retired and gone. The lamps are extinct, the

altar overturned; the light and love are now vanished,
which did the one shine with so heavenly brightness,
the other burn with so pious fervour; the golden
candlestick is displaced, and thrown away as a useless
thing, to make room for the throne of the prince of
darkness; the sacred incense, which sent rolling up in
clouds its rich perfumes, is exchanged for a poisonous,
hellish vapour, and here is, 'instead of a sweet savour, a
stench.' . . . Look upon the fragments of that curious
sculpture which once adorned the palace of that great
King: the relics of common notions; the lively prints
of some undefaced truth; the fair ideas of things; the
yet legible precepts that relate to practice. Behold
with what accuracy the broken pieces show these to
have been engraven by the finger of God; and how
they now lie torn and scattered, one in this dark
corner, another in that, buried in heaps of dirt and
rubbish! There is not now a system, an entire table
of coherent truths to be found, or a frame of holiness,
but some shivered parcels; and if any, with great
toil and labour, apply themselves to draw out
here one piece and there another, and set them together, they serve rather to show how exquisite the
divine workmanship was in the original composition, than for present use to the excellent purposes
for which the whole was first designed. . . . You
come, amidst all this confusion, as into the ruined
palace of some great prince, in which you see here the
fragments of a noble pillar, there the shattered pieces
of some curious imagery, and all lying neglected and
useless among heaps of dirt. He that invites you to
take a view of the soul of man gives you but such

another prospect, and doth but say to you, 'Behold the desolation!' all things rude and waste. So that should there be any pretence to the Divine Presence, it might be said, If God be here, why is it thus? The faded glory, the darkness, the disorder, the impurity, the decayed state in all respects of this temple, too plainly show the great Inhabitant is gone."[1]

IV. The preceding paragraphs have been carrying us into our concluding topic here, viz. the RESULTS OR CONSEQUENCES which sin has entailed on the nature of man. The substance of what Scripture teaches on this subject may be held as condensed in the sentence, "The wages of sin is death." Like the terms "Sin," "Flesh," "Heart," the term "Death" is one of the pivot words of Bible anthropology. To examine how much it means would require a treatise of itself. But we assume for our present purpose that it has three meanings, a legal, a moral, and a physical sense. "In the day that thou eatest thereof thou shalt surely die," clearly means, 'in that day thou art dead,— legally dead, as under condemnation, sentence being pronounced; spiritually dead, as fallen from righteousness and separated from God.' The literal or physical death is a consequence which flows from these; liability to it dated from the moment of the transgression, yet this liability does not surcease with that deliverance which is effected in redemption, for even in the redeemed "the body is dead because of sin," though "the spirit is life because of righteousness." The two latter meanings of the term "Death," namely, the

---

[1] John Howe, *The Living Temple*, Part II. chap. iv. sec. 9.

moral and the physical, cover the ground of our present
question as to the direct consequences of the fall upon
man's own nature. Spiritual inability and physical
dissolution are those results of sin which may in a
sense be called constitutional changes.   In what
sense they can be so regarded it is for us to
inquire.

Spiritual inability, or the loss of " all ability of
will to any spiritual good accompanying salvation,"
is only part of what is generally called spiritual
death; but it is an essential part of it, and is, moreover, that part which alone properly belongs to this
place, as a result of the fall affecting man's moral constitution.   Our interest in it, however, is chiefly negative; that is to say, we are concerned to show that
what is called in the Bible death in trespasses and sins,
is not such a derangement of man's original constitution
as implies either (*a*) a destruction of his free agency, or
(*b*) the loss of any essential element or attribute of his
nature. Under (*a*) it is of some moment to note, that
those who have been most strenuous in maintaining
the Scripture position that fallen man cannot of himself return to God, cannot repent unto life, cannot
believe unto salvation, in his natural mind receiveth
not the things of God, in his carnal state cannot please
God, have nevertheless uniformly and consistently
held that man under sin has not ceased to be a free
and responsible agent. This "natural bondage"—that
is, servitude to sin in a fallen nature—is perfectly consistent with " that natural liberty" wherewith " God
hath endued the will of man, that it is neither forced,
nor by any absolute necessity of nature determined, to

good or evil."[1] Even in times when a controversy
such as that between Luther and Erasmus was
possible, when men might be said to be tilting from
opposite sides of the shield, the Augustinians at least
did not mistake the real issue. In the second age of
Reformed theology the two positions were seen to be
both practically and speculatively consistent, as the
clear and well-balanced lines of the Westminster Confession show. This is now so well understood, that
even those who theologically differ from the Augustinian or Calvinistic view, and maintain the Arminian
position, do not impute to their opponents any real
inconsistency in holding the natural liberty of the will.
That fallen man should be spiritually bound, yet
metaphysically free, is now seen to be a position consistent with Scripture, with sound theology, and with
common sense.[2] (b) In refuting the unscriptural
position that man's death in sin means that by the fall
some element of his constitution was lost or fell into
abeyance, we have to glance at some forms of error
recently revived. Modern trichotomists undertake to
deliver us from a controversy of fourteen centuries'
standing regarding the will, its natural liberty and its

[1] Westminster Confession of Faith, chap. ix. 1.

[2] For an interesting incidental commentary on the ninth chapter of the
Confession, see the late Principal Cunningham's article on " Calvinism and
the Doctrine of Philosophical Necessity," in the course of which he points
out the theological confusions of the philosophers Stewart, Mackintosh, and
Hamilton, as well as the converse oversights of the divines Edwards and
Chalmers. He shows that the position of all the Reformers—the Lutherans,
when cleared of their earlier exaggeration, as well as the Calvinists—was,
like that of Augustine himself, one which entirely conserved the natural
freedom of the human spirit, and which did not involve the question of
man's bondage under sin and deliverance by grace with any philosophical
theory whatever. See Dr. Cunningham's *Reformers and the Theology of the
Reformation*, pp. 471–524.

bondage under sin, by substituting the simple-looking
formula that the *pneuma* in fallen man being dead or
dormant, regeneration consists in the quickening or
awakening of that *pneuma*, the absence or inaction
of which was enough to explain man's spiritual death.
This pretension is very poorly supported.   Indeed,
there is no point where the attempt to construct a
scheme of Christian doctrine in terms of the so-called
"tripartite nature of man" more entirely fails than this.
In the first place, it is impossible to ascertain whether
the writers of this school mean to maintain that this
sovereign power in man's constitution, the spirit, is
since the fall dead, or disabled, or defective, or
dormant, or wholly absent.[1]   Further, the theory
that this defect or absence of the *pneuma* in fallen
man accounts for his spiritual bondage under sin errs
in precisely the opposite direction from that in which

[1] Delitzsch quotes with approval from Zezschwitz, that conscience is the
remains of the spirit in the psychical man (*Pneuma-rest im psychischen
menschen*). "Looking to his substantial nature," he adds in a note, " no
man is without this *pneuma*, but . . . all who stand outside of grace are
ψυχικοί; and in so far as they have extinguished in themselves the last
remains of spirit, the conscience (*inwiefern sie auch den letzten Pneuma-
rest, das Gewissen, in sich ertödtet*), they are absolutely without spirit,
πνεῦμα μὴ ἔχοντες (Jude 19)."   This, after he has said that in regeneration
" the communication of the Spirit again revives the extinguished image of
God in our spirit, and keeps it living : it restores our spirit thereby to its
true nature ; so that man, *who even naturally has not ceased to have a
πνεῦμα*, now for the first time begins to have a πνεῦμα rightly, and to
be πνευματικός."—*Biblische Psychologie*, pp. 337, 338 ; Clark's Transl.
pp. 397, 398.
    Mr. J. B. Heard is still more self-contradictory. Almost every page of
his chapter on " The State of the *Pneuma* in Man since the Fall," contains
the conflicting epithets " dead," " defective," " dormant," as applied to
that " faculty" of which he also says, " When God withdrew from Adam
the presence of His Holy Spirit, the *pneuma* fell back into a dim and
depraved state of conscience toward God."—*The Tripartite Nature of Man*,
pp. 161–186, 4th edit., Edin. 1875, from which the quotations given in the
text are taken.

its supporters seem to think they are moving. Instead
of being a cautious or moderate statement of the consequences of the fall, it is implicitly a very serious
exaggeration.   One of these writers contrasts the
orthodox view with his own by calling the former the
dogma that original sin was something positive, and
the latter the negative or privative idea of birth-sin,
which he holds to be sufficient to explain the facts of
the case.[1] Now the theory of these writers is, that
the *pneuma* in fallen man is a dead organ; that there
is a "defect of that special religious faculty in man
which is called the spirit;" that by the eating of the
forbidden fruit "the spark of the divine image in man
was quenched."   And all this is put forward as "only
saying that birth-sin is privative and not positive,"
and as "enough to account for the condition of man
as we see him to this day." Enough, certainly!
Almost as much more than enough as was that famous
dictum of Flacius, that original sin was a corruption
of the substance of the soul.[2] For according to this
theory man's natural subjection to sin depends upon a
physical defect, the defect of an organ, the dead or
disabled state of the sovereign power of the regulative
pneuma — a "fatal defect," as the upholders of the
theory rightly name it, for it makes man's recovery
inconceivable. The whole of this fallacious train of
statement rests on the incorrect assumption that
Scripture warrants a tripartite analysis of natures or
constituent elements in the original constitution of
man, such as would enable us to give what may be
called a physical explanation of man's fallen state,

[1] *The Tripartite Nature of Man*, p. 184.   [2] See Lect. V.

accounting for it by the absence or abeyance of a
special religious or spiritual faculty.[1]

There is, therefore, no course open to us but to state
the effect of the fall upon the human will in the terms
which have so long exercised the theologians, if we
are to state it philosophically at all. But the profound affirmation of Scripture is that man is " dead in
trespasses and sins." No faculty or element is singled
out as that in which this death takes special effect.
It is an effect upon man's entire moral position.
Hence this doctrine of human inability in spiritual
things presents the same complex problem as that
concerning the sinfulness of concupiscence. The Bible
solution is, that such inability to good on the one
hand, and evil desire on the other, conditioning the
will, are at once sinful and penal. They are sin in one
sense; they are death or the wages of sin in the other
sense. They constitute a moral character at the back
of all acts of will. They characterize man's fallen
nature as depraved, corrupt, in a word sinful, before any
actual transgressions. But they are themselves the consequences of sin—penal consequences—taking effect in
a form conditioned by the federal unity of mankind.
The peculiarity of the Bible view here is that the same
thing is represented as sin and death in one. " O

---

[1] It is the more needful to advert to this, since the tripartite psychology
has been largely adopted by the holders of what is called " conditional
immortality." The Rev. Edward White, whose application of it to eschatological speculations has become noted, speaks according to the same
theory even when he touches on man's spiritual state since the fall. " This
moral ruin consists in the paralysis of the πνεῦμα or spiritual faculty, which
no longer either *sees* or *wills*, as is necessary for a life in union with God.
This is the cause of the sinful life, and ' the wages of sin is death.' "—*Life
in Christ*, p. 280, 3d edit., Lond. 1878.

wretched man that I am, who shall deliver me from
the body of this death?" The principle that in this
region sin and its punishment are practically identical,
is one which receives the attestation of nature, of conscience, and of Scripture alike. Man's will is spiritually
disabled by the fall, because of that profound law that
sin subjects the sinner to a moral fatalism, a *misera
necessitas mali* expressed by our Lord's words : " Whosoever committeth sin is the servant of sin." [1]

Whether *physical death* implies a constitutional change
resulting from the fall, is a question which requires
to be answered with more care than is sometimes
given to it. A general acquaintance with physiological and geological facts has now made the idea
familiar to all educated people, that death is a law
of organized matter. It is not uncommon, however, to
represent the Bible as saying that the sin of man first
introduced physical death into the animated world.
It is plain that the Bible makes no such assertion.
Indeed, the scientific principle that death is a necessary step in organic processes is expressly affirmed by
our Lord and by St. Paul in application to the vegetable world.[2] And there are indications by no means
obscure in the earlier chapters of Genesis that the same
law is recognised as applicable to all animal organisms.
Accordingly, observing that the maxim, "Death by
sin," applies to man alone, the best orthodox divines
have been careful to state that the sentence of death
which followed the fall was not the introduction of any
new physical law or constitutional change even in

---

[1] See Martensen's *Dogmatics*, p. 209 (Clark, Edin. 1866).
[2] John xii. 24 ; 1 Cor. xv. 36.

regard to the human body.[1] The great text on this
subject, Rom. v. 12, " By one man sin entered into the
world, and death by sin," must be read in the light of
the Old Testament narrative on which it is grounded.
Now, when we consider what is stated in Gen. ii. and
iii. with regard to the constitution of the first man, we
see that there is obviously a sense in which he was
created mortal. He was Adam from the *adamah*, the
ground. Dust was the material of his body. Organized
matter has naturally in it the seeds of decay, the certainty of dissolution. That the body of the first man
could not be immortal by its constitution is implied, if
not expressed, in the narrative. " Dust thou art, and
to dust thou shalt return." That is to say, the curse
assumes the form of a prediction, that in consequence
of sin the law of organized matter should be allowed to
have its way, even in the case of man. On the other
hand it is plain that, according to this narrative, man
was not made to die, that he was created for incorrup-
tion. It bears out what Bishop Bull calls the foundation of the whole Catholic doctrine concerning the state
of man in his integrity, namely, that Adam should not
have died if he had not sinned.[2] His constitution, however, even in innocence, implied, to use the language
of the theological schools, not an impossibility of dying,
but only a conditional potentiality of not dying.

Now, in the event that man had not sinned, there
are several conceivable ways in which the "*posse non*

---

[1] See Appendix, Note P.

[2] " I have dwelt the longer in asserting this great truth that Adam should
never have died if he had not sinned, because, this foundation being once
surely laid, it will appear that the whole superstructure of the Catholic
doctrine concerning the state of man in his integrity, and concerning man's

mori" might have issued in a confirmed physical immortality. The favourite patristic view was, that after probation Adam would have passed from the earthly to the heavenly paradise by an Elijah-like translation. Others have supposed that, even remaining on earth, his body would have undergone a change analogous to that which Christians are taught to expect at the second coming of Christ. Others, again, have contented themselves with saying that holiness confirmed and established should have effected such a change on man's physical being as to render it impassible and immortal.[1] There is a good deal to be said for the view favoured by Augustine, Luther, J. Müller, and others, that the narrative itself supplies us with a suggestion on the point. " The tree of life, in the midst of the garden," was the divine provision for effecting this transition. The mention of it may be regarded as the way, proper to this transcendental narrative, of stating that the Creator had prepared a process for man's passing into the immortal or undying life, as a being made up of body and spirit, had he continued obedient. The idea of "the tree of life" is of that original paradisaic sort to which the imagination of mankind in all ages bears witness, when it represents its heroes as seeking to bathe in the fountain of perpetual youth, or toiling in search of some secret " elixir" to counteract the decays of mortality. If physical death be implied in man's original constitution, in so far as he

---

fall by sin, which is to be measured by the former, is firmly built thereon ; which is the reason why Pelagians formerly and Socinians of late have so strenuously opposed this verity." — *The State of Man before the Fall;* Bull's *Works*, vol. ii. p. 60, Burton's edit., Oxford, 1846.

[1] Turretine, *Instit. Theolog. Elench.* Loc. v. Qu. xii. 3, 4.

is of the earth earthy, yet according to Scripture (and the instinct of mankind answers thereto) it was so only as a possibility which could and ought to have been averted. The provision made for averting it lay symbolically and sacramentally in the use of the tree of life, though really and spiritually in man's being so formed in the image of God that perfect obedience was possible to him.[1]

The chief value of this view is, that it simplifies the connection between the fall and that part of its effects under consideration. When man sinned, physical death followed as a natural consequence. The sentence was carried out by no introduction of constitutional change. It was effected simply by denying to man that "immortalizing transition" which would have occurred in his path of progress had he remained holy. This denial was sealed by his expulsion from paradise and consequent exclusion from the tree of life. The dust of which his body was framed, instead of being transmuted into such a garb for the perfect spirit as it should have become by his feeding on that ambrosial nourishment, is left to the law of its own decay and returns to dust. Man in consequence of sin becomes subject to physical death as an inevitable necessity and the law of his being.[2]

[1] See Julius Müller, *The Christian Doctrine of Sin*, vol. ii. pp. 296, 297. So also Bishop Bull. "Now it is certain the tree of life was so called because it was either a sacrament and divine sign, or else a natural means of immortality; that is, because he that should have used it would (either by the natural virtue of the tree itself continually repairing the decays of nature, or else by the power of God) have lived for ever, as God Himself plainly assures us, Gen. iii. 22-24."—At p. 54 of the treatise formerly cited. See also the quotation from Augustine, *De Genesi ad Litteram*, given in Appendix, Note P.

[2] Augustine has put this with epigrammatic effect when, commenting

While, therefore, we repel as unscriptural the absurd position that sin introduced the principle of decay and death into the animated world, yet on the other hand Scripture clearly teaches that death in all its meanings is to man a consequence of sin. No exegesis of texts such as Rom. v. 12 is tolerable which would exclude either the spiritual or the physical sense of the term "death." As Philippi has well said, it lies in the very nature of such biblical notions ["life," "death," "sin"], embracing a rich variety of elements, that often several or even all these elements should appear in combination, the context of the passage deciding how many and which are to be conceived as blended in one.[1] The death which came by sin, the death which is the wages of sin, is no doubt largely spiritual death, but the position of physical death under this general statement is clear. It is a part of the curse. It is a consequence of sin in the sense that had man not sinned it would have been averted. It is an effect of the first sin, of the race-sin, in such a sense that for sin it has come upon those who have not personally and consciously

on Rom. viii. 10, 11, he says, " 'If Christ be in you, the body is dead because of sin.' Paul is very careful to say 'dead,' not 'mortal.' The body was mortal by its nature, yet that mortal did not become dead but on account of sin. . . . And again, 'He that raised up Christ from the dead shall also quicken your mortal bodies.' Paul says not 'your dead bodies,' as before he had said 'the body is dead,' but 'shall quicken,' says he, 'even your mortal bodies,' and that in such a way that not only shall they not be dead, but also no longer mortal." See the whole passage as given in Note P.

[1] See Philippi on *The Epistle to the Romans*, *in loc.*, 3d edit. vol. i. p. 254 (Clark). So also Delitzsch : " Rom. v. 12 plainly means that there is in the world a dominion of death, as there is of sin, introduced by the one man in whom humanity originates ; all men die because that all have sinned, inasmuch as the One sinned. Death is to individuals an inevitable consequence of the sin of that One, even apart from their own proper transgressions."—*Biblische Psychologie*, p. 369.

sinned. To say that "death, as a simple physical fact, is unaffected by moral conditions, that its incidence is natural and lies in the constitution of things,"[1] is to break up the whole scriptural view. Mainly and primarily, no doubt, the death of the soul is death. Sin is the death-dealing thing, but man is always presented in the Scriptures as a unit, and that which is death to him in one element of his nature must extend to all. It is germinant in meaning as in power.

No doubt there is a sense in which decay and death are natural—natural in animals, natural to the body of man as animal; but the Bible consistently represents man from the first as more than animal—as a personal, responsible, and God-related creature. For him death means separation, cutting off: primarily, of his spiritual life from God; secondarily, of his soul from his body. Physical death is for him corruption of the body and deprivation of the spirit. By the New Testament revelation, death is for the Christian greatly transformed. But it is not to be treated by Christians after the fashion of philosophy, either ancient or modern. The extinction of corporeal life in man is a real evil, is in the strictest sense part of the wages of sin. How it is met, modified, and even transmuted into blessing is a leading characteristic of the Christian revelation in regard to man's future.

[1] Prin. Tulloch, *Croall Lecture*, p. 76. This and the similar expression on p. 189, "The physical death of infants, therefore, does not require sin to explain it," are statements irreconcilable with the principles which in the main are followed throughout the book. The author seems to be influenced by a desire to combine fidelity to Scripture theology with some homage to views that are entirely the reverse of scriptural.

LECTURE V.

PSYCHOLOGY OF THE NEW LIFE.

" Toute la foi consiste en Jésus-Christ et en Adam ; et toute la morale en la concupiscence et en la grâce."—PASCAL, *Pensées*, p. 296 (Molinier).

" C'est un des grands principes du Christianisme que tout ce qui est arrivé à Jésus-Christ doit se passer dans l'âme et dans le corps de chaque chrétien ; que comme Jésus-Christ a souffert durant sa vie mortelle, est mort à cette vie mortelle, est ressuscité d'une nouvelle vie, est monté au ciel et sied à la droite du Père ; ainsi le corps et l'âme doivent souffrir, mourir, ressusciter, monter au ciel, et seoir à la dextre. Toutes ces choses s'accomplissent en l'âme durant cette vie, mais non pas dans le corps. . . . Aucune de ces choses n'arrive dans le corps durant cette vie ; mais les mêmes choses s'y passent ensuite."—*Ibid.*, I. 28, 29 (Faugère).

JOHN iii. 3.—" Except a man be born again, he cannot see the kingdom of God."

EPH. ii. 5.—" Even when we were dead in sins, hath quickened us together with Christ."

EPH. iv. 22–24.—" That ye put off concerning the former conversation the old man, which is corrupt according to the deceitful lusts; and be renewed in the spirit of your mind; and that ye put on the new man, which after God is created in righteousness and true holiness."

2 COR. v. 17.—"Therefore if any man *be* in Christ, *he is* a new creature."

GAL. ii. 20.—" Nevertheless I live; yet not I, but Christ liveth in me."

Also

GAL. v. 16–26 and ROM. vii. 5–viii. 14.

LECTURE V.

THE rise of the new life in the soul must be considered a central topic in our theme, for it is here that the supernatural scheme of the Bible merges into human experience. The religion of revelation—a system of supernatural facts—touches at this point the natural scheme of man and his being; for the supernatural, in this form of a personal spiritual change, becomes a fact of consciousness. The doctrine of grace, it has been said, can never perish, for it creates defenders of itself. Fresh witness for its truth arises with every additional human being who becomes the subject of divine grace. He has the evidence in his own person of a divine interposition on man's behalf. The kingdom of heaven is within him.

The spiritual supernatural within man, the entrance of the redemptive power into his nature, or his entrance into its domain, is called in Scripture a birth—a being "born again" or "from above," [1] a quickening and resurrection, [2] a new creation or a new crea-

---

[1] John iii. 3, 5 : ἐὰν μή τις γεννηθῇ ἄνωθεν.

[2] Eph. ii. 5, 6 : συνεζωοποίησε . . . καὶ συνήγειρε. Comp. Col. iii. 1; Rom. vi. 5, 11.

ture.[1]   These expressions indicate, of course, the
entirely divine origination of the change; that in it
God—the Spirit of God—acts upon the human heart
in a direct or immediate transaction.   This divine side
of the fact is that to which the term "regeneration"
is usually restricted in modern evangelical theology.
It follows that in the regenerative act the subject of
the change is passive, and even, it may be, at the
time unconscious of the change, as the analogies of
Creation, Birth, and Resurrection imply.

In what regeneration in this sense consists, has
been carefully and clearly made out in the best schools
of Protestant theology, though, as usual, not without
controversy.   What it chiefly concerns us to notice
here is, that when we speak according to Scripture
we must repudiate all theories of regeneration which
make it consist in a change upon the substance of
the soul, or upon the constitution of human nature,
or even upon any special faculty or element in that
nature.   The first of these erroneous opinions is commonly connected with the name of Matthias Flacius
Illyricus, a name among the most considerable in
the second generation of the German Reformers.   A
man of strong evangelical feeling, but a keen con-
troversialist rather than an exact thinker, he had
allowed himself, in dealing with opponents of the
scriptural doctrine of depravity, to use some incautious expressions which seemed to make sin the
very substance of fallen human nature; and then pro-

---

[1] 2 Cor. v. 17 ; Gal. vi. 15 : καινὴ κτίσις. Comp. Eph. ii. 10, 15 : κτισ-
θέντες, κτίσῃ ; iv. 24 : κτισθέντα ; Col. iii. 10 : κτίσαντος. Comp. also παλιγ-
γενεσία in the only two places where it occurs, Tit. iii. 5, in our present
sense, and Matt. xix. 28, in a dispensational meaning.

ceeded, in spite of the remonstrances of his fellow-Reformers, to elevate this exaggeration into a dogma. His favourite texts on the subject are: " I will take away the hard and stony heart;" "Our old man is crucified with Christ;" "Ye were once darkness," etc. Relying upon such Scripture terms as these, and upon certain expressions of Luther, he contended that the substance of human nature was by the fall changed, corrupted, and depraved. Accordingly he held that in the production of the new spiritual man there is a corresponding substantial change. When charged with Manichæan heresy, he explained that he had never used the phrase quoted against him, " that sin is the substance," but had always asserted that it is the "essential form" of fallen nature. He clung tenaciously, however, to his main position that the corruption of human nature is essential and substantial, not accidental. In the *Formula Concordiæ*, drawn up about two years after the death of Flacius, his opinion is distinctly alluded to and condemned, as destroying the distinction between the substance of human nature—or the man himself as created by God —and that original sin which inheres in his nature or essence and corrupts it.[1] The error of this able, laborious, and much afflicted divine has served chiefly as a foil to bring out with greater distinctness the teaching of the evangelical Church on the point. It is clear that, according to Scripture, neither the fall on the one hand nor regeneration on the other can be regarded as effecting a change in the substance of human nature.

But although the Lutheran symbols are perfectly at

[1] See Appendix, Note Q.

one with those of the Reformed Church in repudiating
all errors of this kind belonging to the age in which
they were written, the doctrine of the regenerate life,
as taught by some Lutheran theologians now, does
suggest the idea of constitutional or substantial
change.   This tendency arises in a way quite different
from that above described.   It is a reflex of the sacramentarian views prevalent in the Lutheran and in
some other communions.   When men teach that our
Lord's humanity is partaken of in the sacraments, it is
easy to see how a general theory might arise to the
effect that the divine humanity of Christ is the basis
of the new life in believers, or that regeneration consists in the communication of His theanthropic life to
the soul.   When this tendency is intensified, as is the
case with some Lutheran divines, by a favour for the
trichotomic partition of human nature, the result may
be anticipated.   Delitzsch, in the section of his *Biblical
Psychology* treating of regeneration, has given full expression to the theory.   "Since the mystery of the
Incarnation was realized, divine influences are at work
which make sinful man partaker of the spirit, soul,
and body of Christ; so that he who, according to his
connection with Adam, is earthy, becomes, according
to his connection with Christ, spiritual and heavenly."
"This," he explains, "does not take place through
physical impartation any more than did the entrance of
man's soul at the first through the divine inbreathing,
or than does the derivation of soul or spirit in children
from their parents.   Yet influences proceed from Christ
according to His tripartite human constitution (*seinem
dreifachen menschlichen Wesensbestande nach*) which

place men in such communion with the spirit, soul,
and body of Christ as exercises a transforming power
over their threefold nature." "In the work of grace,"
he proceeds, "we are made partakers of the spirit of
Christ, whereby is revived and preserved the once extinct image of God in our spirit; of the soul of Christ,
that is, of His blood, which divine-human blood becomes the tincture of our soul to the recovering of its
God-like glory (*doxa*); of the flesh of Christ, which
enters into us without mixing with our sin-pervaded,
material, animal flesh, and which becomes a tincture
of immortality, laying hold of the essence of our flesh
in order to assimilate to itself eventually even its outward appearance, in the resurrection." After such a
statement, it is not surprising to find him closing the
paragraph in words which almost echo the Flacian
exaggeration: "Since the natural spiritual-psychical
constitution of man," he concludes, "is not merely
ethically but substantially affected by corruption, the
restoration of it must be also at once ethical and
substantial." [1]

The opinion that through Christ a constitutional
change is effected upon human nature has been taken
up by a school of writers in this country, who hold it
in a far cruder form than that of the Lutheran theology, and without any sacramentarian proclivity which
could account for it. With them it originates in a
different interest. In support of his theory of "conditional immortality," Mr. Edward White, for instance,
sets forth the doctrine that "God unites the divine

---

[1] *Biblische Psychologie*, pp. 338–340. I have, of course, condensed the
paragraphs, not quoted them *verbatim*.

essence with man's mortal nature in the regeneration
of the individual by the indwelling of the Holy Spirit,
'the Lord and Giver of life,' whose gracious inhabita-
tion applies the remedy of redemption by communicating to good men of every age and generation
God-likeness or immortality, to the soul by spiritual
regeneration, and to the body by resurrection." Like
the Lutheran divines, he holds that this mighty change
is conveyed to mankind through the channel of the
incarnation. But in stating what the change is, a
serious discrepancy occurs. "We hold," he says, "that
the Scripture teaches that the very object of redemption is to change our nature, not only from sin to
holiness, but from mortality to immortality,—from a
constitution whose present structure is perishable in
all its parts, to one which is eternal, so that those who
are partakers of the blessing 'pass from death unto
life,' from a corruptible nature into one which is incorruptible in all its parts, physical and spiritual."[1] And
again: "Apart from such renewal in the divine likeness, life, however intelligent, is perishable, for the
soul has no union with Eternal Love. It is, then,
a moral change in the character of the soul and the
discipline of the body, and not an ontological or
physical change in substance, which is the condition
of salvation and the present result of the indwelling of
the Divine Spirit."[2] How these two paragraphs are
consistent, or how even the two sentences of the last
can be saved from self-contradiction, we leave the
reader to consider. Nor do we concern ourselves at
present with their bearing on the doctrine of man's

[1] *Life in Christ*, p. 117, 3d edit.   [2] *Ibid.* p. 280.

natural immortality. Meanwhile, our business with
this theory is simply to set its startling and confused
view of the change effected in regeneration side by
side with that drawn by the consent of centuries of
evangelical thinking from the statements of Scripture.

After what has been said in the preceding lecture
in refutation of theories which restrict to certain
elements or faculties in man the chief effect of the
fall, it is not necessary that we should now discuss
the corollary from these theories, which would restrict
in a similar manner the act of regeneration. We have
already dealt with the view which makes the great
change in conversion to consist in the re-awakening
of a buried or dormant *pneuma*.[1] It is thoroughly
untenable. To give any significance to the theory, it
is necessary for its defenders to maintain, as Mr. J. B.
Heard does, that this dormant *pneuma* is always ethically
incorrupt, is only affected by depravity in the sense of
being buried before conversion and still weak after it;
and that sanctification acts upon it not in the way
of making it holy, but simply by strengthening its
supremacy. But to assert that "the *pneuma* or god-
like in man," which regeneration quickens and sanctification strengthens, "is not prone to evil,—indeed,
cannot sin,"[2]—is to contradict the whole strain of
Scripture, if not even its express language, when it
declares that in believers themselves there is filthiness
both of the Sarx and Pneuma.[3] But this theory must
fall under a broader and more general condemnation.

[1] In Lecture IV., at pp. 168, 169.
[2] *Tripartite Nature of Man*, p. 218, 4th edit.
[3] 2 Cor. vii. 1.

To make regeneration the re-awakening of any such
dead or dormant faculty is to contravene the Scripture
view that man's whole inward being—his heart—is
the seat of sin, and consequently the subject of renewal. This principle, so characteristic of the Bible,
namely, the unity of our inward life, confronts, indeed,
all theories which would place the seat of regeneration
in any one faculty or department of the soul, as the
intellect, the affections, or the will. It is the whole
inner man, as such, that is spiritually dead. It is the
same that is spiritually made alive. Regeneration
is something which affects the whole man. It is a
quickening, *i.e.* the impartation of a new form of life.
It is a second birth, or the entry into a new spiritual
state. It is the gift from God of a new heart, a new
moral self. The inner man, that is, the human being
in the centre and unity of his life, is the seat or subject of the life-giving power of the Holy Ghost which
produces this new creation; and the new creature is
identified with that abiding or indwelling of God's
Holy Spirit.[1]

Jonathan Edwards has come closest to a definition
of the new life when he says in his *Treatise concerning
Religious Affections* (part iii. sec. 1), " This new spiritual
sense and the new dispositions that attend it are no
new *faculties*, but new *principles* of nature : I use the
word *principles* for want of a word of a more determinate
signification. By a *principle of nature* in this place, I
mean that foundation which is laid in nature, either

---

[1] See all this carefully stated by Dr. Charles Hodge, *Systematic Theo-
logy*, vol. iii. pp. 16, 17, 33–36. In connection with his discussion of the
" Nature of Regeneration," stands another concerning the " Psychology of
Faith," which will be found *ibid.* pp. 42–67.

old or new, for any particular manner or kind of exercise of the faculties of the soul; or a natural habit or foundation for action, giving a person ability and disposition to exert the faculties in exercises of such a certain kind, so that to exert the faculties in that kind of exercises may be said to be his nature. So this new spiritual sense is not a new faculty of understanding, but it is a new foundation laid in the nature of the soul for a new kind of exercises of the same faculty of understanding. So that the new holy disposition of heart that attends this new sense is not a new faculty of will, but a foundation laid in the nature of the soul for a new kind of exercises of the same faculty of will."[1] This definition expresses quite simply, and yet with an approach to philosophical accuracy, the position of the Scriptures upon the nature of the change effected by regeneration. It holds the proper mean between extremes against which the evangelical Church has always contended. There is no change in the substance of the soul. There is no essential or constitutional transformation of man's nature. There is not even the implantation of a new part or faculty. Yet, on the other hand, there is more than the revival of any existing faculty. There is far more than the origination—even though that were admittedly super-

[1] To the same effect we might quote from the Puritan theology ; e.g Charnock says : " Regeneration is a mighty and powerful change wrought in the soul by the efficacious working of the Holy Spirit, wherein a vital principle, a new habit, the law of God, and a divine nature, are put into and framed in the heart, enabling it to act holily and pleasingly to God. . . . The divers expressions whereby the Scripture declares this work of regeneration are included in this term of the *new creature* or the *new creation*. . . . It is a certain spiritual and supernatural principle or permanent form *per modum actûs primi*, infused by God, whereby it is made partaker of the divine nature, and enabled to act for God."—*Works*, iii. p. 88.

natural—of certain conscious acts or actings of the soul itself. This view, which errs in the opposite direction from that of Flacius, was held by the later remonstrants, and has been recently favoured by some adherents of the new school divinity in America.[1] Regeneration lies deeper than consciousness. This is true not only of the act of the Divine Spirit originating it, but in a sense also of the thing originated. Deeper than consciousness and will, the Spirit produces in regeneration that new abiding state, disposition, principle, or habit, which constitutes the regenerated character, which gives it stability and perseverance, and which makes the renewed man's walk and conversation to be what they are.

Taking our stand, then, on the scriptural definition of the new life as something supernatural in itself and supernaturally introduced, we should now proceed to attempt such psychological questions as these :—

1. What ground in human nature though fallen does Scripture indicate as making regeneration possible?

2. How does the principle of spiritual life, supernaturally introduced, the subject being passive or even unconscious, become act or movement consciously realized?

3. How does the new life co-exist with remaining sin, or what are the relations of flesh and spirit in the Christian?

The second of these questions must be passed over. Beyond the general distinction between regeneration viewed as the divine act wrought entirely without the co-operation of the sinner, and conversion as the con-

---

[1] See Dr. Hodge, *ut supra*.

scious turning of the soul to God, there is hardly
anything in this region which evangelical thinkers can
be said with unanimity to have deduced from the
Scriptures. The reformed theology presents no reasoned
connection between regeneration in the stricter sense
and conversion with its fruits. It scripturally affirms,
as we have seen, in all cases a divine work deeper than
consciousness, before that subjective apprehension of
salvation which is the turning-point in the conscious
spiritual life. It more than admits the possibility of
infant regeneration. But it has no uniform theory of
the mode either of production or existence of grace in
the unconscious or habitual state. In those Protestant
communions where the idea of sacramental grace has
retained prominence, there has always been a tendency
to relapse from the evangelical to the Romish view of
conversion. But those who have examined carefully
the opinion of Luther, tell us that his notion of the
faith of infants, begged and obtained for them in their
baptism by the prayers of the Church, is not so divergent as at first it seems from that which has prevailed
in the Calvinistic and Puritan churches. Earnest
Christians build much of their practical religious life
on the correct assumption that grace, habitual and
unconscious, must exist in many cases long before
actual conversion; and that even what are called
sudden conversions may sometimes be the bursting
into flower of what was long preparing in the bud.
The region, however, to which this question belongs
is a difficult one in theology, and it has been the habit
of theologians to avoid it. By modern Continental
divines it is sometimes treated as belonging to Chris-

tian ethics, a study which with us lies as yet almost
wholly uncultivated.[1]

We fall back, then, on the two remaining questions,
the first and the last,—that which relates to natural
conscience, and that which concerns the struggle between sin and grace in believers.   We ask first: How
fallen nature remains capable of a divine redemption;
and then, How redeeming grace conquers man's evil.
The former we can deal with only in a few sentences.

I. It is plain enough that what Scripture recognises
as the thing reserved in man's nature rendering its
recovery by divine grace still possible, is not the
possession of any dead or buried *pneuma.*   Its view, as
we have seen in the last two lectures, is much broader
and simpler.   It is that, notwithstanding the fall, man
continues in an important sense to bear the divine
image, to be by his constitution a temple of the living
God, though the divine inhabitant may have ceased to
dwell in it.   To restore this image to its full glory is

---

[1] Harless, for example, thus states what he considers the fundamental
problem of that study : " With respect to the principle of Christian life and
Christian ethics, in its reality it is just Christ Himself who has taken
possession of me ; and for ethics, the only question is to find an expression
of the consciousness conformable to experience of the way in which I know
myself regulated by Christ as the principle of my moral life, and in which
form of my inner life I have Him as such. . . . For the Christian finds not
within himself the principle of a sound life, but in an objective power which
brings him to restoration.   The beginning of this life he wins not by his
own struggles after good, but he obtains it as a gift of grace to be possessed,
into whose fulness of life he enters."—*System of Christian Ethics,* p. 13
(Clark, 1868).   One section of this treatise is entitled, " The Entrance of the
Blessing of Salvation into the Spiritual Life of the Individual " (*Der Eintritt
des Heilsgutes in das Geistesleben des Individuums*) ; and under it are such
paragraphs as " The Appropriation of Regeneration in our Conversion "
(*Der Besitz der Wiedergeburt in der Bekehrung*).   For some further references
on this subject, see Appendix, Note R.

the end and aim of the whole redemptive process. Calvin, using the term "regeneration" in the wide sense as equivalent to the entire recovery of man from the fall and its effects, says that the scope of it is nothing else than to restore in us that image of God which had been defiled, and only not obliterated, through the sin of Adam.[1]

If we desire to be more specific in our answer to this question, we must go back to the consideration of the sense in which Scripture affirms the image of God to be unobliterated by the fall. The leading peculiarity of the Bible doctrine of man in his origin and constitution, we have seen to be its ascription to him of spiritual personality, formed and upheld by the Divine Maker. This places not the first man only, but all men, in a peculiar and inalienable relation to God: " In Him we live, and move, and have our being."   And it is because the human spirit was, and continues to be, a spirit derived from God that it is possible for it still to conceive or feel after and in a sense comprehend God. It is the other side of the relationship, however, which Scripture employs to throw light upon redemption. Its possibility is secured in the fact that God continues to stand in His relation to all men, "the Father of spirits," "the God of the spirits of all flesh," "for we are also His offspring."   This, indeed, will not of itself give us a cause or reason for the undertaking of redemption.   That is uniformly ascribed in Scripture to grace, love, the highest expression of the divine energy

---

[1] " Uno ergo verbo pœnitentiam interpretor regenerationem, cujus non alius est scopus nisi ut imago Dei, quæ per Adæ transgressionem fœdata, et tantum non obliterata fuerat, in nobis reformetur."—*Instit.* lib. iii. cap. iii. 9.

and nature. But that lost men are His, in a sense
which specially belongs to men in the universe of
being, is the Bible ground of the possibility of redemption. Nay more, it is the basis of that large *præparatio
evangelica* which Scripture recognises everywhere.
Because men are His, God has never left Himself
without witness, nor without avenues of approach to
the human spirit under the most unfavourable dispensations of humanity.

There are still more specific Scripture statements,
telling of an intellectual and a moral aspect of this
universal divine witness, implying a corresponding
capability in the nature of man to receive it. It is
affirmed that the invisible things of God can be perceived from His works, arguing a certain power in men,
as they are, to perceive or apprehend God.[1] It is
declared that the uncodified moral law of nature stirs
the consciences of the heathen, and that this shows the
effect or practical force of divine law to be written on
their hearts.[2] It is not well to press these Scripture
statements into a rigid scientific form,—to insist, *e.g.*, on
the intellectual element alluded to, as a *sensus com-
munis* or organ of revelation, or to speak of " conscience "
as a " law within," self-subsistent and self-acting. But
these indications that God retains for Himself a way
of return to the human spirit and a ground for its
recovery are most valuable. That men everywhere
grope after God ; that the natural ungodliness of men
is only possible through denial and resistance of evidence
which they are capable of receiving ; that the human
spirit is never unvisited by a sense of duty and a

[1] Rom. i. 19–21.   [2] Rom. ii. 14, 15.

corresponding sense of sin, yea, is moved at times by longings for salvation,—these are the natural preparations for the gospel. It is one of the grand credentials of the Bible as a system of revealed truth, that it so clearly and fully recognises these as the heritage of man. It is the supreme proof the religion of the Bible is from God, is a supernatural provision for man's redemption, that it meets these presentiments and carries on these preparations to fulfilment. What pagan religions and human philosophies barely and partially recognise as man's deepest needs, Christianity not only recognises but satisfies.[1]

II. It must be obvious that only in a very modified sense can we speak of a psychology of the new life. That life, we have said, springs from a supernatural principle introduced by a supernatural act. But the renewed life itself also is carried on and sustained in a way that is above nature. The Scripture always treats this new life as really the life of God in the soul of man: "It is no more I that live; but Christ liveth in me." We must not therefore expect that the life of grace could yield us a subject of strict scientific treatment, any more than that its beginning could be accounted for on natural principles. Nevertheless, the kingdom of grace is no exception among the realms of God in respect of fixed and forecast order. Spiritual life, like all other life, has its laws and processes. Its course is continually treated in Scripture as a process of growth.[2] And there is a peculiarity in

---

[1] I need hardly remind the reader under this section of the brief but most eloquent tract of Tertullian, *De Testimonio Animæ.*

[2] Eph. iv. 13–16 ; 2 Pet. i. 5–8, with iii. 18.

N

that growth which brings it into an obvious analogy with other facts and laws of the human being. It is not simply the evolution of the new vital principle implanted in regeneration. This spiritual principle has been introduced into a moral constitution where sin had its seat. Its growth is a growth in the overcoming of evil as well as in the divine life itself. A prominent part of its history, therefore, is that of the opposition between sin and grace, of the struggle between flesh and spirit. The exposition of this conflict leads into the very heart of the doctrine of sanctification. The struggle itself has a large place in the spiritual experience of Christians. It needs hardly be said that the great Pauline passages, Gal. v. 16–26, Rom. vii. viii., where it is discussed, are, more than almost any other parts of Scripture, of moment for biblical psychology. We devote the remainder of this lecture to a rapid consideration of them.

The pre-requisites for the solution of the teaching of these chapters are (a) the settlement of the psychological terms, and (β) the determination of the precise stages of spiritual history delineated.

(a) We have already shown that the psychological terms of the New Testament writers generally, and of Paul in particular, were based upon the corresponding Old Testament expressions. Further, that what is new and peculiar in their meaning they have derived from the growth of divine revelation itself, rather than from any philosophical influences. In regard even to the very prominent terms "flesh" and "spirit," so characteristic of the Pauline passages under consideration, this has been in effect admitted by Pfleiderer, an able representative of the present German theology. " In brief, then," he says, " the real (ethically intensified) dualism of σάρξ and πνεῦμα is not an element of the philosophical anthropology of Paul and a presupposition of his dogmatic, but a somewhat secondary product of his Christian speculation, the psychological reflex of his dogmatic antithesis between sin and grace. The case is exactly the same with the so-called dualism of John. This is the reason why here, as there, it is decidedly inadmissible to rank these contrasts under philosophical categories, or to refer them to the metaphysical dualism of philosophical systems. It produces only confusion and mis-statement." [1] What is of moment to us here is the virtual admission that the meaning of " flesh " and " spirit " in the writings of St. Paul is one newly charged with evangelical content, not an import of extraneous or even of Jewish philosophy. That the writer now quoted attempts, after the manner of his school, to rationalize the process by which the apostle arrived at this meaning, does not invalidate his testimony to the fact that the ideas are peculiar to the Pauline system of the gospel. We prefer the apostle's own account of how he received them.

A consistent view, as we have seen, of the two

---

[1] Kurz also : " der eigentliche (moralisch zugespitzte) Dualismus von σάρξ und πνεῦμα ist nicht ein Element der philosophischen Anthropologie des Paulus und eine Voraussetzung seiner Dogmatik, sondern ist ein ziemlich vermitteltes Produkt seiner christlichen Spekulation, *der psychologische Reflex seiner dogmatischen Gegensatzes von Sünde und Gnade.* Genau ebenso verhält es sich mit des Johannes sogenanntem Dualismus. Diess ist der Grund warum hier wie dort die Anwendung philosophischer Categorieen oder Zurückführung auf den metaphysischen Dualismus philosophischer Systeme entschieden unzulässig ist, und nur Verwirrung und Entstellung erzeugt."—*Der Paulinismus :* " Ein Beitrag zur Geschichte der urchristlichen Theologie," p. 25. Leipzig, 1873.

important terms "flesh" and "spirit,"[1] will not allow
us to narrow them each to a single meaning. A
double sense at least is indispensable. There is,
first, the simply natural meaning, according to which
they respectively denote the lower and higher, or the
material and immaterial elements in man's constitution, characterised, however, rather by their origin
than by their nature—the one as of the earth, and
perishable, the other as immediately from God. But
there is also a sense which is ethical or religious,
the meaning with which the terms are fully charged
in the New Testament, and especially in the Pauline
system. In the passages under consideration, for
example, "flesh" becomes identified with the force
or principle of sin in fallen nature, and "spirit" with
the principle of spiritual life in the new creature.
How the primary passes into the secondary meaning
is a question in the answer to which rationalizing interpreters betray the characteristic weakness of their
system, unwillingness to admit the supernatural.
Pfleiderer, for instance, holds *pneuma* to be "an original transcendent physical conception," and admits it
to have acquired "an ethical application under the
influence of Paul's mystic faith." Accordingly, he
finds it no violent transition that a corresponding
ethical application should have been given by the
apostle to the physical conception of *sarx*. This testimony that there are two such distinct applications in
the Pauline writings of both "flesh" and "spirit," first a
physical and then an ethical, has its value. But when
the concession is virtually retracted by attempting to

---

[1] On πνεῦμα see Lect. II., at pp. 66–72 ; on σάρξ, at pp. 74–82.

show how the secondary meaning was developed by
Paul out of the primary, its value is lessened, and the
failure of the "constructing" becomes conspicuous.
We see at once the superior simplicity and truth of
the view that the higher meaning was poured into the
terms by the increasing volume of divine ideas opened
up to such as Paul by the Holy Spirit. Take first the
two meanings of "flesh," and note how impossible it
is, in a way of mere ratiocination, to develop the one
out of the other. The attempt to get the ethical significance which Paul gives to it out of the elementary
Hebrew conception of the perishable (*i.e.* the bodily)
part of man signally fails.[1] It leaves out the clearly
Scriptural position of the change in human nature
caused by the fall. It is quite inadequate to account
for selfishness, wrath, pride, and other non-fleshly sins
bearing prominently the name "works of the flesh."
To assert that *sarx*, from its primary meaning, "living
material of the body," came by a natural process of
thought and language to mean "the principle of sin,"
is to assume human nature to be subject to sin by
its physical constitution—a view wholly untenable,
because at variance with the most radical conceptions
of the Bible from its earliest to its latest writings.

Then take the correlative term "spirit," and mark
the relation of its two meanings to the psychology of
the passages before us. We have traced the connection between its early and natural meaning of "life as

---

[1] The reader is referred to Pfleiderer's discussion of Σάρξ in his *Paulinismus*, pp. 47–56. Note particularly the weakness of the proofs on which
he rests the assertion that the Old Testament traces the sinfulness of man to
his fleshly origin and fleshly nature. These proofs are merely references to
Ps. li. 7, ciii. 10, 14 ; Isa. xlviii. 8 ; Job iv. 17, xv. 14, xxv. 4–6.

derived from the Creator," and its fullest spiritual
meaning of " the new life implanted in regeneration."
We have said that this latter was arrived at, not by
a mere process of human thought, but by the clearer
discovery of the personal Author of spiritual life, the
Holy Spirit, and by the altogether new revelation of
Jesus Christ, the quickening Spirit, as the Head of a
redeemed humanity.[1] In its natural meaning, however, " spirit" ranges from the mere physical sense of
wind or breath,[2] and from denoting life in general, up
to the indication of man's innermost mental and moral
being.   In the New Testament, and even within the
Pauline epistles, *pneuma* is freely used in this natural
sense : sometimes as the simple psychological correlate
of the flesh or the body ;[3] at other times as the seat

---

[1] Pfleiderer's mode of accounting for the peculiar Pauline use of *pneuma* to
denote the new life in believers is, that " a transcendent physical, or transcendent eschatological idea became of necessity," according to a process
which he undertakes to describe, " an immanent ethical one" (*Dass der
transscendent-eschatologische Begriff zum immanent-ethischen werden musste*).
Or again, " that the eschatological participation of life with Christ is to
the apostle imperceptibly transformed into the ethical new life of the Christian Present" (*Das eschatologische Mitleben mit Christo verwandelt sich
also dem Apostel unter der Hand in das ethische neue Leben der christ-
lichen· Gegenwart*).—*Paulinismus*, pp. 18, 196.   Here, as before, we have a
testimony to the correctness of the evangelical rendering of Pauline ideas.
Pneuma with the apostle acquires the special meaning of the new life, and
that because he regarded believers as supernaturally united to Christ, and
partakers of the supernatural spirit of Christ (πνεῦμα Χριστοῦ).   We are
content to use the testimony on that point of a critic so little biassed in the
evangelical direction.   We do not encumber ourselves with his construction
of what he calls " the genesis of this whole mode of representation."   The
Scriptures themselves give us a better account of it, namely, that Paul and
the other apostles had the "mind of Christ."

[2] Ezek. xxxvii. 8; Hab. ii. 9 ; John iii. 8.

[3] For the use in this sense of "body" and "spirit," see 1 Cor. v. 3,
Jas. ii. 26 ; of "flesh" and "spirit," as exactly equivalent to the other
pair, see Col. ii. 5, 1 Cor. vii. 34.   1 Cor. vi. 20 might be added, but the
reading καὶ ἐν τῷ πνεύματι, κ.τ.λ. is now given up.

of self-consciousness ;[1] or again, as the inner essence of
the man, which, as well as the flesh, is defiled by sin,[2]
and the salvation of which is the aim of all gospel
work.[3]   But it is worthy of our exact attention that in
the great passage, Rom. vii. and viii., where the new
life is to be designated by the term *pneuma* in its intensified spiritual force, *flesh* and *spirit* are not introduced antithetically earlier than the beginning of
chap. viii., when the dominion of the new principle
has been asserted.   The higher elements of the human
being himself to which the law makes its appeal are
denoted in chap. vii., not by *pneuma*, but by " mind "
(νοῦς) and " inward man " (ὁ ἔσω ἄνθρωπος) ; so that
confusion between the two senses of *pneuma* is avoided,
and that term reserved in this connection to denote
the new life introduced by regeneration.[4]

A word or two still falls to be said concerning the
voces signatæ now mentioned,—" mind," and " inward
man."

Nous throughout the Pauline writings is not substance like *pneuma*, but faculty, conscious faculty, and
knowledge both of God and duty.[5]   Even in the heathen
it manifests itself as knowledge of God and law of conscience.[6]   It may become so blinded and blunted as to
be " the mind of the flesh " (νοῦς τῆς σαρκός, Col. ii. 18),
or " reprobate mind " (ἀδόκιμος νοῦς, Rom. i. 28).   On the
other hand, it may be educated and enlightened by the

---

[1] 1 Cor. ii. 11.　　　　[2] 2 Cor. vii. 1.　　　　[3] 1 Cor. v. 5.

[4] Compare what was said on the relation between *pneuma* and *nous* at
p. 90.

[5] 1 Cor. xiv. 19: "I had rather speak five words with my understanding," etc.

[6] Rom. i. 20, ii. 14.

law till the law of God (ὁ νόμος τοῦ Θεοῦ) so dwells in it
as to be appropriately called "the law of my mind"
(νόμος τοῦ νοός μου, Rom. vii. 23). There is therefore
an evident propriety in νοῦς being set over against
σάρξ in Rom. vii., because the field of the struggle
there described is man and his principles of nature
under the law of God. Now it is to the *nous* that the
law of God appeals. It is the *nous* in which it dwells,
and through which it testifies for God against sin.
Here, then, we have the whole field of human nature
divided into two camps. The law of God and the law
of sin are the combatants. But from their encamp-
ment or environment respectively, they are also
designated as "the law of the mind," and "the law in
the members."

Finally, we have the important expression, "the
inward man" (ὁ ἔσω ἄνθρωπος, Rom. vii. 22), which
occurs besides only in Eph. iii. 16, and with a slight
variation, ὁ ἔσωθεν, or, according to the better reading,
ὁ ἔσω ἡμῶν, in 2 Cor. iv. 16, and with which we may
connect as synonymous Peter's "hidden man of the
heart," ὁ κρυπτὸς τῆς καρδίας ἄνθρωπος, 1 Pet. iii. 4. The
primary idea of this expression is evidently one purely
natural. It is contrasted with "the outward man"
(ὁ ἔξω ἡμῶν ἄνθρωπος, 2 Cor. iv. 16), which perishes by
material decay or by the vicissitudes of time. It is the
inner and spiritual nature of man as contrasted with
the outward and fleshly. The use of it is another
guarantee, if any were needed, for the essentially
bipartite character of the Pauline psychology. It
may be taken as the most general expression for the
inner or spiritual factor in the human being. Under

this general expression may be held as included *pneuma*
(spirit), when used to denote the nature of that factor;
nous (mind), as its intellectual or rational aspect; and
kardia (heart), when it is regarded as the practical
centre or fountain of man's life.   But a secondary or
ethical meaning of the phrase "inner man" evidently
lies behind.   Without saying that in its primary sense
it is morally indifferent, it is plain that in its secondary
or ethical sense, where it enters, as in Rom. vii., into a
psychological delineation of spiritual experience, it has
the sense of morally higher nature.   This, of course,
must be stated with caution.   It indicates, not "a
higher or better self left to man at the fall," much
less the "new man" or the "new creature."   Still,
it points to that inward nature which is capable of
regeneration, which is fitted to become the seat of the
new life, the true field for the operation of spiritual
processes.

Thus we see that the terms "flesh," "spirit," "mind,"
"inward man," admit of a consistent explanation,
dependent upon the view of human nature underlying
the apostle's course of thought.[1]

(β) The main thing for us is to make out the spiritual
history which this wonderful analysis is intended to
trace, and the proper position of the passage Rom. vii.
14–25 in that history may be said to be the knot of
the question.   There are almost equal difficulties in
affirming the experience described in these verses to
be that either of a wholly unregenerate or of a fully
regenerate man.   Plainly it cannot refer to that struggle
of the natural conscience with the desires and passions

---

[1] On "The Pauline Anthropology," see Appendix, Note S.

which belongs to all moral life. This conflict is a
broad commonplace in the history of the soul, as
familiar to the readers of Plato and Epictetus as to
the students of the Christian Scriptures. It is not
to be thought that St. Paul, in a treatise professedly
tracing the progress of a soul brought into contact
with the truth of God, if not regenerated by it, should
at this stage introduce the mention of a struggle
which was common to the virtuous heathen, the Stoic
philosopher, and the Jewish proselyte. It is not
altogether incorrect to say that "the whole picture
conveys the idea of the essential war there is in every
conscious moral life betwixt the higher and lower
principles at work within it."[1] But after all, this is
only the frame of the picture. For the chief question
we have to answer is, What are the contending principles
at work within the soul here described? Now it is
expressly said that the holy law of God is one of them,
and that law indeed brought home or become "the
law of the mind." It is certain, therefore, that if this
delineation present a state previous to conversion, that
state is not previous to the entrance of the divine
element into the strife. If it is pre-regenerate, it is
not pre-spiritual. It is not a conflict between man's
own higher and lower powers alone, for a spiritual
visitation of the man by the divine commandment has
already taken place. Further, it is said the man here
described "wills to do good," is distressed because of
his own evil; and that not merely because of evil deeds,
but of motions and desires toward evil. His subjection
to sin, therefore, is not that described in a former

---

[1] Principal Tulloch, *Croall Lecture*, p. 155.

chapter, "yielding your members instruments of un-righteousness unto sin, servants to uncleanness and to iniquity."[1] It is rather that of being sold as a slave against his will,[2] of being brought into captivity by the violence of war.[3] He delights in the law of God after the inward man. That law is the law of his mind, and with the mind he himself is subject to that law even when with the flesh he serves the law of sin. It is impossible that this can be a man unvisited by that divine working which precedes salvation. Instead of enmity against God, which is "the carnal mind," there have entered into the inmost heart of the man consent to the divine law and aversion from sin. Such a position of true willingness toward the good, and absolute unwillingness toward the evil, could not be occupied by any but a spiritually quickened soul. It is a state brought about neither by the aspirations of natural virtue, nor by the unsupported appeals of the moral law, but only by the grace of God.

On the other hand, considerable injustice has been done, not only to the interpretation of an important passage of Scripture, but, what is more serious, to the entire doctrine of sanctification, by some of those who are bent on maintaining that the latter half of the seventh chapter of Romans describes the experience of a converted man. It has been too often read as if it described the ordinary and normal state of a child of God; as if nature and grace were so exactly balanced in believers that "they cannot do the things that they

---

[1] Rom. vi. 13, 19.
[2] πεπραμένος ὑπὸ τὴν ἁμαρτίαν, Rom. vii. 14.
[3] ἀντιστρατευόμενον, ver. 23.

would;" as if the sum and substance of sanctification were this death in life, or this living death expressed by the perpetual cry, "O wretched man that I am!" Now it has been well said, that if this were all that grace did for its votaries, St. Paul would only have proved that it was as futile and insufficient as the law. If all that regeneration could accomplish were only to awaken a sense of inward discord without being able to do it away, this "would certainly destroy the influence of spiritual Christianity and disgrace its character."[1] But the mistake lies in not perceiving that chap. vii. gives us only one side of the picture. The delineation is progressive, and the full account of the conflict is not before us till we pass on to chap. viii., and see how the victory is secured for believers.

Note what are the contending principles. "The law" or principle "of sin," the "law in my members," is on the one side; the divine law, the "law of my mind," is on the other. The former law has its seat, not in me, my now awakened self, but in "my flesh;" that is, in my inherited nature, in my members as constituted through the agency of the flesh.[2] The divine law, on the contrary, makes its appeal to

---

[1] This is the common mode of misunderstanding the evangelical interpretation. Mr. Erskine of Linlathen, for example, puts it thus : " Calvinism, by what I cannot but think a very absurd misconception of the meaning of the 7th chapter of the Epistle to the Romans, teaches that a man may be in a safe state and may be a true believer, whilst he continues carnal and sold under sin, according to the 14th verse."—*Letters of Thomas Erskine*, p. 7, edited by Dr. Hanna, 2d series, Edin. 1877. It would be ungrateful to quote from this volume without allusion to the exquisite character and spirit of these letters. But accurate representation of evangelical opinion is not to be expected from them.

[2] See in Lect. II., at pp. 84, 85.

"my mind;" it has secured the affection or "delight" of my "inward man." That "mind" or "inward man" belongs to the divine image, by which their Maker retains His hold of human souls even when fallen, and which it is the function of grace so to restore that it may be fully possessed and adorned by the life from on high. Speaking roundly and generally, therefore, the two camps in this war might be named "the Flesh" and "the Spirit." They are so named in the less elaborate account to be found in Gal. v. 17, where the result of the conflict at this stage is given in the same terms of moral failure as at the corresponding points in Rom. vii.: "The flesh lusteth against the Spirit, and the Spirit against the flesh: and these are contrary the one to the other; so that ye cannot do the things that ye would." But in the fuller and more detailed delineation of the Epistle to the Romans, the term "spirit" (*pneuma*), as we have remarked (*supra*, p. 199), is not used in chap. vii., but reserved for chap. viii., as the word denoting the new life in its proper seat and power. The man who is in the Spirit and walks after the Spirit is in the main delivered from the body of this death. His own spirit is life because of righteousness. The righteousness of the law is fulfilled in him. The law of the Spirit of life in Christ Jesus hath made him free from the law of sin and death. Thus, in the complete account of the struggle, full justice is done to the results of Christian sanctification.

But now arises the question concerning the relation to one another of the two parts in this whole delineation,—the description of the conflict ending with the

groan, "O wretched man that I am!" and the description of the triumph beginning with the shout, "I thank
God through Jesus Christ our Lord." What is described in the former is a strife not merely of higher and
lower elements in man's own nature, but of contrasted
moral forces that have entered into him. The power
of sin in his flesh strives with the testimony of law in
his mind, the result of which strife is a sort of moral
impotence,—we cannot do the things that we would.
What is described in the latter chapter is grace resolv-
ing the strife. Moral impotence, divided service, is
not the real result of the new principle of regeneration. The new life is that which is delivered from it,
when we walk not after the flesh, but after the Spirit.
Shall we say, then, that the two parts of the description succeed each other in time? that they are spiritual
portraits of the same person drawn at two successive
stages of his religious history? On this understanding,
Rom. vii. 14–25 gives us the portrait of an awakened
Pharisee or of a legal Christian; Rom. viii. 1–14, that
of a fully regenerate man, a free child of God. The
transition from the one to the other takes place when
the Pharisaic Hebrew is converted, and trusts not to
the law but to Christ, both for acceptance with God
and for the Spirit of holiness: or when the legal Christian comes to his second conversion (if the phrase be
allowed), and enters on the higher life of sanctification;
when he ceases to think that he can subdue sin and
attain to holiness under the law and through his own
efforts; when he accepts the whole salvation as a free
gift of righteousness and of the Spirit; in short, when
by God's grace he breaks out of bondage into the

liberty wherewith Christ hath made His people free. Should this historical succession and connection be insisted on, all reasonable comment must agree that the man described in the latter half of chap. vii. is neither, on the one extreme, unregenerate, nor on the other a regenerate man in his proper and normal state. He must be in some such intermediate condition as we have now endeavoured to express, by holding him either to be an awakened legalist or an unemancipated Christian.

It must be confessed, however, that this rendering of the description is not entirely satisfactory. There is another which suggests itself, as more in keeping both with this particular passage and with the whole strain of the epistle. It requires, indeed, that we shall not insist on making the two passages describe two different types of persons, or even two successive stages in the experience of the same person. For has not the determination to find historical sequence and contrast in the two, tended to perplex the meaning? There are such mixed elements in both delineations, that no application of them to distinct stages in conversion and spiritual life is quite satisfactory. It is clear that the two things really contrasted in the successive passages are the bondage of law and the reign of grace. How the contrast comes in here is apparent upon a glance at the broad argument of this epistle, the scope of which is to establish the superiority of grace to the law. In the early chapters of it the apostle has demonstrated that by the law no flesh shall be justified, that justification can come only by grace in the form of faith. Having finished this part

of his argument in chapter fifth, he goes on in chapter
sixth to lay the Christian foundation of holiness, and
in chapter seventh to show that by the law no man,
legalist or Christian, can be sanctified; completing
the demonstration in chapter eighth by showing that
sanctification is of grace—grace in the form of spiritual
life and liberty.   Now on this interpretation there is
no need to suppose that the apostle in the two contrasted passages is describing any other experience
than his own, or that of any other regenerate person.
Neither is it necessary to suppose that he is contrasting two states, stages, or successive experiences even
of the regenerate.   Rather is he presenting two ideal
conceptions of the relations to law and grace respectively of a man in Christ aiming at the attainment of
holiness.   In the first, as given in chap. vii., he
looks simply at himself and the law.   Remember
carefully as you read it that he is not merely describing an experience.   He is conducting an argument.
He is engaged in proving from facts the weakness of
the law, its inefficiency at any stage to produce holiness.   The experience of the sinner proves it; by the
law is only the knowledge of sin.   The experience of
the awakened proves it; the law in him only reveals
and stirs up more sin.   The experience of the regenerate proves it; for even in him, though the renewed
will be present to do good, though the awakened mind
delight in the law of God, there is still that other law
in his members warring against the law of his mind,
and causing him after all to serve the law of sin.
' This is all that the law of God can do,' says he, ' even
for me, a converted man.   Not, indeed, that this is

the fault of the law. God forbid! In an important
sense it is to the honour of the law. This is one great
service rendered by it in the process of redemption,
that it reveals the strength and evil of my sin; yea,
that it helps to discern, to divide between me and the
sin that dwelleth in me. Yet, while it discovers this
terrible inward dissension, it cannot heal, but rather
intensifies it. Wretched man that I am! How much
more wretched had I nothing else! What would
become of me if I had only the law to enable me to
attain holiness?' 'Thank God!' he cries, passing on
to the second and complete conception of chap. viii.,—
'thank God, in Christ Jesus I have something else!
I have the Spirit of Christ. Through the law of the
Spirit of life in Christ Jesus I am delivered from both
the other laws in the sense in which deliverance from
them is salvation. The good and holy law no more
condemns me, for there is now no condemnation to
them which are in Christ Jesus. The base and evil
law of sin no more enthralls me, for the law of the
Spirit of life has made me free from it. The Spirit of
Christ has taken possession of our spirit, that we might
be free to fulfil all righteousness, to mortify all sin,
and to press forward to the blessed perfection, in body
and spirit, of the life to come.'

In this way it will be seen, that though we do not
insist on historic contrast or sequence in the two
passages, we still preserve the progressive character of
the delineation. The two contrasted ideal conceptions
are realized more or less in every true child of God.
The first depicts what he too often is. The second
describes what he ought and what he strives by God's

o

grace to be. The experience described is that of a
double life—the saint's paradox, the believer's riddle.
And this rendering of the description has been countersigned by all the great commentators on a passage
which supremely illustrates the maxim that "the
heart makes the theologian." No interpretation will
satisfy the spiritual mind which does not include in
the normal experience of a Christian what is described
both in the seventh and in the eighth chapter of
Romans. Only it should never be forgotten that the
Christian life really moves from the lower experience
to the higher; that every living Christian is progress-
ing out of the one into the other, until he comes to
dwell in the latter, or rather to dwell habitually in
Christ, and to have the Spirit of Christ dwelling
victoriously in him.

One other point of importance must be noticed
before we pass from this great passage, namely, the
position assigned in it to the responsible personality,
or the relations of the Ego throughout the struggle.
On this point the thought of the apostle is very clear.
The person is never divided. The Ego is never in two
contrasted states or in two hostile camps at the same
time. That is as impossible as that a man can serve
two masters. He may have within him two contending principles; and in the shifting war of the principles
for supremacy, the Ego—I myself—will undoubtedly
undergo a change,—will be seen, in fact, as you nar-
rowly mark the tide of battle, to pass over from the one
camp to the other. When the flesh bears unbroken .
sway, and the natural life is undisturbed, the Ego is
alive in that fleshly, worldly life, *totus in illis*. When

the law comes with spiritual force the Ego dies: its
natural hopes of being right with God are crushed; its
own fancied power to do well utterly departs; the man
exclaims, "It is plain that I am carnal, sold under
sin; in ME, that is, in my flesh, dwelleth no good
thing." But at this point the inward man asserts
itself, wills right, consents unto the law. "Then,"
says he, "I am no more myself the slave of evil. It
is no more I that do the things which I would not."
As the moment of liberation draws on, it is "with the
mind I myself serve the law of God." And as liberty
is realized through the Spirit, "the law of the Spirit
of life in Christ Jesus hath made ME free from the law
of sin and death."

It is impossible to construe the passage without
admitting that the apostle expresses his personality
as identified with two contending elements alternately.
But it is no less true that the passing of the Ego, on
the whole, from being dead in sin, or "alive without
the law," through the intermediate experience of
being visited by "the commandment," to the final
condition of being under grace and walking after the
Spirit, is traceable throughout. The sense and thought
of the whole passage admit no doubling or confusion
of personality, no perplexing of responsibility. Thus
much it seems necessary to say, because Paul's vivid
phraseology here and elsewhere has been perverted
to the support of certain extreme forms of quasi-
evangelical statement. What Flacius found in Romans
vii., "Two men set in the skin of one man," is not
unfrequently the finding of incautious expounders of
this great passage on Christian sanctification. We are

told by them of two Adams, two natures, if not almost
of two persons in the regenerate,—the old and evil,
who will never be sanctified, and with whom the child
of God has nothing to do, or in other words, for whom
he is not responsible; the new, born from above, who
is always right and accepted with God. It need
hardly be said that such teaching is at once mistaken
and dangerous. The "two men in one skin" has a
correct meaning, if we read it according to the Scripture. The "old man" and the "new man" mean
two kinds of power, two laws, two principles of nature.
But whenever these are represented as existing and
contending in one regenerate responsible person, the
"new" is life and living, the "old" is dying and in
effect dead. The Ego is not divided. "Every man
hath an edge. He cuts one way or another. And as
a man's edge is set, that way is he."[1] The renewed
man has his edge set towards eternal life. He lives
after the Spirit. He is crucifying the flesh. He is
mortifying the deeds of the body. He is putting off
the old man with his deeds, and putting on the new.
He is, in short, at one with the Spirit of Christ who
now dwells within him.

'How much is really contained in the new birth?
Why is there so little of the new man in the regenerate?
Why are the spontaneous products of his heart so
corrupt and evil after all? Why deeper than will am
I left so bad? Should not the new birth have done
much more for me than it has done; and especially in
those deep places within to which I cannot reach to do

[1] Dr. John Owen.

it for myself?' Most Christians will concur in the propriety of putting such questions, though there be no exhaustive answer to them.

In regard to the first, it is scarcely necessary to repeat, that we do not find in the psychology of grace anything like the introduction of a new element of being, or the creation of a new faculty, or the implantation in man's constitution of any power, physical, mental, or moral, which it did not contain before. What we find in the new birth is the supernatural gift of a new principle of nature—using "nature" in the sense in which we say popularly that "habit is a second nature." By a special act of divine grace, which we call regeneration, a foundation is laid in the nature of the man for an entirely new exercise of all his faculties in a renewed life. The natural *nidus* or constitutional seat of this new beginning is the inward man (ὁ ἔσω ἄνθρωπος), which may be viewed in respect of substance as the spirit or natural *pneuma*, or in respect of intelligence and conscience as the mind (*nous*), in respect of life and action as the heart[1] (*kardia*), so that regeneration is said to be a permanent transformation of the spirit of our mind, and that which is formed by it dwells in the heart, is the hidden man of the heart. This new principle of spiritual life is called "the new man" (ὁ νέος or καινὸς ἄνθρωπος), and the man under its influence is "a new creature" or "a new creation" (καινὴ κτίσις). But if we attempt any further question in what it really or metaphysically consists, we get the answer, simply, that it is "the law (*i.e.* the principle) of the Spirit of life in Christ Jesus." According to the

---

[1] See above, p. 201.

doctrines of grace, this means that through the media-
tion or ministry of the Holy Ghost, Christ Himself, the
new Head, the second Adam, becomes to each member
of His body " a quickening Spirit," and dwells in the
heart of His own. The difficulty we have in such
passages as Rom. viii. 1–16, and Gal. v. 16–26, to
determine whether "spirit" (*pneuma*), in certain clauses,
means the renewed spirit of the man or the renewing
Spirit of God within him, may be taken as itself an
evidence that it is the divine indwelling which constitutes the new life. Yet it is clear that *pneuma* in
these passages has on the human side its enlarged
significance—that, naturally signifying the inner man,
which is fitted to be the seat of the Holy Ghost, it now
signifies the whole life, in its principles and actions,
which results from that indwelling.

As to how much of actual sanctification this entitles
us to expect or enables us to realize, the great Pauline
passage we have been considering speaks in a way
verified by the experience of most Christians. It is plain
that some of the questions suggested above can receive
no answer. They are in their utterance but the reflec-
tion of Paul's " O wretched man that I am!" The burden
and the mystery of sanctification can never be more
powerfully stated than in that famous passage where
the "unresolved antinomy" stands as a mirror, in
which every spiritually exercised man sees the present-
ment of his own experience. You may prefer to think
the features in Rom. vii. specially those of an awakened
Pharisee, as in Gal. v. they are those of an unen-
lightened or legal Christian. It is better, as we have
seen, to abstract the delineation altogether from time,

succession, and special circumstances in the life of the
awakened soul.   The apostle is not speaking of himself
as regenerate; at least he is not describing the effect
of regeneration.   The antinomy cannot be the right
and normal state of a converted man.   But he may
be fairly held as describing what is experienced in
spite of regeneration, a conflict which even for the
regenerate has not passed away.   That it may describe
the special position of a legal or carnal Christian we
have admitted, but what is of more importance, it is a
permanent description of the difficulty or struggle of
sanctification, and reveals some of its causes.   " The
man who is in Christ—just this very man—is divided
into a man actually living in Christ, and a man who,
though surrounded by the new life, is not yet actually
pervaded by it. . . . In other words, there is even in
the regenerate life a region pervaded by grace, and a
region, so to speak, only shone upon by grace. . . .
Over this latter, a mournful powerlessness of good purposes unaccomplished throws its long dark shadow."[1]
We must note, however, that the transition marked
by the words, " I thank God through Jesus Christ our
Lord " (Rom. vii. 25), if not one in time from an
unripe to a riper Christian stage, is at least one in
idea from what a Christian too often is to what he can
and ought by grace to be.   Since the *pneuma*, in the
sense of the indwelling of Christ within him, is that
from which nothing but good can proceed, he has
only to give himself up to this spirit which dwells in

---

[1] Delitzsch, *Biblische Psychologie*, near the close of the section on
" Regeneration," headed, " Die unaufgehobene Antinomie," one of the most
interesting and able passages in the whole treatise.

him, to walk after it, in order to do good.   Again, as
the sinful flesh was only the principle of the old man,
who died with Christ, it has no further claim on the
new man, who lives with the living Christ; it cannot
and dare not have the mastery over him; he cannot
and dare not any longer be under an obligation to
compliance with it.   Thus evil is for the Christian
as such that which is contrary to his nature; the
power and domination of sin are necessarily abrogated
for the Christian together with the law that was its
provocation.   The requirement, therefore, to keep from
evil and to do good, is for the Christian the self-evident
consequence of his new nature; he has only to exhibit
in action that which he already is in fact, a spiritual
man.   This is not mere abstract statement.   It is a
habit of the inspired writers to pass constantly from
reasoning to exhortation, and here it is very marked.
You see plainly that an ideal and an actual are
being placed side by side.   'This is what you ought
to be, what you must be: then be it.   The Spirit
of Christ dwells in you, and has made you free:
be free.   You are in the Spirit: walk after the
Spirit!'

We cannot close without sketching in a few words
the doctrine developed in the Epistle to the Romans,
as the ground of the experience which we have just
been endeavouring to trace.   It must always be
observed, in order to understand Rom. vii. and viii.,
that chap. vi. has laid the foundation for what follows.
The experience of dying unto sin and living unto
righteousness is supported by the doctrine of dying

with Christ on the cross and rising with Him to
newness of life.

It will be noticed that in chap. vi., parallel to the
expressions, "dead to sin," "freed from sin," there
runs another set of expressions, "dead with Christ,"
"baptized into His death," "buried with Him,"
"planted together in the likeness of His death,"
"our old man is crucified with Him, that the body
of sin might be destroyed." The purport of all this
plainly is, that by the death of Christ a death-blow has
been given to the power of sin in believers—so given
as if it had been actually inflicted when the Lord was
crucified. The earlier part of the argument in chaps.
iv. and v. had gone to show how the cross of Christ
is the ground of pardon, peace, and acceptance with
God: "He was delivered for our offences." The object
now is to show that the cross is also the ground of
our sanctification, particularly of our deliverance from
the power of sin as well as from its guilt and punishment. In the same manner, the objective historical
fact of the resurrection of Christ is made the ground
of our rising to newness of life; and this not simply
as a type or model after which our moral quickening
takes place, nor merely as an expression of allegorical
or mystical resurrection, but in the sense that believers
participate for their new moral life in the supernatural
power of the resurrection, in that supernatural gift of
the Spirit which the risen Christ received to bestow
upon His people. It is the law of the Spirit of life in
Christ Jesus that makes them free from the law of sin
and death. Taking it in both branches, as death to
sin and life to God, the whole is thus expressed by

Paul in a later epistle: "That I may know Him and the power of His resurrection, and the fellowship of His sufferings, being made conformable unto His death."[1]

The significance of thus connecting the believer's dying to sin and living to righteousness with the dying and rising again of his Lord can hardly be overrated. Practically it is all-important as the support of the apostolic exhortations. What comfort could be imparted to Christians by telling them, that since Christ has died and risen, they also are dead to sin and done with it, when they feel every day that this is anything but true? They should be overwhelmed in despair were there nothing more in the saying than a moral appeal to crucify the old nature,—were they left to struggle with what it seems a kind of irony to call the 'remains of corruption within them,' aided only by the consideration that they owe it to so loving a Saviour to live a life of freedom from sin. No! but the doctrine of these chapters is, that the death of Christ, besides being an expiatory death for cancelling guilt and bringing in everlasting righteousness, was implicitly the destruction of the principle of sin in those that are His. It is therefore a most important part of the apostolic doctrine of Christ's redeeming death, that it secures moral renovation as well as justifying grace. It is the supreme glory of the gospel to lay the foundations of practical holiness upon the same sure corner-stone on which are laid those of peace with God. No doubt, its importance is distorted if it be made the chief thing in the apostolic

[1] Phil. iii. 10.

system, and exalted at the expense of the doctrine
of reconciliation which is really the basis of it.[1] No
doubt, also, it can be stiffened and formalized in a
dangerously antinomian manner, if it be cut off from
its proper doctrinal correlatives—if the fact of Christ's
death be represented boldly and by itself in the
emancipation of the soul from actual sin. The principle of living union with Christ, by the entrance of
His Spirit into the heart on the one hand, and by
the exercise of our faith on the other, underlies the
doctrines both of justification and of sanctification.
This principle also secures that holiness must grow
out of reconciliation. It vitally connects the roots
of sanctification with the grounds of justification. In
the act which unites him to a crucified Redeemer, the
Christian dies with Christ in a sense which no doctrinal
explanations can ever exhaust, and that because of
the mystic union then formed between the Redeemer
and the redeemed. His Spirit, taking possession of
their hearts, in that gracious moment deals the being
of sin within them a mortal blow, which is the earnest
and the ground of their final deliverance from its every
motion, and of their appearing in the presence of God
without spot or wrinkle or any such thing. Their sin
died with Christ on the tree, not only as to its guilt
but as to its power; and in this sense, they, being
dead with Christ, are dead indeed unto sin. Like all
the doctrines of grace, this death of the soul to sin
runs back into the mystery of a relationship between
the redeemed soul and Christ its living Head. Each

[1] See, for example, the paradoxical statements of Matthew Arnold in his
St. Paul and Protestantism.

of us apprehends it only as this union with Christ is
realized and becomes the true ground of hopeful and
successful struggle against indwelling sin in the heart.
This identification of himself in idea with Christ is
the key to Paul's whole doctrine of the new life.   The
practical realization of it is the new life itself.

Nor let us fail to remark, that in order to attain
holiness, the Spirit of Christ in believers connects them
vitally with their Lord's future as well as with His
past.   To unfold the fulness of sanctification, we must
fix our faith, like Paul, on two grand events in the
history of our blessed Head and Lord.   Between these
two facts, as the two great pivots of redemption, Paul's
faith travels, and as it goes, weaves out in thought and
puts on in practice the garment wrought in gold of a
complete salvation.   These two are: first, the fact
accomplished, 'He was crucified and rose again; in
Him, with Him, therefore, am I also dead and risen;'
then, the future advent, 'He comes in glory, comes
the second time without sin unto salvation.   In Him
I also anticipate the glory.   For this, even we who
have received the first-fruits of the Spirit wait and
yearn, the manifestation of the sons of God—the
adoption, to wit the redemption of our body.'

Thus we arrive at our concluding topic: the light
which the Bible view of man's nature, and especially
of that nature as redeemed, sheds on the future life
and on the resurrection.

LECTURE VI.

THE BIBLE VIEW OF MAN'S NATURE IN ITS BEARING ON A FUTURE LIFE.

" Thine are these orbs of light and shade ;
Thou madest life in man and brute ;
Thou madest death ; and lo, Thy foot
Is on the skull which Thou hast made.

" Thou wilt not leave us in the dust :
Thou madest man, he knows not why—
He thinks he was not made to die ;
And Thou hast made him : Thou art just."

TENNYSON.

LUKE xx. 35–38.—" They which shall be accounted worthy to obtain that world, and the resurrection from the dead, neither marry, nor are given in marriage: neither can they die any more : for they are equal unto the angels; and are the children of God, being the children of the resurrection. Now that the dead are raised, even Moses showed at the bush, when he calleth the Lord the God of Abraham, and the God of Isaac, and the God of Jacob. For He is not a God of the dead, but of the living : for all live unto Him."

JOHN xi. 24–26.—" Martha saith unto Him, I know that he shall rise again in the resurrection at the last day. Jesus said unto her, I am the resurrection, and the life : he that believeth in me, though he were dead, yet shall he live : and whosoever liveth and believeth in me shall never die."

PHIL. iii. 11, 12, 21.—" If by any means I might attain unto the resurrection of the dead. Not as though I had already attained, either were already perfect : but I follow after, if that I may apprehend that for which also I am apprehended of Christ Jesus. . . . Who shall change our vile body, that it may be fashioned like unto His glorious body, according to the working whereby He is able even to subdue all things unto Himself."

Also,

The Fifteenth Chapter of FIRST CORINTHIANS.

LECTURE VI.

THE last things, life after death, the resurrection, the general judgment, the final destiny of men, are not treated of in Scripture under abstract propositions. What the Bible says on these subjects is said mainly in connection with the revelation of redemption. Moreover, there are two distinct lines on which even these disclosures are set forth. The first is that which we may call "personal," for in it the future is spoken of as part of the development of an individual human being—the after-life and ultimate salvation or destruction of the man. The other is that which we may call "dispensational," when these last events are spoken of on the public scale, as moments in the development of the kingdom of heaven, or of the dispensation of redemption in the hand of the Lord Jesus Christ. Thoroughly to connect these two in a complete system of eschatology, is a task for which our theology is confessedly incompetent. Nor need this be wondered at. The Scripture itself does not give us a complete view of these connections. Even inspired writers declare that here they "know in part and prophesy in part."

The questions of eschatology with which we have to

deal in the present lecture are chiefly those arising in
the line of personal redemption.   They are those directly
related to the view which Scripture takes of man's own
being.   We have to ask, What is the bearing of the
Bible psychology upon its doctrine of the future life?
Does the human being carry in himself the credentials
of an existence beyond the grave?   Does revelation
acknowledge or confirm these?   What foundation does
it lay in its anthropology for a belief and knowledge of
the life to come?   In connection with the details of revelation concerning a future life, arise many interesting
questions as to the separate or intermediate state, the
resurrection, and the resurrection body.   We must
restrict our inquiries to the two topics of the future
state in general, and the resurrection in particular.
The essential unity of the Scripture doctrine on these
two topics, and its close connection with the Scripture
view of man's origin and nature, will come out as we
proceed.

I.

The relation of Bible thought on these subjects to
the religion of the ancient Egyptians, with its vivid but
coarsely physical views of a future life, to Oriental and
Greek beliefs concerning the soul, or even to the
current of Christian speculation, would open up too
wide a field.   We must confine ourselves mainly to
the most simple and central propositions of Scripture.
But the bearing of revelation on man's natural and
instinctive belief that he shall live after death cannot
be passed over.   During most of the Christian centuries,
the Scripture doctrine concerning the life to come has

been held as bound up with and based upon that of the indestructibility of the human soul. Man is a being who must live after death, must live for ever. Conscience declares that present conduct and character are to influence an eternal hereafter. Nay, the very make of the soul tells of the timeless and changeless sphere to which it belongs. This doctrine of the natural and necessary immortality of the human soul has been religiously cherished as of the very essence of the scriptural or Christian belief in a life to come. Not, indeed, that it has escaped question or cavil, even among Christian thinkers. The Greek Fathers had a contention of their own against certain modes of affirming the soul's indestructibility. There were early heretics, refuted by Origen, who held that the soul totally dies with the body, and will be restored to life with it in the general resurrection at the end of the world.[1] During the Middle Ages, the philosophical notion of the soul as the form and essence of the man, and therefore that which necessarily survives death, seems to have reigned almost uncontested in Christian theology. The Reformers, however, amid their many controversies, were soon involved in one upon this subject also. Calvin's tract in refutation of it keeps alive the memory of the psycho-pannychian heresy, which was, that the soul dies or sleeps from death till the day of judgment. Luther is charged with having himself given some countenance to the opinion. The natural mortality of the soul, which is properly the position of materialists and unbelievers, has been repeatedly during recent centuries adopted by Christian thinkers, and combined

[1] Eusebius, *Hist. Eccles.* lib. vi. c. 37.

P

by them, in ways more or less fantastic, with the
Scripture revelation of a future life. The names of
Coward, Dodwell, and Priestley will call up to those
familiar with the history, forms of this belief maintained at successive periods in the eighteenth century,[1]
—a century of which, however, it has been pithily said,
that "the immortality of man was *par excellence* its
dogma."[2] The position is held at present by Mr.
Edward White and other defenders of what they
themselves call the "conditional immortality of man."

More cautious Christian opponents of the prevailing
method of identifying divine revelation as to a future
life with the tenet of the soul's indestructibility, have
preferred to rest the doctrine of survival on the
resurrection of Jesus and the affirmations of Scripture,
without insisting on the soul's natural immortality.
Archbp. Whately and Bp. Hampden in our own country,
with the late Dr. Rothe of Heidelberg among Continental divines, may be cited as representatives of this
position. These opinions are notes of dissatisfaction
arising out of the manner in which the scriptural

[1] Some English divines in the first part of last century joined the materialists Coward and Anthony Collins, in maintaining the natural mortality
of the soul as a positive tenet of Scripture no less than a truth of psychology. The learned Henry Dodwell, a nonjuring churchman deprived of
his chair at Oxford, published several works in which he laboured with
great ingenuity to prove, "from the Scriptures and the first Fathers, that
the soul is a principle naturally mortal; but immortalized actually by
the pleasure of God to punishment; or to reward by its union with the
divine baptismal Spirit. Wherein is proved that none have the power of
giving this divine immortalizing spirit since the Apostles but only the
Bishops" (the words of his title-page). At a later period, Priestley, in
his *Disquisitions relating to Matter and Spirit*, not only held the sleep of the
whole man till the resurrection to be the genuine Christian doctrine, but
argued that it made the soul as much dead as the body, and was only
another and softer name for the same thing.

[2] Erdmann, *Geschichte der Philosophie*, ii. 650.

view of a future life has been bound up with philosophical propositions concerning the nature of the soul,
some of them elaborated in other schools of thought
than that of Christianity.   The real answer to these
dissents should be found by connecting the Bible
revelation concerning the future life with its own
simple philosophy of man.

The Bible does not affirm the immortality of the
soul in any abstract or general form.   Much less does
it define the constitution of the soul as involving its
necessary indestructibility.   So much we may freely
concede.   But when it is said that the notion of a
separable soul or spirit in man is unscriptural, is
nothing but a philosophical figment, and that the soul's
separate existence is no necessary part of Christian
belief, we are prepared on the strongest grounds to
demur.[1] It is plain to demonstration that a view of

[1] As an example of this position, I cite a sentence or two from Dr.
Hampden's *Bampton Lecture* of 1832, a book which was the occasion of
much controversy. In the opening of his seventh lecture he says : "This
notion of the separate existence of the soul has so incorporated itself with
Christian theology, that we are apt at this day to regard our belief in it as
essential to orthodox doctrine. Even in maintaining that such a belief is not
essential to Christianity, I may incur the appearance of impugning a vital
truth of religion. I cannot, however, help viewing this popular belief as a
remnant of scholasticism. I feel assured that the truth of the resurrection
does not depend on such an assumption ; that the life and immortality of
man, as resting on Christ raised from the dead, is a certain fact in the
course of Divine Providence, whatever may be the theories of the soul, and
of its connection with the body."

Again, in a note, he continues thus :

"Are we not disposed, even in these days, to rest too much on the
natural or metaphysical arguments for a future state, and to imagine that
the Christian faith is compromised by a denial of the immateriality of the
soul? I by no means intend to deny its immateriality. . . . But we go
beyond the basis of the facts when we assume, in our abstract arguments
for the natural immortality of the soul, its separate existence apart from
the body. . . . What matters this to the Christian, who is fully assured
that because Christ lives he shall live also ; that ' as by man came death,

the human constitution essentially bipartite is the
doctrine of Scripture, and that the spirit or soul of
man is expressly affirmed to survive the body. The
personal existence of human beings after death is a
doctrine that pervades the whole system of Scripture.
The Bible sustains and illumines, in the most remarkable and varied ways, man's instinctive belief that he
was made for an everlasting existence. Nor is it at
all difficult to see how the scriptural conceptions of
his origin and nature consist with these disclosures
concerning the life to come. The immediate origination of man's life by the breath of the Almighty, the
kinship of man with His Maker, his formation after
the divine image, the possession of spiritual personality as an essential and inalienable part of that image,
—these are the Bible ideas with which the doctrine
of continuance after death naturally allies itself. It
would not, of course, be correct to say that the Scripture constructs out of these propositions any abstract
argument for man's life after death. It would be
clearly incompetent to argue that man's survival is,
in Scripture, based upon his possession of *neshamah*
or *ruach*, even though there be good reason to think
that these expressions are so applied to man as
to imply that he specially belongs to God, who is

by man came also the resurrection from the dead'? I would say, in the
words of Nemesius : 'Ἡμῖν δὲ ἀρκεῖ πρὸς ἀπόδειξιν τῆς ἀθανασίας αὐτῆς ἡ
τῶν θείων λογίων διδασκαλία τὸ πιστὸν ἀφ' ἑαυτῆς ἔχουσα διὰ τὸ θεόπνευστον
εἶναι.

"If we sincerely rely on the clear evidence given of Christ raised from the
dead, as a certain fact in the course of Divine Providence, and believe the
connection of our own immortality with that fact, we may surely regard
all merely philosophical inquiries on the subject as fair matter of disputa-
tion, without offence, and without any fear whatever for the stability of
the real Christian doctrine of the resurrection of the dead."

the Father of spirits.   It would be wrong, however, to
import into these terms the metaphysical idea of an
indissoluble substance, and thus commit the Scripture
to the philosophical argument that the soul cannot die
because it cannot be dissolved or dissipated.   But the
author of the Book of Wisdom seems to be fairly
following the doctrine of Genesis when he says, "For
God created man to be immortal, and made him to be
an image of His own peculiar nature."[1]   The hinge of
comparison between the Original and the copy is not
abstract duration ; it is spiritual personality.   Man is
a personal being, created after the semblance of the
peculiar nature of God.   And upon this ground, which
may be termed at once ontological and ethical, the
Bible doctrine of man's survival rests.   "All souls are
mine."   "They all live unto Him."

It is of importance here to distinguish between the
Bible mode of affirming man's future existence and
the methods of other religions and philosophies, which
founded their doctrine of future life upon a different
idea of man's nature.   This is more especially necessary in regard to that one which has such close
affinities with scriptural doctrine as to have been
greatly identified with Christian eschatology, elaborated by the schoolmen as the foundation of the faith,
and often preached from the Christian pulpit as a
substitute for the fuller light of the gospel on life and
immortality.   The Greeks connected man's survival
of death with his participation of the divine essence.

---

[1] Ὅτι ὁ Θεὸς ἔκτισε τὸν ἄνθρωπον ἐπ' ἀφθαρσίᾳ, καὶ εἰκόνα τῆς ἰδίας ἰδιότητος ἐποίησεν αὐτόν.—Σοφ. Σαλωμών. ii. 23.   Our translators have followed
the less supported reading ἀϊδιότητος, "eternity."   But ἰδιότητος is fully as
germane to the argument in hand.

The scientific presuppositions of the Platonic philosophy in establishing the immortality of man were such as these : That the divine and therefore immortal part of man is derived from the supreme Creator;[1] that the individual soul is of the same nature and character as the universal soul or soul of the world;[2] that it is a simple, uncompounded, and so incorruptible principle,[3] in its own nature indestructible even by its own evil;[4] that it is self-moved and the cause of motion,[5] the divine and contemplative reason.[6] This is a doctrine of immortality which deserves careful consideration from all Christian thinkers. It is well to note both wherein it differs from the scriptural doctrine, and how far it has done good service as an aid to Christian faith. It would be foolish to despise any reasoned plea for immortality, and certainly that developed in the Platonic dialogues is noble. Next to the disclosures of revelation, the reasonings of Plato have furnished the grandest confirmation in literature of man's belief that he survives death; only we must observe that the real strength of the plea does not lie

---

[1] *Timæus*, iii. 34, 35, 41, 69 (Steph.), especially in this last, παραλαβόντες ἀρχὴν ψυχῆς ἀθάνατον, κ.τ.λ.

[2] *Ibid.* iii. 69, 90.

[3] *Phædo*, 78, where the argument turns upon the soul being ἀξύνθετον or μονοειδίς. It has been subtly followed out by Plotinus, *Ennead.* iv. 7.

[4] *Republic*, lib. X. 609, D : Ἴθι δή, καὶ ψυχὴν κατὰ τὸν αὐτὸν τρόπον σκόπει. ἆρα ἐνοῦσα ἐν αὐτῇ ἀδικία καὶ ἡ ἄλλη κακία τῷ ἐνεῖναι καὶ προσκαθῆσθαι φθείρει αὐτὴν καὶ μαραίνει ἕως ἂν εἰς θάνατον ἀγαγοῦσα τοῦ σώματος χωρίσῃ; Οὐδαμῶς, ἔφη, τοῦτό γε. Ἀλλὰ μέντοι ἐκεῖνό γε ἄλογον, ἦν δ' ἐγώ, τὴν μὲν ἄλλου πονηρίαν ἀπολλύναι τι, τὴν δὲ αὐτοῦ μή. Ἄλογον.

[5] *Phædrus*, 245, C : Ψυχὴ πᾶσα ἀθάνατος. τὸ γὰρ ἀεικίνητον ἀθάνατον.

[6] *Ibid.* 249, E : Πᾶσα μὲν ἀνθρώπου ψυχὴ φύσει τεθέαται τὰ ὄντα.
This summary of citations is indicated in a paper on "The Belief in Immortality," by Prin. Fairbairn of Airedale College. See his *Studies in the Philosophy of Religion and History*, pp. 226, 227. 1876.

in the abstract propositions above cited. Plato the
poet, the thinker, is broader than his philosophy. His
plea for a future life is not merely that of the meta-
physician. His moral arguments from the soul's own
aspirations, from the necessity of retribution, from the
divine order and government of the universe, are
common to him with all who have worthily treated
the theme. For this instinct of life after death, "a
specifically human possession," makes philosophy and
religion its tributaries and servants. The nature of
man demands from both what can evoke and satisfy
his aspirations after immortality.

It is upon his own peculiar doctrine of knowing
and being, however, that the argumentative parts of
Plato's teaching on this theme chiefly depend. And
the influence of even these on the current of Christian
thought has been very great. Nor are its results to
be regarded as only injurious. It is the custom at
present very strongly to disparage them. Yet no more
manifest instance of ideas preparing the way for the
reception of the gospel can be cited than this great
legacy of Platonic speculation, to which the Christian
religion served itself lawful heir. Nor can we doubt
that, as the assimilating power of Christianity triumphs,
the precious metal of this Greek amalgam will be
thoroughly extracted, and the base elements rejected.
It is necessary here, in a word, to discriminate what,
in the Greek view of immortality, is akin to Bible
thought, and what is alien from it. The point where
they coincide is in making personality the ground of
continuous existence. Greek thought had too firm a
grasp of the notion of personality, of freedom, of the

ethical principles involved in the government of the
world and in the nature of man, to allow metempsychosis
to obtain a permanent foothold on Grecian soil.[1] Still
less possible was it for the Greek mind to adopt the
dreamier pantheistic forms of belief in a future life
which prevailed in India. On this important common
ground, ˌthen, the Bible religion and the more developed forms of Greek thinking met together, namely,
that man as responsible person, as God-related, must
survive death. But the divergence between the Bible
thought and that of the Platonic philosophy is now very
manifest. Plato analyzed man's nature not only into
separable, but into opposing elements. Greek philosophy concentrated its characteristic dualism upon the
nature of man. One part of him is divine, another
almost anti-divine. One part of him is immortal,
another part of him is perishable and perishes for
ever, — an idea too easily confounded with that
which still speaks in the Christian tongue of man's
nature as made up of an immortal soul and a mortal
body. The Hebrew, the Bible thought, has indeed its
duality of man's nature, as we have shown; but it
is a duality of littleness and greatness, of man's
ephemeral place here on the one side, and of his kinship and friendship with the Almighty on the other.
It did not, it could not, found its doctrine of future
life, as Greek philosophy did, upon the elaborated
distinction between the spiritual and the material in
man. For that distinction, when worked out by
philosophy, led to the indignant and contemptuous
rejection of the resurrection from the dead. Yet so

[1] See Fairbairn, *Studies*, etc., p. 174.

grateful was Christian thought for elaborated argument
to commend belief in a future life, and to set it on a
logical and scholastic basis, that the native opposition
of the Greek mind to the doctrine of the resurrection
was forgiven.   The distinctive character of the scriptural belief was also too much forgotten.   Gradually,
in Christian schools, the Greek influence prevailed,
and even in the Christian Church the idea of the soul's
immortality for long took the place of the Scripture
doctrine of a future life.   During the last century
almost universally,—in some philosophical sections of
Christendom still,—the survival of an immortal essence
of the man is substituted for that " adoption," that
" complete redemption," for which the Spirit teaches
Christian believers to wait and yearn.   The Christian
hope is too often made to appear the hope of release
from the body at death, instead of the body's redemption and a perfected salvation for the whole nature of
the man.

The distinctive peculiarities of the Platonic argument are the existence of eternal ideas and the pre-
existence of the soul.   An exquisitely dramatic passage
in the *Phædo* will be remembered, where Socrates
brings out this crowning solution to relieve and to re-
assure the baffled reasoners.   They had been drawn
on to express the fear, that since the soul is a harmony,
it must cease like music when the frame and the strings
of the lyre are dissolved.   'But what call we that,'
says Socrates, 'which pre-exists the lyre ?   That can
be no mere harmony.   What did not begin with the
body cannot end with the body.   The admission of the
pre-existence of ideas, and therefore of the soul, settles

the question. A harmony is an effect, whereas the soul is not an effect, but a cause.'[1] Here it must be allowed that Greek and Christian thought part company. The Bible, with its distinctive doctrine of creation, renders the pre-existence argument futile and unnecessary. Nor can we admit with Jowett,[2] that the Platonic reasoning—"eternal ideas exist, therefore the soul exists eternally"—is any true parallel to the argument from immortality, among ourselves, drawn from the existence of God. When this latter is properly based as a scriptural and Christian argument, it takes such grounds as man's formation by the one living and true God, and his moral relation to that God—grounds confirmed to us supremely in the disclosures of revelation. There is, it is true, an affinity between the Platonic reasonings and such arguments for the soul's continued existence as those employed by Bishop Butler in the famous opening chapter of his *Analogy*. It may be questioned how far these have been of much real service to the doctrine. To say that the soul is indissoluble is no affirmation of its immortality. That some particular element in man's constitution is incapable of annihilation, is not really to the point as regards his future personal existence. Besides, this mode of reasoning has the disadvantage of hinging too much on a mere logical concatenation of abstract propositions.

It is proper, at this place, to take some notice of those apparent oppositions that have arisen even among Christian thinkers as to the doctrine of the soul's

---

[1] *Phædo*, 89 *et seq.* (Steph.). Consult Jowett's introduction to his translation of this dialogue. Jowett's *Plato*, i. 402.

[2] *Ibid.* p. 420.

immortality. And first, of the assertion so commonly mooted, that some of the Greek Fathers held the mortality of the soul, and especially the annihilation of the wicked. The changes have been rung by Dodwell and by some subsequent writers upon a well-known passage in Justin Martyr's *Dialogue with Trypho,* to prove that this Apologist held both these positions. A famous citation from Tatian, beginning, "The soul is not immortal by itself, but mortal. It is also capable of not dying," is made to do duty to the same effect. And so with several isolated quotations from Theophilus, Irenæus, and others. Olshausen has clearly pointed out in what direction the solution of these passages is to be found.[1] All these writers held, with more or less consistency, the distinction between the *psyche* and the *pneuma ;* so that when they affirm that the soul is mortal in itself, but can become immortal, it must be remembered that it is of the *psyche* they are speaking. According to the views of some of them, the nature of man at the first was that of a body and soul (*psyche*), upheld by the spirit (*pneuma*). Upon the fall, the spirit retires or is extinguished, and the soul dies. In redemption, the spirit is revived or restored, and thus again an immortality of blessedness becomes the possession of the soul. Now it is obvious at a glance, that unless the trichotomic character of their anthropology is kept in view, the modern reader is entirely misled when the opinions of these Fathers are cited concerning the mortality or immortality of the soul.

---

[1] In a brief paper contained in his *Opuscula Theologica,* Berlin, 1836. For an account of Olshausen's view, with the relevant citations from the Fathers, the reader is referred to Note T, in the Appendix.

Of not less importance is it to observe, that in speaking
of the death of the soul, these writers do not invariably,
or even usually, mean cessation of existence.   They
use the expressions " death " and " dying " in an ethical
sense.   The death to which the *psyche* becomes subject upon the loss of the *pneuma* is, accordingly,
ignorance of its divine origin and alienation from God
in this present world, to which is added the darkness
of Hades in the world to come.   To these two lines of
explanation, the tripartite psychology of the Greek
Fathers and their tropical use of the term "death,"
Olshausen has called attention very pointedly.   There
is another consideration, which has been less adverted
to, but which tends in the same direction.   They were
all familiar with the Platonic doctrine of the soul.
Some of them had been once adherents of that philosophy.   Their denial of the soul's immortality, then,
it must be remarked, was not a denial of it in our
sense, but a protest against the theory of its necessary
indestructibility, its essential divinity, and its pre-existence.   In the passage from Justin above mentioned,
this is expressly stated.   " Souls are not immortal," he
says, " for they were created, and their existence depends upon the will of God." [1]   It is plain that this

---

[1] For the sake of the English reader, I subjoin the well-known paragraphs from the *Dialogue with Trypho*, in an excellent translation, *Ante-
Nicene Christian Library*, vol. ii. pp. 93, 94 :—

" ' Those philosophers know nothing, then, about these things ; for they
cannot tell what a soul is.'

" ' It does not appear so.'

" ' Nor ought it to be called immortal ; for if it is immortal, it is plainly
unbegotten.'

" ' It is both unbegotten and immortal, according to some who are styled
Platonists.'

" ' Do you say that the world is also unbegotten ?'

statement bears no relation to the question of the soul's continuance after death. It is simply a denial of its pre-existence, or of its absolute self-subsistence. In view of Justin's repeated and strong expressions elsewhere regarding the eternal punishment of the wicked, it is obviously unfair to quote the isolated passage from the *Dialogue with Trypho*, in the application given to it by such writers as H. Dodwell and E. White. It may be fairly enough cited to show that Justin held the annihilation of the wicked as a thing possible to the Almighty; perhaps also that in his opinion the cessation of their soul's existence was a conceivable solution of the awful mystery of their future. But these are concessions which no one would greatly care to dispute.

It is not necessary now to unearth the opinions on the soul's mortality maintained by Dr. Dodwell, cumbered as these were by his extravagant high churchism.[1] The views of those who in our own day hold the position of dissidents within the Christian

---

" 'Some say so. I do not, however, agree with them.'

. . .   " 'But if the world is begotten, souls also are necessarily begotten; and perhaps at one time they were not in existence, for they were made on account of men and other living creatures, if you will say that they have been begotten wholly apart, and not along with their respective bodies.'

" 'This seems to be correct.'

" 'They are not, then, immortal?'

" 'No; since the world has appeared to us to be begotten.'

" 'But I do not say, indeed, that all souls die; for that were truly a piece of good fortune to the evil. What then? The souls of the pious remain in a better place, while those of the unjust and wicked are in a worse, waiting for the time of judgment. Thus some which have appeared worthy of God never die; but others are punished so long as God wills them to exist and to be punished.' "

[1] *An epistolary discourse, proving from the Scriptures and the first Fathers*, etc. (see this title quoted in full, note on p. 226). London, 1706.

The natural mortality of human souls clearly demonstrated from the Holy Scriptures and the concurrent testimonies of the primitive writers. Being an

Church from the faith of immortality, deserve some
attention.   The chief writers among them are Mr. J.
B. Heard and Mr. Edward White, whose opinions,
however, are far from being exactly coincident.   The
latter declares that "the general object of his book [1]
is to show that in the popular doctrine of the soul's
immortality is the *fons et origo* of a system of theological
error; that in its denial we return at once to scientific
truth and to sacred Scripture; at the same time clear-
ing the way for the right understanding of the object
of the Incarnation, of the nature and issue of redemption
in the Life Eternal, and of the true doctrine of divine
judgment on the unsaved." [2]   He characterizes the
soul's immortality as " an inadmissible assumption." [3]
He groups it among notions which he calls "anti-
scriptural," and "part of the mystery of iniquity;" [4]
and declares that "the assertion of man's natural
immortality is the direct cause of the creation of a
God-dishonouring theology." [5]   On its positive side, the
theory professes to be a doctrine of future life for man
through the incarnation.   According to this writer,
Scripture teaches that the object "of redemption is to
change man's nature, not only from sin to holiness, but

*explication of a famous passage in the dialogue of S. Justin Martyr with
Tryphon, concerning the soul's immortality, etc.* London, 1708.

*A Scriptural account of the eternal rewards or punishments of all that
hear the Gospel, without an immortality necessarily resulting from the nature
of the souls themselves that are concerned in these rewards and punishments.*
London, 1708.

The titles of these treatises of Dodwell suffice to indicate how far his
views are the precursors of those to be immediately considered.

    [1] *Life in Christ*, 3d edit., revised and enlarged. London, 1878.
    [2] *Ibid.* p. 70.
    [3] *Ibid.* p. 104 ; in former editions it was " an intolerable assumption."
    [4] *Ibid.* p. 117.
    [5] *Ibid.* p. 190.

from mortality to immortality; from a constitution whose present structure is perishable in all its parts, to one which is eternal." This stupendous change, conveyed to mankind through the channel of the incarnation, is realized in the individual by the indwelling of the Holy Spirit. "He applies the remedy of redemption by communicating Godlikeness and immortality to the soul by spiritual regeneration, and to the body by resurrection."[1] The theory, therefore, it will be seen, exaggerates the effects of the fall, by assuming that man then lost the divine image in such a sense as to come under the law of extinction at death like the lower animals. "Without redemption, man would certainly go to nothing at death."[2] It makes regeneration, as we have seen, a physical or constitutional change. Its view of a future life is inconsistent and incredible. The eternal life of the saved is, quite scripturally, ascribed to their union with Christ. But to Christ also, upon this theory, must be ascribed the survival of the unsaved in the state of punishment. "To permit· of the reconstitution of the identical transgressor, we hold that his spirit is preserved in its individuality from dissipation in the death of the man, to be conjoined again to the body at the day of judgment. This survival of the 'soul' we attribute exclusively to the operation of redemption, with its graces and corresponding judgments."[3] Thus, "both heaven and hell, the life eternal of the one and the second death of the other, are the results of that

[1] See the quotation given in full at p. 184, in Lect. V.
[2] Heard's *Tripartite Nature of Man*, 4th edit. pp. 247, 248. White's *Life in Christ*, p. 96.
[3] White, p. 119.

meritorious work of Christ."[1] The statement of these
consequences, as drawn by the writers themselves, is
the sufficient refutation of their theory.

The whole scheme bears marks of having been
elaborated under the pressure of sentiment, and with
the desire of arriving at a foregone conclusion, namely,
that eternal punishment is impossible. This theory of
"conditional immortality," or of the ultimate annihilation of the wicked, may claim one advantage over its
rival, the theory of universal restoration. In its appeal
to the certainty of future punishment and to the irre-
vocable character of future destiny, it is somewhat
more in accordance than the other with the findings at
once of conscience and of Scripture. But both theories
are incompetent solutions of the awful problem which
they attempt. It is obvious that neither of them can
be made to consist with the whole doctrine of Scripture
as to the future of man. The one with which we have
been dealing raises far more and greater difficulties
than it solves. It is impossible to make it fit in to the
doctrinal scheme of the Bible. Any moral power it
may possess in the hands of some able and earnest
Christian preachers of it, is more than nullified by its
fatal concessions to scepticism and materialism on
the question of the soul. And its theory of man's
constitution is certainly not that of Scripture.[2]

[1] Heard, p. 251.
[2] If anything further were needed to show the weakness of the theory, it
would be sufficient to point to the exegesis on which it rests. This exegesis
requires that "life" and "death" be taken in Scripture, usually and all
but invariably, to mean "continuance of existence" and "cessation of
existence" for man. This is called "taking Scripture language in its
simplest and most obvious sense." It is strange that men cannot perceive
how under the guise of a law of exegesis they are simply assuming the
whole point in dispute concerning the natural immortality of man. No

We return to our proper subject of the relation which the Scripture doctrine of man's constitution bears to its discovery of a future life. We are not warranted, as we have seen, to insist on any attribution to man's soul or spirit of an absolute necessity of eternal continuance; "God alone hath immortality." But when we view "the souls (*neshamoth*, spirits) which He hath made"[1] as persons, we have taken the proper scriptural position. "Personal continuance of existence has its fundamental postulate in the existence of a personal God, its final ground in the free determinate will of this God, its final reason in the counsel of redemption, for biblical psychology has to seek the solution of this problem in the revealed mystery of God's redeeming purpose."[2]

competent interpreter would ever think of confining to so bald and shallow a meaning in any other connection such deeply-charged expressions as the Bible words for life and death. The same exegesis is of course applied by these writers to the quotations they make from the Fathers. How mistaken it is, Mr. White, for example, in one place enables his reader to see for himself. He quotes Athanasius' saying, that the original sentence of death (Gen. iii.) signifies (and can signify nothing else than) that not only they should die, but in the destruction of death remain (ἀλλὰ δὲ ἐν τῇ τοῦ θανάτου φθορᾷ διαμένειν). Athanasius obviously regarded death in the scriptural sense, not as cessation of existence, but as continuance (διαμένειν) under penalty.

[1] Isa. lvii. 16.

[2] Delitzsch, *Biblische Psychologie*, p. 407. The whole passage, which I have merely summarized in the above sentence, runs thus:—

"Persönliche Fortdauer hat zu ihrer Grundvoraussetzung das Dasein eines persönlichen Gottes, zu ihrem letzten Grunde die freie Willensentschliessung dieses Gottes. Unsterblichkeit aber und persönliche Fortdauer sind in der h. Schrift sich ganz und gar nicht deckende Begriffe. Unsterblich ist nur der mit Gott dem Unsterblichen durch Christum den Auferstandenen vereinigte Mensch. Für diesen hat der zeitliche Tod das Wesen des Todes verloren, für alle anderen Menschen ist dem zeitlichen Tode nur eine Grenze gesteckt. Seinen letzten Grund hat auch das im Erlösungsrathschluss, dessen Selbstverwirklichung den ewigen persönlichen Fortbestand der gesammten Menscheit fordert. Ohne sich also lange bei den im Wesen der Menschenseele gelegenen Wahrscheinlichkeitsgründen für

There are two leading ideas concerning man in the earlier Scripture which naturally connect with its doctrine of his future. These are, his kinship with God by origin and nature, and the unity of his being —an indivisible personality. Add to these, what the later Scripture only fully unfolds, that redemption is based upon the union of mankind with a Divine-human Redeemer. The elements of the revealed doctrine of a future state lie in these three propositions. Mark how the divine kinship of man and the unity of his being support the Old Testament belief of a life beyond the grave. The former of these, in its bearings on our theme, has been eloquently, and with some slight abatement justly, expressed by Canon Perowne: "No philosophic reasoning comes to the aid of the Hebrew as he questions with himself concerning a life hereafter. He can construct no argument for the immateriality of the soul; he can build up no plausible hypothesis. . . . He does not reason: 'I think; therefore I am. I shall continue to think; therefore I shall continue to be.' He does not argue with himself: 'The soul is one and indivisible; therefore it cannot perish.' He does not draw his hopes from the constitution of man, from his memory, his affections, his intellect, his sense of law and duty. Even in face of the terrible problems of life, and in sight of all the prosperous wrong-doing

ihren jenseitigen Fortbestand aufzuhalten, hat die biblische Psychologie die Lösung ihrer eschatologischen Räthsel in dem enthüllten Mysterium des Erlösungsrathschlusses zu suchen."

These sentences show that Mr. White is mistaken in claiming Delitzsch as of his view, as he does at p. 119 of his *Life in Christ*. The words, "eternal personal continuance of the entire human race," set that at rest.

which was so great a trial to his constancy, he does not escape from his perplexity by any chain of reasoning, by any analogies that nature might suggest and philosophy confirm. He does not infer, that because the world is out of joint, God's righteousness must have a larger sphere of action than this world and the short years of man, and so conclude that there is a life to come, in which the vindication of God's moral government shall be complete. His is a grander logic, for it is the logic of the heart. His conclusions are reached, not in the schools, but in the sanctuary of God. . . . There, casting himself into the everlasting arms, he knows that these shall be beneath him, though heart and flesh should fail. There, holding sweet converse with his Eternal Friend, he is sure that the God who has stooped to speak to him as a Friend will not suffer him to drop into the abyss of annihilation. His life is no passing phenomenon. He is not like the tree, or the flower, or the bird, or the beast—creatures of God's hand which know Him not, and do but yield Him the homage of a reasonless praise. He knows God; he has spoken to God; he has heard the voice of God in his heart. This is no illusion, but the most blessed, as it is the most certain, of all truths. Faith and love have won their everlasting victory in those words, which will for all time remain the noblest expression of the soul pouring itself out towards God :—

> ' But as for me, I am always by Thee.
> Thou hast holden me by my right hand.
> Thou wilt guide me in Thy counsel,
> And afterwards Thou wilt take me to glory.
> Whom have I in heaven but Thee?

And beside Thee, there is none upon earth in whom I delight.
My flesh and my heart may fail,
But God is the rock of my heart and my portion for ever.' " [1]

It is no less plain that the other idea now mentioned, namely, the unity of man's being, pervades this and all similar passages of Scripture. " Because He calls the man His friend, because He calls Himself the God of the individual, singled out by name, therefore the whole man must survive the shock of death. It is not the spirit's immortality which alone is secured. It is not a mere prolongation of existence of which the pledge is given. The body as well as the soul is God's. In the body He calls these men His children; on the body He sets the seal of His covenant. And therefore, though the flesh may turn to corruption, and the worm may feed upon it, yet from their flesh shall they see God,—see Him not only in this world, the Avenger of their cause, but see Him in the world to come, the Judge who metes out to them their recompense, the Rewarder of them who diligently seek Him." [2]

Everything the Bible has to say about the life after death is strongly coloured by this fundamental presupposition of the oneness of the man. In that respect it entirely differs from the Greek notion that the soul of man is immortal because it is of the nature of the gods, but that his body is an encumbrance which is cast off and perishes for ever. It is, according to the Bible, the man who endures even under the temporary eclipse of disembodiment, till he be again clothed

[1] " Immortality," the *Hulsean Lecture* for 1868, pp. 75-77. J. J. S. Perowne, B.D.
[2] *Ibid.* p. 84.

upon of God. It is to be noted that the historical instances which stand as proofs of another life in the Old Testament all take this form. It is not an abstract statement of the soul's separate existence after death. It is not the reappearance of departed spirits. It is the translation of an Enoch, "so that he should not see death."[1] It is the unseen departure of Moses "by the mouth of the Lord,"[2] and the withdrawal of his mortal raiment from human ken. It is the rapture of Elijah in his chariot of fire. We have no need to suppose that the Jews drew their doctrine of bodily resurrection from Egyptian or Persian sources. For although, as may be seen in the book of Maccabees, the later Jews drew from such sources errors and exaggerations of it, the doctrine itself is obviously germane to the central idea of their own Scriptures on the subject, namely, that God claims the whole man for the inheritance of a future life.

The idea accounts for a leading feature of Old Testament eschatology. No doubt the record affirms a divine kinship of man as such. But the writers themselves are men who realize it. Consequently, when they write of the future life, it is chiefly of their own hopes concerning it. Their sentiments take the shape not of philosophical speculations, but of piety and religious faith. We have glimpses, indeed, in psalmist and prophet of an under-world where the wicked are ruled over by death;[3] but in the main it is the future as bound up with the hope of salvation that is presented. And this leads to still another remark, that we are fairly entitled to distin-

[1] Heb. xi. 6.   [2] Deut. xxxiv. 5, עַל־פִּי יְהֹוָה.   [3] Ps. xlix. ; Isa. xiv.

guish in the Old Testament between the ideas of an
after-life, current in the age of the writers, and the
revealed hopes to which they clung.   Natural or
traditional notions of Sheol as a gloomy subterranean
abode, with its weak and wavering shades, its almost
entire extinction of existence, may colour the thoughts
of a psalmist under the cloud of spiritual depression,
may lend a cold and sceptic tone to the delineations
of Ecclesiastes, may be dramatically presented in the
poetry of Job ; but the writers themselves teach us
to distinguish these from the truth of revelation, and
attach all their own hopes of a future life to the
revealed doctrines of man's creation and redemption.

Following out these considerations, we may be able
to account for the alleged reticence of the earlier
Scriptures on the subject of a future life.   It has been
common to represent the older revelation as excluding
or disregarding the life after death.   Arguments, even,
for the divine character of the Mosaic system have
been built upon the assumed fact of the absence of
that doctrine from the religion of the ancient covenant.[1]   These theories have long since fallen out of
favour.   Still the fact has to be accounted for, that
comparatively little is said in the older Scriptures of
life beyond the grave.   Canon Perowne gives well the
usual account of this reticence.[2]   There is no haste in
God's teaching.   The heroism of faith needed to be
strengthened.   God alone, without any direct revelation of a future heaven, was to be enough for these
ancient believers.   He cites the reason given by some

[1] E.g., Bp. Warburton's Divine Legation of Moses demonstrated.
[2] At pp. 88, 89 of his Hulsean Lecture.

of the fathers, that the Jewish nation was too rude and ignorant to be capable of receiving truths so lofty. He adds the shrewd surmise of Bossuet, that during the times preceding our Lord the doctrine of the soul's existence after death had been a source of errors. The worship of the departed lay at the bottom of almost all idolatry. Therefore the most primary notion of the soul and of its blessedness was all which the law of Moses gave. It was reserved for the new commencement in the coming of Messiah to lay this foundation of religion afresh.[1]

The chief reason, we apprehend, is to be found in the peculiar character of the divine revelation which the Bible records. A false idea of revelation underlies much of the reasoning on both sides about the Bible doctrine of immortality. If revelation were a series of apothegms or oracles, of abstract utterances even for men's need, it would be hard to understand why the plain discovery of a future life should have been withheld, especially if it could have been conveyed in such simple propositions as, "The spirit in man never dies," or, "Man continues for ever." But the entire revelation is personal and historical. The foundation of all religion, the existence of God, for example, is never given in the Old Testament Scriptures as an abstract proposition. It is taken for granted. But God reveals Himself to man by entering into special relations with men. The religion of redemption becomes the possession of mankind through a series of historical transactions between God and His chosen people. It is no otherwise with the light which reve-

---

[1] Canon Perowne's *Hulsean Lecture*, pp. 131, 132.

lation sheds on man's future life.   Man's own instinctive belief, his natural expectation of life after death,
the Bible takes for granted.   Abstract affirmations or
confirmations in that kind would have been foreign to
its whole character.   The Old Testament expresses the
faith of a future life, chiefly as the assurance of God's
redeemed that they shall dwell with Him for ever.
When it passes beyond this to more direct intimation
of future glory and personal resurrection, these are
almost invariably Messianic, and expressed in a form
primarily applicable to the Head of redeemed humanity.
Peter interprets the clearest of all the psalms on this
subject, "Thou wilt not leave my soul in hell, nor
suffer Thine Holy One to see corruption," as a direct
prophecy of the resurrection of Jesus.   Job connects
his survival of death and his return from the grave
with the appearance of his kinsman-Redeemer at the
latter day upon the earth.   Both in Isaiah and in
Ezekiel the idea of resurrection from the dead is used
as a most clear and splendid figurative description of
predicted deliverances which God was to work out
for Israel.   The most distinct of all Old Testament
words on the subject of return from the grave occurs
in a clearly Messianic passage of Daniel (xii. 2): "And
many of them that sleep in the dust of death shall
awake, some to everlasting life, and some to shame
and everlasting contempt." There is abundant evidence outside of the Old Testament canon that the
ideas of future life and resurrection were making rapid
advances among the Jews in the interval between the
last of the prophets and the coming of our Lord.   Yet
we read in Acts xxiii. 6–9 that these ideas were still

subjects of discussion between Pharisees and Saddu-
cees. It is only when the historical revelation arrives
in the fulness of time at an incarnation, and the personal God of the ancient covenant becomes the God-man
Christ Jesus, that the life beyond the grave and the
resurrection of the body can be fully brought to light
in the gospel. Indeed, even the Lord Jesus brings
life and immortality to light, not so much by words
and sayings, though these certainly He does not with-
hold, as by His own Messianic experience — tasting
death for every man, then, by resurrection from death
destroying death and him that had the power of it,
that we might be delivered from the bondage of its fear.

In a memorable passage of the *Phædo*, one of the
speakers says that if a man can do no better on a
matter of such practical importance as faith in a
future world, "he ought to choose out the best and
most irrefragable of human opinions about it, and
upon that, like a mariner on a raft, risk his way
through the storms of life, unless he can proceed more
easily and safely on the more sure vehicle of some
divine word."[1] It is true enough to say, as Perowne
does,[2] that the divine word for which Socrates was
seeking, Paul had found when he wrote: "For we
know that if the earthly house of our tabernacle were
dissolved, we have a building of God, a house not made
with hands, eternal in the heavens." But it is more

---

[1] Plato, *Phædo*, 85 C (Steph.). Δεῖν γὰρ περὶ αὐτὰ ἓν γί τι τούτων διαπράξ-
ασθαι ἢ μαθεῖν ὅπῃ ἔχει ἢ εὑρεῖν· ἤ, εἰ ταῦτα ἀδύνατον, τὸν γοῦν βέλτιστον τῶν
ἀνθρωπίνων λόγων λαβόντα καὶ δυσεξελεγκτότατον, ἐπὶ τούτου ὀχούμενον, ὥσπερ
ἐπὶ σχεδίας, κινδυνεύοντα διαπλεῦσαι τὸν βίον· εἰ μή τις δύναιτο ἀσφαλέστερον
καὶ ἀκινδυνότερον, ἐπὶ βεβαιοτέρου ὀχήματος ἢ λόγου θείου τινός, διαπορευθῆναι.
(This sentence is put into the mouth not of Socrates, but of Simmias.)

[2] *Hulsean Lecture*, p. 94.

correct to affirm that what Paul and we have is the divine word in a grander sense than these philosophers thought of, namely, the Word incarnate and now glorified, who is our new and living Way to the world unseen. We see from the whole character, therefore, of those divine transactions which the Bible records, why there is a silence and a withholding, as it were, on this theme, in the ancient Scriptures. Mere words, even divinely-given words, could not have satisfied men on the subject of the future. The revelation of blessed life for ever could only come by a Redeemer, the incarnate Hope of men,—could only be unfolded by Him as He lived and died and rose again for men, and so achieved in His own person the right to say, "I AM the Resurrection and the Life."

II.

We pass, then, to our concluding point, the Scripture doctrine of the Resurrection.

It is of much importance to notice, that what our Lord and His followers teach on this subject is the continuance of the person, the redemption of the whole man. Hence it is that personal resurrection, instead of being something thrown in at the end, is the very centre and gist of the gospel discovery of a future life, and shines on its front. Doubly instructive is our Lord's argument for it, drawn from the words which Moses heard at the burning bush: "I am the God of Abraham, and the God of Isaac, and the God of Jacob."[1] He goes for His proof, not to such special texts as plainly allude to the particular

---

[1] Ex. iii. 6 ; Matt. xxii. 32.

event of rising again from the dead, but to one of the
great covenant-words which secure redemption for the
entire nature and being of those on whom God has
set His everlasting love. It is an instructive surprise,
moreover, to find that in these words Jesus reads, not
what we are so apt to think of, the survival of the spirits
of the blessed. When He says, " God is not the God of
the dead, but of the living," and affirms this " touching
the resurrection of the dead," He evidently means
more than that Abraham, Isaac, and Jacob were living
a disembodied life in some unseen region. He means
that the covenant-name is in pledge for their complete bodily restoration. It secures the permanence
of the whole man.

Once illuminated by our Lord's teaching, and still
more by His own rising again, this mode of presenting
the doctrine of a future life prevails with all the
apostles. When Paul went with the Glad Tidings to
Athens, he did not tell the Greeks that man survives
the grave, that his soul lives after death in a separate
state ; this would only have been in the line of their
own philosophy. He preached that which not only
surmounted, but in a sense confronted their surmises.
He seemed to them a setter forth of strange gods
when he preached unto them Jesus and the resurrection. It is always under the influence of this new
fact that the apostles celebrate the victory won for
man by their Lord and Saviour. Men are " begotten
again unto a lively hope by the resurrection of Jesus
Christ from the dead." [1] " He hath abolished death,
and hath brought life and immortality to light through

[1] 1 Pet. i. 3.

the gospel;"[1] "The last enemy which shall be destroyed is death;" "O death, I will be thy plagues: O grave, I will be thy destruction."[2] "For since by man came death, by man (*i.e.* by the God-man, the Head of redemption) came also"—what? survival of death? No; but "resurrection of the dead."[3] Survival of death was not first brought to light by the special revelation which the Bible contains. Man's heart and conscience have witnessed for that in all ages and among all nations. Man's intellect, whenever awakened to thought, speculates and reasons about it. Revelation clears and confirms it. Survival of death was no part of redemption. It was not a thing secured for the first time by the work of Christ. It belongs to man as man. It was " resurrection of the dead" to which our Lord bore witness in His own person, and through which He secured that all in Christ shall be made alive.

We cannot forget that, as regards the last things, all is not light even to the student of the latest revelation. It is under the New Testament, as it was under the older economy, mainly in the way of redemption that we have disclosures of the life to come. We are not told much by our Lord and His apostles concerning the general resurrection. The firm outline of the last judgment sets forth, no doubt, " all the dead, small and great, standing before God," before "the great white throne and Him that sits on it."[4] But how they come, and what their form of existence, are veiled from us. The fact of a bodily resurrection is affirmed plainly enough. Paul declares his "hope

[1] 2 Tim. i. 10.   [2] Hos. xiii. 14.   [3] 1 Cor. xv. 21, 26, 55.   [4] Rev. xx. 12.

that there shall be a resurrection of the dead, both
of the just and of the unjust."[1]   He has conscience
and revelation both with him when he says: "We
must all appear before the judgment-seat of Christ,
that every one may receive the things done in his
body."[2]   Our Lord's words, which seem to redupli-
cate on those already quoted from Daniel, are still
more definite: "All that are in the graves shall hear
His voice, and shall come forth; they that have done
good, unto the resurrection of life; and they that have
done evil, unto the resurrection of damnation."[3]   The
fact is distinct; but as to the mode, anything that is
explicit belongs to the resurrection of the just.   No
doubt the principle, "to every seed his own body," is
one of far-reaching application.   Still it remains true
that what Delitzsch has called "the night side of the
general resurrection," lies buried in shadow.

What we are told as to the way and manner of
the re-awaking, belongs to those that are Christ's, and
to them only.   When we follow the line of personal
redemption we have a clear path of light; and its
course is worthy of great attention.   This "blessed
hope" rests directly on the person of the Saviour, and
becomes ours by reason of our oneness with Him.
Jesus Himself withdraws the sad soul of Martha from
the far-off vista of the general resurrection, to fix it
upon this more vivid and immediate ground of confidence: "I am the Resurrection and the Life."[4]
Again, it is spoken of as the direct result of that
spiritual life of which the Saviour is the source:
"Whoso eateth my flesh, and drinketh my blood,

---

[1] Acts xxiv. 15.   [2] 2 Cor. v. 10.   [3] John v. 28, 29.   [4] John xi. 25.

hath eternal life; and I will raise him up at the last
day."[1]   Further, it is expressly attributed to the
operation of the Divine Spirit, who is the principle
of the new life in believers: "If the Spirit of Him
that raised up Jesus from the dead dwell in you, He
that raised up Christ from the dead shall also quicken
your mortal bodies by His Spirit that dwelleth in
you."[2]   Finally, Paul speaks of it as something which
lay before him as a goal of conscious effort, the
scope of his own strenuous, self-sacrificing faith, which
counted all things loss that he might win it, the
crown of faith's following after, apprehending, reaching
forth, and pressing toward the mark of his high calling in Christ Jesus: "If by any means I might attain
unto the resurrection of the dead."[3]   Here, surely, is
something different from our too common view.   We
think and speak as if resurrection were a bare future
event, an eschatological fact with which our present
working faith had little or nothing to do, an event
which must come in due time alike to all, to those
in and to those out of Christ.   Do not these words
represent it as the crown and completion of that
which union to Christ by grace secures?   Here, surely,
is a Scripture truth which is entitled to our living
regard, and which, had it the due place, would won-
drously transform the outlook of the future from a
mere departure out of the body into an unbroken series
of progressive glorious advances, till we be clothed
upon with our house from heaven.

Of the How, the What, the When of this ultimate
attainment of redemption, Scripture does not warrant

---

[1] John vi. 54.   [2] Rom. viii. 11.   [3] Phil. iii. 11.

us to speak with much detail, but its outlines are firm. "How are the dead raised up?" Had men observed the exact words in which the inspired reasoner allows the question, they should have had an easier path to the answer than that which divines too oft have taken. "The dead raised up." Scripture never speaks, as creeds and apologists have spoken, of "the resurrection of the flesh." It does not even place the emphasis on resurrection of the body, but on the resurrection of the dead, their manifestation, their return from the unseen into the visible glories of a ransomed universe. Had men followed the idea pervading St. Paul's exquisite analogy of the seed-corn, theology should have been preserved from scholastic quibbles about identity of matter and identity of form, when it had to state the relation between the present and the future body. "Thou sowest not that body that shall be, but bare grain, it may chance of wheat, or of some other grain; but God giveth it a body as it hath pleased Him, and to every seed his own body."[1] Had the Church followed the spiritual teaching of this fifteenth chapter of First Corinthians, instead of her own childish memories or pagan traditions, our pulpits should have been long ago delivered from the charnel-house theology of the "Night Thoughts," our popular Christian belief from reproaches irreverently but not quite groundlessly cast upon it.[2] There is no good reason

---

[1] 1 Cor. xv, 37, 38.

[2] "When scientific thought was once more directed to the subject of immortality, it was easily seen that the doctrine of resurrection, in its vulgar acceptation, could not possibly be true, since a case might easily be imagined in which there might be a contention between rival claimants

why we should ever expose apostolic teaching to try
conclusions with modern chemistry.   The difficulties
which science raises in such subjects, riper science will
solve.   On this topic of the resurrection we see the
answer already beginning to take shape.   Science at
the present day stands in a very different and more
friendly attitude towards this belief of man's reappearance in the future world than did the science of
one or two generations ago.   We are now assured
that our present bodies are the same, yet not the same,
that we have had from our birth.   That there is in
the body some principle, law, or specific form, which
remains ever the same amid the flux of particles, is
now an axiom of knowledge.   We may say, in an
almost literal sense, that we pass through the process
of resurrection constantly; that we are always dying
in the flesh, always rising anew by virtue of the
law of organic identity.   Behind this, again, lies the

for the same body. . . . It is, indeed, both curious and instructive to note
the reluctance with which various sections of the Christian Church have
been driven from their old erroneous conceptions on this subject; and the
expedients, always grotesque, and sometimes positively loathsome, with
which they have attempted to buttress up the tottering edifice. Some
deem it necessary that a single material germ or organized particle of the
body at death should survive until the resurrection, forgetting that, under
such a hypothesis, it would be easy to deprive a man of the somewhat
doubtful benefits of such a resurrection, by sealing him up (while yet alive)
in a strong iron coffin, and by appropriate means reducing his whole
physical body into an inorganic mass. . . . According to the disciples of
this school, the resurrection will be preceded by a gigantic manufacture
of shoddy, the effete and loathsome rags of what was once the body being
worked up along with a large quantity of new material into a glorious
and immortal garment, to form the clothing of a being who is to live for
ever! . . . We have only to compare this grotesquely hideous conception
with the noble and beautiful language of Paul, to recognise the depth of
abasement into which the Church had sunk through the materialistic conceptions of the Dark Ages."—*The Unseen Universe*, pp. 57, 58, 5th ed.,
Lond. 1876.

greater law of personal identity—that there is a being
which thinks, feels, and wills, maintains a connected
growth from infancy to age in knowledge and moral
character. This being does not cease at death. The
bearing of such ideas on the identity of the future
body with the present is obvious. They help us to
see how the undivided personality of the man in its
organic unity of soul and body can be the same in a
future state. It is not identity of particles, it is not
resurrection of relics, that we need to render the scriptural belief truly conceivable. It is this conception
in which science and faith concur, namely, that each
human being shall be the same in all that constitutes
the organic personality, that this unchanging life will
put on its nobler form under the conditions of its
nobler state.[1]

When, however, we hear Scripture on the question,
How are the dead raised up? we must rest on the
great Christian propositions. It is in Christ Jesus ; it
is by virtue of the whole nature, corporeal and spiritual
alike, being united to the Saviour ; it is through the
operation of that Spirit who dwells in head and members alike, and quickens both. In short, as we have
said, it rests on the grand central truth of Christianity,
that God, in whose image man was made at first,
becomes in Christ Jesus the quickening Head of a
new because a redeemed humanity. How the body
which is to be, finds a connection with the body that
now is—how that which is laid in the grave becomes the
seed-corn of the resurrection, we must leave with Him

[1] For a careful and interesting statement of this point, see Westcott's
Gospel of the Resurrection, pp. 143–145, 155, 156, 3d ed., Lond. 1874.

R

in whom His people are indissolubly wrapped up for
time and for eternity.

"With WHAT BODY do they come?" He who puts
the question into the mouth of his reader, with a
caution against too curious inquiry, has yet substantially supplied the answer.[1] Instead of corruption, *i.e.*
liability to decay, which is the character of our present
body, the future one, he tells us, shall be incorruptible.
Instead of the dishonour to which all that perishes is
liable, it shall have glory. Instead of weakness, there
shall be power. In a word, instead of a psychical or
soulish body, there shall be raised up a pneumatical
or spiritual body. If Bible psychology has furnished
us with a characteristic and consistent conception, it
is that of spirit or *pneuma* as the distinguishing possession of man. It has traced the *pneuma* in man,
and its development from the elementary idea of
man's life as inbreathed by his Creator, through its
use as a designation for man's free personality, up to
its renewal as the law of the spirit of life—that which
animates the new creature as the Spirit of Christ
Jesus Himself. It has thus prepared us for the
culmination of personal redemption in a spiritual
body. Man was made at first a "living soul"—
an animal, though the crown of the whole animal
creation. It was natural that his earthly frame
should be a "soulish body." But the aim of redemption is that even fallen man may become spiritual—to
lead by a new and more glorious way to that height of
spiritual glory which he was created to attain. How
fitting that its final gift should be that of a body equal

[1] 1 Cor. xv. 42–46.

to his redeemed position ! In any case, man's passage out of trial into bliss would have implied some such change, for flesh and blood cannot inherit the kingdom of heaven. As it is, redemption's crown is the final triumph of the Redeemer's grace, who, according to the energy of His all-subduing power, shall change the body of our humiliation, that it may be fashioned like unto the body of His own glory.[1]

The time, the WHEN of this transformation is a question that would lead us too far afield. Scripture clearly speaks of an interval. It allows us to conceive of a state in which even believers shall be "absent from the body." It describes these blessed ones as "souls" in heaven, "spirits of just men made perfect." But whether they are even there wholly unclothed, devoid of all corporeal vehicle, it scarcely enables us to determine. An opinion which seems on the face of it contrary to Scripture, is that, no longer confined to the followers of Swedenborg, which makes the souls of the blessed at death put on at once the spiritual body as they enter the unseen world, and leave for ever that which is laid in the tomb. Less apparently unscriptural, but cumbrous, is the theory of some of the fathers, who speak of a first and second *stola*,—who take the "white robes" of the Apocalypse to be a provisional body, put on for the intermediate state, worn only till the time come for the marriage garment of the resurrection.[2] Very beautiful, if somewhat mystical, is that of medi-

---

[1] Phil. iii. 21.

[2] Delitzsch refers to Augustine (*Serm.* iv., *in Solennitate Sanctorum*), Gregory, and others, for this distinction.

æval divines, favoured by some recent theologians, which regards the bodiless spirits of the redeemed departed as having meantime a kind of borrowed corporeity, by gathering round the glorified body of their Lord,—finding there "the sanctuary and true tabernacle" of their being as well as of their worship.[1] This coincides at all events with the best thing we know about our friends fallen asleep in Jesus. They have gone to be with Him; they are now with Christ—

> " And in that cloister's stillness and seclusion,
>   They live whom we call dead."

It is not wise for us to attempt to say much as to when or how the spiritual body comes. We know that it shall be the fitting garb of a ransomed and glorified spirit. We know that it shall be itself a pledge and trophy that of all Christ got from the Father He has lost nothing. It shall represent the dust redeemed, the body ransomed from the grave. How it is woven in the hidden secret of the life after death, we may not venture to surmise. If we have watched how the body, even here, puts on a likeness and correspondence to the real man, to the life within, it will not be difficult to think that for the ripening Christian his future body is being prepared by the Spirit of Christ dwelling already in this mortal frame, and quickening within it that which is to live for ever. It will be open to us to believe that the process is being perfected for the spirits of the just in an unseen world,

---

[1] " Interim ergo sub Christi humanitate feliciter sancti quiescunt," quoted from St. Bernard by Delitzsch, *Bibl. Psychol.* p. 416. Comp. Hofmann's ingenious interpretation of Heb. viii. 2 ; *Schriftbeweis*, II. i. 405.

and that all these things shall be made plain when
they shall appear with Christ at His coming, when the
sons of God shall shine forth an exceeding great army,
in the day of the adoption, that is, the redemption of
their body. "Now we see through a glass darkly,
but then face to face." "Now I know in part, but
then shall I know even as also I am known."

Thus we close this endeavour. It is with hasty
footsteps, and touching the mere heads of our theme,
that we have made our way through it. We claim
no novelty for our discussion. To show in what
sense Scripture is a primary fountain for the knowledge of man's own being and destiny, is no new or
alien study in the theological school. From the early
Apologists to the Reformers, it had always been perceived and insisted on that the Bible gives us such
knowledge of ourselves as is fitted to lead us beyond
ourselves to God; that its discovery of man is as
unique and divine, as truly a revelation, as its discovery of God. But it has not been so usual in
theological schools anywhere till recently, and in
those of our country scarcely at all hitherto, to fix
attention on the natural presuppositions and principles
of the Scripture writings concerning man. The intention of this rapid sketch has been to vindicate a
place for biblical psychology in the only sense in which
it commends itself to candid inquiry. It ought to take
its place among us as throwing light on the doctrinal
statements of revelation—as, in short, a torch-bearer
to biblical theology.

But there is a collateral use which such a study may be hopefully expected to effect. The nature of man is a stronghold of modern Christian apologetic. It always has been, indeed, one of the surest defences of the Christian faith, that Christians were furnished by their religion with the most satisfactory answer the human mind and heart have ever received concerning man's own being. That religion has the supreme claim to be divine which best enables man to meet the Sphinx of nature with a solution to the most puzzling of her riddles—the one of which he is himself the subject. If the Bible can tell us whence and what we are, and whither we are going, there is nothing that will more persuasively and surely convince us that it has light from heaven. We can depend upon its revelation of God, verified and countersigned as that revelation is by its self-attesting witness concerning man. The eye of modern scepticism has discerned the value of this position, and round it much of the battle between faith and unbelief is ranged. The challenge of Positivism, for example, is thoroughly pronounced. Here is one of its recent utterances: "Attention is fully fixed now on the nature and mode of development of the human being; and the key to his mental and moral organization is found. . . . The philosophy of human nature is placed on a scientific basis, and it and all other departments of philosophy are already springing forward so as to be wholly incomparable with those of a thousand years ago. By the verification and spread of the science of human nature . . . there will be an extinction of theology. . . . The worst of the contest is

over, . . . the last of the mythologies (that is, the
Christian faith) is about to vanish before the flood of
a brighter light." [1] The utterance would be amusing,
were it not so sad. It is so stale in its falsity, this
favourite prediction of unbelief that Christianity is on
the point to disappear. But the falsity of the anticipation is equalled by the fallacy of the ground on
which it rests, namely, that man's nature can be explained without spirit, without God, and without the
life to come. We may be very sure that the human
heart will never rest in such an answer to its deepest
inquiries. We may be as sure that whatever tends
to elucidate the Bible answer, to concentrate attention
on its sublime Anthropology, will meet with ever-
increasing assent; for it appeals to the testimony,
simple, universal, and divine, of the soul itself,—to that
which is, in the words of Tertullian, " Testimonium
animæ naturaliter Christianæ."

A book which tells of the origin and nature of man
in a way to satisfy the soul's own witness of its
Maker and of its being; a book which solves the great
riddle of humanity, why the constitution of our nature
is so excellent while its condition is so wretched ; above
all, a book which reveals Jesus Christ, the Man of men,
the God-man, approves itself to be as truly human as
divine—the family-book of the human race, as it is the
utterance of the God and Father of men. But, indeed,
the Person who speaks in it and through it is greater
than the book. Of Him give all its writings witness.
He shines through them all ; and He knew what was
in man. His words throw light over the whole cir-

[1] Harriet Martineau, *Autobiography*, ii. 458 *et seq.*

cumference of human living and dying. His life and
deeds grapple with their sin, and He Himself is the
destroyer of their foes. He invites them to go forward,
with their hand in His, to meet the " shadow feared of
man." " Fear not," He says, " for I am the First and
the Last, and the Living One. And I was dead, and
behold I am alive for evermore, and have the keys of
Hades and of death." From the page of revelation to
Him who is its Subject and its Author we lift our
gaze and cry, "With Thee is the fountain of life; in
Thy light shall we see light ! "

APPENDIX.

NOTES.

APPENDIX.

—◆—

NOTES ON LECTURE I.

NOTE A, PAGE 26.

HOFMANN AND DELITZSCH ON BIBLICAL PSYCHOLOGY.

DELITZSCH in his second edition has quoted and replied to Hofmann's attack on the so-called science which the former so much favours. All that is here given, therefore, will be found substantially in Clark's translation of Delitzsch's *Biblical Psychology*, but in preparing the extracts I have made constant reference to the original of both authors. Hofmann's words are : "A true Biblical Anthropology and Psychology have, it is true, been got together, but without finding any justification in Scripture, of which Harless rightly says that we must not expect from it natural description and natural knowledge, because these were not intended to be given there.[1] That putative science is based merely upon such Scripture texts as do not teach what the nature of man is, but, on the hypothesis that it is understood what kind of creature is meant when man is spoken of, declare his relation or deportment towards God. It is replied that the Scripture does nevertheless give, almost in its first sections, disclosures which are deliberately anthropologic and psychologic, seeing it narrates the process of man's creation. It is further alleged that

[1] So in the preface to the 4th edition of his *Christliche Ethik* ; but the remark seems to be withdrawn in the latest edition.

it must be worth while to bring together its anthropological and psychological presuppositions, since they cannot
be so trivial as to be matter of course, nor so inconsequent
and unconnected as to be capable of no scientific arrangement.
But as regards the disclosures, they only serve the purpose of
rightly defining the relation of man to God and to the world
at large, without the knowledge of which relation there can
undoubtedly be no anthropology and psychology corresponding
to the reality.   As to the presuppositions, it is subject to no
doubt that one may group them together, without, however,
being justified in the expectation that they will form a
scientific whole.   For they only come to light in so far as
they are employed for the expression of facts, which, while
they touch on the anthropologic and psychologic region, themselves belong to another.

   " A Biblical Psychology is just as little a psychological
system as a Biblical Cosmology is a cosmological system.
And if one finds it feasible to call it theological instead of
biblical, it will also be allowable to say that there is a Theological Psychology only in the same sense in which one can
speak of a Theological Cosmogony."—*Der Schriftbeweis*, i. 284,
285, 2te Aufl., 1857.

   To this Delitzsch replies, that he is very far from denying
that all Scripture psychology is bound up with the revelation
of redemption.   What he maintains is, that in pursuance of
its great design of declaring salvation for man, the Bible has
to say so much on man's spiritual and psychical constitution,
that it must proceed upon a psychology distinct from that
of mere natural knowledge.   He retorts upon Harless and
Hofmann that both use largely in their respective treatises
exactly those utterances of Scripture which refer to the most
fundamental questions in psychology.   Hofmann especially,
while asserting that Scripture teaches nothing on the subject,
is constantly attempting to answer from Scripture such psychological questions as—How is man's soul related to his spirit ?
How is the spirit in man related to the Spirit of God ?   Is

man's constitution trichotomic or dichotomic? How is man as a nature distinguished from man as a person?

"Whether, then," he goes on, "we call this teaching or not, Scripture gives us on all these questions at least the explanations necessary for a fundamental knowledge of salvation. These explanations must be exegetically set forth, and because they are of a psychological nature, must be psychologically digested; must be adjusted according to their connection *inter se*, as well as with the living whole formed by the historical and personal facts of redemption.

"And here at once is a system, to wit, a system of Biblical Psychology, as it is fundamental to the system both of the facts of salvation and of the revelation of salvation; and such a system of Biblical Psychology is so necessary a basis for every biblical summary of doctrine, that it may be rightly said of the doctrinal summary which Hofmann's *Schriftbeweis* seeks to verify by Scripture, that from the beginning to the end, from the doctrine of the creation to the doctrine of the last things, a special psychologic system, or (if this expression be objected to) a special complex of psychological primary conceptions, lies at the basis of it. What Scripture says to us of .cosmology might certainly appear insufficient to originate a system of biblical cosmology; but it says infinitely more to us about the spirit and soul of man than about Orion and the Pleiades. And I would not assert that Scripture offers to us no natural knowledge of the soul; I believe it rather to the honour of God's word to be compelled to maintain the contrary. For example, that the constitution of man is dualistic, *i.e.* that spirit and body are fundamentally of distinct origin and nature, that is surely a natural knowledge—a tenet with which, in spite of all the objections of rigid scientific investigation, we live and die. And although such utterances as Scripture gives us to ponder—*c.g.* in Gen. ii. 7 and 1 Cor. xv. 45—may deserve no other name than 'finger-pointings,' yet an investigation in Biblical Psychology which takes the way indicated by these finger-signs will be justified. . . . We desire to bring out exegetically the views of Scripture regarding the nature, the life, and the life-destinies of the soul as these are determined in the history of its salvation. And we also desire, according to the unavoidable exigence imposed upon our thinking when engaged in the region of Scripture, to bring these views into systematic connection. . . .

" The task which I propose to myself is practicable; for under the name of Biblical Psychology I understand a scientific presentation of the doctrine of Scripture on the psychical constitution of man as it was created, and the ways in which this constitution has been affected by sin and redemption. There is such a doctrine of Scripture. It is true that on psychological subjects, just as little as on dogmatical or ethical, does Scripture contain any system of dogmas propounded in the language of the schools. If it taught in such a way, we should have no need at all to construct from it Psychology, and as little Dogmatic or Ethic. But still it does teach. . . . There belongs essentially to the Holy Scripture a quite definite psychology which is equally fundamental to all the sacred writers, and which essentially differs from that multiform system lying outside the circle of revelation. The task of Biblical Psychology, therefore, can be executed as a unity. We have no need first to force the doctrinal matter of the Bible into oneness; it is one of itself. The Biblical Psychology so built up is an independent science which coincides with no other, and is rendered superfluous by no other in the entire organism of theology. It is most nearly related to the so-called Biblical Theology, or rather to Dogmatics. For what is usually designated by the former expression—an extremely unfortunate one—more properly falls in with the history of redemption on the one hand, or the history of revelation on the other. Biblical, or, as one may also call it, Theological Psychology (to distinguish it from the scientific-empirical and philosophic-rational) pervades the entire material of Dogmatics, inasmuch as it discusses all those phases of man's psychical constitution that are conditioned by the facts and relations—

so full of significance in the history of salvation—which form the content of Dogmatic Theology. At all the points of contact, however, it maintains its own special character. For of what is common to it with Dogmatics it only takes cognisance in so far as that common factor throws light or shadow upon the human soul, draws the soul into co-operation or sympathy, and tends to clear up its obscurities. Much which is only incidentally dealt with in Dogmatics is a principal subject for the subsidiary science of Psychology: as, for example, the relation of the soul to the blood, a point of some importance for the doctrine of propitiation, or the question whether the soul is propagated *per traducem*, which is of moment for the doctrine of original sin. On the other hand, the scriptural doctrines of the Trinity, of good and evil angels, of the divine-human personality of Christ, which in Dogmatics are main themes, come to be treated by Psychology only in so far as they are connected with the divine image in man, with the good or evil influence of the spirit-world upon him, and with the restoration of true human nature. The new relation of God to humanity in Christ, which is the centre of our entire theology, is also the centre of Psychology, as of Dogmatics. The business of Dogmatic is to analyze and systematize the believing consciousness of this new relationship—a consciousness which relies upon and rests in the Scripture. The business of Psychology, on the other hand, is with the human soul, and through the soul with that human constitution which is the object and subject of this new relationship.

"From this conception of our science, which we are still convinced will stand the crucible of criticism, we turn to the method of its realization."—Delitzsch, *Biblische Psychologie*, pp. 12–16, 2te Aufl., 1861.

NOTE B, PAGES 22, 31, 34, 36.

THE TWO CREATION-NARRATIVES.

[FOR the character of these narratives the reader may refer to all competent commentators on Genesis. I have found it useful to gather what may be said from very different points of view, by reference to some more special discussions of the subject: *e.g.*, Quarry *On Genesis* (" On the Purport of the Introductory Chapters of the Book of Genesis ; " " On the Use of the Names of God in the Book of Genesis," etc. ; two dissertations, Lond. 1866) ; Macdonald, *Creation and the Fall* (" A Defence and Exposition of the first three Chapters of Genesis," Edin. 1856) ; Ewald's two papers referred to on p. 30 (viz. " Die Schöpfungsgeschichte nach Gen. i. 1–ii. 4," to be found at p. 77 of Ewald's *Erstes Jahrbuch der biblischen Wissenschaft*, 1848 ; then " Die spätere Schöpfungsgeschichte Gen. ii. 5," etc., in *Zweites Jahrbuch* (1849), p. 132. There is also a third paper on the subject of the Creation, entitled, " Die sonst in der Bibel zerstreuten Vorstellungen über die Schöpfungsgeschichte," *Jahrbuch* 1850, p. 108). Numerous references to the subject will also be found in Hofmann's *Schriftbeweis.* I find myself much in accord with the views presented in two papers by Professor James Macgregor in the *British and Foreign Evangelical Review*,—" The Place of Man Theologically Regarded," Jan. 1875 ; " The Christian Doctrine of Creation," Oct. 1878. The first of these papers, especially, I have found suggestive on the whole theme of this lecture.]

I. THE FIRST NARRATIVE AS A COSMOGONIC REVELATION.

It is not uncommonly asserted that this account of the creation of the world was, up till a recent date, taken by all theologians either in a literal sense or as in some way scientific, whereas nearly the reverse of this is the truth ; it is a comparatively modern idea to take this as an account of the formation of the world in six days. It is a still more modern idea to view it as a vision or foretelling of scientific truths. The most ancient Christian interpreters did not take the six days literally. Some of them thought the world was created in an instant of time, and that the six days were expressed as a mode of indicating gradation and order in creation, and as laying a foundation for the observance of the seventh-day rest. We are now in a position to do more justice than these ancient interpreters could to the magnificent general ideas of creation, of its unity, order, progress, and scope, contained in this divine cosmogony; but the true foundation of a right exegesis is to regard it mainly, as they did, from the religious point of view, as an expression of belief in God, in a Creator, and in a plan of Creation, ideas which all belong properly to an inspired system of spiritual truth. It is not necessary to refer to the countless and shifting modes of reading into this chapter the discoveries and often merely the conjectures of science which have prevailed within the last fifty or sixty years. That which has become most favourably known in this country is the theory of Kurz, so luminously and poetically expounded by Hugh Miller. It is based upon the conjecture that " the knowledge of pre-Adamite history, like the knowledge of future ages, may have been communicated to Moses, or perhaps to the first man, in prophetic vision; that so, perhaps, vast geological periods were exhibited to the eye of the inspired writer, each appearing to pass before him on so many successive days." The result aimed at was to establish a correspondence between the discoveries of modern science as to the different geological eras, and the various steps in this sublime passage of Scripture. No one who cares for the subject can fail to be acquainted with the gorgeous prose poem on this theme which the stone-mason of Cromarty evolved out of his scientific knowledge, acted on by a brilliant and devout imagination. A wise and weighty dictum of his own, however, is well worth considering in connection with it : " Were

s

the theologians ever to remember that the Scriptures could not possibly have been given to us as revelations of scientific truth, seeing that a single scientific truth they never yet revealed, and the geologist that it must be in vain to seek in science those truths which lead to salvation [or satisfy the spiritual needs of man], seeing that in science these truths were never yet found, there would be little danger even of difference between them, and none of collision."—*Testimony of the Rocks*, p. 265. This is exactly the principle which it is necessary for us to carry through all our treatment of Scripture. And it is particularly applicable to this narrative, for it is just here that there is a strong temptation to make the Bible appear scientific. That the main purpose of this chapter is religious cannot be doubted. It is meant to teach the unity of God,—a protest against the gods many of the nations; the distinction between God and the world,—a protest against pantheism; the fact of the divine origin of the world,—a protest against atheism, as involved in the notion of the eternity of matter; above all, to show God's relation to man and the relation of man to the world, that the God of revelation and the God of creation are one, and that the God of grace —the Lord Jehovah God, who sealed His mercy to Israel with the special institution of the Sabbath, is the same who made the world in six days and rested on the seventh.

That along with these spiritual ideas concerning God and man there are also given in this chapter certain principles of creation, some great lines of physical and cosmical truth, must not, of course, be overlooked. No one can be satisfied to believe that the writer who conveys here such grand thoughts about the world and its becoming as those of the original uprise of all things,—the chaos of earth's primitive state—the birth of light long before the formation of the sun—the orderly succession of existences, inorganic, vegetable, animal, human,— was left in framing these thoughts to the false and inadequate ideas of nature prevalent in his own time. It is clearly quite otherwise. These grand principles of natural truth coincide so thoroughly with the findings of science, that we are compelled to say, This is inspiration. It is the unity of truth. It is the harmony of the Divine Mind. The light of the same Spirit who framed the world lies on this first page of the great World-Book. This divine light upon God and creation and man's place there is true to the world of fact and nature, and will never, therefore, contradict, but always harmonize with whatever of scientific truth man shall scientifically discover for himself. But it is not science; and we must protest against this creation-narrative being interpreted as an illuminated transcript of scientific discovery in all its details before the time. The incompetence of such a style of exegesis becomes more apparent the more we think of it. Scientific discovery and scientific guess or hypothesis, going hand in hand, are always moving,—the guesses shifting rapidly, like a framework or scaffolding; the discovery creeping slowly on, like a noble building rising solidly tier by tier. But how could a prophecy of such discovery be given beforehand, or how could a view of the world's becoming in its scientific shape be given to those who had no science, or even to those who, like us, have an unfinished and imperfect one? It is all but certain that geological and anthropological theories which at present prevail will change, and those speculative readings of geology into Genesis which have found such favour will be left dry and baseless. No! the real spirit of this world-picture is very different. It is a view of the creation which is to serve for all ages of human history, to fit into every single age's need. Each being an age in which scientific research is only at one of its stages, this sublime view of the divine work of world-making, in order to serve its proper purpose, must deal with great spiritual and cosmical principles, and with these alone.

II. THE TWO NARRATIVES AS AN ACCOUNT OF MAN'S FORMATION.

There can be no doubt that the creation of man is the point of importance and of junction in the two narratives. The partial account given in the second of the origin of plants and animals occasions some difficulty to those who are bent on harmonizing the two. The main difficulties are —(a) the introduction of a vegetable creation along with man ; (b) the apparently subsequent origination of beasts and birds. In both these points the second appears to diverge from the first narrative. One explanation is that which takes the *fauna* and *flora* of the second narrative as those of the present geological era, or of the human period. Those described in the former narrative are, on this hypothesis, held to belong to the past epochs of life on the globe, of which palæontology reads us the record laid up in stone. This belongs, however, to the style of interpretation against which we wish to guard ourselves. Another explanation is, that the former narrative contains the grand principles of the rise of life on the globe ; the latter, the production and grouping of life, vegetable and animal, in the Edenic region, which took place simultaneously with the origination of man. This is certainly the natural impression which the two narratives respectively make on the mind. But, as we have said, the second is not strictly a creation-narrative at all, except as it bears upon the human being.

That man is *terminus ad quem* of creation, is the sum and substance of both narratives. In the words of Hofmann : "Die Schöpfung der Welt ist Schöpfung des Menschen. Die Schöpfungsgeschichte ausgeht in die Schöpfung des Menschen, auf diese abzielt, mit ihr sich abschliesst." The same author thus expands this idea as expressing the whole Bible view of the earth, with its works and its changes : " Dass die Erde, als sie nun das Feld der menschlichen Thätigkeit ward, in Folge der Sünde des Menschen eine Stätte des Fluchs geworden ist, wo

Dorn und Distel wächst; dass die Entartung der Menschheit aus dem Himmel droben den Strom der Regenfluth, aus der Tiefe drunten die verschlossenen Wasser gerufen, und so eine Wandelung der Welt, Himmels und der Erde, herbeigeführt hat; dass Kanaan um der Gemeinde Gottes willen eine Stätte des Segens werden soll, wo Friede wohnt, und dass das Gericht Gottes über die Feinde derselben Himmel und Erde verzehren wird; dass der Mensch Christus Jesus über alles Geschaffene erhöht ist, und seine Gemeinde einer neuen Welt Himmels und der Erde wartet—alles dies dient zur Bestätigung jener in dem Schöpfungs-berichte ausgesagten Thatsache."—*Schriftb.* i. 283.

Keeping in view this substantial harmony, let us, however, look at the two narratives in the distinct features which characterize respectively their account of the origin of man.

(1.) *Peculiarities of the First Account of Man's Creation.*

Let us first note just what we find on the face of the narrative, Gen. i. 26–30.

a. The creation of man is here very particularly defined as a distinct section in the narrative, by the fact of its being set down, not as a distinct day's work, but as following a completed creative act, that of the land animals (in three divisions), with its appended sentence marking a stage—"God saw that it was good" (ver. 25).

b. This act, however, stands in line with the other creative acts, and especially with the creation of all other living beings, by three marks—(1) That it takes place on the same day as that of the land animals; (2) that it comes last in the whole series of the creation; (3) that man's relation to the other creatures is expressly defined as that of their climax, crown, and superior.

c. It stands out of or above the line of the other creative acts by these features—(1) The solemn and formal resolution of the Creator to create man. (2) The discovery of "the inseparable and eternal plurality of Godhead "[1] in connection with this act: "Let *us* make man in *our* image." (3) The directness of creative act expressed over against the mediate creation word for the lower animals: "Let the waters bring forth," etc.; "Let the earth bring forth," etc. (vers. 20, 24). (4) The express declaration of an image or model for man's creation, in contrast to the terms, "after their kind," "after his kind," used of all the lower animals. These were made each after a type or model devised in the divine mind, and apparently perpetuated. Man is made not after the animal type, not after any of these already created types, not even after one of his own, but in the image of God.

The remaining statements of the chapter do not directly affect the account here given of man's origin, but have their interest as bearing upon his original state. They are as follows:—

d. The creative act is emphasized by its repetition three times in ver. 27, over and above the formal and solemn resolution to create of ver. 26. The creation in the divine image is also repeated and emphasized. The creation of woman is put alongside that of man in this narrative as both of direct divine formation and in the divine image; though the expression, "male and female created He them," may be explained as a generic description in keeping with the whole character of this first narrative—where, it is true, there is as yet no mention of *Issha*, the woman, but the term *Adam* is used to include both sexes. "The race" (so we might paraphrase it) "was created by God male and female."

e. The "blessing" of God pronounced over them is not peculiar, for a similar blessing, accompanied with a fiat of propagation and production, is pronounced over the winged and finny tribes in ver. 22. The distinction here is, that the words describing fertility and fecundity are in ver. 22 spoken by God as concerning the creatures; but here (ver. 28) are spoken to mankind.

f. The gift or office of dominion over the earth and all the

[1] Luther.

creatures is expressly conveyed to man by God in connection with this blessing. The fact of the subordination of all living creatures to man is stated in this form of a donation or charter, as it is also evidently grounded upon the divine image in man (ver. 28).

g. The grant to man for food of the seed-bearing herbs and the fruit-bearing trees, and the grant to the beasts and birds of the "green herbs" for meat, closes the description of the creation and placing of man as here given (vers. 29, 30).

Clearly, however, the great features of this first description are the solemn and formal preparation for man's introduction, and his creation after the divine image. Here the scriptural view of man's origin and of his nature is seen to be homogeneous. Every view of these two things must follow the law of consistency. And this view is clear and consistent. Man is an animal among the animals, breathes the breath of life as they do, yet is represented as occupying a different position from that of all the other creatures, not only in relation to them, as supreme over them, but in relation to God his Maker. With all this the account of his special creation coincides.

(2.) *Additional Particulars of Man's Formation supplied by the Second Narrative.*

We have spoken in the text of the relation between the two accounts as bearing on man. Their full coincidence is accompanied by characteristic differences. The first was the generic account of man's creation, the second is the production of the actual man. Accordingly, we find here, instead of the verb בָּרָא, "to create," so prominent in the earlier narrative, the word יָצַר, "to form" or "knead." And again, in connection with the detailed account of the formation of Eve, another verb still, viz. בָּנָה, "to build," is employed.

The additional facts brought out by the second narrative are these :—

a. The formation of man's body from the dust of the ground.

This makes much more emphatic than the former narrative man's place in the line of the animal creation. And with this agree those other passages which speak of him as " dust " (עָפָר, Gen. iii. 19 ; Eccles. iii. 20, xii. 7) and " clay " (חֹמֶר, Job xxxiii. 6), and as " of the earth earthy," ἐκ γῆς χοϊκός (1 Cor. xv. 47). On the other hand, עָפָר may be held to denote not *de limo terræ*, not a solid mass, a clod of the earth, but the finest part of earth's material. Thus, also, both אֲדָמָה and חֹמֶר are special in their meaning, " red earth," " virgin soil," " potter's clay." Here, then, we have in popular phraseology substantially what the nomenclature of science expresses with regard to the human frame: " It is well known that the animal body is composed, in the inscrutable manner called *organization*, of carbon, hydrogen, oxygen, nitrogen, lime, iron, sulphur, and phosphorus, substances which in their various combinations form a large part of the solid ground." —Macdonald, *Creation and Fall*, p. 326.

Considerable difference of opinion prevails as to the etymology of the name Adam. The common etymology of Kimchi, Rosenmüller, and others, deriving it from *adamah*, " the ground," looks natural and reasonable. The objection to it is that it seems to derive a root from its derivative, or at least a simpler form of a word from another and less simple form of the same word. Accordingly, Gesenius, Tuch, Hupfeld derive both words from the root אָדַם, " to be red or ruddy." Josephus interprets the name *Adam* as having reference to *red* earth, that is, virgin and true earth. Heard (*Tripartite Nature of Man*, p. 41) apparently mis-states Josephus when he refers to him the interpretation of *Adam* as derived from the red colour of the skin. He gives other derivations, as from דְּמוּת, shortened into דָּם, with reference to Gen. i. 26 ; or from דָּם, " blood." Meier and Fürst propose an Arabic root = " to hold together." Keil thinks the derivation of Adam from *adamah* may be paralleled by that of *homo* from *humus*, or from χαμά, χαμαί. *Man* and *Mensch*, he thinks, on the other hand, may be connected with a Sanscrit word equivalent in meaning to *mens,* " the mind" (*Comm. in loc.*). Macdonald (*Creation and Fall,* p. 329) mentions, but only to discountenance, the curious conjecture that it has a connection with *red* as denoting a particular race. He says there is "no evidence whatever" for such a conclusion. But Sir H. Rawlinson has already pointed out that the Babylonians recognised two principal races—the *Adamu* or dark race, and the *Sarku* or light race. And George Smith, in his most recent book (*Chaldean Account of Genesis,* Lond. 1876), reads the tablets on "Man's First State and Fall" as referring to the Zalmat-quqadi or "dark race," and says that in various other fragments of these legends they are called *Admi* or *Adami*.

The article *Adam u. seine Söhne* in Herzog has these remarks : "Der Name Adam (אָדָם, LXX. 'Αδάμ, Lat. *Adamus,* oder *Adam, Adœ*) wird gewöhnlich irrig von אֲדָמָה, Erde, das Einfachere aus dem Entwickelteren in der Form abgeleitet, oder formell richtiger von דָּם, Blut, und אָדַם, roth sehn, im Sinne der Schönheit des röthlich glänzenden Menschen als des Unterschieds zwischen einer weissen (rothen) und schwarzen Urrace der Menschen. (Josephi *Antiq.* 2. 1. Targum Jonathan *zu Genes.* ii. 7. Leusden, *Onomasticum Sacr.,* s. v. 'Adam'; Marck, *Historia Paradisi,* ii. 5 ; Gesenius, Wörterbuch, u. d. W.) Sir William Jones will sogar von dem Sanscr. *Adim* = Erster ableiten. Richtiger gewiss von dem alten Zeitwort אָדַם feststampfen, festfugen, woher auch אֲדָמָה (Fürst, *Hand-wörterbuch,* u. d. W.)."

Delitzsch holds that although the name *Adam* is derived from the *adamah,* and hence denominates man from his lower nature, yet this arises from the fact that it is man's distinction among all creatures, his characteristic dignity, that he, the earthly one, can bear the image of God. This it is which constitutes him the point of union of two worlds, the spiritual and the corporeal,—the *centre, copula,* or *focus* of all created being, just as Ps. viii. declares that he bears his likeness of God in an earthen vessel. Hence the importance of man's body in relation to this topic of the divine image. It is not that his body is a part of the likeness, but that his embodied condition lends its peculiar force to the fact that he bears it, though the image itself which he bears consists primarily in his invisible nature. This is substantially the idea expressed by Theodorus, that man is the link which was formed to bind together the whole creation, σύνδεσμον ἁπάντων τὸν ἄνθρωπον κατεσκευάσεν.

b. The other detail which adds to our information from the former narrative is, that the Lord God breathed into the nostrils of the form so moulded from dust "the breath of life or lives," and "man became a living soul," or "an animated being." Here also we have man described as in the line of the other living creatures. For although the "breath" with which he is endued is expressed by a word (נִשְׁמָה) which does often signify the human spirit, yet it is sometimes used both of men and animals (e.g. Gen. vii. 22); and the expression "living soul" (נֶפֶשׁ חַיָּה) has been used in the first narrative (Gen. i. 30) of the lower animals. For these reasons we cannot with confidence build the distinction between man and the other animals in their creation on the use of neshamah, which is sometimes groundlessly asserted to be the specific designation of the human soul-life (see Beck, Umriss der biblischen Seelenlehre, p. 7, note), or to be "invariably applied to God or man, never to any irrational creature" (Murphy, Critical and Exegetical Comm. on the Book of Genesis, p. 92). Neither can we base it on the formation of man's body by the Lord God Himself, for the same phrase that He "formed" them out of the ground is said of the beasts (Gen. ii. 19) and the fowls. Yet, though we may not place the distinction in the act of formation from the dust, nor in the animating principle man possesses, we are entitled to base it on the divine act of inbreathing into his nostrils. That this point, moreover, was deemed of the utmost moment by the other Scripture writers, may be seen by such expressions as those of—

Job xxxii. 8, where נִשְׁמַת שַׁדַּי is said to give man understanding;

Job xxxiii. 4, where the רוּחַ־אֵל has made (עָשָׂה) him, and the נִשְׁמַת שַׁדַּי has given him *life;*

Job xxvii. 3, where life is described as the continuance of the רוּחַ אֱלוֹהַּ in his nostrils;

Isa. xlii. 5, where God is described as the Giver (נֹתֵן) of breath (נְשָׁמָה) and spirit (רוּחַ) } to the people of earth.

We may fairly enough interpret it (with Delitzsch) as meaning "that it is not merely the general life principle imparted to the world which individualizes itself in man, but that God breathes directly into the nostrils of man the fulness of His personality, . . . that in a manner corresponding to the personality of God, man may become a living soul." We may justly infer that "it was the foundation of the preeminence of man, of his likeness to God, of his immortality: for by this he was formed into a personal being, whose immaterial part was not merely soul, but a soul breathed entirely by God " (Keil, *in loc.*).

We may conclude, then, that on the one side this second narrative presents man's formation as the prime thing of the earth, that even on the lowest side of his nature it was earth's highest excitation. It may even be held as suggesting that the human physical was connected with the previous nature or natures, and was brought out of them; that is, it was made from the earth in the widest sense of the term (see Tayler Lewis' note at p. 211 of Lange *On Genesis*). On the other side, the communication of life to man is described as a peculiar and distinct act of God. The superiority and distinction in his origin thus indicated no doubt corresponds to that point in the former narrative where man's creation in the divine image was signalized.

It is interesting to find that Lord Bacon directs attention to the emphasis laid by this narrative on the immediate production of man's soul, as contrasted with the mediate production of the life of the lower animals indicated in the former narrative. He grounds upon the distinction a peculiar view of man as possessed of two souls [of which see further in

Note G of this Appendix]; but the remark is of moment in exegesis of our passage. "We have noted," he says, "those two different emanations of souls which in the first creation of them both offer themselves unto our view—that is, that one hath its original from the breath of God, the other from the matrices of the elements; for of the primitive emanation of the rational soul, thus speaks the Scripture: *Deus formavit hominem de limo terræ et spiravit in faciem ejus spiraculum vitæ.* But the generation of the unreasonable soul or of beasts was accomplished by these words: *Producat aqua, Producat terra.* And this irrational soul, as it is in man, is the instrument only to the reasonable soul, and hath the same original in us that it hath in beasts, namely, from the slime of the earth; for it is not said, *God formed the body of man of the slime of the earth,* but, *God formed man*—that is, the whole man, that *spiraculum* excepted."—*De Augmentis,* lib. iv. c. iii. § 1; English version by G. Watts, Oxford, 1640.

NOTE C, PAGES 37, 43.

RECENT SCIENTIFIC MODIFICATIONS OF THE EVOLUTION THEORY.

IMPORTANT divergences among those who have pursued the methods of study stimulated by the great evolution hypothesis deserve attention. M. Naudin, an eminent French botanist, owned by Darwin himself as one of his precursors, who, before the English naturalist, compared the action exercised by the natural forces in the production of species to the methods used by man in obtaining races, now proposes an evolution theory which entirely excludes the hypothesis of natural selection, and rejects the idea of gradual transmutations. He substitutes the doctrine of abrupt transformism. According to this view, "when species vary they do so in virtue of an intrinsic and innate property, which is only a remains of the primordial plasticity." He insists upon the suddenness with which most of the variations observed in planets have been produced, and regards it as a representation of what must have taken place in the successive genesis of living beings. It is obvious that in his theory of a "primordial plasticity" or "evolutive force" inherent in organisms, M. Naudin has taken up a position entirely distinct from that of Darwinism. It is a position clearly not inconsistent with Theism, with Creationism, nor even with the acceptation of the early chapters of Genesis. In his view, the Mosaic account of man's origin is full of instruction. How he proposes to read it is briefly stated in *The Human Species*, by A. De Quatrefages, p. 124 (International Scientific Series, vol. xxvi.), where a *resumé* of the theories of M. Naudin will be found.

It is well known, also, that A. R. Wallace, who may be called one of the founders of Darwinism, has entirely diverged from the doctrine of natural selection in the case of man. This great traveller and naturalist, reasoning from the observations he has made upon many savage tribes, declares that natural selection by itself is incapable of producing from an anthropoid animal a man, such even as we find in the most savage nations known to us. Proceeding on the principle that natural selection must be determined by immediate utility, he argues that it is perfectly certain that natural selection could not have produced the present appearance of the human skin, or the development of the moral sense as it now exists even in many savages. While, therefore, holding that natural selection is capable of accounting for the rise of all inferior races, and even of a race having almost all the physical characters of man as he is now, this author is constrained to hold that an unknown cause, or the intervention of a superior intelligence, is necessary to the production of the human species. Whether we fix our attention on the confession thus made, by one of its original propounders, of the insufficiency of the Darwinian theory of the origin of species to account for the origin of man, or whether we regard it as, on the part of its author, an unintentional confession of the failure of the theory of natural selection to account for the rise of species in general, the position now announced by Mr. Wallace is worthy of special notice.

Besides these and many other divergences among evolutionists themselves, those who desire to form a complete judgment regarding the present state of the question will do well to consider the objections offered by a large body of competent scientific inquirers to the whole theory of gradual transformism, as well as to its application to the human race. Among these objections are—(1) the purely hypothetical character of the theory ; (2) more particularly, the absence of any positive instances of the production of species in this way ; and (3) that the age of the earth is not such as to allow of the enormous lapse of time demanded for the origination of species by insensible modifications.

(1.) *The Hypothetical Character of the Evolution Theory forbids its being received as Science.*

The conference of the Association of German Naturalists and Physicians at Munich, in September 1877, was rendered memorable by a weighty protest, uttered in the name of science, against the dogmatism of the extreme evolutionists. The demand made by Professor Haeckel of Jena (well known in this country by his books, written in the extremest form of Darwinism), that the *Descendenztheorie* should be taught under public sanction as an established fact of science, brought out the answer of Dr. Virchow, delivered to the assembled *savants*. As it exists only in pamphlet form, a few of its pungent sentences may be cited. It is entitled, *Die Freiheit der Wissenschaft im modernen Staat* (" The Freedom of Science in the Modern State ;" authorized Eng. transl., London, John Murray, 1878).

In his preface written for the English translation of his paper, Dr. Virchow says :

" It seemed to him high time to utter an energetic protest against the attempts that are made to proclaim the problems of research as actual facts, the opinions of scientists as established science, and thereby to set in a false light, before the eyes of the less informed masses, not merely the methods of science, but also its whole position in regard to the intellectual life of men and nations. With a few individual exceptions, this protest has met with cordial assent from German naturalists. They feel themselves set free again from the tyranny of dogmatism. They have regained the certainty that, in natural science as in all else, real work, if it produces only isolated results, is a better security for the durability of progress than the most ingenious speculation. Let us hope that men of science in England also will not fail to examine this most serious question, whether the authority of science will not be better secured if it confines itself strictly to its own province, than if it undertakes to master the whole view of nature by the premature generalizing of theoretical combinations."

In the address itself he thus enforces the same topic :—

" We must not forget that there is a line of demarcation between the speculative province of science and the domain which she has actually won and fully settled. What is required of us is, that this boundary shall be marked with continually greater precision ; not only occasionally, but that in general it shall be so far fixed that every individual shall be more and more conscious where the boundary lies, and how far he can demand of others the admission that what he teaches is the truth. This, gentlemen, is the task at which we have to work *among ourselves.* . . . When Dr. Haeckel says that it is a question for the educators, whether the theory of evolution (*die Descendenztheorie*) should be at once laid down as the basis of instruction, and the protoplastic soul (*die Plastidul-seele*) be assumed as the foundation of all ideas concerning spiritual being,—whether the teacher is to trace back the origin of the human race to the lowest classes of the organic kingdom, nay, still further, to spontaneous generation,—this is, in my opinion, an inversion of the questions at issue. If the evolution theory is as certain as Dr. Haeckel assumes it to be, then we must demand, then it is a necessary claim, that it should be introduced into our schools. How could it be conceivable that a doctrine of such moment, which lays hold of every one's mind as a complete revolutionary force, the direct result of which is to form a new religion,[1] should not be imported in its completeness into the scheme of our schools ? ...

"It is easy to say that 'a cell consists of small portions, and these we call *plastidules;* and that plastidules are composed of carbon, hydrogen, oxygen, and nitrogen, and are endowed with a special soul, which soul is the product or sum of the forces which the chemical atoms possess.' To be sure, this is possible. I cannot form an exact judgment about it. It is one of the positions which are for me still unapproachable. I feel like a sailor who puts forth into an abyss, the extent of which he cannot see. But I must plainly say that, so long as no one can define for me the properties of carbon, hydrogen, oxygen, and nitrogen, in such a way that I can conceive how from the sum of them a soul arises, so long am I unable to admit that we should be at all justified in importing the 'plastidulic soul' into the course of our education, or in requiring every educated man to receive it as scientific truth, so as to argue from it as a logical premiss, and to found his whole view of the world upon it. This we really cannot demand. On the contrary, I am of opinion that, before we designate such hypotheses as the voice of science,—before we say, 'This is modern science,'—we should first have to conduct a long series of elaborate investigations. *We must therefore say to the teachers in schools, 'Do not teach it.'*"

As Virchow meets Haeckel, so does M. A. De Quatrefages in his latest work meet Darwin himself. That purely hypothetical character of the theory which forbids its being taught

[1] "Die unmittelbar eine Act von neuer Religion schafft."

as science, also forbids its being received as a sufficient
account of the rise of species.   The veteran French naturalist
writes thus :—

"In the last editions of *The Origin of Species*, Darwin refuses
to admit that fertility among mongrels is general, taking his
stand upon our *ignorance* on the subject of crossings between
wild *varieties (races)*.   Thus, in order to admit the physiological transmutation of race into species, a fact which is contrary to all positive facts, Darwin and his followers reject the
secular results of experience and observation, and substitute
in their place a *possible accident*, and the *unknown*.   The
Darwinian theory relies entirely upon the possibility of this
transmutation.   We see upon what data the hypothesis of
this possibility rests.   Now, in a *truly liberal spirit*, I ask
every *unprejudiced* man, however little he may be conversant
with science, the question, Is it upon such foundations that
a general theory in physics or chemistry would be founded ?

"Moreover, the argument, of which we have just seen an
example, may be found in every page of Darwinian writings.
Whether a fundamental question, such as we have just been
examining, or a minor problem, as the transmutation of the
tomtit into the nuthatch, is under discussion, *possibility*,
chance, and *personal conviction* are invariably adduced as con-
vincing reasons.   Is modern science established upon such
foundations ?   Darwin and his disciples wish that even our
ignorance on the subject of certain phenomena should be
considered as in their favour.   The question has often been
argued on the ground of palæontology, and they have been
asked to point out a single instance of those series which
ought, according to them, to unite the parent species with its
derivatives.   They admit their inability; but they reply
that the extinct *fauna* and *flora* have left very few remains ;
that we only know a small part of these ancient archives ;
that the facts which favour their doctrine are doubtless buried
under the waves with submerged continents, etc.   'This
manner of treating the question,' Darwin concludes, 'dimin-

T

ishes the difficulties considerably ; it does not cause them to disappear entirely.'   But I again ask this question, In what branch of human knowledge, except these obscure subjects, should we regard problems as solved, for the very reason that we possess none of the requisite knowledge for their solution ?

"I do not intend to reproduce here the entire examination which I have made elsewhere of the transmutation theories in general, or of Darwinism in particular.   The above observations will suffice, I hope, to show why I could not accept even the most seductive of these theories.   In certain points they agree with certain general facts, and give an explanation of a certain number of phenomena.   But all without exception attain this result only by the aid of hypotheses which are in flagrant contradiction with other general facts, quite as fundamental as those which they explain.   In particular, all these doctrines are based upon a gradual and progressive derivation, upon the confusion of race and species. Consequently, they ignore an unquestionable physiological fact ; they are entirely in opposition with another fact, which follows from the first, and is conspicuous from every point of view—the isolation, namely, of specific groups from the earliest ages of the world, and the maintenance of organic order through all the revolutions of the globe.

"Such are my reasons for refusing my adherence to Darwin's theories."—*The Human Species,* pp. 100–102, Lond. 1879.

(2.) *Scientific Objections to the Theory from the Absence of Necessary Links.*

This weak point of the Darwinian theory in its application even to physical man is exposed by Virchow in the field of pre-historic evidence ; by other writers, on structural and physiological grounds.   Virchow, in the paper above referred to, thus deals with the lack of evidence in the past for man's connection with the lower animals :—

" There are at this time few students of nature who are not
of opinion that man stands in some connection with the rest
of the animal kingdom, and that such a connection may
possibly be discovered, if not with the apes, yet perhaps, as
Dr. Vogt now supposes, at some other point. I freely acknowledge that this is a desideratum in science. I am quite
prepared for such a result, and I should neither be surprised
nor astonished if the proof were produced that man had
ancestors among other vertebrate animals. You are aware
that I am now specially engaged in the study of Anthropology,
but I am bound to declare that every positive advance which
we have made in the province of pre-historic Anthropology
has actually removed us farther from the proof of such a connection. . . . On the whole, we must really acknowledge that
there is a complete absence of any fossil type of a lower stage
in the development of man.   Nay, if we gather together the
whole sum of the fossil men hitherto known, and put them
parallel with those of the present time, we can decidedly
pronounce that there are among living men a much greater
number of individuals who show a relatively inferior type
than there are among the fossils known up to this time.
Whether it is just the highest geniuses of the quaternary
period that have had the good luck to be preserved to us, I
will not venture to surmise !   Our usual course is to argue
from the character of a single fossil object to the generality of
those not yet found. This, however, I will not do. I will
not affirm that the whole race was as good as the few skulls
that have survived.   But one thing I must say, that not a
single fossil skull of an ape or of an ' ape-man ' has yet been
found that could really have belonged to a human being.
. . . As matter of fact, we must positively recognise that
there still exists as yet a sharp line of demarcation between
man and the ape.   We cannot teach, we cannot pronounce it
to be a conquest of science, that man descends from the ape
or from any other animal.   We can only indicate it as an
hypothesis, however probable it may seem, and however

obvious a solution it may appear (Wir können das nur als
ein Problem bezeichnen, es mag noch so wahrscheinlich
erscheinen und noch so nahe liegen)."—*Die Freiheit der
Wissenschaft*, pp. 29, 31.

M. de Quatrefages urges the same objection from considerations of structure :—

" Although the distance between anthropomorphous apes
and man appears to be but small to Haeckel, he has nevertheless thought it necessary to admit the existence of an
intermediate stage between ourselves and the most highly
developed ape. This purely hypothetical being, of which not
the slightest vestige has been found, is supposed to be detached
from the tailless catarrhine apes, and to constitute the twenty-
first stage of the modification which has led to the human
form. Haeckel calls it the *ape-man*, or the *pithecoid-man*.
He denies him the gift of articulate speech, as well as the
development of the intelligence and self - consciousness."
Again he says : " Two beings belonging to two distinct types
can be referred to a common ancestor, whose characters were
not clearly developed, but the one cannot be the descendant
of the other. ... The consequence of these facts, from the
point of view of the logical application of the law of *permanent characterisation*, is that man cannot be descended from
an ancestor who is already characterised as an ape. . . . A
walking animal cannot be descended from a *climbing one.*
This was clearly understood by Vogt. In placing man among
the *primates*, he declares, without hesitation, that the lowest
class of apes have passed the landmark (the common ancestor)
from which the different types of this family have originated
and diverged. . . . Thus, since it has been proved that, according to Darwinism itself, the origin of man must be placed
beyond the eighteenth stage, and since it becomes in consequence necessary to fill up the gap between marsupials
and man, will Haeckel admit the existence of *four unknown
intermediate groups*, instead of one ? Will he complete his
genealogy in this manner ? It is not for me to answer."

M. de Quatrefages further quotes results in various branches of anatomical research adverse to the simian genealogy of man, even upon Darwinian principles :—

" M. Pruner Bey, resuming the descriptive and anatomical works which have been carried on till within the last few years, has shown that the comparison of man with the anthropomorphous apes brings to light a fact which is subject to very few exceptions—the existence, namely, of an inverse order in the development of the principal organs. The researches of Welker upon the sphenoïdal angle of Virchow lead to the same conclusion; for in man the angle diminishes from the time of birth, whilst in the ape it is always increasing, so much so that sometimes it is effaced. It is upon the base of the cranium that the German anatomist has remarked this inverse order, the importance of which cannot escape notice.

" A similar contrast has been remarked by Gratiolet upon the brain itself. The following are his observations upon this subject. In the ape, the temporal sphenoïdal convolutions which form the middle lobe, make their appearance and are completed before the anterior convolutions which form the frontal lobe. In man, on the contrary, the frontal convolutions are the first to appear, and those of the middle lobe are found later.

" It is evident, especially after the most fundamental principles of Darwinism, that an organized being cannot be a descendant of another whose development is in an inverse order to its own. Consequently, in accordance with these principles, man cannot be considered as the descendant of any simian type whatever."—*The Human Species*, pp. 105-111.

(3.) *The Time Difficulty.*

This scientific objection to the theory of gradual transformism, as an account of the origin of the various orders of life on the globe, is heard from various quarters. " ' According to the most recent calculations,' says M. Naudin, ' the *maximum* duration of animal life upon our globe can be approximately estimated at about fifty millions of years at the very most, and the farther progress of science will never raise this estimate, but on the contrary will tend to restrict it.' Now fifty millions of years may seem a very good figure; but in reality it is absolutely insufficient to explain the production of all the organic forms, if we suppose them produced by insensible modifications. Not millions of years, but thousands of millions of ages would be required."—Janet, *Final Causes*, p. 293 (Edin. 1878).

W. Carruthers, F.R.S., of the British Museum, in a paper on *The Testimony of Fossil Botany in reference to the Doctrine of Evolution*, along with other considerations, such as " the sudden and simultaneous appearance of the most highly organized plants at particular stages in the past history of the globe, and the entire absence among fossil plants of any forms intermediate between existing classes or families," alludes to the serious difficulty created by the demand upon time : " The single species *Salix polaris* carries us back beyond the glacial period. Several specific forms existed, as we have seen, during the cretaceous epoch. Beyond this we want geological periods, which are the geologists' time-divisions, to carry back by slow and imperceptible changes the cretaceous *salices* and the rich associated flora of still existing generic types to the generalized angiosperm, and on to the gymnosperm. The whole evidence supplied by fossil plants is, then, opposed to the hypothesis of genetic evolution."

But it is by scientific men, working in a totally different region from that of the naturalist and physiologist, that this limit to the scope of the evolution hypothesis has been most sharply drawn. Evolutionists, borrowing the assumption of current geology, construct their theory on the supposition that they have almost unlimited time in the earth's past to draw upon, even since the first appearance of life upon the globe. Considerations derived from the secular cooling of the earth, the appreciable retardation of her daily rotation, and the constant dissipation of energy within the physical universe, go to prove that a period comparatively moderate must be fixed for the duration of the whole solar system. Considerably within this, of course, must be the period when life could have been possible on earth. What havoc these considerations will work on the requirements of the Darwinian hypothesis may be seen by consulting what has been written on the subject by Sir W. Thomson, Professor Tait, and others. An amusing and instructive summary will be found in the *Quarterly Review* for July 1876, in an article headed, " Modern Philosophers on the Probable Age of the World."

Such facts and citations in the history of the Evolution theory are open to all readers. It is not for us to pronounce upon the correctness of conflicting scientific opinions. It is for scientific men to settle these questions among themselves. But the lesson for the interpreter of Scripture from such variations in science is plain. For him to hasten to propound schemes of conciliation, of mutual interpretation between the Mosaic account of the rise of the animated world, and the Darwinian or Haeckelian pedigree of the lower animals and man, would be to repeat an old and now unpardonable blunder. There is, as we have said in the text, a sense in which the general principle of Evolution is at variance neither with Theism nor with Scripture. In that sense the Mosaic record and the wisest Christian philosophy may be said to pave the way for its reception. But the opinions above quoted, and they are specimens of a much larger number, suggest that we are probably on the eve of still more important modifications in the form of the Evolution hypothesis. No hypothesis framed with a strict and true scientific purpose should be met with theological anathemas. On the other hand, science itself will in time avenge religion by the sure demolition of all propounded hypotheses of which the motive has been anti-theological. There is no abiding place in science for constructions, the

preponderating aim of which has been the abolition of God
rather than the investigation of nature.

The allusion on p. 43 is to the mode of constructing primitive man adopted by H. Spencer, Sir J. Lubbock, and similar
writers. The following trenchant remarks upon that method
I take from Dr. A. M. Fairbairn's *Studies in the Philosophy of
Religion and History*, Lond. 1876 :—

" Existing peoples, savage as little as civilised, can be used
as types or models of primitive. Mr. Herbert Spencer's primitive man, physical, emotional, intellectual, is a purely
imaginary being. He is built up by an inductive, but built
upon a deductive process. His deduction is by no means
unassailable either as to principles or method, but we are not
concerned with it meanwhile, only with the induction. And
how does it proceed ? Whence come the facts inducted ?
Mr. Spencer says : ' We must be content to fill out our general
conception of primitive man, so far as we may, by studying
those existing races of men, which, as judged by their physical
characters and their implements, approach most nearly to
primitive man.' And as these races present him with a most
bewildering multitude of differences, he has to select from
these the features he considers primitive. And what is the
principle of selection ? ' To conceive the primitive man as
he existed when social aggregation commenced, we must
generalize as well as we can this entangled and partially conflicting evidence (of the differences between the various
savage races) ; led mainly by the traits common to the very
lowest, and finding what guidance we may in the *à priori*
conclusions set down above.'

" Now, the method is bad, most unscientific, and the principle of selection is worse. The savage races are as old as
the civilised, as distant, therefore, from primitive man.
Change, too, has been as busy in them as in us—perhaps
busier. Their customs are less persistent, their memories
shorter, their past far less extended and powerful. The most
distinctive features of the primitive man are exactly those

least discoverable in the savage. His energy, his resolution, his inventiveness, his capacity for progress and discovery. The implements may be the same, but the skill is not. The physical characters may be alike, but what of the mental? If alike, how does the savage after so many ages happen to be savage, while we are civilised? Then why select the traits common to the very lowest as the most primitive? Do the inferior members of a species best preserve the features of the primitive type? Does palæontology 'fill out its conception' of an extinct plant or animal by combining the traits common to the members of the lowest and most degenerate species within the genus to which it belonged? Palæontology is one thing; zoology or botany another. If the development of life on the earth is to be studied, it must be through the once living forms preserved in its successive strata, not through the lowest and most degenerate forms of vegetable and animal life now on its surface. So, if the growth of mind and the progress of man are to be understood, it must be by the method of palæontology—the comparative study of the peoples in the past who have made our present" (pp. 251, 252).

NOTE D (CLOSE OF LECTURE FIRST).

UNITY AND ANTIQUITY OF THE HUMAN RACE.

I HAD meant to incorporate with Lecture First some remarks on the relation to Scripture teaching of the most recent scientific theories on the unity and antiquity of man. But after a considerable amount of miscellaneous reading, the attempt was abandoned, on the ground of a general principle stated in the preceding Note. The time has not come when any adjustment can be profitably attempted between the rapidly-shifting theories of science on these subjects, and the account of primitive mankind given in the Bible.

In regard to the UNITY of the race, the case at present as between science and theology is comparatively one of agreement. The scriptural position, as commonly understood, is that of the derivation of all men from a single pair,—a position which, as Hase pithily puts it (*Hutterus Redivivus*, p. 157), is probable according to nature's law of parsimony, is reconcileable with the diversity of races, is important for the recognition of the equality and brotherhood of all men, and is theologically all but essential to the conception of original sin (see the allusion in Lecture IV. at p. 149). When looked at from the side of scientific and historic inquiry, it may be regarded as a double question,—one either of unity of the human species, or community of origin for the human race. These two are not absolutely identical. But those who, like Agassiz, contend that men are not all of one stock, generally hold that the diversities of race are equal to different species; whereas those who admit men to be all of one species make no stand against community of origin, though it is, of course, conceivable that men might be of one species and yet have a few different centres of origin. Even this, were it scientifically established, could hardly be said to invalidate the Scripture view that God hath made of one blood all nations of men.

It is well known, however, that the whole current of scientific opinion at present runs in favour of community of origin for the race. Besides the speculative reasons which lead almost all evolutionists to favour this view, the more strictly scientific labours of comparative philology tend strongly in this direction. "The comparative study of languages shows us that races now separated by vast tracts of land are allied together and have migrated from one common primitive seat. The largest field for such investigations presents itself in the long chain of Indo-Germanic languages, extending from the Ganges to the Iberian extremity of Europe, and from Sicily to the

North Cape " (Alex. v. Humboldt, *Cosmos*, ii. 471, 472, Otte's Transl.). " The evidence of language is irrefragable, and it is the only evidence worth listening to with regard to pre-historic periods. There is not an English jury now-a-days, which, after examining the hoary documents of language, would reject the claim of a common descent and a legitimate relationship between Hindu, Greek, and Teuton " (Max Müller, quoted in Cabell's *Unity of Mankind*, pp. 228, 229). From the side of physiology, such writers as M. de Quatrefages are equally clear and definite. The leading naturalists, Linnæus, Buffon, Lamarck, Cuvier, Geoffrey, Humboldt, Müller, arrive at the conclusion that all men belong to the same species, and that there is but one species of man.

While there is thus a returning consent of science to the opinion that the human race is one, and has a common origin, coinciding so far with the usual theological position, it must be remembered that this reappearance in scientific circles of the conception of human unity is accompanied with a tendency to expand enormously the conception of the period during which man has occupied the earth.

The ANTIQUITY of man is a question at present regarded as the special property of the recent science of pre-historic archæology. Forty years have scarcely elapsed since scientific men began to attribute to the human race an antiquity more remote than that which is assigned them by history and tradition. Now, the existence of man at a very much earlier date than the 6000 or 7000 years of traditional chronology is assumed as almost an established fact of scientific research. This state of the question has produced the usual result of hasty attempts on the part of over-confident interpreters of Scripture to meet scientific conjectures. Some writers, such as M'Causland (*Adam and the Adamite*, Lond. 1864) and S. Baring-Gould (*Some Modern Difficulties*, Lond. 1872), have not scrupled to revive the exploded theory of Isaac de la Peyreira, an eccentric writer of the seventeenth century, to the effect that Scripture itself supposes the existence of older races of men than the Adamic. With a great deal of solid learning, Rawlinson, on the other hand, shows how the pre-historic or unhistoric races of the geologists and archæologists may be accounted for on the hypothesis of a Scythian or Hamite migration far earlier than that of the Semitic and Aryan races, which form the historic nations.

The main points to be borne in mind by the student of Scripture on this question of man's antiquity are these :—(1.) That the enormous periods of thousands and even millions of centuries claimed for man upon earth by Sir Charles Lyell, Darwin, Wallace, etc., are mere guesses, which the writers themselves and the progress of research are constantly modifying. (2.) That the interpretations of Scripture which fix the age of man at the Ussherian era of 4004 B.C., or any similar date, are entirely traditional. Chronologists have for fifteen centuries been endeavouring to make Bible facts fall in with the preconcerted arrangements of their systems. The Bible is not committed to any of these systems. It is evidently incompetent to draw up a record of years or centuries from the genealogical tables of Genesis, which reckon on a wholly different principle. It should be recognised that there is an important sense in which the date of man's origin is left in Scripture an entirely open question. The remark of Bishop Ellicott is thoroughly to the point when he says : " The history of the genesis of the earth is told in the Bible only in broad and general outlines, admirable alike for their simplicity and their now recognised scientific truth. It may be exactly the same in reference to the history of the genesis of the race. The history may be told in similar broad and general outlines, which future discovery will as abundantly verify as it has already verified the revelation as to the home of the race and the formation of the phenomenal world. Nay, more ; on these subordinate questions faith may owe much to science, if faith will but resolve to remain patient and confident " (see his paper in a volume entitled *Credentials of Christianity*, p. 233).

[Any one who wishes to see the present state of this question should consult, in addition to the well-known works of Sir Charles Lyell (*Geological Evidences of .the Antiquity of Man*, 4th edit. Lond. 1873), of Sir John Lubbock (*Origin of Civilisation and Primitive Condition of Man*), of Tylor (*Primitive Culture*, etc.), the more cautious statements of Professor D. Wilson in his *Pre-historic Man* (3d edit. 2 vols. 1876); the counter-evidence adduced by Southall, *Recent Origin of Man as Illustrated by Geology*, etc. (Lond. Trübner, 1875,—a large volume teeming with facts); the strictures of Professor Piazzi Smyth, *The Antiquity of Intellectual Man* (Edin. 1871); together with the laborious collection of opinions on Bible chronology given in Herzog's *Real-Encykl.*, art. " Zeitrechnung." The forthcoming *Rhind Lectures* of Dr. Arthur Mitchell on Archæology, in its application to the question of the age of man and his civilisation, will be looked for with an interest corresponding to that which they awakened in their oral delivery.]

NOTES ON LECTURE II.

NOTE E, PAGE 58.

MAN'S NATURE A UNITY.

AMONG recent writers on Bible psychology it is a favourite assertion that the Bible treats humanity as an integer; that man is the true monad; that in the language of Scripture and of early Christian writers the soul is not the man, and the body is not the man, but man is the *tertium quid* resulting from their union. There is a sense in which these statements are correct. But, as I have shown in the text, they bring no support to the one-substance theory of modern philosophers. To say that the Bible language on this point " agrees in an unexpected manner with the deductions of recent science,"[1] is at the best only to overrate the accidental agreement of non-analytic language with the terms of a false analysis. To go farther, and say that the Bible has no notion of a separable soul and spirit in man, that it regards death as the destruction of the man, is to place oneself in hopeless antagonism to the facts. The Bible, which regards man as possessed of a dual constitution, composed of a higher and a lower element, God-given and earth-derived, attaches the personality to the higher, and views human beings as capable of existence apart from their present visible corporeity. It is impossible to identify the Bible view in any way with that of the positive or monistic philosophy. When, however, the assertions above referred to are intended to bring out the Bible view of the oneness of man's nature, they are fitted to

[1] White, *Life in Christ*, p. 94.

do good service. It is certain that the Bible mode of speaking of man's nature differs essentially from much of the
language which an alien philosophy has imposed upon religion. To speak so exclusively of the soul as has been so
long the practice in religious and moral teaching, is to show
much disregard of man's position in the world, and strange
inattention to the language of Scripture. It seems to have
been forgotten that man's one though complex nature is to
be his nature for ever. The Bible never loses sight of this.
It never overlooks the ministry of the body. From that
great first text which describes man's original constitution,
through those passages which speak of his dominion over earth
and the creatures, in all those which represent work done
through the agency of the body as divine service and human
victory, onward to those which represent the redemption of the
body as the climax of salvation, it is evident that the Bible
system of religion is based upon the unity of man's nature.

It is therefore quite just to regard all attempts in philosophy and in science to appreciate the real unity of our
nature as in the proper sense a return to truth, and an agreement with Scripture. " This harmony between the outer and
the inner man," says Mr. Heard (*Tripartite Nature of Man*,
pp. 58, 59), whom I am glad to quote once with a sense of
concurrence, " the interdependence of sense on thought and
thought on sense, is the point on which our soundest physi-
ologists are advancing every day. Discarding the old materialism, which made thought a secretion of the brain or blood,
and the old spiritualism, which taught that the spirit of man
was probably that of some fallen dæmon imprisoned for a
while in flesh, we are advancing in the right direction when
we maintain the separate existence of the mind and body, and
yet regard the former as perfectly pervading the latter, nay,
as being the formative principle by which it is constructed
and adapted to our nature and use.

" The goal to which modern research is tending is the point
where the old dualism between mind and body will not dis-

appear, but combine instead under some higher law of unity which we have not as yet grasped. Physiology and psychology will not stand contrasted then as they do now, but rather appear as the two sides of the same thing seen in its outward and inward aspect. The resurrection of the body, which at present is a stumbling-block to the spiritualists and foolishness to materialists, will then be found to be the wisdom of God as well as the power of God, and so the Scripture intimations of the unity of man's true nature in one person will be abundantly vindicated.

" According to Scripture, the body is neither the slave of the soul nor its prison-house, as philosophy, with its dualistic views of body and mind, has constantly taught. The relation of the two may be described as sacramental ; the body is the outward and visible sign of the inward and spiritual mind. The mind is not seated in one part of the body, but in the whole ; it does not employ one class of organs only, but all. Hence the well-known Hebraism, ' All my bones shall praise Thee ;' and the other expression, ' Naphshi,' which we render as ' My soul,' but which might be better expressed ' Myself.' The entire nature of the mind breathing through the entire body."

The idea of man's constitution as at once a unity and a complex is well expressed by St. George Mivart in his *Lessons from Nature* (London, 1876). The principle announced by Mr. Mivart contrasts very favourably with the one-sidedness of prevailing scientific methods. He speaks of lessons to be derived from " nature in the broad sense of that word, as a great whole of which the mind of man forms a part." " Observation and experience," he says, " have convinced me of the narrowing and misleading effects upon the mind of an incomplete conception of what is meant by the term ' Nature.' It is too generally taken as denoting the assemblage of phenomena external to and apart from the human mind, which none the less is one of the most important objects which presents itself to our perception. Hence arises a necessary imperfection. But a worse evil follows. ' Nature,' taken in this limited sense, is often made use of to explain that which has been tacitly excluded from it. Thus it is that the facts and processes of reason are apt to be first ignored, in order that they may be afterwards treated as if the mere pheno- mena of irrational nature were sufficient to explain them."

" The lesson, then, concerning man, which we seem to gather from nature as revealed to us in our own conscious- ness and as externally observed, is that man differs funda- mentally from every other creature which presents itself to our senses. That he differs absolutely, and therefore differs in origin also. Although a strict unity, one material whole with one form or force (not made of two parts mutually acting, according to the vulgar notion of soul and body), yet he is seen to be a compound unity in which two distinct orders of being unite.

" He is manifestly ' animal,' with the reflex functions, feelings, desires, and emotions of an animal. Yet equally manifest is it that he has a special nature ' looking before and after,' which constitutes him ' rational.' Ruling, comprehend- ing, interpreting, and completing much in nature, we also see in him that which manifestly points above nature. We see this, since we know that he can conceive mind indefinitely augmented in power, and devoid of those limitations and imperfections it exhibits in him. Manifestly a contemplation of nature must be futile indeed which neglects to ponder over those ideas of power, wisdom, purpose, goodness, and will which are revealed to him in and by his own nature as he knows it to exist, and therefore as conceivably existing in a far higher form in that vast universe of being of which he is a self-conscious fragment."—Pp. 190, 191.

NOTE F, PAGES 61, 66, 94.

MODERN FORMS OF THE TRIPARTITE THEORY.

THE revival of biblical psychology in recent times may be
identified with the recall of attention to the fact that the
distinction between the terms "soul" and "spirit" in Scripture is real and of importance. Its divergence, however,
from the track of valid biblical science may be measured by
the degree in which this real trichotomic usage has been mistaken for the assertion of a tripartite nature in man. The
father of modern biblical psychology, M. F. Roos, in his little
treatise in Latin (1769), now accessible only in the translation by Cremer, *Grundzüge der Seelenlehre aus heiliger Schrift*
(Stuttgart, 1857), has avoided this error. He distinguishes
the terms in their natural sense, and has marked carefully the
spiritual import of the contrasted terms in the later scripture
(cf. pp. 41, 42, 53–62, of the German edition). The whole
performance is simple, and, as Delitzsch says, somewhat
mechanical and dictionary-like; but it is a true, if unpretend-
ing, account of Bible phraseology on the subjects it embraces.
The overweening tendency to philosophize all religious truth
and all scriptural statement is to blame for the rash theorizing
which, for the most part, marks the treatment of our subject
since Roos.

    How Delitzsch has cleared himself of any adhesion to a
tripartite theory I have discussed in the text. But it may
be here further remarked, that he not only repudiates the
theory of two souls or of two distinct inner natures; he even
guards against the mistake too commonly made by writers on
this subject in our country, that soul and spirit represent
lower and higher faculties. "The distinction," he says, " of
so-called higher and lower powers of the soul has, as we shall
be convinced farther on, its substantial truth witnessed for

also by the Scriptures; but, for the rest, the false trichotomy consists exactly in that way of distinguishing soul and spirit which refers these two to distinct departments of being. There is no special need of a refutation of this trichotomy from the Scriptures, since it is absolutely incapable of being established on scriptural authority. . . . We maintain the dualism of nature and spirit as strenuously as we maintain the dualism of God and the world, and in the same degree we regard the body and the spirit of man as being of distinct natures. But the soul belongs to the side of the spirit. The essential distinction between a human nature-psyche (*Natur-psyche*) and the human thinking spirit (*Denkgeist*) is an invention contrary to Scripture and to experience. The dualism of Psyche and Pneuma, under which man, considered ethically, is groaning, is a consequence of sin, which has sundered within itself his life-principle received immediately from God. For it is one principle from which are derived both his bodily and his spiritual life. There is no nature-psyche between spirit and body, but only a soulish life which springs from the spirit itself" (*Bibl. Psych.* p. 94; Clark, p. 113). This is so far clear and satisfactory. How the author reconciles it with his repeated assertion that soul and spirit, though of one nature, are distinct substances, it is not for us to say.

The late Dr. J. T. Beck of Tübingen was much earlier in the field than Delitzsch, the substance of his treatise, *Umriss der biblischen Seelenlehre*, having been delivered to a semi-academic audience well - nigh forty years ago. The work, which has only recently become accessible in English (Clark, 1877), appears to have undergone very little modification since its first issue in 1843. It abounds in subtle and often original remarks. The position taken by Beck on the tripartite theory is not in reality very far from that which most cautious interpreters would be willing to admit as the fair result of the Scripture usage, namely, that the Scripture view of man's nature is really dichotomic. Man is made up of body and spirit, but the personality is often designated by

the mediating term "soul." These simple facts, however,
Beck weaves into a philosophical theory. The following
sentences give his view in brief:—" Alles Lebendige auf Erden
(was ein leibliches Eigenleben führt) auch eine Seele hat, und
alles Fleisch wiederum (seelische Leibesleben) nur vermöge
des Geistes existirt (Job xii. 20). Der Geist bildet denn
auch für das Einzel-Leben das Princip und die Kraft, in der
es besteht; die Seele bildet den Sitz desselben, seinen Träger
und Leiter, der Leib das Gefäss und Organ, so dass jedes
eigenthümlich ist in seiner Art, aber nur in Verbindung mit
den andern (Matt. x. 28; 1 Thess. v. 23). Indem nun die
eigenthümliche Grundlage der aus Geist und Erde gebildeten
Menschen-Natur, das eigentliche Subject oder Ich die Seele
ist (1 Cor. xv. 45) welche die innere Lebens-kraft des Geistes
und das äussere Lebens-Organ des Leibes zusammenknüpft
zu Einer lebendigen Individualität: setzt die Seele im Leibe
das innere Leben in ein äusseres und offenbares Leben um,
während sie in und mit dem Geiste das unsichtbare und vom
Leibe unabhängige Innenleben darstellt (1 Cor. v. 3, vi. 20,
vii. 34). Wie denn das Leben in seiner Gebundenheit an
den Leib ein Leben im Fleische ist (Gal. ii. 20), so in einer
Abgezogenheit vom Leibe ein Seyn im Geiste (*Offenb.* i. 10,
iv. 2, xvii. 3); daher die abgeschiedenen Menschen Geister
heissen (Ebr. xii. 23; 1 Pet. iii. 19), Seelen aber noch, wo das
frühere Leben im Leibe oder die im Blute dauernde, organische
Existenz berücksichtigt ist (*Offenb.* vi. 9, xx. 4; 3 Mos.
xix. 28, xxi. 11; 4 Mos. xix. 11, 13).

 "Wenn der Mensch nicht selber Geist ist, sondern nur hat,
Seele aber ist, so ist er doch nur lebendige Seele geworden
durch das Eingehen des Geistes; diesem kommt seiner Natur
nach das Lebendigmachen, belebende Wirksamkeit zu, der
Seele nur das Lebendigseyn, und zwar eben nur vom Geiste
aus; so bildet dieser die nothwendige Lebensbedingung für
das menschliche Ichleben, und ist in richtigem Lebensstand,
vermöge seines Zusammenhangs mit dem göttlichen Geist, für
die Seele die tragende Trieb-und Belebungskraft (1 Cor.

xv. 45, mit 1 Mos. ii. 7; 2 Pet. i. 21; Röm. viii. 14)"
(pp. 35, 36).

"Da die Seele Geist in sich und über sich, Leib an sich
und um sich hat, so dass eine zwiefache Lebens-Sphäre und
Thätigkeit (geistige und leibliche) in Einem Organismus und
Einer Oekonomie zusammenbesteht: weist diess auf einem
Einheits-Punkt hin als die Lebens-Mitte, welche für den
Lebensstrom, wie er von innen nach aussen und von aussen
nach innen geht, nach seiner geistigen und leiblichen Fülle
und Kraft den Quell- und Sammel-Punkt bildet, und dieser
Bestimmung gemäss ihre besondere organische Eigenthümlich-
keit und Bedeutung hat. Diese Stellung weist die Schrift
dem Herzen zu" (pp. 70, 71).

C. F. Göschel, a follower of Beck and Delitzsch, adheres
very closely with the former to the idea of soul as the uniting
link between body and spirit; but he puts it in a form still
more open to objection. He finds in Gen. ii. 7 three *momenta*
or elements of man's being, distinguished from one another.
According to this passage the soul is that which takes its rise
from body and spirit, earth and breath; that which has become
personality, the synthesis of that thesis and antithesis. The
soul is neither mere spirit nor mere body, rather both at once;
but not as two, rather as one. The trichotomy, therefore, he
considers to be grounded upon this prime text, and to pervade
the whole Scripture in a living and powerful way. The soul
is neither mere spirit nor identical with body, therefore a
Third which takes its rise from the two former *momenta*, "aus
dem Gebildeten und Eingegossenen hervorgeht, aber unmittelbar
weder gebildet noch geschaffen ist, sondern ohne Weiteres aus
Beiden wird" (see his article "Seele" in Herzog). To this
position Delitzsch objects that a mixed nature (*Mischwesen*)
arising at once out of body and spirit is entirely inconceivable.
But Göschel, also, carefully repudiates the notion of two souls
in man. I append a sentence or two from his booklet, *Der
Mensch nach Leib, Seele und Geist diesseits und jenseits*, Leipzig,
1856:—"Wirklich ist die Seele das Dritte im Bunde, so dass

sie nicht allein aus dem Geiste, sondern auch aus dem Leibe, näher aus dem Leibes-Blute stammt. Nicht sind etwa zwei Seelen im Menschen, eine natürliche und eine geistige, sondern die Geistes-Seele ziehet die Leibes-Seele in sich zu einer einigen Seele, welche Leib und Geist zu einen bestimmt ist, *una alma sola* (Dante, *Prg.* xxv. 74). Ueberall, wo ein Gegensatz ist, welcher sich nicht widerspricht, sondern sich nur ausschliesst, um sich einzuschliessen, da fehlt auch das Dritte nicht, welches beiden Seiten angehört, und darum auch beide zu einigen bestimmt ist, nur dass zuvor das Fremdartige und Widersprechende ausgeschieden werde. Diess ist die Trichotomie des Menschen, welche die Schrift lehrt, und darum auch die Wissenschaft anerkennen muss zu weiterer Verständigung. Der Mensch gehört zweien Welten, zweien Reichen an, der natürlichen und der übernatürlichen Sphäre : die Seele ist das Band zwischen beiden Reichen. Weil die Seele in der Mitte ist, so gehört sie nach der einen Seite der Natur an,—darum nennt die Schrift den natürlichen d. i. den der Natur auschliesslich verfallenen Menschen auch seelisch (1 Cor. xv. 45–49); aber nach der andern Seite gehört sie dem Geiste an,—darum stehet geschrieben : ' Fürchtet euch nicht vor denen, die den Leib tödten, aber die Seele nicht zu tödten vermögen' (Matt. x. 28, xvi. 26 ; Marc. viii. 27). Nach jener Seite ist Seele und Leib Eins, als natürlich, nach dieser ist Seele und Geist Eins, als übernatürlich. Aber damit ist die Trichotomie nicht widerlegt, sondern recht eigentlich bestätigt " (pp. 6, 7).

The view of G. F. Oehler is accessible to the English reader in his *Theology of the Old Testament* (Clark, 1874). In the section headed " Elements of Human Nature " (Body, Soul, Spirit), i. p. 216, he has succinctly and carefully traced the Old Testament usage of soul and spirit. " In the soul, which sprang from the spirit, and exists continually through it, lies the individuality,—in the case of man his personality, his self, his *ego ;* because man *is* not רוח, but *has* it—he is soul." His conclusion is thus stated : " From all it is clear that the Old

Testament does not teach a trichotomy of the human being
in the sense of body, soul, and spirit being originally three
co-ordinate elements of man ; rather the whole man is included
in the בָּשָׂר and נֶפֶשׁ (body and soul), which spring from the
union of the רוּחַ with matter; Ps. lxxxiv. 3 ; Isa. x. 18 ; comp.
Ps. xvi. 9. The רוּחַ forms partly the substance of the soul
individualized in it, and partly, after the soul is established,
the power and endowments which flow into it and can be
withdrawn from it" (i. p. 219). This author's article on
" The Heart" (*Herz*), in Herzog's *Real-Encykl.*, is one of the
most valuable of recent contributions to biblical psychology.

Dr. J. H. A. Ebrard occupies a position very similar to that
of Oehler. He is sometimes quoted as apparently a tricho-
tomist. It may be well to note, therefore, that he distinctly
rejects that position. Only,'like the author just quoted, he
endeavours to assign a psychological value to the distinction
between πνεῦμα and ψυχή, though his construction of it is
different. "Das richtige Gesammt-resultat aus den oben ange-
führten Stellen," he says, " ist vielmehr dies, dass während
Seele dem Begriff des Individuums zukommt, Geist vielmehr
dem der Person angehört. Wer eines ethischen Verhaltens,
eines bewussten Verhältnisses zu Gott fähig ist, ist ein πνεῦμα.
Daraus aber, dass πνεῦμα selbst wieder für das den Körper
belebende gebraucht wird (wie Luc. viii. 55), ergibt sich, dass
πνεῦμα und ψυχή nicht zwei Theile, zwei Stücke des Menschen
sind. Das Ich des Menschen ist πνεῦμα, wiefern der Mensch
als Subjekt die Welt in sich hat und so mit Gott zusammen der
unpersönlichen Creatur gegenübersteht ; es ist ψυχή, wiefern
er in der Welt, d. h. als leiblicher, einzelner ein Naturwesen
ist, und einen mikrokosmischen Leib um sich bildet, und von
seinem Leibe als von sich redet. Und eben weil es zum
Begriff des menschlichen Geistes gehört, in leiblicher Form
einzeln zu sein, so bleibt sein Ich auch während der (abnormen)
Trennung von Leib eine Seele, d. h. fähig, in einem Leibe zu
existiren und hierzu organisirt. Wenn also Paulus, 1 Thess.
v. 23, sagt : Euer Leib, Seele, und Geist müsse unsträflich

behalten werden, so berechtigt dies nicht mehr zu einer
Trichotomie, als wenn er gesägt hätte ' Euer Verstand, Wille
und Gefühl, u. s. w.,' zu einer substanziellen Trennung dieser
drei Existenzformen des Einen Ichs berechtigen würde."—
Christliche Dogmatik, i. 262, 263.

The opinions of Olshausen, who is a pronounced tricho-
tomist, will be found in his tract, " De Naturæ Humanæ
Trichotomia N. T. Scriptoribus recepta," contained in his
Opuscula Theologica, Berlin, 1834. They have been rather
superseded by more recent writing.

In our own country, such writers as Ellicott, Alford, Liddon,
fully recognise the importance of the trichotomic usage, but
none of them has investigated its real meaning. All of them
adopt the mistaken interpretation that the distinction between
soul and spirit is that between a lower and a higher soul, and
accordingly all of them lean towards the evident result of this
exegesis, which is that Scripture is committed to the theory of
a tripartite nature in man. Of those named, Ellicott's view,
as given at some length in a sermon on "The Threefold
Nature of Man," from 1 Thess. v. 23, is the most pronounced
(*The Destiny of the Creature*, and other sermons, Lond. 1863).
Yet their utterances on the point are little more than *obiter
dicta*. Not one of these authors has seriously and consistently
taken up this peculiar scheme of human nature. Unfortunately for the cause of biblical psychology, it has been
mainly represented in this country by writers who advocate
the extreme form of the tripartite theory. The leading
English work on the subject is that of Mr. J. B. Heard, *The
Tripartite Nature of Man, Spirit, Soul, and Body* (4th edition,
Clark, Edin. 1875), which has been before the public for
some considerable time. The book abounds in vigorous
strokes of thought, but any value it possesses is lessened by
the extravagance of the thesis which it seeks to maintain.
Any one who chooses to see its numerous inconsistencies
patiently traced out will find the task accomplished in an

article in the *London Quarterly Review* for April 1879. A greatly more cautious treatise, though more elementary, and much less known, is that of the late Jonathan L. Forster, entitled *Biblical Psychology* (London, Longmans, 1873). It is the more necessary to advert in some detail to this English form of the tripartite theory, that it has been recently adopted to prop up the eschatological views of the propounders of a so-called " conditional immortality." The summary which follows is drawn chiefly from the work of Mr. Heard. I have shown in the text of the Lecture that none of the Continental defenders of a scriptural trichotomy have committed themselves to the extreme theory of a tripartite nature. Even Mr. Heard is understood to admit only in a qualified manner the eschatological conclusions which some of his followers have reached, and which by their obviously unscriptural character will probably soon lead to the collapse of the entire system.

The outlines of the system are these :—

Man is a τριμερὴς ὑπόστασις, a union of three, not of two natures only. With this simple key it is proposed to unlock the main positions as to man's Original Standing, the Fall, Regeneration, the Intermediate State, and the Future Glory.

Out of the union of three natures in one person result two tendencies, the flesh and the spirit. " Soul," the union point between " spirit " and " body," was created free to choose to which of these two opposite poles it would be attracted. The equilibrium between flesh and spirit is the state in which man was created, and which he lost by the fall. Adam was created innocent and capable of becoming holy, endowed with inherent capacities for becoming spiritual, capable of becoming pneumatical through the native powers of the *pneuma*. This was the sense in which man was made in the divine image.

The fall was an inclination given to the whole nature of Adam in the direction of the flesh, by which the spirit or image of God was deadened in him; and this bias to evil descends to his posterity. There also descends, however, the germ or remains of the fallen *pneuma*, variously described as a dead organ, a rudimentary organ without corresponding function, or a bare spiritual capacity ; an integral part of man's nature which could not be destroyed by the fall, and which still makes itself felt as conscience. It is proposed by this theory to resolve the quarrel of fourteen centuries' standing between the Augustinian and Pelagian view of man's present natural state. It proposes a return to the position on this subject said to have been held by the Greek Fathers in consequence of their attending to the distinction between πνεῦμα and ψυχή—a position lost to Latin theology by the obliteration of the distinction, and which the Reformers, Lutheran and Calvinistic alike, failed to restore. Any account of original sin from a dichotomic point of view is thought to make more difficulties than it solves. Upon the bipartite hypothesis of man's being, if original sin be something positive, it must be a transmitted *virus*, which, like a physical disease, should either have worn itself out or should wear out the race. The *reductio ad absurdum* of the Augustinian position was the view of Flacius Illyricus that original sin corrupted the nature of the soul. The negative or privative idea of birth-sin is quite sufficient to explain the facts of the case, but still only upon the tripartite view of man. For the privative idea when applied on a bipartite psychology results in the utterly insufficient theory of the Pelagian—a far more serious defect than Pelagians allow can alone account for the facts of human nature as we see them; that is, the defect of the *pneuma*. When Adam fell, God withdrew from him the presence of His Holy Spirit, and thus the *pneuma* fell back into a dim and depraved state of conscience toward God. We need not suppose more than this fatal defect allowed to continue, and Adam to propagate a race under the unspiritual condition into which he had fallen, and we have enough to account for the condition of man as we see him now. Original sin is by the help of this psychology seen to be privative only, but so serious in its privation as defect of the regulative or sovereign *pneuma*—a defect which sufficiently accounts for

universal depravity. [For some remarks on the inconsistencies and exaggerations of this part of the scheme, see
Lect. IV. pp. 167-170.]

This dormant existence of the πνεῦμα in the natural man
is further insisted on as giving us assurance of the possibility
of regeneration or conversion, and insight into its method.
Were the πνεῦμα in man supreme, as by his constitution it
ought to be, there would be no need of regeneration. As
Butler says of it under the name of conscience, " had it power
as it had manifest authority, it would absolutely govern the
world;" on the other hand, were it wholly obliterated,
regeneration would be impossible. Men would be beyond the
reach of redemption, as devils are with reason supposed to be.
Thus the rudimentary existence of the πνεῦμα in all men in
their unconverted state is the ground of the possibility of their
recovery by grace. In the same way this theory suggests the
possibility and mode of sanctification. The Evangelical view
of fallen human nature is said to land in a dilemma those who
hold man as a compound of soul and body only. For if the
immaterial nature of man is wholly corrupt, desperately
wicked, and that nature is a unit, no *nidus* in human nature
is reserved into which the Divine Spirit can descend and
purify all within. How can a good thing come out of an
evil ? Upon this view the heart is desperately wicked, and
remains so, even in the regenerate, who nevertheless are led
by the Spirit of God, and walk not after the flesh but after
the Spirit. How this can be is as unexplained as how a deaf
man can hear, or a lame man can walk. Let but the distinction
between ψυχή and πνεῦμα be seen, and all is clear and consistent. The ψυχή is like the flesh prone to evil, and remains
so even in the regenerate. But the πνεῦμα—the God-like in
man—is not prone to evil, indeed it cannot sin. Its tendency
is naturally upwards to God. Regeneration, then, is the
quickening of this πνεῦμα. Sanctification is the carrying on
of that which conversion began. Conversion or the first
quickening of the *pneuma* may be dated either from the first

moment of conviction by the law (Rom. vii. 9), or from the time when the *pneuma* is practically acknowledged to be the master principle, and our members are yielded as instruments of righteousness unto God. The gradual character of sanctification and the conflict implied in it thus explains itself. It is the working out of that which was begun at conversion. The seminal principle, then quickened, grows and asserts its presence by asserting its mastery over the lower part of our nature, until the true harmony of man's constitution, spirit, soul, and body, overturned by the fall, is completely restored.

Besides the groundless and unscriptural assumption that there is any part or faculty in fallen man which is "not prone to evil and cannot sin," this whole theory of regeneration and sanctification differs from that of the Bible as being almost purely naturalistic. With the exception of once bringing in the supernatural in the regenerating or reawakening act, it makes the whole a natural process; whereas the scriptural view of the renewed life is that it is a standing miracle, a supernatural life. It is a miracle to begin with, and precisely such a miracle as is here disparaged, "bringing a clean thing out of an unclean." And it is a continuous miracle; exactly such a miracle, too, as was shadowed forth in the healing works of Him who made "the blind to see, the deaf to hear, and the lame to walk." Were this tripartite theory correct, theology must be recast, and so also must Christian preaching. Evangelical teachers must change their note (as Mr. Heard's critic in the *London Quarterly* puts it), and instead of calling men to repentance, must say, "Develop your *pneumata*."

When it enters on questions connected with the future life, this tripartite theory breaks up in confusion. Its supporters are hopelessly divided among themselves. Mr. Heard treats the moral and metaphysical arguments for a future life with respect. He considers them to be presumptions, and presages rather than proofs, intimations more than arguments. But to Mr. E. White, the doctrine of the soul's immortality is the

root of all evil in theology. Since the fall, man naturally goes
to nothing at death. Mr. Heard knows that when the early
Fathers speak of the mortality of the *psyche*, they may fairly
be taken "to mean no more than this, that the existence of the
wicked in the place of punishment depends on the appointment of God, not on the necessary immortality of the soul."
(See further as to this in Note T of this Appendix.)   Of the
soul as the seat of self-consciousness, he will affirm neither
mortality nor immortality.   He thinks the soul or self-consciousness can only exist through its union with the spirit or
God-consciousness, so that the proof of the life everlasting
must rest, not on the argument for the natural immortality of
the *psyche* (who argues for this ?), but on the gift of eternal
life to the *pneuma*, when quickened and renewed in the
image of God.   But he admits that there may be an evil-
possessed *pneuma* in man as well as a divinely quickened
pneuma.   The duration of punishment and malignity of evil
must bear some proportion to each other.   So far, therefore,
from denying eternal punishment, he declares that Uni-
versalism seems to shut its eyes to all those passages which
speak of spiritual wickedness.   He wishes to discover some
middle truth between the Augustinian theory of a *massa
perditionis*, the undistinguishable misery of all out of Christ,
and the Universalist doctrine that all punishment is remedial.
He concludes with Bengel that the doctrine of final retribution
is not one fit for discussion.

All this is treated in a much less tentative way by Mr.
Edward White.   Having started with the proposition that the
fall changed man's constitution to one perishable at death,
like the lower animals ; having set out with the bold general
denial of man's natural immortality, and yet being loyal
enough to Scripture to preach judgment to come for all mankind, he is in sore straits to find a ground for the survival of
the impenitent.   For the eternal life of the saved he finds
sufficient ground in their union to Christ, the act of regeneration having changed their constitution from mortality to

immortality.   But for the rest, he is compelled to say that
it is the incarnation and work of the Redeemer which secures
their reservation to future punishment, though there is for
them no continuous or immortal existence in the world to
come.   Some disciples of the school seem to imagine that the
trichotomy affords ground for a solution of the terrible
problem.   They apply it in a very crude and simple fashion.
Since natural men have only the *psyche*, and since the
pneuma is added or bestowed only in regeneration, immortal
existence belongs to those alone who are possessed of the
pneuma.   All others by and by pass into nothing by the very
law of their nature.   But this denial of the *pneuma* altogether,
as an element of being, to natural men, this addition of it as a
faculty in the case of the regenerate, this attempt, in short, to
construct an eschatology out-of-hand upon the basis of the
tripartite theory, is too obviously irreconcileable with fidelity
to Scripture to command the support of the present leader of
the, school.   He is aiming at the same conclusion, viz. that
none but those who are in Christ live for ever.   But he
cannot be content so to snatch at it.   How little Mr. White
really makes of the trichotomy will be seen in his succinct
and fair statement of the question at pp. 274–279 of his
Life in Christ.   He sees clearly that no ontological distinction
is implied in the difference between *psyche* and *pneuma*;
consequently he is shut up to assume that by the *pneuma* in
regeneration our Lord meant the "spiritual and eternal *life*
secured by the indwelling of the Holy Spirit, not the addition
of a wholly new faculty to humanity."

NOTE G, PAGES 71, 94.

THE TRICHOTOMY IN ITS HISTORICAL CONNECTIONS.

PROCEEDING on the general principle that the historical method is the right one for the elucidation of the psychological terms of Scripture, I have endeavoured to show that a close observation of Old Testament usage will enable us to understand how the trichotomic language of the New Testament arose, and what is its exact force. But a great deal that is interesting in the way of collateral illustration of the Bible trichotomy might be got together. I am only able to add a few scattered notes on the various ancient sources which shed light on the Pauline or sacred trichotomy either by contrast or by resemblance.

As indicated in the Lecture (pp. 93, 94), the main parallels in ancient philosophy, though differing all of them essentially from the scriptural trichotomy, are those of the Platonic and the Stoic schools before the rise of Christianity, and of the Neo-Platonic after it. Even in the Stoic psychology, however, I am unable to find any exact parallel, except in a writer subsequent to Paul, viz. the Emperor Marcus Aurelius.

Some profess to find a trichotomy indicated by Pythagoras. If we may believe Diogenes Laërtius (viii. 20), the highest power in man according to that philosopher was that designated by the Greek term φρένες. He says: τὴν δὲ ἀνθρώπου ψυχὴν διαιρεῖσθαι τριχῆ, εἴς τε νοῦν καὶ φρένας καὶ θυμόν. Νοῦν μὲν οὖν εἶναι καὶ θυμόν καὶ ἐν τοῖς ἄλλοις ζώοις, φρένας δὲ μόνον ἐν ἀνθρώπῳ. But Olshausen, who gives this reference, adds: " I can hardly persuade myself that Pythagoras would attribute νοῦς to all living creatures." He also quotes Stobæus (Ecl. phys. p. 878), who assigns quite another division to Pythagoras,

viz. of man εἰς λογισμὸν, θυμόν, καὶ ἐπιθυμίαν; but this is
clearly Platonic. It is best to confess that no one knows
what Pythagoras held on these subjects.

The Platonic tripartition is familiar. It consists in the
assertion of three principles as constituting the inner nature
of man, τὸ λογιστικόν, τὸ θυμοειδές, τὸ ἐπιθυμητικόν, the
rational, irascible, and concupiscible; often also represented
by ὁ λόγος, ὁ θυμός, αἱ ἐπιθυμίαι. At first sight this appears
to be only a trichotomy of the soul, leaving the body out of
account. It does not seem to be inconsistent with the ordinary dichotomic language which Plato also freely uses of our
whole nature as made up of body and soul. But as he goes
on to teach that the rational or intelligible part of the soul is
immortal, necessarily partaking of eternity with those eternal
ideas which it contemplates, while the two others, the irascible and concupiscible parts, are mortal, we see how it has
been usual to attribute to him the doctrine of three souls.
Again, when we observe him saying (*Timæus*, 72 D) of the
soul that a certain part is mortal and another part divine, we
may more properly speak of him as teaching a doctrine of
two souls in one body. Finally, when he speaks of a tripartite universe made up of νοῦς, ψυχή, σῶμα, we may consider
that man, who is an image or copy of it in little, consists of
the same three parts. Thus we arrive at a Platonic tripartition of man's nature into Reason, Soul, and Body.

In the *Republic*, book iv. (440, Steph.), will be found a
passage where the threefold division of the soul is insisted on,
τὸ λογιστικόν, τὸ θυμοειδές, τὸ ἐπιθυμητικόν. The object of
the reasoning is to prove that the *second* of these principles
sides with the *first*; that it is at war with the *third*, and is
clearly distinct from them both (Οὗτος μέντοι, ἔφην, ὁ λόγος
σημαίνει τὸν θυμὸν πολεμεῖν ἐνίοτε ταῖς ἐπιθυμίαις ὡς ἄλλο
ὂν ἄλλῳ); that this spirit or courage (θυμός) is on the side of
reason (ξύμμαχον τῷ λόγῳ γιγνόμενον τὸν θυμόν); that the
contrary is never known to take place, viz. that θυμός should
be on the side of the desires when reason decides the other way.

At first sight, τὸ θυμοειδές may appear to be of the order of the desires; but now we should say the contrary, that much rather in the conflict of the soul it takes arms for the rational principle (πολὺ μᾶλλον αὐτὸ (τὸ θυμοειδές) ἐν τῇ τῆς ψυχῆς στάσει τίθεσθαι τὰ ὅπλα πρὸς τοῦ λογιστικοῦ). Still further, he goes on to make sure that τὸ θυμοειδές is distinct from τὸ λογιστικόν; that it is not merely a kind or species of reason (λογιστικοῦ τι εἶδος), but that, as there are three classes in the state,—traders, auxiliaries, counsellors,—so there are three principles in the soul, and that this third element of courage or spirit must be distinct, and is, when uncorrupted, an auxiliary of reason (οὕτω καὶ ἐν ψυχῇ τρίτον τοῦτό ἐστι τὸ θυμοειδές, ἐπίκουρον ὂν τῷ λογιστικῷ φύσει, ἐὰν μὴ ὑπὸ κακῆς τροφῆς διαφθαρῇ). This is plain when we prove that courage (θυμός) is distinct from reason (λόγος), as we have already proved it distinct from desire (ἐπιθυμία); and this is proved by the case of children, who from the very first have spirit (θυμός), though they may never have reason (λόγος).

In these passages πνεῦμα never once occurs—as, indeed, it could not, having in classical Greek a totally different meaning of a merely physiological kind; and as for ψυχή, it is used by Plato for the whole inward nature of man, as appears from the use of σῶμα for its correlative. The two master-principles above named, τὸ λογιστικόν and τὸ θυμοειδές, as counsellor and warrior combined, are said to rule and defend the whole soul and the whole body (ὑπὲρ ἁπάσης τῆς ψυχῆς τε καὶ τοῦ σώματος). It is also evident that the τὸ λογιστικόν here does not correspond with the New Testament πνεῦμα in any sense, though it may with νοῦς. Τὸ θυμοειδές may be more like the לֵב, καρδία, of the Scriptures, but this too may be questioned. The parallel between αἱ ἐπιθυμίαι and the τὰ μέλεα of Paul is a good deal more close; and an interesting question of possible parallelism arises when we take this Platonic division as on the whole a division into higher and lower powers of the soul.

x

Beside the above let us place that other passage in the *Republic*, book ix. (589, Steph.), where, in allegorical fashion, Plato pictures the soul as a human figure containing within it a hydra, a lion, and a smaller man.   He then reasons that the noble course is that which subjects the beast to the man, or rather to the divine in man, the ignoble, that which subjects the man to the beast (τὰ μὲν καλὰ τὰ ὑπὸ τῷ ἀνθρώπῳ, μᾶλλον δὲ ἴσως τὰ ὑπὸ τῷ θείῳ τὰ θηριώδη ποιοῦντα τῆς φύσεως, αἰσχρὰ δὲ τὰ ὑπὸ τῷ ἀγρίῳ τὸ ἥμερον δουλούμενα), and asks, how would a man profit who should take money to enslave the noblest part of him to the worst?   The two beasts and the inner man' here, all covered by the outward form of man, answer to the three principles of the former passage.   There is a slight contradiction, for he supposes here that the two lower (hydra and lion) may combine against the higher, the man, but says the wise will seek an alliance with the lion-heart.   Again, the exquisite figure in the *Phædrus* (246, Steph.), where the nature of man is compared to a charioteer driving two winged horses, one of them noble and of noble origin, the other ignoble and of ignoble origin, may be held to illustrate his theory of the composite and even paradoxical constitution of man.   It is usually assumed that the *Phædrus* was an early treatise.   And this allegory does not easily fit into Plato's more mature scheme of man's composition. Nevertheless the passage is extremely characteristic.   When taken along with the reasonings based upon the allegory, *e.g.* that such a constitution cannot be intended to be immortal, it contrasts strikingly with the simple biblical idea of the unity of man's nature.   Besides these divisions of the whole inner nature of man into three principles, we find in the *Timæus* (30, Steph.), a division into νοῦς, ψυχή, and σῶμα (νοῦν μὲν ἐν ψυχῇ, ψυχὴν δὲ ἐν σώματι ξυνιστὰς τὸ πᾶν ξυνετεκταίνετο).   It is true that this is given in connection with the *anima mundi*, but commentators have always understood it as referring to the human being as well.   Delitzsch seems, therefore, to be mistaken in ascribing this division first to Plotinus.   For the full Platonic doctrine of two souls in one body, *vide Timæus*, 69, 70.

An Aristotelic trichotomy is sometimes spoken of (*e.g.* by Delitzsch, p. 93), but it is plain that Aristotle differed fundamentally from Plato in his view of man's constitution. His subtle and profound doctrine of the ψυχή has pervaded philosophic speculation ever since his own day.   He meant to conceive of ψυχή as a principle manifesting itself in an ascending scale through vegetable, animal, and human life. But his theory of its vegetative, sensitive, and noetic functions by no means favours a trichotomy.   Much rather, his view of ψυχή as "the simplest actuality (ἐντελέχεια) of a physical body potentially possessing life" laid the foundation for the strict philosophical dualism which has prevailed through all the centuries of Christian thought.   It may, with some appearance of plausibility, be even held to favour the monistic view of modern Positivism.   It is to be noted, on the other hand, that Aristotle finds in man νοῦς παθητικός and νοῦς ποιητικός, a passive and an active intellect.   And as Plato claimed immortality only for that highest of his two souls which as λόγος or νοῦς constituted the real man, so Aristotle says (*De Anim.* iii. 5), τοῦτο (*i.e.* ἀπαθὴς νοῦς) μόνον ἀθάνατον, . . . ὁ δὲ παθητικὸς νοῦς φθαρτός.   Still with him these are only two modes of reason. They are not, as for Plato, several souls.   According to Aristotle, the active or creative reason (νοῦς ποιητικός) is apparently impersonal.   Its survival of death, its everlasting existence, is not the continued personal existence of the man.   [For the bearing of Aristotle's view on the question of a future life, see Westcott's *Gospel of the Resurrection*, pp. 147–152.]

The psychology of the early Stoics seems to have been of a ruder and lower kind than either of the preceding.   They assimilated man's rational activity to the activity of the senses. But they upheld the oneness of the soul's being with greater vigour than did either Plato or Aristotle.   Reason, τὸ ἡγεμονικόν (otherwise called διανοητικόν, λογιστικόν, or λογισμός), is with them the primary power.   From it the other parts of

the soul are only derivatives. From it, like the arms of a
cuttle-fish, the seven divisions of the soul reach to the body.
At a later period, among the Stoics, and also among the
Epicureans, this scheme appears to have become that of the
ascription to man of a rational and an irrational, or of an
intelligent and an animal soul—a tendency which stretched
far on, as we shall see, into the philosophy of modern
Europe. The most remarkable parallel to the biblical trichotomy is that found in the writings of the last of the Stoical
philosophers, the emperor M. Aurelius Antoninus. In his only
extant treatise, Τῶν εἰς ἑαυτὸν, βιβλία ιβ΄, he says: "What I
am consists entirely of the fleshly and spiritual, and the chief
part," ὃ τί ποτε τοῦτό εἰμι, σαρκία ἐστὶ καὶ πνευμάτιον, καὶ
τὸ ἡγεμονικόν (lib. ii. § 2). Again: "Body, soul, mind; to
thy body belong senses; to thy soul, affections; to thy mind,
assertions (decreta)," Σῶμα, ψυχὴ, νοῦς· σώματος αἰσθήσεις,
ψυχῆς ὁρμαὶ, νοῦ δόγματα (lib. iii. § 16). Once more:
"There are three parts of which thou art composed,—the
bodily, the spiritual, and the mind," Τρία ἐστὶν ἐξ ὧν
συνέστηκας, σωμάτιον, πνευμάτιον, νοῦς (lib. xii. § 3). It is
not possible to agree with T. Gataker (the Cambridge editor,
1652) when he says, in a note on the second of the passages
quoted, "Parilis distributio et in sacris literis reperitur
1 Thess. v. 23, σῶμα, ψυχὴ, πνεῦμα qui et νοῦς, Rom.
vii. 25;" or with Sir A. Grant (Ethics of Aristotle, vol. i.
Essay vi. p. 297), who thinks that we find in Aurelius
"the same psychological division of man into body, soul, and
spirit as was employed by St. Paul." To make this out it is
necessary to say, as the last-quoted writer does, that the
πνεῦμα of St. Paul answers to the νοῦς or ἡγεμονικόν of
Antoninus. Now any one who follows the line of investigation
we have indicated, will see at a glance the differences between
these two trichotomic schemes. St. Paul would totally deny
that the νοῦς is the ἡγεμονικόν. The real governing principle
according to him is πνεῦμα, and πνεῦμα in a sense entirely
different from that in which it is used by Aurelius. For

though πνευμάτιον in the Stoic scheme is an addition to the
Platonic language, there is no change or advance upon the
Greek idea which identifies πνευμάτιον and ψυχή, whereas
everything in the scriptural scheme turns upon the natural
and moral distinction between ψυχή and πνεῦμα. Lastly, the
σῶμα and the σάρξ of the two schemes are only seemingly
parallel. The Stoic depreciates the σῶμα, considers τὰ σαρκία
as the mere prison of the mind; but there is nothing in the
stoical σάρξ answering to what St. Paul understood by that
term in relation to the depraved nature of man. His conception is wholly biblical.

This peculiar form of the Stoic psychology is later than
Paul. But of any influence exercised even by earlier Stoical
schools upon the Pauline psychology it is vain to speak. An
Alexandrian influence would have been more probable. But
Philo's trichotomy is purely Platonic, and differs, therefore,
essentially from that of the apostle. Older and simpler influences, as we have seen, sufficiently account for the rise of
this last. The idea of a trichotomy was rendered familiar to
Paul, as to other Hebrews of his time, by the current language
of philosophy, both Stoic and Alexandrian; but the form and
contents of that which appears in the New Testament were
moulded by Old Testament psychology, while its special terms
were prepared in the Greek of the Septuagint. The Seventy
were doubtless familiar with the philosophical language of the
Greek schools, yet they have remained entirely true, in their
translation, to the genius of the Hebrew Scriptures. Accordingly, the term νοῦς, so prominent in Greek philosophy for the
higher aspect of the soul, never occurs in the Septuagint in
that connection (see Note H). Πνεῦμα and ψυχή are of
constant occurrence,—the former as the uniform translation
of רִיחַ, and sometimes of נְשָׁמָה (which is also, at times,
rendered by πνοή); the latter as the equivalent of נֶפֶשׁ and
חַיָּה, sometimes of כָּבוֹד. The general names for body are σῶμα
and σάρξ. The terms of the simple trichotomy, spirit, soul,
and body, are evidently thus provided for in that version of

the ancient Scriptures with which Paul was so familiar, and need not be sought in any extraneous source whatever. The application of it in the Christian system belonged to the new revelation.

It would be overstrained to build much on occasional traces of philosophical influence in the language of the Septuagint, *e.g.* Job vii. 15, Ἀπαλλάξεις ἀπὸ πνεύματός μου τὴν ψυχήν μου, where our present Hebrew text has no such distinction; or Ps. li. 12 (Heb. v. 14; Sept. l. 12), πνεύματι ἡγεμονικῷ στήριξόν με, where we have probably a purely undesigned coincidence with the philosophical ἡγεμονικόν. It is clearer, however, that Josephus had a favour for the current trichotomy when he paraphrases Gen. ii. 7 thus:—Ἔπλασεν ὁ Θεὸς τὸν ἄνθρωπον, χοῦν ἀπὸ τῆς γῆς λαβών· καὶ πνεῦμα ἐνῆκεν αὐτῷ καὶ ψυχήν (*Antiqq.* I. i. β), instead of giving the simple and untechnical rendering of the Septuagint. A similar favour for what became the New Testament trichotomic usage is traceable in the Wisdom of Solomon, in such passages as xv. 11: Ὅτι ἠγνόησε τὸν πλάσαντα αὐτὸν, καὶ τὸν ἐμπνεύσαντα αὐτῷ ψυχὴν ἐνεργοῦσαν, καὶ ἐμφυσήσαντα πνεῦμα ζωτικόν; and xvi. 14: ἐξελθὸν δὲ πνεῦμα οὐκ ἀναστρέφει, οὐδὲ ἀναλύει ψυχὴν παραληφθεῖσαν. In the Apocrypha generally, the leading psychological terms are used with much the same latitude as in the Old Testament. But among other traces of Greek influence, we may reckon the more pronounced dualism of " body and soul " which begins to appear in these writings: *e.g.*, σῶμα, ψυχή, Wisd. i. 4, 2 Macc. vi. 30, xv. 30; πνεῦμα, σπλάγχνα, Baruch ii. 17; a hint of pre-existence, Wisd. viii. 20; and most noticeably, the Greek notion of the body as the fetter of the soul, Wisd. ix. 15,—this last passage containing also the very terms of the later Greek trichotomy, σῶμα, ψυχή, νοῦς.

The only other illustration of a trichotomy which it is necessary to adduce from non-Christian philosophy is that of the Neo-Platonists. This was rather a trinity of the universe, however, than a tripartition of human nature. The first principle of the universe was the One (τὸ ἕν), a mysterious unity, out of which all things emanated. The second principle is that which contemplates the One and requires only it to exist. This is pure intelligence (νοῦς). The third principle is the universal soul (ψυχή), which is produced by and reposes on intelligence, as intelligence derives from the original Unity. The soul in the very power of its weakness forms to itself a body, endows blind matter with form and thought. (For an account of this tripartition, see Archer Butler's *Lectures on the History of Ancient Philosophy*, ii. p. 354 et seq.) When this scheme is applied to human nature, the soul is reckoned as the image and product of intelligence, and inferior to it, though divine. Then, the soul permeates the body as fire permeates air. It is more correct to say that the body is in the soul, than that the soul is in the body. The soul contains the body. The divine extends from the One to the soul. We might identify this system with the Stoic trichotomy, σῶμα, ψυχή, νοῦς, but the character of the Plotinian thinking was theosophic rather than philosophic. It was a bold jumble of all the philosophies, pervaded by mysticism, and intended to rival Christianity,—a mere inflated imitation, which owed all that was really new in it to the sacred thought which it obviously parodied.

To trace the history of the trichotomy in the hands of early Christian writers would be a difficult task. The whole subject of the psychology of these writers is obscure and uncertain. That the Pauline trichotomy does not appear in the Apostolic Fathers proves nothing against its acceptance in the early Church, for the range of topics and therefore of Scripture quotation, in their extant writings, is necessarily very limited. In the Greek Apologists, on the other hand, the use of a trichotomy is frequent. The Pauline terms even are easily traced. But though they use the scriptural *pneuma* and *psyche*, their thinking is really Platonic or Stoic. They protested against the results of the Platonic psychology (see Note T of this Appendix), but they could not shake themselves free of its influence. Accordingly, they are ruled by the notion of two principles in man, a lower and a higher; a creaturely soul (*psyche*), and a divine or incorruptible spirit (*pneuma*). This was undoubtedly an unscriptural view, and it soon led to such results — Gnostic, Manichæan, Apollinarian — as drew forth the protest of the Church in her general councils. How great was the influence of the ancient philosophy, even with Christian writers, may be seen in Clemens Alexandrinus and Origen, both of whom favour the Platonic trichotomy. Even Tertullian is disposed to accept it as not alien to the faith (*De Anima*, xvi.), while he disparages the biblical distinction between soul and spirit.

Long after these early controversies were forgotten, the Aristotelic philosophy perpetuated the distinction between a vegetative and a rational element in the human ψυχή. The distinction was promoted by William of Occam, 1347, into a doctrine of two souls differing in substance from one another,—the sensitive soul joined to the body *circumscriptivè*, so as to dwell in separate parts of it; the intellective soul separable from the body and joined with it *diffinitivè*, so that it is entirely present in every part. A similar view is ascribed to the Italian philosopher Bernardinus Telesius (1508–88). But it is of more interest to find something akin to it in the writings of the father of modern inductive science. Lord Bacon suggests a trichotomy of man's nature in this way : having observed that " there were two different emanations of souls in the first creation of them, viz. one that had its original from the breath of God, and another from the matrices of the elements," he proposes to distinguish these in man as the *spiracle* or *inspired substance* on the one hand, and the *sensible* or *product soul* on the other. It is in connection with his consideration of the former, in proposing to ask whether it be native or adventive, separable or inseparable, mortal or immortal, how far it is tied to the laws of matter, how far not, and the like, that he utters the suggestive sentiment that there are questions in philosophy which must be bound over at last unto religion [see extract given in title-page of Lecture I.]. In speaking of the second, he says that this is in beasts the principal soul, whereof the body of beasts is the organ; but in man this soul is itself an organ of the rational soul, and should bear the appellation, not of a soul, but rather of a spirit. His trichotomy then would be soul, spirit, and body, — *soul* denoting the divine spark, the in-breathed principle of rationality; *spirit*, the unreasonable soul, "which hath the same original in us as in beasts, namely, from the slime of the earth." This is a tripartite theory, for it seems to demand a rational principle ruling over two distinct organs or organisms, the animal soul and the animal body.— *De Augmentis*, lib. iv. cap. iii.

From the time of Lord Bacon, the trichotomy may be said to have fallen greatly out of sight, until the revival of biblical psychology in the end of the last and beginning of the present century. There is probably no instance since the ancient councils in which a psychological article has been introduced into church symbols, except that of the later Helvetic Confession. In this document the strict dualism of the human constitution is insisted on in words which reflect some forgotten controversies: "Dicimus autem constare hominem duabus ac diversis quidem substantiis, in una persona, anima immortali, utpote quæ separata a corpore, nec dormit, nec interit, et corpore mortali, quod tamen in ultimo judicio a mortuis resuscitabitur, ut totus homo inde, vel in vita, vel in morte, æternum maneat. Damnamus omnes qui irrident, aut subtilibus disputationibus, in dubium vocant immortalitatem animarum, aut animam dicunt dormire, aut partem esse Dei." —*Conf. Helvet. posterior*, c. vii.

NOTE H, PAGE 91.

LEADING TERMS IN BIBLE PSYCHOLOGY.

[THE most useful works for this subject are those of Roos, Delitzsch, and Beck, and a suggestive tract by Zeschwitz, entitled, *Profangræcität und biblischer Sprachgeist* (Leipzig, 1859). F. Böttcher's *De Inferis* (Dresden, 1845) is in great part a careful lexical study of Old Testament terms, as bearing upon psychology and eschatology. Dr. B. Weiss' *Lehrbuch der biblischen Theologie des N. Test.* (Berlin, 1873) is more detailed than such handbooks usually are, both on what he calls "die urapostolische" and "die paulinische Anthropologie." Cremer, as might be expected from his antecedents, is full and good in his treatment of psychological terms (*Biblico-Theological Lexicon of New Testament Greek*, 2d ed., Clark, Edin. 1878). I append a few notes supplementary to what has been said in the Lecture.]

SPIRIT (רוּחַ, נְשָׁמָה, πνεῦμα).—To begin with the New Testament word Πνεῦμα. The meanings in *ordinary Greek* are three,—(*a*) air or wind, (*b*) breath, the air we breathe, (*c*) life in general. " Thus in a *physiological* sense we often find it in the classics, especially in the poets and in later Greek; in a *psychological* sense, as the element of human existence and personal life, never " (Cremer). It is only in the LXX. and in the New Testament that πνεῦμα has the sense of a spiritual being, or refers to man in his higher mental aspects, and thus is a good example of the language-building and enriching power of the religion of the Bible. In the *Scriptures*, however, we find it used (A) in the classical senses,—"wind," John iii. 8; "breath, breath of life," Ezek. xxxvii. 8; Hab. ii. 19; "life" (in the physiological sense, but drawing rather to the meaning "soul"), Luke viii. 55; Jas. ii. 26; Rev. xi. 11, xiii. 15.

The additional idea which is even on this side introduced
into the term is that it is life, or a life-principle, from God.
So in the LXX. as = רוּחַ or נְשָׁמָה, Isa. xlii. 5.   Both of men and
brutes, Eccles. iii. 19, 21; Ps. civ. 29, 30.   (B) The senses
special to the Scriptures are these :—(1) It denotes the
distinctive, self-conscious, inner life of man, 1 Cor. ii. 11,
v. 3, 5; Col. ii. 5; Matt. v. 3; Luke i. 80, ii. 40; Mark
viii. 12.   (2) Connected with the former or physiological
sense, as life which is God-derived, comes the πνεῦμα in its
religious sense, Ps. xxxi. 6, xxxii. 2, xxxiv. 19, li. 12, 19,
lxxviii. 8; Prov. xvi. 2; Isa. xxvi. 9, xxix. 24, xxxviii. 16,
lxi. 3, lxvi. 3; Ezek. xiii. 3; Rom. i. 9.   Then (3) its highest
and specially Pauline meaning of "the new nature," Rom.
viii. 2, 6, 10, 16; Gal. iii. 6, v. 16, 17, 18; Jude 19.   See
the gradual rise of πνεῦμα in these three meanings traced in
the lecture, pp. 67–74.

For the relation of πνεῦμα τοῦ ἀνθρώπου to τὸ πνεῦμα τὸ
ἅγιον, τοῦ Χριστοῦ, the chief passages are Rom. viii. 16 (comp.
1 Cor. ii. 11, 12), and the whole context of Rom. viii. 1–17;
Gal. iii. 5; Philem. 25.   "Inner assurance depends upon the
contact of the Spirit newly given of God with the spirit in us
which is ours conformably with nature; and the vitality and
power of this divine life-principle depend upon the indwelling
or communication of the Spirit of Christ.   We must always
understand by πνεῦμα the divine life-principle by nature
peculiar to man, either in its natural position within his
organism, or as renewed by the communication of the Spirit.
But we must keep fast hold of the truth that this newly
given life-principle does not become identical with the spirit
belonging to man by nature, nor does it supplant it.   It
cannot be said of it, τὸ ἐμόν, ὑμῶν πνεῦμα; and we must
distinguish between the texts where it is spoken of as now
belonging to man, and those where it appears as independently
existing.   Still this is not a difference of subjects, as if a
different πνεῦμα were meant, but simply a difference in the
relation of the πνεῦμα to man; so that when reference is thus

made to the Spirit, though it be the personal Holy Spirit that
is meant, yet He is regarded as the agent who in and for
man accomplishes the work of redemption" (Cremer, *sub voce*).
With some slight wavering, the opinion of Cremer on the
whole appears to be, that in the Christian there is simply a
natural πνεῦμα and the divine Holy Spirit, and that it is
the divine Holy Spirit acting on the natural πνεῦμα in man
which produces the quickened or renewed πνεῦμα. He
seems to say that this renewed πνεῦμα must not be held
identical with the πνεῦμα belonging to man by nature—that
it is non-individual, that it is the Holy Spirit acting in the
man. Is this a *tetrachotomy* of the Christian into body, soul,
spirit, and the Holy Spirit?

To understand πνεῦμα, especially in its antithesis to ψυχή,
attention should be given to the use of πνευματικός in the
New Testament. With one exception (Eph. vi. 12), it always
denotes that which belongs either directly to the Lord, the
Spirit (*e.g.* 1 Cor. x. 3, 4), or to the renewed spirit in
believers. 1 Cor. ii. 11–16 and xv. 42–47 are the two main
passages determining its force. No careful reader of 1 Cor. ii.
could avoid seeing that the distinctive character of the human
πνεῦμα is present to the mind of the writer. The clear
description of the πνεῦμα in ver. 11 as the self-consciousness
in man, and its comparison with the τὸ πνεῦμα τοῦ Θεοῦ,
make this undeniable. That in this connection the man
blind to spiritual-divine things should be called ψυχικός, and
the spiritually enlightened πνευματικός, is a clear recognition
that in the writer's mind ψυχή and πνεῦμα have the respective
values that have been accorded them in modern biblical psychology. The whole passage is moulded, like that in the same
Epistle, xv. 42–47, upon the antithesis of ψυχή and πνεῦμα,
and both passages would be unintelligible without the assumption of that antithesis. It might be possible to reckon 1 Thess.
v. 23 rhetorical amplification, but Heb. iv. 12 and the two
passages now named refuse to bend to such an hypothesis.

רוּחַ is the complete Old Testament equivalent of πνεῦμα.

The Septuagint is on the whole faithful to this rendering. נְשָׁמָה is a strictly parallel expression in Hebrew. It can be used along with רוּחַ of the mere principle of life even in animals (Gen. vii. 22). Like רוּחַ, also, it can denote the innermost function of the human spirit (Prov. xx. 27). The LXX. have rendered it frequently by πνοή, especially when a parallelism with רוּחַ occurs in the original (e.g. Job xxvii. 3, xxxii. 8, xxxiii. 4; Isa. xlii. 5, lvii. 16), and this probably indicates accurately the distinctive shade of meaning. There does not seem to be the slightest foundation for the notion favoured by Beck, that נְשָׁמָה denotes the specific difference between the life of man and that of animals (Umriss, x. p. 7, note: the passages cited by him, especially the verses Deut. xx. 13, 14, 16, seem to me to disprove the distinction). The idea is of Rabbinic origin. So also is the still less scriptural notion of making נְשָׁמָה and רוּחַ denote separate spiritual elements, or even distinct souls in man. We find the Rabbinical writers sometimes quoted as making three inner principles. Olshausen cites Jalkut Rubeni, fol. 15 : " In homine est רוּחַ et נֶפֶשׁ et נְשָׁמָה, sed quando peccat, נְשָׁמָה ab eo abit et adscendit, נֶפֶשׁ et רוּחַ manent, ita ut homo adhuc vivere possit." But so arbitrary were these distinctions, that according to another form of the Rabbinical terminology, נֶפֶשׁ was the intelligent, immortal principle, נְשָׁמָה, on the other hand, the animal soul which passes away with the body (Delitzsch, p. 154, note). The more usual trichotomy of the Rabbins, נֶפֶשׁ for the lower soul, רוּחַ for the spirit of life, and נְשָׁמָה for the intelligent soul, may be noted as ministering to the confused usage through which, with some writers, spiritus came to signify the animal soul, and anima or mens the higher soul. See Lord Bacon's psychology as described in the preceding Note.

SOUL (נֶפֶשׁ, ψυχή).—The original use of נֶפֶשׁ is (a) for the principle of life as embodied in individual instances, and this either with חַיָּה, as Gen. i. 20, 30, or by itself, as Ex. xxi. 23; Job xxxi. 39; Jer. xv. 9. This life-principle is viewed as

seated in the blood, Gen. ix. 4; Lev. xvii. 11; Deut. xii. 23.
In this sense it is simply *anima*, the soul of the flesh. Then
(*b*) it becomes equivalent to *animus*, as the subject of all
activities, even of the highest in man, Deut. iv. 29, vi. 5;
Ps. xix. 8, xlii. 2; Isa. lxi. 10; and is used also of God
Himself, Jer. li. 14, on which the reader may consult Origen
(Ante-Nicene Lib. x. 118), *De Anima*. We then advance to
(*c*) its use to denote the individual possessing life. This
usage pervades the Scriptures. It proceeds on the distinction
that the נֶפֶשׁ or ψυχή is the subject of that personal life, the
principle of which is רוּחַ or πνεῦμα. But "soul," in the Old
Testament sense of the word, does not of itself constitute
personality. Delitzsch's remarks on this point are acute and
just (*Bibl. Psych.* p. 153). The use of soul (נֶפֶשׁ) for a
"dead body" is peculiar to the Old Testament, Lev. xxi. 11;
Num. vi. 6, ix. 6, 7, 10, xix. 13. It is most simply explained by Oehler on the principle of euphemism, just as we
speak of a "dead person" without meaning to say that the
personality lies in the body. Delitzsch's idea, that it may
allude to the impression made by a corpse immediately after
death, as if the soul still lingered by it, is more fanciful. In
the Septuagint and in the New Testament the use of ψυχή
is wider and higher than that of נֶפֶשׁ in the Old, for it has
often to stand for the Old Testament לֵב, the heart.

The adjective ψυχικός originally signified in classical Greek
that which pertains to life; then it came to be used in
antithesis to σωματικός. In Old Testament Greek it occurs
only in 4 Macc. i. 32 (ψυχικαί over against σωματικαί), and
in 2 Macc. iv. 37, xiv. 24 (in the adverbial form, equivalent
to "heartily"). In the New Testament it takes the remarkable meaning of a contrast, not to σωματικός, but to πνευματικός. (See passages referred to above under that word.)
On its peculiar use in Jude 19 the remark of Cremer seems
to be just, viz. that the ψυχικοί are not denied to possess
πνεῦμα as a constituent of human nature, which would have
been expressed by μὴ πνεῦμα ἔχοντες, but that they are not

so possessed of the πνεῦμα as they might have been. Beck
leans to a contrary conclusion (*Bibl. Seelenlehre*, p. 38). He
says man, by becoming mere *man with soul*, loses the stamp
of the spirit. This view of Beck probably arises from his
identifying "soul" with the human ego.

Of the relation of "soul" and "spirit" to each other, we
have spoken in the text, pp. 67–74. The following examples
of the combination of רוּחַ and נֶפֶשׁ in the same context may be
noted :—Ps. xxxi. 6, 8 ; Isa. xxvi. 9 (with which may be
compared the combination of לֵב and רוּחַ in Ex. xxxv. 21).
The antithesis of רוּחַ and נֶפֶשׁ in Job xii. 10, for human life
as contrasted with life in other creatures, is entirely singular.
The New Testament passages in which πνεῦμα and ψυχή stand
together are the well-known ones, Luke i. 47 (with which compare 1 Sam. ii. 1), Phil. i. 27 (where the English has "spirit"
and "mind") ; 1 Thess. v. 23 ; Heb. iv. 12.

BODY (σῶμα).—Its Hebrew equivalents are very various.
Böttcher, *De Inferis*, p. 20, arranges them as (1) proper, and
(2) metaphorical. Under (1) he gives, as the oldest terms
derived from the leading parts of the body, גְּוִיָּה, *truncus*,
1 Sam. xxxi. 10 ; עֶצֶם, *os, ossa*, Prov. xvi. 24 ; בָּשָׂר, *cutis, caro*,
flesh, Gen. ii. 24. As the second and third stages, he
remarks the use of a proper word for "body," גּוּפָה (*a cavitate*),
1 Chron. x. 12 ; גֶּשֶׁם (*contrectabile*), Dan. iii. 27. He further
notes, as an Old Testament usage, the employment of "flesh"
and "bones" for the whole body, Gen. ii. 23, Job ii. 5. It
is worthy of attention that "flesh and blood," which is not
an Old Testament expression, first occurs in the Apocrypha,
Sir. xiv. 18, xvii. 31 (see a conjectural emendation of this
singular passage in Böttcher, p. 35), 1 Macc. vii. 17, and so
passed into the current language of the New Testament.
Under (2) there occur in the Old Testament only Job iv. 19,
בָּתֵּי חֹמֶר (*houses of clay*), and Dan. vii. 15, נִדְנֶה, *a sheath*. But
with these may be compared the New Testament οἰκία τοῦ
σκήνους (2 Cor. v. 1), ναός (1 Cor. vi. 19), σκεῦος (2 Cor. iv. 7).

Of Flesh (בָּשָׂר, σάρξ) in its various uses we have spoken, pp. 74–86. The rise of the ethical meaning of σάρξ will probably remain the subject of considerable difference of opinion. That בָּשָׂר in its Old Testament meaning ever goes farther in an ethical direction than the physical weakness and frailty of human nature, has not been conclusively proved. Eccles. ii. 3 and v. 6 are quite insufficient proof. A philosophic origin has been asserted for the ethical force of σάρξ, and Lightfoot avers that such use of it has been traced to Epicurus (*On Philippians*, p. 285, note).

MIND.—*Νοῦς* is a word of which the scriptural use can be easily traced. It occurs very seldom in the Septuagint. In the few places where it does occur, it represents לֵבָב, לֵב, except in Isa. xl. 13, where νοῦν Κυρίου stands for רוּחַ יְהֹוָה; and the rendering is retained in 1 Cor. ii. 16. The apocryphal writers have used it a few times, and in a sense more distinctively Greek. The passage Wisd. ix. 15 is singularly unbiblical, suggesting, as we have said, the Stoical trichotomy, σῶμα, ψυχή, νοῦς. In the New Testament the entire absence of νοῦς, with one exception (Luke xxiv. 45), from the Gospels and from the writings of the older apostles (leaving Rev. xiii. 18, xvii. 9, out of sight), shows how clearly they adhere to the Old Testament psychology, from which the very notion represented by νοῦς was absent. To note its frequent use by Paul, and that especially definite and almost delicate antithesis in which it contrasts with σάρξ in one connection (Rom. vii.) and with πνεῦμα in another (1 Cor. xiv.), will complete its history.

CONSCIENCE.—*Συνείδησις* is a word of late introduction into the Scriptures. As Old Testament Greek, it occurs only once in the canonical books (Eccles. x. 20), where it renders מַדָּע, but obviously rather with the meaning " consciousness " than " conscience." The force of it in Wisd. xvii. 11 is more nearly our own. It does not occur in the Gospels, except in John viii. 9, a passage not usually reckoned genuine. In the

Epistle to the Hebrews and in the epistles of Paul and Peter
its occurrence is plentiful, and its force equivalent to that
which it has received in modern speech.   It is a function of
πνεῦμα if we regard it as self-consciousness, or of καρδία
when regarded as moral approval or disapproval.   It may also
be viewed as a function of the renewed πνεῦμα in believers
(see Rom. ix. 1).   The Old Testament לֵב covered what idea
of conscience was akin to Hebrew thought.   And it is to be
noted that St. John uses καρδία in a connection where St.
Paul would certainly have used νοῦς or συνείδησις (1 John
iii. 19–21).   To trace the advance of the term from its literal
meaning of self-consciousness to its full ethical import would
be of interest.   Its clear recognition in the latter sense in
Pagan literature is also significant.   Lightfoot speaks in somewhat strong terms of this word, as " the crowning triumph of
ethical nomenclature," which, " if not struck in the mint of
the Stoics, at all events became current coin through their
influence."   He cites it as a special instance of " the extent
to which Stoic philosophy had leavened the moral vocabulary
of the civilised world at the time of the Christian era " (Essay
on " St. Paul and Seneca" in his *Commentary on the Epistle to
the Philippians*, at p. 301).   On the place of conscience in
biblical psychology, see the slightly conflicting views of Harless,
Christliche Ethik, Pt. I. c. i. § 8, and Delitzsch, *Biblische
Psychologie*, III. iv. ; Beck's remarks, *Umriss*, etc., § 18, 22,
are also worthy of attention.

NOTES ON LECTURE III.

PASSAGES IN GEN. I. V. AND IX.

[THE subject of the divine image is one carefully discussed by all the leading commentators and theologians. I may name some instances of its special treatment from different points of view. It has been dealt with by Sebast. Schmidt, professor of theology at Strasburg, in his *Tractatus de Imagine Dei in Homine ante Lapsum* (Argent. ed., sec. 1701). The position of the author is strictly Lutheran, the mode of treatment laborious and scholastic. Bp. Bull's *State of Man before the Fall* (in vol. ii. of the Oxford edition of his works, 1846) is a tract full of patristic learning, and evinces also a very evident favour for the patristic view, that a special supernatural endowment in unfallen man could alone account for his primitive rectitude. Macdonald's excursus on "Man the Image of God," in his *Creation and the Fall* (p. 296 et seq.), is a cautious statement of the evangelical position. Schultz, in his *Voraussetzungen der christlichen Lehre von der Unsterblichkeit* (Göttingen, 1861), has touched upon the subject in a clear and interesting way, but diverges in the direction of "conditional immortality." On the three texts in Genesis I append a few further words.]

Gen. i. 26, 27. Besides those referred to in the lecture, another note of the specialty of the creation of man lies certainly in the plurals, "Let US make man in OUR image after OUR likeness." It is easy enough to be impatient with the mode of importing everything into every text of Scripture

which finds here already a full discovery of the trinity of
persons in the Godhead. But since *Elohim* has usually the
singular verb, it would be rash to conclude that there is no
peculiarity here at all, except the employment of a *pluralis
majestatis* to give dignity to the description of man's creation.
We may reasonably also think of something less jejune than
an address including with God Himself angels, or other pre-
created beings. We may think of a plurality in God of more
than powers and attributes—a hint of hypostases more distinctly unfolded as revelation grows. And it is surely not
without significance as to the relations between God and man,
that this hint of the plurality in Godhead occurs in connection
with the formation of man.

Gen. v. 1–3. The chief interest for us in this passage is
the bearing of the recapitulation in ver. 1 of man's formation in
the divine likeness (בִּדְמוּת with בְּ, instead of כְּ as in i. 26) on
the statement that Adam begat Seth "in his own likeness,
after his image." Some find in this latter an expression of
man's degeneracy by the fall,—that being himself created in
the divine likeness, he should beget a son only in his own.
Others go so far on the other side, as to find here a direct
proof that the divine image is propagated (Oehler, i. 210).

Gen. ix. 6. This passage connects itself directly with Gen.
i. 27, because of the use of צֶלֶם without וּדְמוּת, and because it is
followed by the renewal of the " divine command to be fruitful,
and multiply," etc. It is valuable in its strong assertion of
an inalienable divine property inherent in human nature, in
consequence of its formation at the first after the divine image.
This idea, moreover, is intimately connected with the institution of magistracy, which is in Scripture invariably represented
as a copy of the divine government. Note particularly the
use of *Elohim* for "judges," Ex. xxi. 6, xxii. 8, 28, and the
whole of Ps. lxxxii. (where Hupfeld is surely wrong in rendering " angels "). Rulers are still in the New Testament
Θεοῦ διάκονοι, λειτουργοί, Rom. xiii. 4, 6. They are God's
delegates, bearers of His image ; for here, in Gen. ix. 6, He

transfers to mankind His own prerogative of blood-avenging
(see story of Cain), and therefore His representatives among
mankind are also themselves called *Elohim*.

The remarks of Hofmann, on the inalienable aspects of the
image as indicated in these passages, are worth quoting:
" Dass sich der Erstgeschaffene zu einer Gottesbildlichkeit
geschaffen wusste, welche ihm allein eignete, von allen anderen
körperlichen Wesen ihn unterschied, spricht sich in dem
ersten Schöpfungsberichte darin aus, dass die Erschaffung des
Menschen als die Verwirklichung eines in den Worten כִּדְמוּתֵנוּ
נַעֲשֶׂה אָדָם בְּצַלְמֵנוּ sich aussagenden Gotteswillens dargestellt
wird.   Den Unterschied zwischen צֶלֶם und דְּמוּת, welchem
man eine viel zu grosse Bedeutung gegeben hat, beschränkt
Hävernick mit Recht darauf, das jenes das Concretum, Abbild,
letzteres das Abstraktum, Aehnlichkeit, ist . . . Gott hat
den Menschen geschaffen als sein Bild, ihn so geschaffen, dass
er ihm gleicht; dies besagen die Worte, und es fragt sich
nur, worin die Gottesbildlichkeit desselben bestehen soll.
Dass eine Aehnlichkeit der Gestalt des Menschen mit der
Gestalt Gottes gemeint sei, fällt mit der oben abgewiesenen
Behauptung, als sei der Gott, welcher dem Menschen erscheint,
darum auch ein körperlich gestalteter.   An die Gottähnlichkeit eines sittlich heiligen Wesens lässt der Zusammenhang
nicht denken, in welchem ja die Erschaffung nicht des Menschen
Adam im Unterschiede von dem nunmehr sündigen Gesch-
lechte, sondern der Menschheit in ihrem Unterschiede von der
Thierwelt berichtet ist.   Am wenigsten lässt sich ein Beweis
für diese Deutung aus Gen. v. 3 entnehmen.   Nicht von der
sittlichen Aehnlichkeit der Söhne Adam's mit ihrem Vater
ist dort die Rede, sondern von der Gleichartigkeit von Vater
und Sohn, vermöge welcher das Geschlecht, so lange es sich
natürlich fortpflanzt und nicht in jene (Gen. vi. 1, 2) erzählte
wiedernatürliche Entartung geräth, sich gleich und dasselbe
bleibt, als welches es von Gott geschaffen worden.   Gegenüber
der Thierwelt und den Lichtkörpern des Himmels ist der
Mensch gottähnlich, daher auch mit וַיִּרְדּוּ als Folge seiner

Gottähnlichkeit, nicht aber als Inbegriff derselben, bezeichnet wird, dass er über die Thierwelt herrscht. Sonne und Mond haben eine Herrschaft, aber als leblose Körper; die Thiere sind lebendige Wesen, aber sie füllen nur Luft, Wasser und Land. Der Mensch dagegen herrscht über die Erde und ihre Thierwelt als nicht blos lebendiges, sondern persönliches Wesen. In eben dem also, was ihn befähigt, die welt um ihn her zu beherrschen, besteht auch seine Gottesbildlichkeit. Ein bewusst freies Ich, ein persönliches Wesen zu sein, ist er geschaffen, und verhält sich dadurch als geschaffenes und körperliches Wesen zu seiner Umgebung, wie sich die Gottheit, welche Geist ist, zur Welt überhaupt verhält. Dass diese Bestimmung der Gottesbildlichkeit des Menschen eine unzureichende sei, wird sich wenigstens aus Gen. i. und Ps. viii. nicht erweisen lassen.

"Nicht ein sittliches Verhalten bedeutet demnach die Gottesbildlichkeit, sondern ein sittliches Verhältniss. Daher wird sie fortgepflanzt auch von dem sündig gewordenen Erstgeschaffenen; und nicht von dem heiligen Menschen, sondern von dem Menschen, darum dass er Mensch ist, heisst es nachmals, er trage Gottes Bild. Die Menschen, wie sie jetzt sind, nennt Jakobus τοὺς ἀνθρώπους τοὺς καθ᾽ ὁμοίωσιν θεοῦ γεγονότας, und weist damit natürlich nicht blos auf die Erschaffung des ersten Menschen zurück, so wenig als Paulus, wenn er das Wort des heidnischen Dichters anerkennt τοῦ γὰρ καὶ γένος ἐσμέν, oder David wenn er von dem Menschen, wie er jetzt ist, zu Jehova spricht

מָה־אֱנוֹשׁ כִּי־תִזְכְּרֶנּוּ וּבֶן־אָדָם כִּי תִפְקְדֶנּוּ וַתְּחַסְּרֵהוּ
מְעַט מֵאֱלֹהִים וְכָבוֹד וְהָדָר תְּעַטְּרֵהוּ

—*Schriftbeweis*, i. pp. 287, 288.

Note J, Page 116.

RECENT VIEWS OF THE DIVINE IMAGE.

THE following sentences present a brief summary of the considerably divergent opinions put forth by the five modern Continental theologians named in the Lecture.

SCHLEIERMACHER notes its emphasis in Gen. i. 26, 27, as expressing the type of man; not referring to the first man in his individuality, but rather as he is the first copy of the human species; he finds it sets forth the nature of man in its supereminence above that of all other creatures. As for any direct information to be further derived from the expression, he is inclined to hold that little or nothing can be made of it, because of the untenable consequences in which one is landed by every attempt to reason from man the copy to God the original,—reasonings which leave only an alternative of gross pantheism on the one hand, or still more gross anthropomorphism on the other, or at least an impure mixing up of the divine and human, which leads either to the ascription of properties to God not to be conceived as divine, or to man of such as are not conceivably human. This (says he) is an example how little biblical expressions, especially in connections not expressly didactic, are to be transferred *brevi manu* to the language of dogmatics. He does not therefore wonder that many theologians, seeing these consequences of a rigid interpretation of that divine declaration (about the image), incline with the Socinians to refer it rather to the plastic and governing (*bildende und beherrschende*) relation of man to outward nature than to man's inner being. Gathering so little from the sacred narrative, it is to him matter of indifference whether it be intended to be historical or not. He does not expect to be able to evolve from it any information how the first man was educated or came to the know-

ledge of God.   He is content with the position demanded by
his own scheme of Christian belief, viz. that since piety or
religion is a common element of all human life, it must be as
old as the human race itself; and the first human beings must
have been in a position to effect the development of the God-
consciousness in those who immediately succeeded them.
This constitutes for him " the original perfection of the
human being," and is quite consistent in his view with an
incapacity long to resist temptation.   Of this theory of man's
original state it may be not unfairly said, that it represents
him as created in a condition of unstable moral equilibrium.
It is not much, if any, higher than the Pelagian view.
[*Der christliche Glaube*, i. 326 et seq.   For Schleiermacher's
view of original righteousness, see *infra*, Note M.]

HOFMANN maintains that the scriptural doctrine of the
image was never meant to express what kind of being man
is, but only in what relation to God he was created.[1]   So he
values his own definition of the "image," because it says
nothing about the constitution of human nature, but only sets
forth the double relationship of that nature to God.   In discussing Gen. i. 26 (see quotation given in Note I), he defines
wherein, according to him, the divine image in man consists.
That it refers to similarity of form, falls with the assumption that God appeared to man in a bodily shape.   The connection will not suffer us to think of a similarity in holy
moral being, for the thing described is not the formation of
Adam as distinguished from his now sinful posterity, but of
mankind in contradistinction from the animal world.   Neither
is it the dominion alone.   This is a consequence of the divine
likeness, but not the content of it.   Man rules over the earth
and the animal world as a personal being.   The divine image
therefore consists in that which makes him capable of ruling
over the world around him.   He is created to be a free,
conscious ego; and in virtue of this, he, a created and corporeal

---

[1] It is at this point that he makes objections to the possibility of biblical
psychology, in a passage already quoted, Note A.

being, is related to his environment, as the Godhead, which is
a spirit, is related to the universe at large. The divine image
therefore denotes not a moral condition, but a moral relation.
Hence it is propagated even by the first man after his fall
(Gen. v. 1), and is predicated of man not as holy, but of man
as he is man (Gen. ix. 6; Jas. iii. 9; 1 Cor. xi. 7). We
say, then, in accordance with Scripture, that the image consists
in the personality of man the corporeal being, and we have
also Scripture for us if we go farther and express the double
relationship of man to the divine. Since, on the one side,
man is a conscious, free personality, on the other side a nature
or being serving himself by means of himself (*sich zum
Mittel seiner selbst dienende Natur*), he thus becomes the
image of God in a twofold manner. He occupies on the
one hand a relation to God like to that inner relation of
the Godhead which has become inequality. He becomes on
the other hand a created copy of God, who is the archetypal purpose of the universe. We can only draw our proof
of this, says Hofmann, from the New Testament doctrine of
Christ, not from the Old Testament account of man's creation.
And he argues against Delitzsch, who will have man to be an
image of the Trinity, that both positions are true; just as of
Christ it may be said all fulness of the Godhead dwells in
Him (Col. ii. 9), and yet that in the sense of John xiv. 9 He
is the image of the invisible God, *i.e.* of the Father (Col.
i. 15; Heb. i. 3). Thus we may quite consistently affirm
that man's relation to his environment is an image of the
relation of the Godhead in general to the world, and also
that humanity has a more defined relation to the Father
in the Son; so that as the divine likeness in the Son is
more accurately expressed by saying that He is the image
of the Father, the divine likeness in man is more fully defined
by saying that he is the image of the Son, or rather that the
relation of man to God is a relation to the Father in the
Son; that humanity is δόξα Χριστοῦ, as the woman is δόξα
ἀνδρός (*Schriftbeweis*, i. 283-291).

JULIUS MÜLLER is more consistent in working out a similar
line of thought. He does not start with saying that the
expression tells only of man's relations, and not of his being
or nature.   He holds that צֶלֶם and דְּמוּת denote a resemblance
in character between the image and its original, rather than in
the relation which each bears to something else (*Christian Doctrine of Sin*, ii. 351); that not only is there no positive proof
in Scripture that the image wherein man was created was lost
in the fall, but that there are statements proving the presence
in man of God's image still; that the distinction of theologians
between a wider and a stricter sense of the image is a make-
shift, to bring the texts into harmony with their doctrine
concerning the forfeiture of the divine image (ii. 353).   The
way in which the divine image is introduced in Genesis
suggests, he says, that it is "something in man which
specially distinguishes him from all other existences in
nature."   He holds, therefore, that it consists manifestly in
man's personality.   Other beings show forth His power and
Godhead, but beings in His image are a revelation of God,
not for others only, but for themselves; who not only are,
but know that they are; who are conscious of themselves, and
therefore of God also.   That IN GOD man lives, etc. (Acts
xvii. 28, 29), implies that man must be a self-conscious *ego*,
a person, for he can be in God so far only as he is, in the
highest sense, in himself; and for this very reason he is the
" offspring " of God (τοῦ γένος ἐσμέν), God and man,—
absolute and relative personality,—being a γένος distinct
from all impersonal existence.   The truth that IN HIM we
live, that we are of His kind, is stated as a guarantee that
" we can feel after Him and find Him" in His world.   Man
should not let himself be hindered from knowing and loving
God, as like to himself, by any deistic or pantheistic abstrac-
tions which would deny him this fellowship.   God, in creating
man, made him in His image.   There is therefore no
anthropomorphism when man conceives of God as a being
like himself, a Spirit who knows and wills.   " If, then, the

divine image in man is spiritual personality, it cannot be a merely transitory gift, but is an essential part of his constitution, still possessed by him, though in a state of sin, leading to his dominion over the creatures, and fully realized in the image of Christ wrought out in him by redemption " (ii. pp. 354, 355).

OEHLER holds that Gen. i. 26 expresses the very idea of man, that this divine image is propagated (Gen. v. 1, 3), and that it is clear from Gen. ix. 6 that the divine image lies inalienably in man's being. In answer to the question what is to be understood by it, he posits the *whole dignity of man* (כָּבוֹד וְהָדָר, Ps. viii. 6), in virtue of which (1) human nature is sharply distinguished from that of the beasts, as proved by the unique divine act of human origination, by the fact that there was no mate for man among the animals, and by the permission to kill the beasts, but not man; and (2) man is set over nature as a free personality, designed for communion with God, and fitted to take God's place on earth (*Old Testament Theology*, i. 211, 212).

DELITZSCH holds that the image of God in man refers primarily to his *invisible nature*, founding this remark upon his exegesis of Ps. viii. "Thou hast made him fall a little short of the nature of the Elohim, *i.e.* of the divine and angelic," which must be incorporeal and purely spiritual. Then, as distinguished from the angels, it is peculiar to man that God created him, the earthly one, after His image. He thinks it not erroneous to regard the spiritual nature of man as the image, in so far as that is something common to men and angels. However, this view of the Fathers, which seems to satisfy a later theology, that the divine image subsists in the νοερὸν καὶ αὐτεξούσιον, or, as we say, in personality, he holds to be quite insufficient, for fallen man is also a person. But he rejects the distinction of a broader or physical and a narrower or ethical aspect of the image, the first of which cannot be lost, and the second of which has been lost, as subject to the charge of an unreconciled dualism, felt even by the dogmatists who have invented it.   Scripture, he says, only knows of one likeness of God in man, which is at once moral and physical, and which cannot be lost morally without being at the same time physically ruined.   Scripture nowhere says that fallen man possesses the *imago Dei* still in living reality; it places the dignity of man now only in the fact that he has been created after the image of God.   This strikes us as exceedingly correct and acceptable, provided it be not bound up with any theory as to the πνεῦμα in man, which would commit us to view the image as physically constituted in creation and physically destroyed by the fall.   What he goes on to add in his latest edition as to the image in man being a creaturely copy of the entire absolute life of the Triune God, and not merely of the Logos, belongs to the dreamy theosophy which is the least valuable feature in the productions of Dr. Delitzsch.

NOTE K, PAGE 123.

INTELLECTUAL FEATURES OF THE IMAGE.

The general principle that rationality enters into the notion of the divine image as a radical element is well stated by the late Prin. Fairbairn in his *Cunningham Lecture* (pp. 37, 38):—

" Undoubtedly, as the primary element in this idea (of the divine image) must be placed the intellect, or rational nature of the soul in man; the power or capacity of mind, which enabled him in discernment to rise above the impressions of sense, and in action to follow the guidance of an intelligent aim or purpose, instead of obeying the blind promptings of appetite or instinct.   Without such a faculty, there had been wanting the essential ground of moral obligation; man could not have been the subject either of praise or of blame; for he should have been incapable, as the inferior animals universally

are, of so distinguishing between the true and the false, the
right and the wrong, and so appreciating the reasons which
ought to make the one rather than the other the object of
one's desire and choice, as to render him morally responsible
for his conduct. . . . And made as man was, in this respect,
after the image of God, we cannot conceive of him otherwise
than as endowed with an understanding to know everything,
either in the world around him or his own relation to it,
which might be required to fit him for accomplishing, without
failure or imperfection, the destination he had to fill, and
secure the good which he was capable of attaining. How far,
as subservient to this end, the discerning and reasoning faculty
in unfallen man might actually reach, we want the materials
for enabling us to ascertain; but in the few notices given of
him, we see the free exercise of that faculty in ways perfectly
natural to him, and indicative of its sufficiency for his place
and calling in creation." After adducing as instances the
naming of the creatures and the recognition of Eve, Dr. Fairbairn goes on: "These, of course, are but specimens, yet
enough to show the existence of the faculty, and the manner
of its exercise, as qualifying him—not, indeed, to search into
all mysteries, or bring him acquainted with the principles of
universal truth (of which nothing is hinted)—but to know the
relations and properties of things so far as he had personally
to do with them, or as was required to guide him with wisdom
and discretion amid the affairs of life. To this extent the
natural intelligence of Adam bore the image of his Maker's."

The late Hugh Miller carries this idea of correspondence
between the intellectual processes of man and the working of
that Supreme Intelligence which framed the world, into some
striking applications. He finds one of these, for example, in
the exact coincidence of those most correct natural systems of
scientific classification at which men have now arrived, with
the order suggested in the successive production of the
structures themselves. In the opening pages of his *Testimony
of the Rocks*, he says: "Now that a wonderful opportunity

has occurred of comparing, in this matter of classification, the human with the divine idea,—the idea embodied by the zoologists and botanists in their respective systems, with the idea embodied by the Creator of all in geologic history,—we cannot perhaps do better, in entering upon our subject, than to glance briefly at the great features in which God's order of classification, as developed in palæontology, agrees with the order in which man has at length learned to range the living productions, plant and animal, by which he is surrounded, and of which he himself forms the most remarkable portion. In an age in which a class of writers, not without their influence in the world of letters, would fain repudiate every argument derived from *design*, and denounce all who hold with Paley and Chalmers as anthropomorphists, that labour to create for themselves a god of their own type and form, it may be not altogether unprofitable to contemplate the wonderful parallelism which exists between the divine and human systems of classification, and, remembering that the geologists who have discovered the one had no hand in assisting the naturalists and phytologists who framed the other, soberly to inquire whether we have not a new argument in the fact for an identity in constitution and quality of the divine and human minds,—not a mere fanciful identity, the result of a disposition on the part of man to imagine to himself a God bearing his own likeness, but an identity real and actual, and the result of that creative act by which God formed man in His own image."

The same charming writer furnishes from his own favourite science illustrations in several departments of what he calls "correspondence of nature and intellect between the two workers, human and divine." He finds in the construction of the ancient organisms which the geologist brings to light, " mechanical contrivances" which have a "human cast and character" about them, —which indicate, in short, a certain identity of mind in the constructive department between the creative Worker and His creature workers. In the æsthetic region, again, he instances some very curious facts, as, for example, that one of the most popular of Lancashire calico patterns was found to be identical with a recently discovered Old Red Sandstone coral; and he goes on to state in more general terms the intellectual image of God which man still retains: " I must hold that we receive the true explanation of the *man*-like character of the Creator's workings ere man was, in the remarkable text in which we are told that ' God made man in His own image and likeness.' There is no restriction here to moral quality: the moral image man had, and in large measure lost; but the intellectual image he still retains. As a geometrician, as an arithmetician, as a chemist, as an astronomer,—in short, in all the departments of what are known as the strict sciences, man differs from his Maker not in kind, but in degree,—not as matter differs from mind, or darkness from light, but simply as a mere portion of space or time differs from *all* space or *all* time. I have already referred to mechanical contrivances as identically the same in the divine and human productions, nor can I doubt that, not only in the pervading sense of the beautiful in form and colour which it is our privilege as men in some degree to experience and possess, but also in that perception of harmony which constitutes the *musical* sense, and in that poetic feeling of which Scripture furnishes us with at once the earliest and the highest example, and which we may term the *poetic* sense, we bear the stamp and impress of the divine image. Now, if this be so, we must look upon the schemes of creation, revelation, and providence, not as schemes of mere adaptation to man's nature, but as schemes also specially adapted to the nature of God as the pattern and original nature."—*Testimony of the Rocks*, p. 243.

NOTE L, PAGE 129.

WAS MAN CREATED IN THE IMAGE OF THE SON ?

WHAT Scripture clearly teaches as to the Christological rela-
tions of the| divine image can be very briefly stated. It has
two lines of statement connecting the Son of God with the
formation or constitution of mankind,—the one referring to
creation, the other to redemption. Man is represented in
Scripture as the crown or goal of that earthly creation of
which the eternal Word is the Author. Again, the eternal
Word, image of the invisible God, is declared to be also the first-
born of the whole creation—the absolute Heir and sovereign
Lord of all. There is thus a propriety in holding man to be
in this sense a copy of the Logos, to be created κατ᾽ εἰκόνα
τοῦ εἰκόνος. But there is no express Scripture assertion of
this resemblance of man, as at first created, to the eternal Son.
On the contrary, it is always the image or likeness of God
that is spoken of in this connection. That the Logos is He
through whom, and in whom, and for whom man is created,
is, of course, implicitly asserted in Scripture. But, as Delitzsch
says (with evident reference to such statements of Hofmann as
those I have quoted in Note J), it would be a mistake to affirm
that man was created after the image of the Son, and not of
the Father or of the Holy Spirit. Everywhere Scripture says
that man was created after the image of the Elohim, or of the
Godhead. Man is called (1 Cor. xi. 7) εἰκὼν καὶ δόξα Θεοῦ,
not Χριστοῦ.

When we come to the new creation, the language of Scripture is explicit in asserting that the Son is the prototype of
redeemed or renewed humanity. The divine image is restored
in those who are predestinated " to be conformed to the image
of His Son " (Rom. viii. 29), συμμόρφους τῆς εἰκόνος τοῦ υἱοῦ
αὐτοῦ; we are renewed in the spirit of our mind only as we

" put on the new man, which is renewed in knowledge after the image of Him that created him " (Col. iii. 10, 11), τὸν ἀνακαινούμενον εἰς ἐπίγνωσιν κατ᾽ εἰκόνα τοῦ κτίσαντος αὐτόν; and in this new creation Christ is all in all, ὅπου . . . τὰ πάντα καὶ ἐν πᾶσι Χριστός. Our likeness to His image is only to be completed when in the final manifestation (ἀποκάλυψις) of the Redeemer and of the redeemed as sons of God, we shall see Him as He is (comp. Rom. viii. 19 with 1 John iii. 2). Then the resemblance shall extend even to the outward form our humanity is to wear, for " He shall transform the body of our humiliation that it may be made conformable to the body of His own glory" (Phil. iii. 21),ʽΟς μετασχηματίσει τὸ σῶμα τῆς ταπεινώσεως ἡμῶν, εἰς τὸ γενέσθαι αὐτὸ σύμμορφον τῷ σώματι τῆς δόξης αὐτοῦ. " As we have borne the image of the earthy, we shall also bear the image of the heavenly " (1 Cor. xv. 49), that is, of the second Man, the Lord from heaven (ver. 47).

All this is clear. But when we attempt any more detailed connection between these two lines of statement, we find little in Scripture to support us. When we endeavour to connect in thought the relation of the Logos to humanity in the first creation with the relation of the incarnate Redeemer to renewed humanity, we enter upon a somewhat " dim and perilous way." It looks very tempting to say that man must have been created at first in the image of Him who was afterwards to be incarnate for man's redemption; that there must have been a special relation of the pre-existent Logos to mankind, preparatory to that near relation which He was afterwards to assume when He became flesh. But it leads directly to the theory of an incarnation apart from the necessity of redemption. And the evangelical Church has always been jealous of speculations leading that way. The theory appears in Christian theology as early as Irenæus (see *Contra Omnes Hæreticos*, V. xvi. § 2). It was a favourite speculation of the Schoolmen, such as Hales, Aquinas, Occam, and Bonaventura. It was mooted by Osiander, a kind of Schoolman among the

Reformers.   But Reformation theology distinctly disowned it (see Calvin, *Instit.* II. xii. 4–7 ; Mastricht, *Theologia*, i. 441), consequently the proposition on which it was based has also been looked upon with disfavour.   S. Schmidt (*Tractatus de Imagine Dei*, p. 339), alluding to opinions held by disciples of Origen, and in the Middle Ages by P. Lombardus, represents the view that Christ only was the prototype of Adam's creation as one rejected by the Church, and rejected because of the terms of the original edict of man's formation in the image of God.

Earnest thinkers in theology have often sighed for some pathway that would lead direct from an original relation of the eternal Logos with the human race to the actual incarnation of the Redeemer.   Some have even said that the theory of expiation cannot " retain its place in the thoughts of the Church unless it can be shown that the death of Christ as a propitiation and a sacrifice for the sins of men is the highest expression of an eternal relation between Christ and the human race " (Dale on *The Atonement*, p. 405).   Doubtless there is something more in the great texts (Col. i. 15–17 ; Eph. i. 10–22 ; Rom. viii. 18–23, etc.) which combine the relation of the Son to the universe with that of the glorified Redeemer to the " restitution of all things," than the Church has ever formulated.   In that direction there is theological territory to be possessed.   But it would serve no end of conquest to open toward it mere hypothetical gateways. For to affirm that man was at first created an image of the Logos is but a hypothesis, and one at best but slenderly supported.

NOTE M, PAGE 133.

ORIGINAL RIGHTEOUSNESS.

SCHLEIERMACHER criticises the phrase in a passage of some interest, and points out what he considers its disadvantages. He thinks it inconvenient not only because *righteousness* requires for its development a social state, but chiefly because the proper conception of *righteousness* as a virtue is that of something arising or acquired in the course of the development of a personal life, not that of a fundamental state or condition from which the development is to take its rise. So that a most undesirable conventional or technical meaning must attach to the expression *righteousness* when applied to the original condition of man, such as it never has in any other connection. . . . If nothing more be meant by representing the first man's actual condition as one of original righteousness, than simply to oppose the Pelagian position by maintaining that it could not have been one of sin, he thinks it may be unconditionally accepted. But if it be meant to imply an actual power which has elevated the higher faculties over the lower, then it would be impossible to conceive of anything else than a continual progression of this power to higher and further degrees (*i.e.* apparently, it would be impossible on this hypothesis to conceive of sin and the fall as ever actually taking place). This is probably the reason why the Romish Church, he says, has conceived of the original state as caused and maintained by an extraordinary divine influence, which, of course, commits the holders of it to a Pelagian view of human nature. It may not be so detrimental in its consequences, but it is just as perplexing to the true conception of the *ursprüngliche Vollkommenheit*, when some of our (Protestant) expounders of the faith affirm that our first parents were in their original condition partakers of the Holy Spirit.

" It seems, then," he goes on, " to be fruitless to attempt to
define more precisely the original condition of the first human
beings, whether we try to think of it as corresponding to what
afterwards becomes known as the advancing development of
the original perfection, or to that which appears to us as a
back-step (*Rückschritt*) in the development. For the Pelagians,
going upon this latter supposition, obtain a twofold advantage,
—(1) that they assume no original perfection which was lost,
and (2) that from the point of commencement which they
assume a continuous development can find place, with the
twofold disadvantage—(1) that goodness with them is not the
original state, and (2) that in the development of goodness
the Redeemer appears only as a single member. The Church
doctrine, on the other hand, obtains the twofold advantage—
(1) that goodness is represented as something immediately
drawn from God; and (2) that when, after the loss of this
original condition, the development is broken off, and a new
point of commencement rendered necessary, the Redeemer can
step forward as the turning-point, with the twofold disadvantage—(1) that the goodness which in appearance was already
attained (by our first parents) could be lost despite of the
upholding divine omnipotence; and (2) that the only purpose
for which we can be tempted to imagine to ourselves the
original condition of the first man, namely, to have a point of
commencement for the genetic presentation of all that follows,
cannot be reached. Consequently, it is more to the point to
define nothing precisely regarding the first condition of the
first man, and just to evolve the original perfection of nature
out of the higher self-consciousness considered in its universality. But would we see in one single human appearance all
displayed that can be evolved out of such original perfection,
this must not be sought for in Adam, in whom it must again
have been lost, but in Christ, in whom it has brought gain to
all."—*Der christliche Glaube*, i. 341, 342.

Whether intentionally or not, this author has clearly
admitted the superiority over all others of the evangelical

view of man's original moral standing. That we are unable to construe in our own minds its mode and habit is no valid objection to its actuality. And it is confessedly the only point of commencement which is consistent with the entire history of human sin and redemption as given in the Bible. Schleiermacher's own view is really no better than that of the Pelagians, for through a confounding of the possibility of a thing with the germ of it, he posits, what even Müller also seems to admit, a " germ of evil" in primitive man. No position, save that man's original righteousness was a state of knowing and doing right which the Creator Himself had originated, will carry us consistently through the whole Bible doctrine regarding man's moral history.

NOTES ON LECTURE IV.

NOTE N, PAGE 143.

THE PROBLEM OF EVIL NECESSARILY INSOLUBLE.

THE origin of evil need not be sought. The nature of evil is
that it must be inexplicable,—an additional confirmation of
the position that it rises in an act of free-will, for in vain
do we seek a cause beyond the will itself. It is in this very
connection that Augustine asserts that the question of the
origin of evil can have no solution : " Si enim dixerimus quod
ipse eam (voluntatem malam) fecerit, quid erat ipse ante voluntatem malam nisi natura bona, cujus auctor Deus, qui est incom-
mutabile bonum ? Qui ergo dicit eum qui consensit tentanti
atque suadenti . . . ipsum sibi fecisse voluntatem malam, quia
utique bonus ante voluntatem malam fuerit ; quærat cur eam
fecerit, utrum quia natura est, an quia ex nihilo facta est : et
inveniet voluntatem malam non ex eo esse incipere quod
natura est, sed ex eo quod de nihilo natura facta est. Nam
si natura causa est voluntatis malæ, quid aliud cogimur
dicere, nisi a bono fieri malum, et bonum esse causam mali
si quidem a natura bona fit voluntas mala ? Quod unde
fieri potest, ut natura bona, quamvis mutabilis, antequam
habeat voluntatem malam, faciat aliquid mali, hoc est, ipsam
voluntatem malam ? *Nemo igitur quærat efficientem causam*
malæ voluntatis: non enim est efficiens, sed deficiens ; quia nec
illa effectio est, sed defectio. Deficere namque ab eo quod
summe est, ad id quod minus est, hoc est incipere habere
voluntatem malam. *Causas porro defectionum istarum, cum*
efficientes non sint, ut dixi, sed deficientes, velle invenire, tale est

ac si quisquam velit videre tenebras, vel audire silentium : quod
tamen utrumque nobis notum est; neque illud nisi per oculos,
neque hoc nisi per aures; non sane in specie, sed in speciei
privatione.   Nemo ergo ex me scire quærat, quod me nescire
scio, nisi forte ut nescire discat, quod sciri non posse scien-
dum est."—*De Civitate Dei,* lib. xii. cc. vi. vii.

So also Pascal : " Le peché originel est folie devant les
hommes, mais on le donne pour tel.   Vous ne me deves donc
pas reprocher le defaut de raison en cette doctrine, puisque je
la donne pour estre sans raison.   Mais cette folie est plus sage
que toute la sagesse des hommes, ' sapientius est hominibus.'
Car sans cela, que dira-t'on qu'est l'homme ?   Tout son estat
depend de ce point imperceptible, et comment s'en fust-il
apperceu par sa raison, puisque c'est une chose contre la
raison, et que sa raison bien loin de l'inventer pas ses voyes
s'en éloigne quand on le lui présente ? "—*Pensées* (Molinier),
i. pp. 293, 294.

Neander puts the same thing with much point: "According
to my conviction, the origin of evil can only be understood as
a fact—a fact possible by virtue of the freedom belonging to a
created being, but not to be otherwise deduced or explained.
It lies in the idea of evil that it is an utterly inexplicable thing,
and whoever would explain it nullifies the very idea of it.
It is not the limits of our knowledge which make the origin
of sin something inexplicable *to us,* but it follows from the
essential nature of sin as an act of free-will that it must
remain to all eternity an inexplicable fact.   It can only be
understood *empirically* by means of the moral self-consciousness.   Τὸ ἐρώτημα ὃ πάντων αἴτιόν ἐστι κακῶν, μᾶλλον δὲ ἡ
περὶ τούτου ὠδὶς, ἐν τῇ ψυχῇ ἐγγιγνομένη, ἣν εἰ μή τις ἐξαιρε-
θήσεται, τῆς ἀληθείας ὄντως οὐ μή ποτε τύχοι, *Ep.* II. Platon.
Whoever in his arrogant littleness can satisfy himself with
mutilating human nature, and reducing it to a minimum, with
substituting thinking in a certain form in place of the whole
man, may adjust after his own fashion all the phenomena
in the moral world; but the unconquerable voice of Nature

will know how to assert her rights against all such fine-spun theories." — *Planting and Training of the Christian Church*, i. 423, note (Bohn).

So also Dr. John Duncan, in his characteristic way evidently drawing upon recollections of the passage quoted from the *De Civitate:* " I cannot get out of the meshes of Augustinianism on the privative nature of sin. Evil is a defect, just as death is a privation, the loss of what once was, and therefore of what is needful for health and completion of existence. Inanimation is the negation of life, and what death physical is to the body, viz. the withdrawal of life, sin is to the soul, the withdrawal of its life. God is not the author of sin, because sin has no author. Sin is an off-cutting, a degeneracy, a cancer or corruption consequent on privation. . . . As to its essence and its origin, beyond this that I have said, it always seems to me that our speculations are directed to find the *rationale* of the only irrational thing in the universe, and of the only thing that has *no cause*. Suppose it to have one; well, is not that causal volition of the creature a sin, equally with all that follows from it? If so, whence came it? From God? μὴ γένοιτο. If not from God, whence? *From naught.* . . . It is causeless and irrational. It is monstrosity—a thing horrible in a God-made universe just *because* it is causeless."—*Colloquia Peripatetica*, pp. 3–6.

NOTE O, PAGE 144.

REALITY OF THE TEMPTATION NARRATIVE.

As to the actual character of the temptation, we must take the same ground as that assumed in the account of Paradise. It is no myth or fabulous clothing of a philosophical conception. Neither is it an allegory or sensuous presentation of an inward or spiritual transaction. It is the record of a real but entirely unique and primitive event in the unfolding of humanity. But in maintaining the real character of the narrative, we must be careful not to betray our position by insisting on a prosaic literalness of interpretation. Van Oosterzee, rejecting the mythical and allegorical modes of interpretation, views the narrative from "the standpoint of the historic conception." "We have here," he says, "a *Sage*, if we want to use this word, but one of which the kernel is undoubtedly history." He admits that there are in it "elements which cannot possibly be literally apprehended," and says that in so far as this is the case it may be regarded as a history "which, though not real, is nevertheless an infallibly true one." Much of what seems strange and incredible in the narrative, he adds, disappears "when we only know how to get through the shell to the kernel, and consider that we are here moving in a higher sphere than that of a dead-level, every-day reality" (*Dogmatics*, pp. 403, 404). So Martensen: "The Mosaic account of the fall of man is a combination of history and sacred symbolism—a figurative presentation of an actual event." "We must remember," he adds, "that the human consciousness by which these events are now presented is one to which both Paradise and the fall are transcendental and prehistoric, for which reason there can be no immediate knowledge of them, but only a knowledge that is mediate, as in a glass darkly" (*Christian Dogmatics*, p. 155). Nitzsch, who quotes Martensen, has used an expression open to misunderstanding when he says that "the Mosaic 'Hamartigenie' is to be held as a true but not an actual history." Ebrard condemns the phrase as a merely prudent way of yielding up the Scripture history to the mythico-allegorical theory. Nitzsch defends himself by saying that the fall of David or of Peter can be presented to us in its actuality (*Wirklichkeit*), but that of Adam only in its truth (*Wahrheit*)—a truth of which we could only be made aware through the Word of God (*System der christlichen Lehre*, p. 228).

Müller thinks it " very difficult to decide what is symbolic clothing and what is real fact " (*Christian Doctrine of Sin*, ii. p. 386), and declines " to enter on the very difficult and critical question whether the narrative be throughout historical." " The hypothesis now in vogue," which regards it as " only the philosophising of some thoughtful Israelite or Oriental concerning the origin of evil, written under the garb of history," he summarily rejects, for in that case, he says, " Christian theology could make no use of it." He points out in a note that this view is improperly called the " mythical," because, according to the proper definition of the *mythus*, that term cannot be applied to a didactic fable deliberately composed by some one. The supposition, he says, is simpler (though also not to be wholly approved of) which regards the narrative as one " wherein history and imagination, truth and fiction, are blended." For, he argues, even upon this theory we must recognise an historical germ, about which elements of fiction gathered during the crystallizing process of national tradition (pp. 347–349).

The real historical character of the narrative is conclusively established when we have regard to these lines of proof :—(1) The manner in which it is referred to in the Scriptures themselves (*e.g.* Job xxxi. 33 ; Hos. vi. 7 ; 2 Cor. xi. 3 ; 1 Tim. ii. 14). (2) The clearly historic view derived from the narrative both by the Jews and by the primitive Church. The Old Testament apocryphal books are unusually rich in their references to Paradise and the fall, and their tone on these points is unmistakeable. Ancient biblical literature, both Jewish and Christian, points strongly in the same direction. For although the tendency to allegorize these primitive facts in the sacred history is a very strong one in the Jewish-Alexandrian, in the Rabbinical, and in the early Christian schools, the very mode of allegorizing is such as to show that the writers assumed the actual character of the things to which they gave a secondary spiritual interpretation. (3) A very interesting proof of the historical character of the temptation narrative is, at the moment we write, receiving fuller illustration at the hand of scholars than in any previous period of biblical study, viz. that which arises from a comparison of the Mosaic narrative with Oriental and other ethnic traditions concerning the entrance of evil. This subject is being carefully studied not only in the sacred books of Persia and India, but in the inscriptions and monuments of Assyria and Chaldea. And although in some instances speculative grasping at affinity with the sacred narrative " has outrun the bounds of scientific method," the general result is daily becoming clearer that these remains speak not of a philosophic myth or of an allegorical conception, but of an actual event, the remembrance of which has been conveyed in veiled and traditional forms along the stream of historic religions. See the writings of Rawlinson, Layard, G. Smith, Friedrich Delitzsch, Lenormant, and others.

NOTE P, PAGES 172, 174, 175.

THE RELATION OF PHYSICAL DEATH TO SIN.

THAT according to the original constitution of man in innocence, his physical part was mortal, is admitted by the most thoughtful divines. In the light of their interpretations, given many of them long before science had propounded her maxims, it will be seen at once that Scripture is nowhere committed to the absurd position that the fall of man introduced into the world the principle of decay in animal organisms. But these divines are as careful, on the other hand, to maintain the scriptural position, that for man death in all its forms is a consequence of sin.

AUGUSTINE, *De Peccatorum Meritis et Remissione*, lib. I. cap. iv., thus quotes and comments on Rom. viii. 10, 11 : " *Si*

autem Christus in vobis est, corpus quidem mortuum est propter
peccatum, etc. . . . *qui suscitavit Christum Jesum a mortuis,*
vivificabit et mortalia corpora vestra, per inhabitantem spiritum
ejus in vobis.   Puto quod non expositore, sed tantum lectore
opus habet tam clara et aperta sententia.   *Corpus,* inquit,
mortuum est, non propter fragilitatem terrenam, quia de terræ
pulvere factum est, sed *propter peccatum ;* quid amplius quæ-
rimus ? et vigilantissime non ait, mortale ; sed, *mortuum.*
(v.) Namque antequam immutaretur in illam incorruptionem,
quæ in sanctorum resurrectione promittitur, poterat esse
mortale, quamvis non moriturum ; sicut hoc nostrum potest,
ut ita dicam, esse ægrotabile, quamvis non ægrotaturum.
Cujus enim caro est, quæ non ægrotare possit, etiamsi aliquo
casu priusquam ægrotet occumbat ?   Sic et illud corpus jam
erat mortale ; quam mortalitatem fuerat absumptura mutatio
in æternam incorruptionem, si in homine justitia, id est
obedientia, permaneret : sed ipsum mortale non est factum
mortuum nisi propter peccatum.   Quia vero illa in resurrectione futura mutatio, non solum nullam mortem, quæ facta est
propter peccatum, sed nec mortalitatem habitura est, quam
corpus animale habuit ante peccatum, non ait, *Qui suscitavit*
Christum Jesum a mortuis, vivificabit et mortua *corpora vestra ;*
cum supra dixisset, *Corpus mortuum :* sed, *vivificabit,* inquit,
et mortalia corpora vestra : ut scilicet jam non solum non sint
mortua, sed nec mortalia, cum animale resurget in spirituale,
et mortale hoc induet immortalitatem, et absorbebitur mortale
a vita."—*Augustini Opera* (Benedictine ed.), tom. x. p. 193.

   So again, *De Genesi ad Litteram,* liber vi. cc. 24, 25 :
"Denique non ait Apostolus, Corpus quidem mortale propter
peccatum ; sed, *Corpus mortuum propter peccatum.*   Illud quippe
ante peccatum, et mortale secundum aliam, et immortale
secundum aliam causam dici poterat : id est mortale, quia
poterat mori ; immortale quia poterat non mori.   Aliud est
enim non posse mori, sicut quasdam naturas immortales
creavit Deus : aliud est autem posse non mori, secundum
quem modum primus creatus est homo immortalis ; quod ei

præstabatur de ligno vitæ, non de constitutione naturæ : a quo ligno separatus est cum peccasset, ut posset mori, qui nisi peccasset posset non mori. Mortalis ergo erat conditione corporis animalis, immortalis autem beneficio conditoris. . . . Ac per hoc illud animale et ob hoc mortale, quod propter justitiam spirituale fieret et ob hoc omni modo immortale, factum est propter peccatum non mortale, quod et antea erat, sed mortuum, quod posset non fieri, si homo non peccasset." —*Opera (ut supra)*, tom. iii. p. 343.

GROTIUS, in his *De Satisfactione Christi*, a defence of the orthodox position against Socinus, says on this subject of man's original constitution: " Ut recte intelligatur hujus peculiaris controversiæ status: non negamus hominem, cum conditus est, fuisse χοϊκόν (terrenum), cui adfuerit vis quædam vitalis, non autem vis vivifica, ut nos Paulus docet 1 Cor. xv. 45, 46, ac proinde eam fuisse corporis conditionem, ut Deo non sustentante interitura fuerit: attamen ex divino decreto non fuisse eum moriturum si in innocentia perstitisset contendimus . . ." And farther on, after quoting the passage from the Book of Wisdom, " For God created man to be immortal, and made him the image of His own peculiar nature (ἰδιότητος). Nevertheless through envy of the devil came death into the world: and they that do hold of his side do find it " (c. ii. 23, 24), he proceeds: " Mortem hic, quam Deus dicitur non condidisse, nec velle, voluntate scilicet peccatum antecedente, qualemcunque intelligi ostendit oppositum ἀφθαρσία (*immortalitas*), in cujus spem homo dicitur conditus, eaque spes pars fuisse divinæ imaginis, aut certe ejus consequens non obscurè indicatur. 'Αφθαρσία (*immortalitas*) autem mortem omnem sive violentam, sive non violentam excludit. Et quod Apostolus dixit, per hominem et per peccatum intrasse mortem, auctor hic non minus verè dixerat, per diaboli invidiam mortem introisse."—*Opera*, tom. iii. p. 302 (Amstel. 1679).

His contention is that death is not to be taken (as the Socinians would have it) as a thing naturally incident to man, even by his constitution at first. But his argument is not that the human frame possessed, in the state of innocence, imperishable life; only, that with the natural possibility of dying there was conjoined a possibility also of living, through the favour of God; and that the excellence of man in creation implied a design for more than a temporary use of him.

JULIUS MUELLER excellently states in what sense death is natural to the body, and in what sense unnatural to the human being and an effect of sin: "Death in nature is simply the annihilation of the animal, its return into the universal life of nature. The death of man, on the contrary, is the dissolving of a living union between a reasonable soul and an organized body. Viewing human death thus, in its universality, and as distinct from death in nature, we can easily regard it as the effect of sin. To divide and isolate thus a living unity is the distinctive characteristic of sin. But what is the effect of this dissolution? Body and soul do not both continue to live after their separation, but the body returns to corruption; and when decay begins to show itself in the body, it seems only natural and even necessary for the soul to withdraw itself, and to live apart from the wasting organism. But as for the body, mortality would seem, as a matter of course, to belong to it in common with all merely corporeal existences. Are we then to say that in it death has sin for its principle and cause? Is what seems to be its essential constitution to be attributed to sin? This surely cannot be maintained, save upon dualistic principles, opposed alike to Christian ideas of the creation, and to the Christian doctrine of our redemption by the incarnation of the Son of God."—*Christian Doctrine of Sin*, vol. ii. p. 295.

According to the Christian doctrine of immortality, "death is undeniably a stumbling-block. If the body, as well as the soul, be destined for an imperishable existence, how comes this destruction of the body in death, accompanied, as it almost always is, with pain and conflict, and being, even when seemingly a placid sleep, an unnatural and violent

rending asunder of what had been developed in living unity?
Arguing from this unity, the more natural though still un-
defined inference would be, that man, having finished his
course in this present life, would be translated, not by a
destructive separation of body and soul, but by an elevation
of his bodily nature to a more perfect state, answering to his
higher inner life.   Now that this is not the case,—that the
transition is effected by a destructive process, the subduing
force of which man is utterly powerless to resist, involving, as
it does, the decomposition of the body and the deprivation of
the soul,—this, while ever a source of horror to one's natural
feelings, must necessarily be a strange anomaly in the eye of
Christian faith."—*Ibid.* ii. p. 290.

DR. OWEN, commenting on the words, "It is appointed
unto men once to die, but after this the judgment," says:
" The Socinians do so divide these things that one of them,
namely death, they would have to be *natural;* and the other,
or judgment, from the *constitution* of God : which is not to interpret, but to contradict the words.   Yea, death is that which
in the first place and directly is affirmed to be the effect of
this divine constitution, being spoken of as it is penal, by the
curse of the law for sin ; and judgment falls under the same
constitution, as consequential thereunto.   But if death, as
they plead, be merely and only natural, they cannot refer it
unto the same divine constitution with the future judgment,
which is natural in no sense at all.

" Death was so far natural from the beginning, as that the
frame and constitution of our nature were in themselves liable
and subject thereunto; but that it should actually have
invaded our nature unto its dissolution, without the intervention of its meritorious cause in sin, is contrary unto the
original state of our relation unto God, the nature of the
covenant whereby we were obliged unto obedience, the
reward promised therein, with the threatening of death in
case of disobedience."—*On the Hebrews, in loc.;* Dr. Owen's
Works (Goold's edition), vol. xxiii. pp. 408, 409; so also in

his *Theologoumena Pantodapa* (vol. xvii. of same edition), lib. i. c. iv. § 7, occurs this sentence : " *Cùm ideo Adami immortalitas in statu suo primigenio, ex principiis naturæ internis nequaquam dependerit,* sed ex solo et liberrimo Dei beneplacito, semotâ per peccatum causâ illâ externâ conservante, necesse erat ut Adamus certo quodam tempore moreretur," etc.   The point has been recently put clearly and succinctly in Dr. A. B. Bruce's *Humiliation of Christ* (the sixth series of the Cunningham Lectures), pp. 277, 278.

NOTES ON LECTURE V.

NOTE Q, PAGE 181.

THE FLACIAN HERESY.

A SPECIMEN of the explanations made by Flacius may be quoted from the minutes of what was called *Colloquium cum Colero*, first published ten years after his death. His main position is re-asserted in a letter to his friend Matthias Ritter, considered to be one of the last pieces which proceeded from his pen. These extracts are taken from a life of Flacius by J. B. Ritter, Frankfort, 1725. Some of his words at the conference with Colerus ran thus :—

"Non ergo transit essentia hominis in essentiam peccati, sed idem homo, præsertim ille internus cordis, jam lux est, jam tenebræ. Caro hominis non physicè sed spiritualiter, aut theologicè loquendo et intelligendo, mala est.

"Forma hominis, in qua est conditus, alia animalis, alia Deo similis, et rationalis. In forma animali homo utcunque mansit. Nunquam neque ab initio neque nunc propositionem illam, peccatum est substantia, ita nude et simpliciter proposui, sed declarationem semper addidi, etc. Nunquam sum usus ista phrasi : peccatum est substantia, sed ea semper, peccatum est forma essentialis. Concedo, quod in lapsu hominis peccatum fuerit accidens, sed formâ, in qua tum est mutatus homo, non est accidens, sed semper est et manet una eademque substantia hominis, sed tamen post lapsum substantia corrupta et depravata, mutata. . . . Dixi terminos Lutheri me retinere. Rem ipsam adversarii mihi concedunt ; Phrasin tantum impugnant, qua tamen Scriptura et orthodoxi usi sunt."

In his letter to M. Ritter, he thus defends his identification of depravity with a depraved nature :—

"Ego sane non video, quidnam sit aliud corruptio aut putredo in corrupto pomo aut alia putrefacta re, quam illa corrupta caro pomi aut certe essentialis, corruptaque forma carnium ipsius. Non sane est quoddam externum accidens agglutinatum aut ab extra infusum : sed ipsamet optima caro illa, massa aut materia pomi versa est in contrariam pessimamque. Huc valde facit quod Spiritus Sanctus passim in Scriptura illud malum amovendum, substantialissimis vocibus nominat, veterem hominem aut Adamum, corpus peccati et mortis, carnem crucifigendam ac abolendam, cor lapideum exscindendum, etc., sic et contrarium bonum, aut imaginem Dei in homine, reædificandum, itidem substantialissimis vocibus nominat, seu substantialia esse dicit, docens esse novum hominem, novum spiritum, internum hominem, novam creaturam. Certe si voluisset affirmare esse tantum quædam accidentia, non defuissent ei tales voces."—M. Matthiæ Flacii, Illyrici, *Leben und Tod*, pp. 276, 277, 293.

In the *Form of Concord* his opinion is condemned in the following terms :—

"Non unum et idem est corrupta natura seu substantia corrupti hominis, corpus et anima aut homo ipse a Deo creatus, in quo originale peccatum habitat (cujus ratione natura, substantia, totus denique homo corruptus est), et ipsum originale peccatum, quod in hominis naturâ aut essentiâ habitat eamque corrumpit; quemadmodum etiam in lepra corporali ipsum corpus leprosum et lepra ipsa in corpore non sunt unum et idem, si proprie et distincte eâ de re disserere velimus. Discrimen igitur retinendum est inter naturam nostram, qualis a Deo creata est hodieque conservatur, in quâ peccatum originale habitat, et inter ipsum peccatum originis, quod in naturâ habitat. Hæc enim duo secundum Sacræ Scripturæ regulam distincte considerari, doceri et credi debent et possunt."

NOTE R, PAGE 190.

REGENERATION AND CONVERSION.

THE theological distinction between these two could not be
more exactly put than it has been by Charnock.   After the
definition of regeneration already quoted (footnote on p. 187),
he thus proceeds: " It differs from conversion.   Regeneration
is a spiritual change; conversion is a spiritual motion.   In
regeneration there is a power conferred; conversion is the
exercise of this power.   In regeneration there is given us a
principle to turn; conversion is our actual turning; that is,
the principle whereby we are brought out of a state of nature
into a state of grace; and conversion the actual fixing on God,
as the *terminus ad quem*.   One gives *posse agere*, the other
actu agere.

" Conversion is related to regeneration, as the effect to the
cause.   Life precedes motion, and is the cause of motion.   In
the covenant, the new heart, the new spirit, and God's putting
His Spirit into them, is distinguished from their walking in
His statutes, Ezek. xxxvi. 27, from the first step we take in
the way of God, and is set down as the cause of our motion :
' I will cause you to walk in my statutes.'   In renewing us,
God gives us a power; in converting us, He excites that
power.   Men are naturally dead, and have a stone upon them;
regeneration is a rolling away the stone from the heart, and a
raising to newness of life; and then conversion is as natural
to a regenerate man as motion is to a living body.   A principle of activity will produce action.   In regeneration, man is
wholly passive; in conversion, he is active: as a child, in its
first formation in the womb, contributes nothing to the first
infusion of life, but after it hath life it is active, and its
motions natural.   The first reviving of us is wholly the act of
God, without any concurrence of the creature; but after we

are revived, we do actively and voluntarily live in His sight; Hosea vi. 2 : 'He will revive us, He will raise us up, then shall we follow on to know the Lord.' Regeneration is the motion of God in the creature; conversion is the motion of the creature to God, by virtue of that first principle; from this principle all the acts of believing, repenting, mortifying, quickening, do spring. In all these a man is active; in the other merely passive; all these are the acts of the will, by the assisting grace of God, after the infusion of the first grace. Conversion is a giving ourselves to the Lord, 2 Cor. viii. 5 ; giving our own selves to the Lord is a voluntary act, but the power whereby we are enabled thus to give ourselves is wholly and purely, in every part of it, from the Lord Himself. A renewed man is said to be led by the Spirit (Rom. viii. 14), not dragged, not forced ; the putting a bias and aptitude in the will is the work of the Spirit quickening it; but the moving the will to God by the strength of this bias is voluntary, and the act of the creature. The Spirit leads, as a father doth a child by the hand : the father gave him that principle of life, and conducts him and hands him in his motion; but the child hath a principle of motion in himself, and a will to move. The day of regeneration is solely the day of God's power, wherein He makes men willing to turn to Him, Ps. cx. 3 ; so that, though in actual conversion the creature be active, it is not from the power of man, though it be from a power in man ; not growing up from the impotent root in nature, but settled there by the Spirit of God."—*Works*, Nichol's edition, iii. pp. 88, 89.

The reference to Luther's opinions on p. 189 of the Lecture is made with a view to bring out the radical agreement of the Reformers on regeneration. The Lutheran Church is too open to the charge of having relapsed into a dogma of baptismal regeneration. But when we observe how much stress Luther himself laid on what he called the " faith " wrought in the child, and the manner in which he believed it to be wrought, we see that his view, however peculiar in its form, did not differ essentially from that more familiar to us as the evangelical or Puritan doctrine. His aim was to maintain that in all cases where regeneration did really take place, it was conversion or faith in the germ. In an early sermon (1518) Luther taught that a child receives baptism on the ground of *aliena fides.* In the earliest form of the *Comm. on Gal.* (1519), proceeding on the principle that in order to baptism faith is requisite, even in the case of infants, he taught that by the word spoken over the child in baptism the Spirit is given and faith is produced, the operation being facilitated by the receptivity of a little child. This passage was afterwards dropped from the *Commentary.* In his great work on the Babylonian captivity of the Church, Luther lays down the position, which was thereafter maintained by him with some unessential modifications, that " sicut verbum Dei potens est etiam impii cor mutare, quod non minus est surdum et incapax quam ullus parvulus, *ita per orationem ecclesiæ offerentis et credentis, cui omnia possibilia sunt, et parvulus fide infusâ mutatur, mundatur, et renovatur.*" Even an adult may be renewed thus, in any sacrament, through the prayer of the Church.

The above is the account of Luther's view given by Köstlin (*Luther's Theologie,* i. p. 353). In another part of the same work it is represented thus : " Children in baptism have faith —faith that is their own, which God works in them through the prayer and the presentation of them by the sponsors in the name of the Christian Church ; the children are not baptized in the faith of the sponsors or of the Church, nevertheless the faith of the sponsors and of the Church begs and obtains for them that faith of their own wherein they are baptized."—Köstlin, ii. 92.

NOTE S, PAGE 201.

THE PAULINE ANTHROPOLOGY.

FROM the mass of treatises on Paul and his doctrines, the following may be selected as giving prominence to his psychology, and, if we may so speak, to his philosophy :— *Entwickelung des paulinischen Lehrbegriffes*, by L. Usteri (a scholar of Schleiermacher; 2te Ausg., Zürich, 1829); Ernesti, *Vom Ursprunge der Sünde nach paulinischem Lehrgehalte* (1855 and 1862, 2 vols.); Holsten, *Zum Evangelium des Paulus und des Petrus* (Rostock, 1868); Otto Pfleiderer, *Der Paulinismus* (Leipzig, 1873; translation, Williams & Norgate, 2 vols. 1877). The most thorough treatise, exactly on this subject, is Lüdemann's *Die Anthropologie des Apostels Paulus und ihre Stellung innerhalb seiner Heilslehre* (Kiel, 1872). Interesting discussions on the topic will also be found in more general works; *e.g.*, in F. C. Baur's *Vorlesungen über Neutestamentliche Theologie* (Leipzig, 1874), in Bernh. Weiss' *Lehrbuch der biblischen Theologie des N. Testaments* (Berlin, 1873), and in Hausrath, *Neutestamentliche Zeitgeschichte* (3ter Theil, Heidelberg, 1875).

These writers are of various ways of thinking. Holsten is nearest to a rationalistic construction of Paul's doctrine. Weiss and Ernesti most fully represent the evangelical view. It should be noted that writers of rationalistic leaning tend to sharpen the distinction between Pauline thought and that of the New Testament generally. This tendency accompanies their exaggerated view as to the influence of individual genius within the sphere of the sacred literature. No one can doubt, however, that both the individuality and the training of St. Paul have influenced very deeply the form of revealed doctrine which the Church has received by him. And there can be as little doubt that to understand the psychology of this most analytic and introspective of all Scripture writers is an essential aid to the apprehension of New Testament theology.

The most radical subject of discussion within the range of Pauline anthropology is that which concerns his so-called dualism. By several of the authors named above it has been considered as a question to what extent his antithesis of flesh and spirit, so vital to his religious system, is the outcome of an underlying dualism, philosophical and metaphysical.

HOLSTEN has taken up the position that, according to Paul, σάρξ, or the living material substance of man, is evil, so that man stands on that account, in the Pauline system, in an absolute opposition to God (see at pp. 396, 398 of the treatise named). He goes the length (p. 387) of gravely disputing the genuineness of 2 Cor. vii. 1. Its expressions are for him *unpaulinisch*, *i.e.* they will not square with his view; for if σάρξ is the principle and fountain of all defilement, the phrases are inconsequent.

USTERI maintains what amounts to the same thing in placing the root of all sin in " die Sinnlichkeit des Menschen " (" ἡ σάρξ ist der Reitz der Sinnlichkeit," p. 30), a view sufficiently refuted by the strong emphasis laid on non-fleshly sins as " works of the flesh." The acme of sin, according to Paul, 2 Thess. ii. 4, is something very different from sensuality.

PFLEIDERER, as we have seen, thinks the metaphysical dualism of philosophical systems inapplicable to the apostle's views. He holds that Holsten has erred in identifying σάρξ with the whole man, and thus making the substantial essence of humanity to be ἁμαρτία, " which is quite un-Pauline and Manichæan." Yet he himself interprets σάρξ and πνεῦμα as two substances in their very nature antagonistic. Thus, he holds, from the opposition of physically different substances results the Pauline dualism of antagonistic moral principles. Out of σάρξ, as merely spiritless substance, grows a causality opposed to the Spirit (Rom. vii. 5, viii. 6). He claims Lüdemann as with him here (pp. 53, 54). The struggle of Pfleiderer to show how σάρξ, on his interpretation, can include non-fleshly sins is notable (pp. 54, 55). He has to admit that his view makes sin necessary to man.

HAUSRATH (pp. 75–80) ascribes to Paul what he calls an anthropological dualism, resting, he alleges, upon the native Jewish dualism which in the later Hebrew Scriptures (*zumal in den späteren Büchern*) divides the All into two regions, earth and heaven. This is the postulate of the Pauline theology (*die Voraussetzung der paulinischen Theologie*). The distinction of flesh and spirit, and of the outer and inner man, are instances of this dualism, which at last culminates in an ethical dualism, behind which the metaphysical may be looked for; so that it was not to be wondered at that thoroughgoing disciples like Marcion should have completed the circle of thinking in that direction, and that thoroughgoing opponents should have made him, under the name of Simon Magus, answerable for the entire Gnostic system. Like Pfleiderer, however, Hausrath acknowledges that, after all, such metaphysical dualism could have no place in the mind of the apostle; that his Jewish idea of God was so powerful as to exclude entirely self-existent matter or self-existent evil; that his anthropological dualism was, in short, the outcome of the deep spiritual feeling of his own sinfulness and of God's grace, arrived at as a result of his own conversion.

The most complete discussion is that of LUEDEMANN, who combats Holsten at great length. Like most of his school, he identifies σάρξ with the living material of the body. But his defence of the originality of Paul's philosophy is worth quoting. As his work is not accessible to the English reader, I give a pretty full digest of his remarks:

The signification attached to σάρξ by some is, that it is identical with the essence of human nature in general. In this case the meaning of the antithesis between σάρξ and πνεῦμα corresponds to that between man and God. Holsten finds it consequently intelligible " that the religious relation should be represented as the relation of the πνεῦμα, the nonmaterial, spiritual substance, to the σάρξ, the material, sensuous

substance ; " and he arrives in this way at the result already
alluded to.   If this relation be in its abstract generality that
of the finite and infinite, we can understand how for Paul the
notion of σάρξ is the expression for the notion of the finite.
Holsten reaches this conclusion by working out consequently
the absolute transcendence of the πνεῦμα over human nature
(*Menschenwesen*) as such, by means of the notions ψυχή,
νοῦς, πνεῦμα.   If we ask under what historical canon this
antithetical foundation of the Pauline world - apprehension
(*Weltanschauung*) falls, Holsten thus formulates his answer :
" That the new feeling of life involved in faith in the Messiah
(*das neue Lebensgefühl des Messias - Glaubens*), Paul in his
theology has apprehended and raised to consciousness in the
religious categories of the Jewish world-apprehension, in the
speculative categories of the Hellenistic."

To settle the legitimacy of this position of Holsten, we
require to ask, Can the speculative categories of Hellenism be
applied off-hand and without modification to the religious
categories of the Jewish consciousness, and yet express a
homogeneous system of thought ?   To answer this question
satisfactorily we must start two others : (1) What is dualism ?
(2) How does the religious consciousness of Judaism relate
itself to it ?   As to the first, we may say generally that to
constitute a dualistic antithesis it is necessary to have two
notions which are co-ordinate, inconsistent with one another,
and contrary opposites.   We see that this is the character
of dualism in Plato's philosophy.   He lays the full stress of
being on the side of spirit, of idea.   This is the only real.
All non-spiritual is unreal, non-existent, mere appearance.
But this carried him too far ; and so, to explain phenomena as
they stood, he had to accept the non-spiritual as antithesis of
the ideal, the principle of separateness and multiplicity of evil,
in short.   Philo, too, wavers, but in his anthropology clings to
Plato's first view, thus bringing out a characteristic of dualism
that you can never have a harmonious synthesis of the two
principles ; the one, in so far as it is at all asserted, is asserted

inevitably at the expense of the other. Philo's anthropology
is : In man there meet two spheres of the universe, the ideal and
the material. Properly he belongs to one of them, the ideal.
The natural history of the nexus of these two principles is
wrought out on the basis of Plato's speculations anent the pre-
existence, the fall, the return of souls. Such is a general
definition, with historical illustrations, of what is meant by
dualism.

(2) We ask, What is the relation of the Jewish religious
consciousness to this ? First of all you have the unity of an
almighty will dominating the universe ; there is no power or
principle thought of in the Jewish religious consciousness
of the Old Testament which is co-ordinate with the Creator
Jehovah.   On the other hand, you find undoubtedly an
antithesis between the transcendent majesty and worth of
the infinite Being, and the comparative insignificance of the
finite. But this antithesis cannot be regarded as a dualism.
It is with contradictory opposites, not contraries, we are here
brought into contact. The finite is purely privative ; this
attitude of thought corresponds to Plato's first and non-
dualistic standpoint. The finite must become positive, active,
co-ordinate as against the infinite before you have a real
dualism. This being the only duality of principles in the Old
Testament, we may expect that there will be as little evidence
of a really dualistic anthropology. Man's earthly constitution is not inconsistent with indwelling of the divine (Gen. vi.
3), and in a religious reference he is regarded as in his own
nature capable of appreciating a revelation from God. Nay,
in this reference we find the material part of man itself taken
as the representative of his ego. We find precisely the
בָּשָׂר placed in religious connection with God ; and mankind
in general represented precisely under the designation כָּל־בָּשָׂר
as recipients of divine revelation (Ps. xvi. 9, lxiii. 2, lxv. 3,
lxxxiv. 3 ; Isa. xl. 5, lxvi. 23, 24 ; Joel iii. 1, *orig.*). On the other
hand, in virtue of his finitude, man can occupy the position of
antithesis to God. In this case he apprehends himself from his

378 NOTES ON LECTURE FIFTH.

sensuous material side, and once again it is the term בָּשָׂר which
becomes the designation of his absolute frailty and nothingness
(Jer. xvii. 5 ; Deut. v. 23 ; Ps. lxxviii. 39, lvi. 5—cf. 12 ; Isa.
xl. 6, xlix. 26, lxvi. 16). Frequently it is also human nature
in its totality which in this way becomes conscious of its
great alienation from the divine infinity (Gen. xviii. 27 ; Job
iv. 19, xxxiii. 6). It is the אֱנוֹשׁ as such who has to acknowledge his inferiority (Ps. ix. 21, x. 18, lvi. 12). Let us now
sum up the state of the case. In the Old Testament we
have the contradictory antithesis of infinite and finite; in
Hellenism, the dualistically contrary antithesis of spirit and
matter. In the Old Testament we have man as a unity of
spirit and body (*eine geist-leibliche Einheit*) standing in the
region of the finite under the designation בָּשָׂר, at times in
communion with the divine infinite, at times with the
emphatic application of this term to his entire being, in a
relation to God of the humblest subjection. In Hellenism
we have man consisting of a material element and a spiritual
which is akin to the divine ; these two being dualistically
kept apart, and capable of consisting only at the expense of
one of them. These two systems of thought being so radically
different, it is clear the one cannot be expressed in terms of
the other.

As a matter of fact, the sense attached by Holsten to σάρξ
is neither Jewish nor Hellenistic. It is not Jewish, for the
Old Testament בָּשָׂר can never be taken so strictly as to
characterise man as a purely material unity, and thus furnish
a pretext for placing him as finite being in genuinely dualistic
antithesis to the divine. It is not Hellenistic, for the Hellenistic category of σάρξ was never meant to characterise human
nature as forming in its totality the dualistic antithesis of the
spiritual-divine (*zum Geistig - Göttlichen*). The Hellenistic
category σάρξ restricts itself exclusively to the body as the
material constituent of man. Hence it follows that (1) σάρξ
as the representative of בָּשָׂר cannot form one term of a
dualism. (2) If we start with a metaphysical dualism, this

must reproduce itself in our anthropology, and in that case σάρξ will just have the Hellenistic signification of the material of the human body.   The religious categories of the Jewish consciousness are therefore incompatible with, disparate from, the speculative categories of Hellenism.

Our investigation may have put us on the way, however, to discover Paul's real position.   Though the identification of Jewish and Hellenic categories has demonstrated itself in the concrete to be impossible, yet alongside of a Judaism just grazed by Hellenism on the surface, a third relation of the two spheres of consciousness is at least conceivable, in terms of which the Hellenic dualism so permeates an originally purely Jewish consciousness, that within the forms of intuition of the Jewish world of thought (*Vorstellungswelt*) there evolves itself a really *contrary* antithesis, the religious anti-thesis of the finite and infinite remodels and hardens itself into a dualism (*sich dualistisch umbildet und verfestigt*), in consequence of which there must simultaneously appear a dualistic moment within the anthropology also.   In such modified consciousness the Hellenistic categories would never indeed occur in entire purity, but partly alongside of purely Jewish standpoints (*Betrachtungs-weise*), partly mixed up with the Jewish categories; perhaps bent on a contest with these latter, and in their consequences gradually sublating and interpenetrating that foundation of the Jewish consciousness which was so pure at its first appearance.   Does not the Paulinism of the four great Epistles exhibit precisely such a form of consciousness?   In that signification of σάρξ accepted by us at the outset as equivalent to " man " and " finitude," we recognised in Paul a moment of the Old Testament mode of thought and expression.   The fact is, he really does at times give expression to the feeling of the inferiority of all that is human by the antithesis of σάρξ and πνεῦμα (Gal. i. 11, 16, ii. 17; Rom. iii. 20; 1 Cor. i. 29, peculiarly Old Testament ἐνώπιον αὐτοῦ).   Reverting to the proper meaning of σάρξ, we find it opposed to πνεῦμα in Rom. i. 3, 4,

ii. 28, 29 ; also Rom. ix. 27 ; 1 Cor. ix. 11 ; 2 Cor. x. 4 ;
Gal. iv. 23, 29. No doubt the Old Testament antithesis of
finite and infinite lies at the root of such passages as 1 Cor.
xv. 34 ff. But clearly there is something more than this
conveyed in the uniform character of the predicates, which are
almost exclusively privative and passive, and seem intended
to designate the essence of the ἄνθρωπος χοϊκός, of the ψυχὴ
ζῶσα in its totality. Still we do not get out of these predicates a real dualism ; the antithetical principles are not co-
ordinate. Over against the absolutely transcendent glory
and absolute reality of the πνεῦμα, the σάρξ as φθορά, ἀτιμία,
ἀσθένεια, never comes to life at all, never lifts itself above the
horizon of genuine reality. That Paul does not occupy the
pure Old Testament position appears from the intentional and
carefully elaborated antithesis which is exhibited in this
passage, opposing attributes being piled on, pair after pair.
And when we note that the expression σάρξ καὶ αἷμα, which
Paul himself employs for human nature generally, e.g. Gal.
i. 16, is applied here (1 Cor. xv. 50) to the purely material
side of man's nature, the question suggests itself, whether the
purely physical use which we claimed for σάρξ at the outset,
and in terms of which we saw σάρξ recur in the signification
of matter, and as we believe also in the phrase ἔξω ἄνθρωπος
(with διαφθείρεται, 2 Cor. iv. 16),—whether this use of the
word be not better fitted to bring the Pauline notion of σάρξ
into analogy with the Hellenistic-speculative, dualistic category
of matter, than that other would be which after the manner
of the Old Testament unmistakeably embraces the whole of
human nature, and with which Holsten makes the attempt.

Holsten would explain certain passages by saying Paul
shared the view of his time concerning a purely external
relation of the spirit to body. But this is not a proper
explanation. In what sense was it the belief of his time ?
It was different from the two most prevalent theories of his
time. 1. From the Platonism of Philo. Philo has two distinct
views, though he avoids making them glaringly inconsistent.

(a) A pure dualism, spirit and matter having nothing in common. (b) Into his κόσμος γεγονώς and σωματικός he imports the Jewish distinction of φθαρτόν and ἄφθαρτον, earthly and heavenly. Paul, on the other hand, never attains the Hellenistic dualism of spirit and matter. There is wanting to him—and in this he is and remains a Hebraistic Jew —the abstract conception of pure spiritual being. 2. He differs from the contemporary Jewish views. They had not the dualism of ideal and real, spirit and matter, as Hellenists. Their antithesis was the heavenly and the earthly. But though wide apart and variously distinguished, they are but parts of a whole. Man, notwithstanding his material body, is capable of having revelations made to him, and of converse with God. They are very far indeed from speaking of the flesh in the way Paul does, or from treating it like him as not really a constituent element of true human nature. The Jew cannot think of man apart from his body. And it is characteristic of the genuine national standpoint, that Judas Maccabeus (2 Macc. xiv. 46) expresses a hope that he will receive at the resurrection, in the complete identity, even the bowels he himself has torn out. Compare and contrast Paul in 1 Cor. vi. 13 : τὰ βρώματα τῇ κοιλίᾳ, καὶ ἡ κοιλία τοῖς βρώμασιν· ὁ δὲ Θεὸς καὶ ταύτην καὶ ταῦτα καταργήσει. Paul therefore held not what may be stated roughly as the view of his time, but more accurately that modified view indicated above (Die Anthropologie des Ap. Paulus, pp. 22–38).

For the ethical and religious view of σάρξ and πνεῦμα the reader must be referred to Ernesti and Weiss, as well as to the longer-known writers on that side, such as J. Müller, Neander, and Tholuck.

NOTE ON LECTURE VI.

NOTE T, PAGE 235.

THE GREEK FATHERS ON THE IMMORTALITY OF THE SOUL.

THIS subject has been very succinctly and pointedly handled by Olshausen in his tractate entitled, *Antiquissimorum Ecclesiæ Græcæ Patrum de Immortalitate Animæ Sententiæ Recensentur*, which will be found in his *Opuscula Theologica*, pp. 165–184. He confines his remarks to the opinions of Justin Martyr, Tatian, and Theophilus. He considers Irenæus, though a Greek writer, to belong by his leanings to the Western Church. Clement of Alexandria he thinks should, on such subjects, be reckoned along with Origen, whose views of the soul's pre-existence, to say nothing of his many eschatological whims, put him in a totally different category from the earlier Greek Fathers. It is further very properly remarked, that the three writers named above stand in such close conjunction as to throw light on each other's opinions. Athenagoras, who for some reasons might well have been grouped with these three, is put aside because of his distinct Alexandrian tendency. So far as the doctrine of immortality is concerned, Athenagoras, following the Greek philosophers, declares once and again that souls are immortal by their very nature—a proposition which was abhorrent to Justin and the others, as belonging to a school of thought which they had renounced when they adopted Christianity.

On this topic, as on so many others, a misleading method of referring to the opinions of the Fathers has prevailed. The habit of too many writers is, when amassing citations and opinions on any subject, to dip into the Fathers for isolated quotations, as some farmers cart stones from an ancient ruin to build into a modern farm wall. The consequence is that these ancient writers are made to support opinions with which they had no sympathy, and to seem to say what they have never said.

Olshausen has exposed this mistake very thoroughly in application to the point in hand. Had the considerations he adduces been present to the minds of those writers in our own day who have revived Dodwell's citations from the Fathers in support of the theory of "conditional immortality," it is impossible that the old quotations could have been made to figure so complacently in their new amalgam. As Olshausen's tract is not within reach of all, I take from it the following paragraphs :—

"Plurimum enim confert ad sententias de quocunque dogmate cognoscendas, ea comparasse, quibuscum tam arcte sunt conjuncta, ut efficacia ipsorum illius facies mutetur. Ita v. g. doctrina de immortalitate animæ copulata est cum anthropologia; quæritur enim, utrum inter ψυχήν et πνεῦμα distinguat ille, de cujus placitis sermo est, si quid de immortalitate senserit exploratur. . . . Patres autem Græci eam naturæ humanæ divisionem adhibebant, de qua ante hoc biennium disputavimus, animam non solum a corpore, sed a spiritu quoque segregantes: qua re tota de immortalitate disputatio immutatur. De spiritu enim libentissime concedunt, quod nostri animæ tribuunt, imo plus etiam spiritui dant, dicentes spiritum esse æternum, ἄφθαρτον, imo ζωοποιοῦν, at longe aliam volunt esse ψυχῆς conditionem. Hæc post hominis lapsum a spiritu sejuncta θνητή est atque tum demum immortalitatis particeps erit, si cum spiritu denuo fuerit conjuncta. Multum tamen abest, ut interituras esse animas existimarent, si forsan cum spiritu non conjungerentur, nihil enim in rerum natura prorsus deleri atque interire posse persuasum iis erat, quamobrem omnium hominum tam πνευμα-τικῶν quam ψυχικῶν resurrectionem docebant. Attamen ea

conscientia veræ originis carere animas malas censebant, qua
gaudent bonæ, cum spiritu copulatæ ; atque hac carere ipsis
erat *mors*.   Patet itaque sententiam patrum de immortalitate
animæ recte percipi non posse, nisi cum placitis ipsorum de
anthropologia, resurrectione et morte componatur, quæ quam
longissime distant a sentiendi ratione, temporibus nostris
insueta.   Aliud quid est ψυχή patribus et mors, aliud nobis ;
necesse est itaque ut aliter sententiam : anima mortalis est,
intelligant, quam ex loquendi more nobis usitato nos eam
intelligere solemus.   Hoc autem discrimen gravissimum, quod
inter antiquiorem et recentiorem cogitandi atque loquendi
rationem intercedit, qui negligerent, eos a vero longe aberrasse,
nemo est qui mirabitur.   Misere enim priscorum ecclesiæ
doctorum   sententia, mortalem esse animam, corrumpatur
necesse est; si ex nostris opinionibus intelligatur. . . .

 " Patet itaque longe alium esse sententiæ illius sensum, quæ
offensioni plerisque esse solet, *animam esse mortalem*, quam
qui vulgo ei tribuitur.   Si recte vim sententiæ percipimus,
haud ita longe ab *Irenæi* et *Origenis* placitis de immortalitate
animæ abest.   Lugdunensis episcopus disertis quidem verbis
profitetur, animas esse immortales, eosque oppugnat, qui
negant immortalitatem, quoniam anima nascitur ; quamobrem
qui historiam dogmatum conscripserunt, longe aliter Irenæum
de immortalitate animæ locutum esse censent, quam Justinum
et qui cum ipso faciunt ; at graviter falluntur viri eruditi, dis-
sentiunt patres quoad verba, consentiunt autem quoad rem.
Irenæus enim, ut Justinus, vim vivificantem vocat spiritum,
ita ut sine spiritu anima mortua sit, eandem naturæ humanæ
divisionem cum Justino adhibens.   Hac autem in re totius
disputationis cardo vestitur, quamobrem *Origenis* quoque
sententia haud admodum illi adversatur, in qua recensenda
versamur, quoniam inter ψυχήν et πνεῦμα eandem differentiam
intercedere existimat, quam Justinus, Tatianus, Theophilus
ponunt.   At cum Origenes præexistentiam animæ doceat et
hanc ob causam lapsum hominum aliaque sua ratione exponat;
admodum diversa esse videntur, quæ de animæ immortalitate

proponit. Neque tamen revera tantopere discrepant; nam ψυχή e coelis delapsa, moritur, ex opinione Adamantii et in vitam restituitur, cum spiritu iterum copulata; quod eadem ratione *Tatianus* docet. Prorsus autem dissentit *Tertullianus* a nostris. Nam cum discrimen inter animam et spiritum tollat, illam natura sua immortalem esse docet; quod, ut supra innuimus, *Athenagoras* quoque fatetur, de cujus anthropologia tamen certi quidquam constitui nequit.

"Jam autem ut finem disputationi imponamus, *Justini, Theophili, Tatiani*, de immortalitate animæ opinionem, cum sententia S.S. componimus, qua cum saltem haud coacte comparari potest. Nam quamvis nemo facile infitias iverit, rudes esse et e usu loquendi dogmatico, parum polito, enatas formulas: θνητὴ ἡ ψυχή, πολυμερής, λύεται, quas jure rejicit S.S. hoc tamen patribus dandum est, nusquam legi in libris sacris, *animam esse immortalem;* de Deo potius prædicatur, eum tenere solum immortalitatem; ὁ μόνος ἔχων ἀθανασίαν (1 Tim. vi. 16), et de Christo: ἐγώ εἰμι ἡ ἀνάστασις καὶ ἡ ζωή (John xi. 25). Christus itaque fons vitæ est, et vitam cum genere humano, a morte oppresso communicavit. Ut ipse dicit: ὁ πιστεύων εἰς ἐμὲ, κἂν ἀποθάνῃ, ζήσεται, quibus verbis innuere videtur, morituros esse in morte non credentes. Videmus itaque haud ita longe remotam esse doctrinam S.S. ab opinione patrum recte percepta; nec abesse potest, cum autores sacri inter animam et spiritum discrimen ponant, qua differentia tota hæc sententia nititur. Hoc enim discrimine admisso, anima non per se vitam habet, sed percipit ex conjunctione cum spiritu, fonte vitæ æternæ. Nihilo secius tamen male dicitur, animam esse mortalem; plerisque enim mors est deletio substantiæ; anima autem prorsus deleri nequit. Rectius ita de anima disseritur, vivit anima, a spiritu sejuncta, animantium more, sine conscientia *originis cœlestis* et divinæ prosapiæ, qua gaudet; vita, quæ merito mors vocatur; cum spiritu autem copulata, originis cœlestis conscientiam tuetur et vitam vivit, vere vitam appellandam. Ita S.S. loquitur, ita patres quoque, in quorum placitis

2 B

recensendis versati sumus, sentiunt, quanquam non satis apte sententiam verbis exprimant. Procul dubio itaque propius ad veritatem accedit eorum sententia, quam vana illa philosophica de immortalitate animæ opinio, nostris temporibus haud paucis recepta. Nimirum hæc animæ tribuit, quod spiritui soli dandum est, nam θεὸς μόνος ἀθανασίαν ἔχει καὶ ὁ πιστεύων ἐν αὐτῷ, sine Deo viventes in morte sunt, et morientes vivunt."—*Opuscula Theologica*, pp. 170–172, 181–183 (Berlin, 1834).

I subjoin the main quotations from the writings of the three Greek Fathers themselves.

The well-known passage from THEOPHILUS of Antioch, which will be found in his only extant work, *Ad Autolycum*, lib. ii. c. xxvii., runs thus :—

Ἀλλὰ φήσει οὖν τις ἡμῖν· Θνητὸς φύσει ἐγένετο ὁ ἄνθρωπος; Οὐδαμῶς. Τί οὖν ἀθάνατος; Οὐδὲ τοῦτό φαμεν. Ἀλλὰ ἐρεῖ τις· Οὐδὲν οὖν ἐγένετο; Οὐδὲ τοῦτο λέγομεν. Οὔτε οὖν φύσει θνητὸς ἐγένετο οὔτε ἀθάνατος. Εἰ γὰρ ἀθάνατον αὐτὸν ἀπ᾽ ἀρχῆς πεποιήκει, θεὸν αὐτὸν πεποιήκει· πάλιν εἰ θνητὸν αὐτὸν πεποιήκει, ἐδόκει ἂν ὁ θεὸς αἴτιος εἶναι τοῦ θανάτου αὐτοῦ. Οὔτε οὖν ἀθάνατον αὐτὸν ἐποίησεν οὔτε μὴν θνητόν, ἀλλά, καθὼς ἐπάνω προειρήκαμεν, δεκτικὸν ἀμφοτέρων, ἵνα, εἰ ῥέψῃ ἐπὶ τὰ τῆς ἀθανασίας τηρήσας τὴν ἐντολὴν τοῦ θεοῦ, μισθὸν κομίσηται παρ᾽ αὐτοῦ τὴν ἀθανασίαν καὶ γένηται θεός, εἰ δ᾽ αὖ τραπῇ ἐπὶ τὰ τοῦ θανάτου πράγματα παρακούσας τοῦ θεοῦ, αὐτὸς ἑαυτῷ αἴτιος ᾖ τοῦ θανάτου. Ἐλεύθερον γὰρ καὶ αὐτεξούσιον ἐποίησεν ὁ θεὸς τὸν ἄνθρωπον. Ὁ οὖν ἑαυτῷ περιποίησατο δι᾽ ἀμελείας καὶ παρακοῆς, τοῦτο ὁ θεὸς αὐτῷ νυνὶ δωρεῖται διὰ ἰδίας φιλανθρωπίας καὶ ἐλεημοσύνης ὑπακούοντος αὐτῷ τοῦ ἀνθρώπου.

The following is the original of the passage from JUSTIN MARTYR'S *Dialogue with Trypho*, quoted in a note on pp. 236, 237. It occurs at the beginning of chap. v. of the *Dialogue* :—

Οὐδὲν οὖν ἴσασι περὶ τούτων ἐκεῖνοι οἱ φιλόσοφοι, οὐδὲ γὰρ ὅ τι ποτέ ἐστι ψυχὴ ἔχουσιν εἰπεῖν.

Οὐκ ἔοικεν.

Οὐδὲ μὴν ἀθάνατον χρὴ λέγειν αὐτήν, ὅτι εἰ ἀθάνατός ἐστι, καὶ ἀγέννητος δηλαδή.

Ἀγέννητος δὲ καὶ ἀθάνατός ἐστι κατά τινας λεγομένους Πλατωνικούς.

Ἦ καὶ τὸν κόσμον σὺ ἀγέννητον λέγεις;

Εἰσὶν οἱ λέγοντες, οὐ μέντοι γε αὐτοῖς συγκατατίθεμαι ἐγώ.

Ὀρθῶς ποιῶν. Τίνα γὰρ λόγον ἔχει, σῶμα οὕτω στερεὸν καὶ ἀντιτυπίαν ἔχον καὶ σύνθετον καὶ ἀλλοιούμενον καὶ φθίνον καὶ γινόμενον ἑκάστης ἡμέρας μὴ ἀπ᾽ ἀρχῆς τινὸς ἡγεῖσθαι γεγονέναι; Εἰ δ᾽ ὁ κόσμος γεννητός, ἀνάγκη καὶ τὰς ψυχὰς γεγονέναι καὶ οὐκ εἶναί ποι τάχα, διὰ γὰρ τοὺς ἀνθρώπους ἐγένοντο καὶ τὰ ἄλλα ζῶα, εἰ ὅλως κατ᾽ ἰδίαν καὶ μὴ μετὰ τῶν ἰδίων σωμάτων φήσεις αὐτὰς γεγονέναι.

Οὕτως δοκεῖ ὀρθῶς ἔχειν.

Οὐκ ἄρα ἀθάνατοι.

Οὐκ, ἐπειδὴ καὶ ὁ κόσμος γεννητὸς ἡμῖν ἐφάνη. Ἀλλὰ μὴν οὐδὲ ἀποθνήσκειν φημὶ πάσας τὰς ψυχὰς ἐγώ· ἕρμαιον γὰρ ἦν ὡς ἀληθῶς τοῖς κακοῖς. Ἀλλὰ τί; Τὰς μὲν τῶν εὐσεβῶν ἐν κρείττονί ποι χώρῳ μένειν, τὰς δὲ ἀδίκους καὶ πονηρὰς ἐν χείρονι, τὸν τῆς κρίσεως ἐκδεχομένας χρόνον τότε. Οὕτως αἱ μέν, ἄξιαι τοῦ θεοῦ φανεῖσαι, οὐκ ἀποθνήσκουσιν ἔτι, αἱ δὲ κολάζονται, ἔστ᾽ ἂν αὐτὰς καὶ εἶναι καὶ κολάζεσθαι ὁ θεὸς θέλῃ.

The remainder of this section or chapter continues the discussion, the writer asking whether the case of the human soul may not be that which Plato affirms of the world itself— viz., that though in itself perishable, it may be upheld in an unending existence on account of the will of God. The passage which immediately succeeds, however, is the one more frequently quoted. It forms the whole of chap. or sec. vi., and runs as follows:—

Οὐδὲν ἐμοί, ἔφη, μέλει Πλάτωνος οὐδὲ Πυθαγόρου οὐδὲ ἁπλῶς οὐδενὸς ὅλως τοιαῦτα δοξάζοντος. Τὸ γὰρ ἀληθὲς οὕτως ἔχει· μάθοις δ᾽ ἂν ἐντεῦθεν. Ἡ ψυχὴ ἤτοι ζωή ἐστιν ἢ ζωὴν ἔχει. Εἰ μὲν οὖν ζωή ἐστιν, ἄλλο τι ἂν ποιήσειε ζῆν, οὐχ ἑαυτήν, ὡς καὶ κίνησις ἄλλο τι κινήσειε μᾶλλον ἢ ἑαυτήν. Ὅτι δὲ ζῇ ψυχή, οὐδεὶς ἀντείποι. Εἰ δὲ ζῇ, οὐ ζωὴ οὖσα ζῇ, ἀλλὰ μεταλαμβάνουσα τῆς ζωῆς, ἕτερον δέ τι τὸ μετέχον τινὸς ἐκείνου οὗ μετέχει. Ζωῆς δὲ ψυχὴ μετέχει, ἐπεὶ ζῆν αὐτὴν ὁ θεὸς βούλεται. Οὕτως ἄρα καὶ οὐ μεθέξει ποτέ, ὅταν αὐτὴν μὴ θέλοι ζῆν. Οὐ γὰρ ἴδιον αὐτῆς ἐστι τὸ ζῆν ὡς τοῦ θεοῦ, ἀλλὰ ὥσπερ ἄνθρωπος οὐ διὰ παντός ἐστιν οὐδὲ σύνεστιν ἀεὶ τῇ ψυχῇ τὸ σῶμα, ἀλλ' ὅταν δέῃ λυθῆναι τὴν ἁρμονίαν ταύτην, καταλείπει ἡ ψυχὴ τὸ σῶμα καὶ ὁ ἄνθρωπος οὐκ ἔστιν, οὕτως καί, ὅταν δέῃ τὴν ψυχὴν μηκέτι εἶναι, ἀπέστη ἀπ' αὐτῆς τὸ ζωτικὸν πνεῦμα καὶ οὐκ ἔστιν ἡ ψυχὴ ἔτι, ἀλλὰ καὶ αὐτὴ ὅθεν ἐλήφθη ἐκεῖσε χωρεῖ πάλιν.

TATIAN, *Address to the Greeks*, § 13 :—

Οὐκ ἔστιν ἀθάνατος, ἄνδρες Ἕλληνες, ἡ ψυχὴ καθ' ἑαυτήν, θνητὴ δέ. Ἀλλὰ δύναται ἡ αὐτὴ καὶ μὴ ἀποθνήσκειν. Θνήσκει μὲν γὰρ καὶ λύεται μετὰ τοῦ σώματος μὴ γινώσκουσα τὴν ἀλήθειαν· ἀνίσταται δὲ εἰς ὕστερον ἐπὶ συντελείᾳ τοῦ κόσμου σὺν τῷ σώματι, θάνατον διὰ τιμωρίας ἐν ἀθανασίᾳ, λαμβάνουσα. Πάλιν τε οὐ θνήσκει, κἂν πρὸς καιρὸν λυθῇ, τὴν ἐπίγνωσιν τοῦ θεοῦ πεποιημένη. Καθ' ἑαυτὴν γὰρ σκότος ἐστίν, καὶ οὐδὲν ἐν αὐτῇ φωτεινόν. Καὶ τοῦτο ἔστιν ἄρα τὸ εἰρημένον. Ἡ σκοτία τὸ φῶς οὐ καταλαμβάνει. Ψυχὴ γὰρ οὐκ αὐτὴ τὸ πνεῦμα ἔσωσεν, ἐσώθη δὲ ὑπ' αὐτοῦ, καὶ τὸ φῶς τὴν σκοτίαν κατέλαβεν. Ἡ λόγος μέν ἐστι τὸ τοῦ θεοῦ φῶς, σκότος δὲ ἡ ἀνεπιστήμων ψυχή. Διὰ τοῦτο μόνη μὲν διαιτωμένη πρὸς τὴν ὕλην νεύει κάτω, συναποθνήσκουσα τῇ σαρκί· συζυγίαν δὲ κεκτημένη τὴν τοῦ θείου πνεύματος οὐκ ἔστιν ἀβοήθητος, ἀνέρχεται δὲ πρὸς ἅπερ αὐτὴν ὁδηγεῖ χωρία τὸ πνεῦμα, τοῦ μὲν γάρ ἐστιν ἄνω τὸ οἰκητήριον, τῆς δὲ κάτωθέν ἐστιν ἡ γένεσις. Γέγονε μὲν οὖν συνδίαιτον ἀρχῆθεν τὸ πνεῦμα τῇ ψυχῇ· τὸ δὲ πνεῦμα ταύτην ἕπεσθαι μὴ βουλομένην αὐτῷ καταλέλοιπεν. Ἡ δὲ ὥσπερ ἔναυσμα τῆς δυνάμεως αὐτοῦ κεκτημένη, καὶ διὰ τὸν χωρισμὸν τὰ τέλεια καθορᾶν μὴ δυναμένη, ζητοῦσα τὸν θεὸν κατὰ πλάνην πολλοὺς θεοὺς ἀνετύπωσε, τοῖς ἀντισοφιστεύουσι δαίμοσι κατακολουθήσασα. Πνεῦμα δὲ τοῦ θεοῦ παρὰ πᾶσιν μὲν οὐκ ἔστι, παρὰ δέ τισι τοῖς δικαίως

πολιτευομένοις καταγόμενον καὶ συμπλεκόμενον τῇ ψυχῇ διὰ
προαγορευσέων ταῖς λοιπαῖς ψυχαῖς τὸ κεκρυμμένον ἀνήγγειλε·
καὶ αἱ μὲν πειθόμεναι σοφίᾳ σφισὶν αὐταῖς ἐφείλκοντο πνεῦμα
συγγενές, αἱ δὲ μὴ πειθόμεναι καὶ τὸν διάκονον τοῦ πεπονθότος
θεοῦ παραιτούμεναι θεομάχοι μᾶλλον ἤπερ θεοσεβεῖς ἀνεφαί-
νοντο.

INDEX OF AUTHORS AND TOPICS.

INDEX OF SCRIPTURE PASSAGES.

ERRATA.

For " and " " and " *read* " und " " und," p. 69, *note.*
For " thrice " *read* " twice," p. 100, line 16.
For " earthly " *read* " earthy," p. 135, line 4 from foot.
Insert quotation marks before " Kurz also," p. 195, *note.*
For 1836 *read* 1834, p. 235, *note.*
For " Act " *read* " Art," p. 288, *note.*
Comma after " multiplicity," *not after* " evil," p. 376, line 5 from foot.
Insert " note the " *before* " peculiarly," p. 379, line 3 from foot.

For Isa. lxvi. 3 *read* 2, p. 331, line 12.
For Deut. v. 23 *read* 26, p. 378, line 3.
For Gal. ii. 17 *read* 16, p. 379, line 3 from foot.
For Rom. ix. 27 *read* ix. 3–8, p. 380, top line.
For 1 Cor. xv. 34 ff. *read* 43 ff., p. 380, line 4.

MORRISON AND GIBB, EDINBURGH,
PRINTERS TO HER MAJESTY'S STATIONERY OFFICE.

In Two Volumes, demy 8vo, price 21s.,

COMMENTARY ON ST. PAUL'S EPISTLE TO THE ROMANS.

By FRIEDRICH ADOLPH PHILIPPI.

Translated from the Third Improved and Enlarged Edition.

'A serviceable addition to the Foreign Theological Library.'—*Academy.*

'A commentary not only ample for its critical stores, but also valuable for its sober exegesis.'—*John Bull.*

'Philippi brings to the interpretation of the Greek text a penetrating analytical power, which lays bare every separate element in the Apostle's thought, and traces it to its very root. His synthesis is equally admirable.'—*Baptist.*

'Will be found of exceptional value, as offering the results of most searching and independent criticism of the sacred text.'—*Dickinson's Theological Quarterly.*

'May be safely commended to devout and intelligent students.'—*Freeman.*

'If the writer is inferior to Meyer in critical acumen, he is at least equal to him in theological learning and religious insight; and his Commentary has independent worth—it is no mere repetition of other men's labours.'—*Church Bells.*

'Sound. scholarly, and, if we may use such a word, sensible—not loaded with details—the work is really helpful.'—*Churchman.*

In Two Volumes, demy 8vo, price 21s.,

HISTORY OF THE REFORMATION
IN
GERMANY AND SWITZERLAND CHIEFLY.

By Dr. K. R. HAGENBACH.

Translated from the Fourth Revised Edition of the German.

'We highly appreciate for the most part the skill and the proportion, the vivid portraiture and fine discrimination, and the careful philosophic development of ideas by which this most readable and instructive work is characterized.'—*Evangelical Magazine.*

'Dr. Hagenbach has produced the best history of the Reformation hitherto written.'—*British Quarterly Review.*

'Dr. Hagenbach undoubtedly has in an eminent degree many of the higher qualifications of a historian. He is accurate, candid, and impartial; and his insight into the higher springs of the Reformation is only equalled by his thorough knowledge of the outward progress of that movement.'—*Scotsman.*

'A thoroughly readable and interesting, as well as trustworthy account of the German and Swiss Reformations.'—*Church Bells.*

'The work before us will have a distinct sphere of usefulness open to it, and be welcome to English readers.'—*Church Quarterly Review.*

'This work. in the quality of historical accuracy and impartiality, is much to be preferred to that of D'Aubigné.'—*Christian Union.*

'By the study of this book a more just and real acquaintance with the actors in the Reformation period may be made than by the use of any other book we know.'—*Weekly Review.*

'English readers will find that it adds something to their appreciation of these often-treated events.'—*Literary Churchman.*

KEIL AND DELITZSCH'S
INTRODUCTION TO AND COMMENTARIES ON THE OLD TESTAMENT.
In 27 Volumes, demy 8vo.

MESSRS. CLARK have resolved to offer complete sets of this work at the Original Subscription Price of £7, 2s. 0d. Single volumes may be had, price 10s. 6d.

In crown 8vo, Eighth Edition, price 7s. 6d.,

THE SUFFERING SAVIOUR;
OR, MEDITATIONS ON THE LAST DAYS OF THE SUFFERINGS OF CHRIST.
By F. W. KRUMMACHER, D.D.

BY THE SAME AUTHOR.

Just published, Second Edition, in crown 8vo, price 7s. 6d.,

DAVID, THE KING OF ISRAEL:
A PORTRAIT DRAWN FROM BIBLE HISTORY AND THE BOOK OF PSALMS.

In demy 8vo, price 7s. 6d.,

SERMONS TO THE NATURAL MAN.
By WILLIAM G. T. SHEDD, D.D.,
Author of 'A History of Christian Doctrine,' etc.

In One Volume, crown 8vo, price 5s., Third Edition,

LIGHT FROM THE CROSS:
SERMONS ON THE PASSION OF OUR LORD.
Translated from the German of A. THOLUCK, D.D.,
Professor of Theology in the University of Halle.

www.ingramcontent.com/pod-product-compliance
Lightning Source LLC
LaVergne TN
LVHW021629180125
801630LV00001B/106